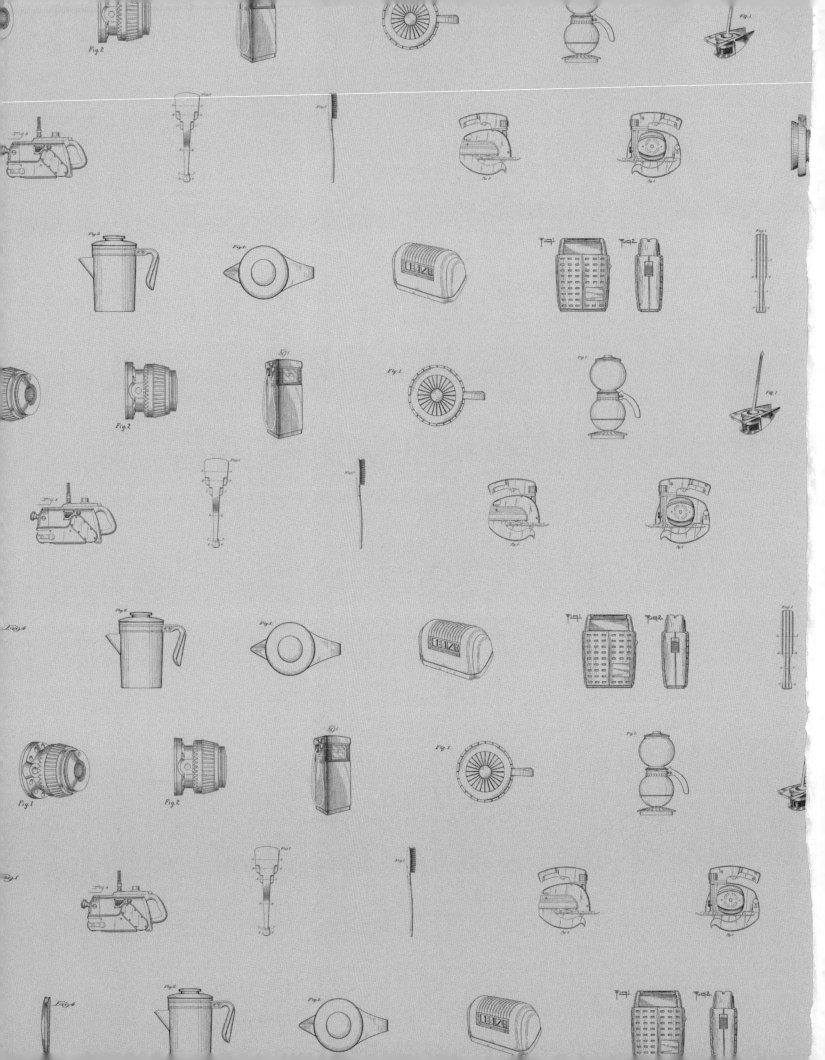

SILVER *to* STEEL

Silver to Steel: The Modern Designs of Peter Muller-Munk
Carnegie Museum of Art, Pittsburgh, November 21, 2015–March 14, 2016

Support for *Silver to Steel: The Modern Designs of Peter Muller-Munk* is provided by the Kaufman Endowment; the Henry L. Hillman Fund; the National Endowment for the Arts; The Fellows of Carnegie Museum of Art; Richard, Priscilla, Bill, and Janet Hunt; Trib Total Media; the Alan G. & Jane A. Lehman Foundation at the request of Ellen Lehman and Charles Kennel; the Bessie F. Anathan Charitable Trust at The Pittsburgh Foundation at the request of Ellen Lehman; Edith H. Fisher; the Alexander C. & Tillie S. Speyer Foundation; Richard L. Simmons; The Roy A. Hunt Foundation; and Sheryl and Bruce Wolf.

Published in 2015 by Carnegie Museum of Art and DelMonico Books · Prestel

Publications Department
Carnegie Museum of Art
4400 Forbes Avenue
Pittsburgh, Pennsylvania 15213
www.cmoa.org

CARNEGIE MUSEUM OF **ART**

ONE OF THE FOUR CARNEGIE MUSEUMS OF PITTSBURGH

DelMonico Books, an imprint of Prestel, a member of Verlagsgruppe Random House GmbH
Prestel Verlag
Neumarkter Strasse 28
81673 Munich
Tel.: +49 89 4136 0
Fax: +49 89 4136 2335

Prestel Publishing Ltd.
14–17 Wells Street
London W1T 3PD
Tel.: +44 20 7323 5004
Fax: +44 20 7323 0271

Prestel Publishing
900 Broadway, Suite 603
New York, NY 10003
Tel.: +1 212 995 2770
Fax: +1 212 995 2733
E-mail: sales@prestel-usa.com
www.prestel.com

Editors: Michelle Piranio, Katie Reilly
Design: MGMT. design
Production Manager: Luke Chase, DelMonico Books · Prestel
Rights and Reproductions: Laurel Mitchell
Imaging: Bryan Conley
Printed in China

ISBN 978-3-7913-5463-7

Library of Congress Cataloging-in-Publication Data

Silver to steel : the modern designs of Peter Muller-Munk / [compiled and written by] Rachel Delphia and Jewel Stern ; with Catherine Walworth.
    pages cm
"Carnegie Museum of Art, Pittsburgh, November 21, 2015-March 14, 2016."
  Includes bibliographical references.
  ISBN 978-3-7913-5463-7 (hardback)
  1. Industrial design--Exhibitions. 2. Industrial designers--United States--Biography. 3. Industrial designers--Germany--Biography.
  4. Silverwork--Exhibitions. 5. Muller-Munk, Peter--Exhibitions. I. Delphia, Rachel. II. Stern, Jewel. III. Muller-Munk, Peter.
  T180.P58C376 2015
  745.2092--dc23
                    2015018464

NOTE TO THE READER

Throughout much of the book, the authors refer to Peter Muller-Munk by the name he gradually adopted both personally and professionally. He was born Klaus-Peter Wilhelm Müller. By 1926 he had informally added his mother's family name, Munk; he formalized this change legally in Germany in 1930. An anglicized version of his name appeared by 1928 as "Peter Mueller-Munk," but variations both with and without the umlaut show up in published sources throughout his lifetime. By the 1950s both the man and his firm were widely known by the American pronunciation [mull-er munk].

SILVER *to* STEEL

The Modern Designs of Peter Muller-Munk

RACHEL DELPHIA AND JEWEL STERN

WITH CATHERINE WALWORTH

Carnegie Museum of Art, Pittsburgh

DelMonico Books · Prestel

Munich | London | New York

Contents

Director's Foreword

LYNN ZELEVANSKY

Henry J. Heinz II Director of Carnegie Museum of Art

———

At Carnegie Museum of Art we are delighted to present the first comprehensive exhibition on the work and career of modernist silversmith and noted industrial designer Peter Muller-Munk. Over the course of his career, Muller-Munk both contributed to and reflected the great social and technological changes of the twentieth century. He began as a silversmith in Germany and then New York, making vanguard modernist pieces, exquisite in their refinement. He left silversmithing for industrial design to make products that would improve the lives of ordinary citizens, and used that calling to inspire students over his ten years as a professor.

Muller-Munk was one of the earliest instructors in the country's first university degree-granting industrial design program, at Carnegie Institute of Technology (now Carnegie Mellon University). He founded his firm, Peter Muller-Munk, Product Design (later Peter Muller-Munk Associates, or PMMA), in 1938, making an international design career with Pittsburgh as his home base. His years in this city, from 1935 to 1967, were a time when it was teeming with the energy of multiple industries. Toward the end of his career, when he began to worry about the impact on the environment of the glut of products, he created systems calculated to improve urban life. In that, he was a precursor of much of today's urbanist thinking around sustainability.

A leader in his profession, Muller-Munk was president of the Society of Industrial Designers, and cofounded the International Council of Societies of Industrial Design, which included seventeen nations. He helped his major client US Steel refine the Unisphere, the central theme of the 1964 New York World's Fair; won an Alcoa design award for the Super Graphic Graflex camera, the quintessential press camera of the time; and worked with the US government on international trade fairs as part of Cold War soft-power diplomacy. In the 1950s he established offices in Israel and Turkey, funded by the State Department, where he trained the local populations in modern design methods.

Despite these remarkable credentials, Muller-Munk has received relatively little attention within the history of design, perhaps because the field tends to focus more on signature style than on functionality, and on work done in New York, Chicago, and Southern California. This exhibition and book will rectify that situation. I am extremely grateful to Jewel Stern, who conceived of an important Muller-Munk exhibition two decades ago, and had the insight and fortitude to stay with it until it could be brought to fruition. Rachel Delphia, Carnegie Museum of Art's Alan G. and Jane A. Lehman Curator of Decorative Arts and Design, has spent years researching Muller-Munk's work, and her dedication, scholarly rigor, and keen intelligence are manifest in this show. With the essential contribution of the museum's capable and resourceful staff, she and Jewel Stern have created a groundbreaking exhibition. Kevin W. Tucker, Margot B. Perot Senior Curator of Decorative Arts and Design at the Dallas Museum of Art, was an early partner in this exhibition and made formative contributions to it. We are all grateful for his collegiality in sharing his research and insights.

As always, we are all enormously grateful to our funders, whose generosity has made this exhibition possible. Major funding for *Silver to Steel: The Modern Designs of Peter Muller-Munk* has been provided by the Kaufman Endowment; the Henry L. Hillman Fund; the National Endowment for the Arts; The Fellows of Carnegie Museum of Art; Richard, Priscilla, Bill, and Janet Hunt; Trib Total Media; the Alan G. & Jane A. Lehman Foundation at the request of Ellen Lehman and Charles Kennel; the Bessie F. Anathan Charitable Trust at The Pittsburgh Foundation at the request of Ellen Lehman; Edith H. Fisher; the Alexander C. & Tillie S. Speyer Foundation; Richard L. Simmons; and The Roy A. Hunt Foundation.

Finally, our profound appreciation must go to Peter Muller-Munk himself, who strove to make the world a better place, and whose ingenuity, vision, and moral core must be an inspiration to all.

Preface

RACHEL DELPHIA AND JEWEL STERN

———

"The things we live with, the things we fashion for ourselves to make our work, our leisure, our homes, and our public places conform to our standards of what is right and acceptable—TV sets, jukeboxes, jet planes, power dams, modular kitchens, and four-tone Cadillacs, all of our myriad machines and gadgets—they will inevitably form a pattern for future historians as to what we stood for and whether the shape and tempo of our world was worth perpetuating."[1]

—Peter Muller-Munk, addressing the American Society of Industrial Designers as its outgoing president, 1955

Nearly a century ago, a determined and resourceful young silversmith, Peter Muller-Munk, sailed to New York from his native Germany. Against the odds, he enjoyed swift success and affirmation of his talents as American collectors and museum curators, enchanted with his modern sensibilities, purchased and acquired his hand-wrought silver wares. By midcentury, however, the art establishment that had seized upon his silver appeared to be indifferent to his latest achievements: modern designs for mass production. He scolded the critics and the museums—including Carnegie Museum of Art in his newly adopted home of Pittsburgh—for their lack of enthusiasm for household objects that represented good design for daily life.

How pleased he would be, then, to learn that today we find value in the entire scope of his world, from candelabra to gasoline pumps—*Silver to Steel*. Indeed, we envision this project—the first publication and exhibition on the life and career of Peter Muller-Munk—as meaningful in many ways, though three aspects are especially pertinent. First, Muller-Munk was a multitalented émigré artist who improbably rose from the anonymity of the silversmith's bench at Tiffany & Co. to become a remarkably successful design entrepreneur, eventually leading a firm of nearly fifty employees. Surveying the breadth and quality of his output from the late 1920s through the late 1960s is both staggering and inspiring.

Second, the design arts are so inextricably woven into the fabric of everyday experience that this project serves as a case study of American cultural history over half a century. Muller-Munk's creations variously conjure the Roaring Twenties, Depression-era austerity, 1930s industrial streamlining, the moral imperatives of World War II, the optimistic postwar consumer revolution, Cold War posturing and diplomacy, and the cultural and political upheaval of the 1960s. Third, this project offers a new portrait of Pittsburgh, revealing the manufacturing capital and Fortune 500 city as a crucible not only for steel and aluminum but also for creative product designs for every type of industry. The history of American industrial design in coastal centers, particularly in the East, has been documented more thoroughly than that of the interior. This project posits a vital design locus in Western Pennsylvania that served national and international clientele.

Muller-Munk is far from unknown to decorative arts and design historians, but the existing knowledge base is cursory. Since his death in 1967, the majority of published references have offered little more than a paragraph, if not merely a sentence, or broadly include Muller-Munk's name in lists of artisans/designers with short biographical entries. Most illustrations depict the same few objects: the silver tea service from the Metropolitan Museum of Art [**P. 42, FIG. 24**], the silver candelabra at the Detroit Institute of Arts [**PP. 30–31, FIG. 10**], the Normandie pitcher for Revere Copper and Brass [**P. 49, FIG. 34**], or occasionally the Waring Blendor [**P. 76, FIG. 3**].[2]

In the 1970s and 1980s, art historians accorded Muller-Munk his first scholarly recognition by examining his silver and early product designs through one of two established approaches: material-based studies (focusing on silver or metalworking) or the history of style (e.g., art deco, machine age, streamlining, and midcentury modern).[3] One of the earliest is Donald J. Bush's *The Streamlined Decade* (1975), which included an image of the Normandie pitcher. *Antiques and the Arts Weekly* illustrated the Metropolitan's tea service as a loan to the 1979 exhibition *Treasure House: Museums of the Empire State*.[4] At the same time Muller-Munk silver appeared on the secondary auction market, at Phillips in 1979, and Sotheby Parke Bernet in 1980.[5] During the height of the art deco revival in the 1980s, Muller-Munk silver was illustrated in numerous publications, including Jessie McNab's *Silver* (1981); Karen Davies's *At Home in Manhattan: Modern Decorative Arts 1925 to the Depression* (1983); W. Scott Braznell's seminal 1984 article in *Antiques*, "The Advent of Modern American Silver"; and Alastair Duncan's *American Art Deco* (1986). Noting the acclaim for Muller-Munk's silver, Duncan asserted, "No silver-smith's work of this period excites wider enthusiasm today."[6]

In the 1980s and 1990s, Muller-Munk works were also shown in major exhibitions: *High Styles: Twentieth-Century American Design* (Whitney Museum of American Art, 1985); *The Machine Age in America, 1918–1941* (Brooklyn Museum, 1986); *Design 1935–1965: What Modern Was* (Musée des Arts Décoratifs de Montréal, 1991); and *Craft in the Machine Age, 1920–1945: The History of Twentieth-Century American Craft* (American Craft Museum, 1995) with the catalogue essay "Striking the Modern Note in Metal," by Jewel Stern.[7] In the new millennium scholars continued to rely on the same Muller-Munk mainstays, primarily the Normandie pitcher and the Metropolitan Museum of Art's tea service, which were selected for *American Modern, 1925–1940: Design for a New Age*, at the Met in 2000, and for *Art Deco 1910–1939* (Victoria and Albert Museum, 2003). An exception was Muller-Munk's silver-plated, industrially produced Silvermode line reintro-duced by Stern in *Modernism in American Silver: 20th-Century Design* (Dallas Museum of Art, 2005) **[P. 47**, **FIGS. 32, 34]**.[8]

Muller-Munk also received attention from historians of the industrial design profession and of design education, such as Jeffrey Meikle in his pioneering book *Twentieth Century Limited: Industrial Design in America, 1925–1939* (1979).[9] The most illuminating and deeply researched account was written by Arthur J. Pulos, a former student at Carnegie Institute of Technology, who became head of the industrial design pro-gram at Syracuse University. Pulos produced in two volumes the first comprehensive historical survey of the American industrial design profession. *American Design Ethic: A History of Industrial Design to 1940* (1983) mentions Muller-Munk and illustrates his silver on view at the Metropolitan Museum of Art **[P. 33, FIG. 12]**. The companion volume, *The American Design Adventure: 1940–1975* (1988), describes Muller-Munk's diverse contributions to industrial design, from his role as a pioneering educator at Carnegie Tech to his leadership within national and international professional societies and his over-seas design work for the United States government.

Muller-Munk is not alone in awaiting scholarly attention. Indeed, of the fifteen founding fellows of the Society of Industrial Designers, about half have been the subject of scholarly

monographs since the late 1990s. A smaller set has had solo ret-rospectives: Henry Dreyfuss and Russel Wright (Cooper-Hewitt, Smithsonian Design Museum, 1997 and 2001, respectively); Raymond Loewy (Hagley Museum and Library, 2002); Brooks Stevens (Milwaukee Art Museum, 2003); and Norman Bel Geddes (Harry Ransom Center, University of Texas at Austin, 2012). These exhibitions demonstrate the relatively recent burgeoning of interest in the careers of industrial designers.

One of the obstacles, as Glenn Adamson has pointed out in his work on Brooks Stevens, has been access to archival materials. A full treatment of Muller-Munk would not have been possible without newly consolidated resources. An additional historical challenge has been the reluctance of art museums to embrace industrial design. It was a concern identified by Muller-Munk in his lifetime. He was critical of the acceptance by museums of only product designs that could pass as sculpture, and he lobbied for the elevation of functional design within cultural discourse, noting in 1951 that "a certain section of industry and public still seem to identify the work of the industrial designer mainly with chrome and colored lucite [*sic*]."[10] He further bemoaned the lack of formal vocabulary among critics who judged "industrial products on the basis of abstract aesthetics only, as though a refrigerator were subject to the same critical approach as the Venus de Milo."[11] No wonder that Muller-Munk's luxurious silver, his streamlined Normandie pitcher, and his skyscraper-styled Waring Blendor received earlier and greater recognition than his cameras or cookware did.

In this context, *Silver to Steel*, which considers hand-crafted objects and industrial products alike, is the result of a remarkable confluence of interested parties and unswerving patience and persistence. The initial idea took form in late 1995, shortly after the American Craft Museum opened the exhibition *Craft in the Machine Age*, for which Jewel Stern was curator and essayist of the metalwork section. Stern approached Rachel Layton (later Elwes), then Carnegie Museum of Art's assistant curator of decorative arts, who had an interest in silver, with the proposal for an exhibition on the modern hand-wrought work of Muller-Munk and Tommi Parzinger, another German émigré silversmith who catered to the American luxury market in the 1920s and 1930s. It was envisioned as a small "jewel-like" show of precious silver objects. Layton gathered archival materials at the Carnegie, and Stern researched, sought objects, and conducted inter-views. Simultaneously, the Carnegie's curator of decorative arts, Sarah C. Nichols, was deeply involved in organizing the major traveling exhibition and catalogue *Aluminum by Design: Jewelry to Jets*, scheduled to open in 2000. After Layton relocated to London in 1996, the Muller-Munk/Parzinger exhi-bition went by the wayside and was never realized.

When Nichols retired in 2006, she encouraged Stern to

return to the silver exhibition project, and Stern picked up the conversation a year later with Nichols's successor, Jason T. Busch, and then assistant curator of decorative arts Rachel Delphia, a Carnegie Mellon industrial design alumna. At this point Kevin W. Tucker, then Dallas Museum of Art's Margot B. Perot Curator of Decorative Arts and Design, with whom Stern had worked closely on *Modernism in American Silver*, expressed interest in the Muller-Munk/Parzinger project while suggesting as an alternative a solo exhibition on the full scope of Muller-Munk's career from silversmith to professor to industrial designer. Busch and Delphia embraced the idea, and discussions continued in May 2008 in Pittsburgh with Stern, Tucker, Busch, Delphia, and two retired Peter Muller-Munk Associates designers, Paul R. Wiedmann and George R. Scheuring. The designers opened the door to a vast array of previously unknown archival material from the firm, including Muller-Munk's scrapbooks and thousands of slides, providing the documentation for a comprehensive narrative. Independently, Stern began to build a collection of Muller-Munk industrial objects, which she recently donated to the Carnegie. Many of these objects are included in the exhibition and illustrated in this catalogue. The vagaries of museum scheduling intervened again as the Carnegie and Dallas curators completed other projects. Finally, in 2012, seventeen years after Stern proposed an exhibition highlighting Muller-Munk silver, *Silver to Steel: The Modern Designs of Peter Muller-Munk* was formally approved. Unanticipated circumstances prevented the Dallas Museum of Art from continuing with the project, and in 2014 the Carnegie took the lead in realizing the exhibition.

This publication is the culmination of nearly two decades of work and the persistent belief that Muller-Munk's story deserved to see the light of day. The book serves both as a biography and as a catalogue of the exhibition at Carnegie Museum of Art. It comprises six chronological essays addressing Muller-Munk's life and accomplishments. In the first chapter, Stern reveals Muller-Munk's German bourgeois upbringing and introduces influential family figures—his professorial father, artistic mother, and pioneering aunt in German jurisprudence—and documents Muller-Munk's formal education. In chapter two, Stern follows Muller-Munk's move to New York, his meteoric rise as a silversmith, and his initial forays into industrial design.[12] Delphia continues the story in chapter three with Muller-Munk's relocation to Pittsburgh as assistant professor of industrial design at Carnegie Institute of Technology and chronicles his development as an educator and a practicing designer. In chapter four, Delphia shows Muller-Munk hitting his stride as the founder and leader of a major design consultancy, Peter Muller-Munk Associates, while simultaneously rising to national and international prominence as spokesperson for his profession. In chapter

five, Delphia and curatorial research assistant Catherine Walworth explore the challenges and triumphs of a mature designer facing a rapidly changing field, ending in unexpected tragedy. Finally, in the epilogue, Delphia and Walworth portray the adaptation and reinvention of a firm that lost its visionary leader and assess Muller-Munk's legacy.

Interspersed between the chapters are five short essays exploring selected subjects in depth. Stern probes one of Muller-Munk's most iconic yet underdocumented designs, the Waring Blendor. Walworth delves into Muller-Munk's contributions to broad cultural trends such as the post–World War II "do-it-yourself" movement, the virtual explosion of color and innovation in product and environmental design, and the dramatic rethinking of that most essential of domestic spaces, the kitchen. Finally, Delphia unpacks another of Muller-Munk's more complicated legacies—the Unisphere, the thematic focus of the 1964–65 New York World's Fair. Five selected writings by Muller-Munk, spanning nearly forty years, reveal his inimitable voice and give the reader a sense of the man's intellect, drive, and persuasive abilities. Indeed, throughout the book, the authors argue that Muller-Munk's success—as a silversmith, professor, and designer—was due not only to his artistic talent but also to his charisma and communication skills. For future scholars, the book includes partial client, patent, and firm employee lists.

We envisioned this book as an informative, scholarly presentation, as well as one that would be readable, compelling, and, dare we say it, *fun*. As curators it has been an honor to convey Muller-Munk's life story. Rarely is there an opportunity to work with material previously unknown, and we were blessed, too, with a trove of fascinating objects to study. As if speaking to us directly, Muller-Munk once offered up a characteristically droll and self-effacing witticism: "If some future biographer finds some skeletons in the PMM closet, I guess that cannot be helped, and it will at least protect him from boredom."[13] Our endeavor has conjured many emotions, Peter, but we thank you for the fact that boredom was *never* among them. We hope you, the reader, will find his story as exhilarating as we have.

Acknowledgments

RACHEL DELPHIA AND JEWEL STERN

———

Silver to Steel: The Modern Designs of Peter Muller-Munk is the product of many minds and hands, and we are tremendously grateful to everyone who helped realize our vision. We thank Lynn Zelevansky, The Henry J. Heinz II Director at Carnegie Museum of Art, for her enthusiastic endorsement of the concept and for her steadfast support. We also thank Sarah Minnaert, deputy director and former director of exhibitions, for her guidance and capable administration from start to finish. Catherine Evans, chief curator, lent unwavering support and encouragement. Her predecessor, Jason T. Busch, now deputy director for curatorial affairs and museum programs at Saint Louis Art Museum, saw great potential in this project and passionately shepherded its early development. Kevin W. Tucker, The Margot B. Perot Senior Curator of Decorative Arts and Design at the Dallas Museum of Art, was for six years our partner and cocurator. We are grateful for his formative intellectual contributions, his administrative acumen, and his ongoing collegiality. Curatorial research assistant Catherine Walworth provided tireless support across all facets of the project, most significantly as an adept researcher and writer. We applaud and thank her for scholarly contributions to this volume.

We are grateful for the professionals, inside and outside of Carnegie Museum of Art, who contributed to this book. Our thanks go to Katie Reilly, director of publications, graphics, and photographic services, for her project leadership, her generous feedback, and her forging of the relationship with our copublisher, DelMonico Books/Prestel. We thank publisher Mary DelMonico and her team Luke Chase, Karen Farquhar, and Ryan Newbanks. Our editor Michelle Piranio provided thoughtful feedback that made this a stronger publication. Designers at MGMT.design, Alicia Cheng, Sarah Gephart, and Olivia de Salve Villedieu, set our text into this beautiful volume. Laurel Mitchell, manager, rights and reproductions, and photographic services, secured hundreds of images and their associated permissions; and Bryan Conley, imaging technician, kept pace with our ongoing requests for scanning and photographing of archival materials.

The dedicated staffs of Carnegie Museums of Pittsburgh and Carnegie Museum of Art contributed far beyond the bounds of the catalogue. We thank Jo Ellen Parker, president, Carnegie Museums of Pittsburgh, for her leadership and support. We are extremely grateful for the efforts of Hannah Silbert, exhibition manager, whose diligence, patience, and attention to detail kept the project on track, and to Emily Rice, exhibition designer, who gave compelling, period-inspired shape to the exhibition in tandem with Alicia Cheng at MGMT. Marilyn Russell, curator of learning and community engagement; Lucy Stewart, associate curator, creative engagement; and their educational team helped us articulate our ideas and engage our visitors. Ellen Baxter, chief conservator and paintings conservator; Michael Belman, objects conservator; and Carolyn Arp, former conservation technician, oversaw the cleaning and treatments of objects often plucked from the dusty shelves of domestic spaces. Orian Neumann, chief registrar; Gabriella DiDonna, assistant registrar, exhibitions and loans; and Elizabeth Tufts-Brown, associate registrar, managed the packing, shipping, and tracking of sundry loans and Internet purchases, and we are especially appreciative of their patience with nontraditional museum objects. John Lyon, manager of maintenance and operations, went so far as to drain the Freon from the Westinghouse appliances. Kurt Christian, chief preparator, and his team, Mark Blatnik, Ramon Camacho, Rob Capaldi, Dale Luce, and Steve Russ, oversaw mount making, framing, and installation. We are also grateful to Tom Fisher, multimedia producer; Neil Kulas, web and digital media manager; and Norene Walworth, graphic designer, who creatively implemented labels and wall texts and interactive digital experiences in the galleries. Brad Stephenson, director of marketing; Jonathan Gaugler, media relations manager; Neil Kulas; Susan Geyer, design services manager; and Matt Newton, associate editor, along with Big Picture Communications, dreamed up innovative ways to spread the word about our project. Aaron Martin, director of development, and his predecessor, Jamie McMahon, identified crucial support for our project with notable contributions in Carnegie Museums of Pittsburgh's central development office from Arlene Sanderson, development writer, corporate and foundation giving, and Daryl Cross, assistant director of sponsorship. Kelsey Small, financial manager, kept both incoming and outgoing funds on track. We also acknowledge and thank former Carnegie Museum of Art staff members: Rosemary Burk, Kelly Englert, Ian Finch, Jeffrey Inscho, Jeff Lovett, Kevin Mercer, Tracy Myers, and Maureen Rolla.

Within the department of decorative arts and design, we owe sincere thanks to Katie Clausen, curatorial assistant, who willingly took on countless tasks that would otherwise have fallen through the cracks. Many university students also contributed, including Milton Fine Museum Professional Fellows Emily Mirales and Chanelle Labash; and interns Lydia Andeskie, Kelsey Kresse, Daniel Letson, Monica Marchese, Melissa Quarto, Kathryn Scheuring, and Laura Winkler. We extend special, heartfelt thanks to Dawn Reid and Amanda Seadler, former longstanding members of the decorative arts and design department, who contributed immeasurably to the project. We also thank Ellen Lehman and Charles Kennel, and Richard Simmons for substantial and ongoing support.

We acknowledge the many contributions of our colleagues at the Dallas Museum of Art, an early project partner, especially Maxwell L. Anderson, The Eugene McDermott Director; Tamara Wootton Forsyth, associate director of collections, exhibitions, and facilities management; Joni Wilson, exhibitions manager; Eric Zeidler, publications manager; Ebony McFarland, former curatorial administrative assistant for decorative arts and design; and Kim McCarty and Emily Schiller, former McDermott Interns for Decorative Arts and Design. We also thank the DMA for introducing us to Quin Mathews, and we extend our heartfelt thanks to Mathews and to Manny Alcala at Quin Mathews Films for so generously portraying Muller-Munk in a short promotional film.

Numerous museums, institutions, and individuals generously loaned or donated objects for the exhibition. We thank our colleagues Terry Irwin at Carnegie Mellon University; Gretchen Anderson at Carnegie Museum of Natural History; Maxwell L. Anderson and Kevin W. Tucker at Dallas Museum of Art; Graham W. J. Beal, Alan P. Darr, and Kenneth J. Myers at Detroit Institute of Arts; Alex Forist at Grand Rapids Public Museum; Neil Bauman at The Hearing Aid Museum; John Hawks at Kenneth Berger Hearing Aid Museum, Kent State University; Angéline Dazé at The Liliane and David M. Stewart Program for Modern Design; Thomas P. Campbell and Beatrice Galilee at The Metropolitan Museum of Art; Matthew Teitelbaum, Nonie Gadsden, and Caroline Cole at Museum of Fine Arts, Boston; Gary Tinterow and Cindi Strauss at Museum of Fine Arts, Houston; Steven Kern and Ulysses Grant Dietz at the Newark Museum; Mary Lynn Bruce at Pittsburgh Corning; Nicolette A. Dobrowolski at Special Collections Research Center, Syracuse University Libraries; Jock Reynolds, Patricia E. Kane, and John Stuart Gordon at Yale University Art Gallery; and private collectors John C. Axelrod; Robert Dobrin; Jacqueline Loewe Fowler; Dr. and Mrs. Kenneth M. Hamlett; David A. Hanks; Sherry Hayslip and Cole Smith; James P. Karlen and Elaine K. Crawshaw; Pam Kueber; Kenneth D. Love; George R. Scheuring; Janna and Richard Taninbaum; Dirk Visser; John C. Waddell; Paul R. Wiedmann, and those who wish to remain anonymous. We also are exceedingly grateful to local entrepreneurs and artisans who replicated the top of the 1969 Mobay couch: Stephen Streibig, Craig Scheuer, all their colleagues at Iontank, and upholsterer Beth Quail.

Peter Muller-Munk still lives in the memories of family, friends, and professional colleagues, and we are enormously grateful to those—some of whom are no longer with us—who shared their recollections. Oral histories and documents brought our subjects to life, and our project is considerably richer as a result. Thanks go first to the family members: Jerry, Matthew, and Abby Tallmer, and Dr. Margo Tallmer; to close friends Edith H. and James A. Fisher and David and Alisoun Kuhn (children of Sally and J. Craig Kuhn); and to Muller-Munk's longtime right-hand man Paul Karlen. We extend our deep gratitude to Paul R. Wiedmann, torchbearer and steward of all things PMMA, without whom we could not have pieced together Muller-Munk's story, and to George R. Scheuring for sharing his knowledge, enthusiasm, and research. We also thank Carole Wiedmann for delicious lunches and conversation during research breaks. We are grateful for the time, effort, and generosity extended by PMMA employees, significant others, and their descendants: Anders Anderson, Elisa Behnk, Annette (Parisson) Betts, Kurt Budke, Ned and Joann DeForrest, Joanne Parisson Gaus, Robert Gaylor and Suby Bowden, H. Kurt Heinz, Tina Jockel, James P. Karlen and Elaine K. Crawshaw, Wesley E. and Bobbie Jo Lerdon, Leonard and Sylvia Levitan, Curtiss D. Lischer, Raymond LoTurco, Kenneth and Diane Love, Walter Mansfeld, Glenn Monigle, Diana Riddle, Jackie Rothenberg, Jon Rothenberg, Donald Sentner, Christina Smith Short, Deborah Smith, Eric Smith, Walton E. and Maggie Sparks, and Arnold Wasserman. For recollections we also thank Jim Kozbelt, Robert Lanza, and Mildred Schmertz.

Special thanks go to Richard Brook for sharing his extensive research on the lives of Peter's father, Franz Muller, and his second wife, Susanne Bruck (Richard's paternal aunt); to Oda Cordes for her expertise on Marie Munk, Gertrud Muller-Munk, and the Munk family, and for her extraordinary and generous help with translations of many passages from her seminal book *Marie Munk und die Stellung der Frau im Recht: Wissenschaftliche Studie über Leben und Werk von Marie Munk in drei Teilen*; to Renate Reiss for her translations of German documents, especially Muller-Munk's records from the University of Berlin and the 1930s correspondence between Paula and Marie Munk; to Florence Goujon of Paris, for her personal visit to Fayence to assist in research on the experiences of the Muller and Mombert families during their residence at the farm at Banégon; to Oliver Gorf, professor at Florida International University for his translation and interpretation of Gertrud Muller's essay "Paris"; and to Karen V. Kukil, associate curator of special collections, William Allan Neilson Library, Smith College.

We wish to acknowledge the following institutions and individuals for generous assistance and moral support: Jane Adlin; Eric Anderson, Mark Baskinger, Daniel Boyarski, Terry Irwin, Sarah Johnson, and Steve Stadelmeier at Carnegie Mellon, School of Design; Paola Antonelli and Paul Galloway at the Museum of Modern Art; Archiv Bildende Kunst, Akademie der Künste, Berlin; Martin Aurand, Katie Behrman, Julia Corrin, Mary Catherine Johnsen, Gabrielle V. Michalek, and Patrick Trembeth at Carnegie Mellon Libraries; Timothy Babcock at Pennsylvania State University, The Fred Waring Collection; Ron Baraff at Rivers of Steel National Heritage Area; Gail P. Bardhan and Elizabeth Hylen at the Corning Museum of Glass, Rakow Research Library; Gary Bass; Jennifer Belt and Ryan Jensen at Art Resource; Sam and Debbie Berkovitz; Rickard Bindberg at Husqvarna Fabriksmuseum; W. Scott Braznell; Elizabeth Broman, Sarah Coffin, and Cara McCarty at Cooper-Hewitt, Smithsonian Design Museum; Melissa M. Caldwell at Philadelphia Art Alliance; Sarah Cassella and Tom Muscatello at US Steel; William Kevin Cawley at Notre Dame Archives; Wendy Crawford at Western Australian Museum Library; Bill Chase at Cleveland Public Library; Judith Childs, Elizabeth Dodge, and Meredith Dodge; Barbara Cline, at Lyndon Baines Johnson Presidential Library; Michael T. Cohen; Charles F. Cummings at New Jersey Public Library; Tim Cunningham and Vijay Chakravarthy at Daedalus, Inc.; Nicole C. Dittrich at Special Collections Research Center, Syracuse University Libraries; Kelley J. Elliott at Corning Museum of Glass; Özlem Er, Istanbul Technical University; Marcie Farwell, Cornell University, Division of Rare Books and Manuscript Collections; Rebecca Federman at the New York Public Library; Aimee Fernandez-Puente at Elizabeth (NJ) Public Library; Claudia Fitch at Louisville Free Public Library; Gary Forgione; Frick Art Reference Library; Marilyn F. Friedman; Sabine Friedrich at Universitätsarchiv, Humboldt Universität zu Berlin; Mimi Gaudieri; Rev. James W. Garvey at Most Holy Name of Jesus Parish, Pittsburgh; Todd Gilbert at New York Transit Museum; Brother Joseph Grabenstein, at La Salle University; David R. Grinnell and Marcia Rostek at University of Pittsburgh Libraries; Nancy Grinnell at Newport Art Museum & Art Association; Eric Grotzinger at Carnegie Mellon, Mellon College of Science; Todd Gustavson at George Eastman House; John Hall; William Inman Sr.; Barbara Jaffee at Northern Illinois University; Dick Jarmon; Wendy Jimenez and Louise Weinberg at the Queens Museum; Linda Johnson, Megan Reddicks, and Garrett G. Swanson at Detroit Institute of Arts; Nancy Johnson at SUNY Oswego, Penfield Library; John Jowers; Antje Kalcher at the University of the Arts, Berlin; Richard Kaplan at Carnegie Library of Pittsburgh; Sue Kapusta at US Steel Foundation; Rick Katz at

Mine Safety Appliances; Mary E. Lamica and company at the North American Glass Club, Lowell Innes Chapter; Rachel E. C. Layton Elwes; Jeffrey Leonard and Mary Ann Prignon at Thermo Fisher Scientific; Jim Lesko; David Lewis; Library of Congress, Prints and Photograph Division; Frank Luca and Nicolae Harsanyi at Wolfsonian-FIU Library; Anne P. Madarasz, Kathleen A. Wendell, Jaclyn G. Esposito, and Matthew Strauss at the Senator John Heinz Regional History Center; George Manos and Donald Manges both formerly at US Steel; Daniel Martinage at IDSA; Brother James Martino, FSC, Brothers of the Christian Schools-District of Eastern North America; Victoria Matranga; Janet McCall and Kate Lydon at the Society for Contemporary Craft, Pittsburgh; Jason McClelland; Cayce Mell; Ken Metcalf; R. Craig Miller; Cynthia Morton, associate curator and head of botany, Timothy Pearce, assistant curator and head of mollusks, and John Rawlins, director, Center for Biodiversity & Ecosystems and curator of invertebrate zoology at Carnegie Museum of Natural History; Museum of Modern Art Libraries; New York Public Library; Sarah Nichols; Alison Oehler; William A. Peniston at the Newark Museum library; Walter Piroth at Radioear Corporation; Matt Prentice; Kris Piscitella; Alexandra and Cathy Raphael; Sabine Rasche at Thüringer Universitäts- und Landesbibliothek; Chris Reinecke, Lori Huisman, and Doug Medema at Bissell Homecare, Inc.; Amy Reytar at National Archives at College Park, Maryland; Elisabeth Roark and Rachel M. Grove Rohrbaugh at Chatham University; Dean M. Rogers at Vassar College Libraries; Charles Sable at The Henry Ford Museum; Annamarie Sandecki and Amy McHugh at Tiffany & Co.; Prof. Dr. Uwe Schaper, director, and Dr. Susanne Knoblich at Landesarchiv Berlin; Paul E. Schlotthauer at Pratt Institute Library; Florian Schreiber and Catleen Reichenbach at Universitätsarchiv Heidelberg; Minette Seate at WQED Pittsburgh; Nancy M. Shawcross at University of Pennsylvania Library; Graham Shearing; Graham Sherriff at Yale University, Beinecke Rare Book and Manuscript Library; Daniel Short at Robert Morris University; Jeanne Solensky at the Winterthur Museum, Garden, and Library; Lauren Stark at College Art Association; John A. Stuart; Amy Surak at Manhattan College; Jenny Swadosh at New York School of Fine and Applied Art; Al Tannler; Rebecca Tilghman, Mehgan Pizarro, Kendra Roth, and Julie Zeftel at The Metropolitan Museum of Art; Jason Tracy; US National Archives and Records Administration; Sarah Webster Vodrey at the Museum of Ceramics, East Liverpool, Ohio; Craig Vogel at the University of Cincinnati; Thomas J. Watson Library, Metropolitan Museum of Art; Hampton Wayt; Barbara Welker at Centrum Judaicum Archiv, Berlin; Philip Wittenberg; and Susan and Steven Zelicoff.

Finally, on a personal note, we thank Michael and Elizabeth Delphia, Casey Helfrich, Geneva Helfrich, Lori Schainuck, and Victoria and James Schainuck.

Berlin: Family

JEWEL STERN

———

"I was born in Berlin, Germany, long enough ago to have spent a careless and delightful youth in the lovely house of parents where literature, music, painting, and medicine contributed to an atmosphere of culture and breeding…. It should be easy for Mr. Freud's roving investigators to retrace my career to the lasting and ineradicable impressions I received from my family and my teachers and no greater compliment could indeed be paid to me, for I would choose the very same ones again were I given the choice."[1]

Klaus-Peter Wilhelm Müller was born on June 25, 1904, in Charlottenburg, then an affluent, independent town on the western periphery of Berlin, the capital of the German Empire under the rule of Wilhelm II.[2] The expansion of Berlin had accelerated following the unification of Germany in 1871, and by the turn of the century the population had more than quadrupled to about two million. In 1904 the massive modernist Wertheim department store on Leipziger Platz, designed by the prominent architect of the period Alfred Messel, was still expanding, and the construction of Messel's AEG (Allgemeine Elektricitäts-Gesellschaft) administration building was imminent. The city was fast becoming the most powerful industrial and technological center in Europe and was portrayed by one observer at the time as a place of opportunity where "everything is intensive life, unlimited ambition, energy, a desire to shift mountains.... In Berlin, modern life stands at its height, automatic, splendid, and flashing like a fully loaded cannon. In addition, it contains something fever like, capricious and American."[3] Others compared the dynamism and rapid industrialization of Berlin to American cities. Mark Twain, who visited in 1892, dubbed Berlin the "Chicago on the Spree," and the contemporaneous German sociologist and economist Werner Sombart referred to it as "a suburb of New York."[4] By the turn of the century, no major European city had experienced such rapid transformative growth and reinvention.[5]

Klaus-Peter Wilhelm, called Peter, was the son of Gertrud Munk (1880–1969) and Franz Müller (1871–1945).[6] Peter's only sibling was a younger sister, Karin Margit, called Margit (1908–1959). The influence of the close-knit Munk family on Peter was substantial, while that of the Müller family is largely unknown. Gertrud was the eldest child of Wilhelm Munk (1844–1929) and Paula Joseph (1855–1936). Wilhelm, the son of a businessman, was born into a Jewish family in the city of Posen (Poznan), in the Polish province of the same name (after the Revolution of 1848, the province was Prussian until 1871, when it was absorbed into the German Empire). He studied jurisprudence at the Heidelberg University, a school that attracted Jewish students because of its liberal orientation, graduated as valedictorian of his class, and received an early appointment as a judge (*Ladgerichtsrat*) in Berlin, where he became distinguished professionally.[7] His daughter Marie later claimed, "Had he not been of Jewish descent, he would certainly have been appointed to the Supreme Court of Germany."[8]

Paula Joseph was born in Stargard, Pomerania, which bordered on the Baltic Sea, in what is now northwestern Poland. She was the youngest of five children of a grain merchant. Paula was described as artistic and exhibited ability in painting both before and after she married, though she adapted to the role of mother and homemaker efficiently and with élan. Later in life, her aesthetic flair apparently enchanted the young Peter and Margit, who became her "most fervent admirers."[9]

frontispiece
FIG. 1
Peter Muller-Munk, 1935

above
FIG. 2
Unter den Linden, c. 1900, with equestrian statue of Frederick the Great at center and Preußische Akademie der Künste (Prussian Academy of Art) at right, located near the Friedrich-Wilhelms-Universität

Gertrud and her younger siblings, Ernst (1883–1915) and Marie (1885–1976), were born in a four-family apartment house that was owned by their father. The house, at Kronbergerstrasse 24, in the vicinity of the Grunewald, was located in "one of the best residential districts in Berlin."[10] Marie Munk described family life:

[We] grew up in a typical German family of the so-called upper middle class. These were characterized by economic security and social standing. They were not families of great wealth, but with the means for comfortable living. They occupied spacious apartments or "villas."... They employed at least one, but usually two or more domestic servants. Their greatest aim was to give their children a good education so that their offspring would climb higher on the social ladder. Expenses for books, theatres, concerts, or travel were not considered luxuries, but as educational factors and necessities.... The father or head of the family was either a professional man, e.g., doctor, lawyer, or civil servant of at least medium rank, or an officer in the army or navy, or a "landed" business man of high standing.[11]

Emphasis on education and travel was a hallmark of the Munk family and scholastic independence a requisite. Gertrud and Marie attended a private high school for girls and learned French, English, and Italian conversation from private tutors, opportunities that showed how "very progressive" their parents were, as Marie later observed.[12]

In 1895, when Gertrud was fifteen, Wilhelm and Paula Munk officially left the Jewish community of Berlin (Jüdischen Gemeinde zu Berlin), converted to Christianity, and adopted the Protestant faith.[13] It is not known what prompted the decision, but it was not uncommon in the last half of the nineteenth century for German-Jews to convert to Christianity as a means of assimilating into German society.[14] Another factor may have been a virulent wave of anti-Semitism that had emerged in the country in the 1880s.[15]

On December 14, 1901, Gertrud married Franz Müller. Less than a month before the wedding, Franz, who was born into a Jewish family, officially left the Berlin Jewish community.[16] Franz was the son of Wilhelm Müller (1830–1887), whose origin is unknown, and Emma Landau (1837–1908), of Lublinitz (Lubliniec) in southern Poland. Wilhelm became a manufacturer in Berlin.[17] His scholarly son Franz eschewed the family business and gravitated instead to the natural sciences and medicine, which he studied at the Rubrecht-Karls-Universität (Heidelberg University) and the Friedrich-Wilhelms-Universität zu Berlin (University of Berlin) between 1890 and 1898.[18] He was an assistant to Rudolf Gottlieb at the Heidelberg Institute of Pharmacology and had already published before becoming, in 1900, a coworker in experiments with Nathan Zuntz, a Berlin pioneer in high-altitude physiology.[19] In 1902 Franz was appointed as a lecturer to the medical faculty of the Friedrich-Wilhelms-Universität, the first important position on the pathway to professorship.[20]

Peter and Margit were born when the family lived in an apartment building at Schlüterstrasse 30.[21] When Franz's mother died at the end of 1908, his inheritance may have facilitated the expanded family's move to Kastanienalleestrasse 6, in a leafy, upper-middle-class residential neighborhood on a street named for its chestnut trees.[22] The home was located within walking distance of a new station for the Berlin U-Bahn, the rapid-transit underground railway inaugurated in 1902, giving Franz easy access to central Berlin, where he taught at the imposing Friedrich-Wilhelms-Universität on Unter den Linden [FIG. 2].

It was a period of accomplishment for the Munks and Müllers. In 1908 universities in the Prussian state accepted women as full-time matriculated students for the first time.[23] Marie was the first female student at the law school in Bonn in 1909, and one of the first female law students in Germany, receiving her doctorate in jurisprudence from Heidelberg University in 1911.[24] In 1912 Franz Müller was elevated to a nontenured professor of pharmacology, placing him among the elite of the medical profession [FIG. 3].[25] That year the family moved to their permanent home nearby at Kastanienalleestrasse 39, a single-family residence that still stands, though in somewhat altered form.[26]

The Munk and Müller families belonged to the *Bildungs-bürgertum*, the educated, professional bourgeoisie class that had emerged in the mid-eighteenth century in Germany and was rooted in the rationality and individualism of the Enlightenment (*Aufklärung*). It represented a cultural elite whose social status was derived primarily from earned educational attainment. *Bildung* was a humanistic ethic that valued higher education and the lifelong pursuit of self-cultivation and refinement.[27] Stellar proponents of *Bildung* included Johann Wolfgang von Goethe, Friedrich Schiller, and Wilhelm von Humboldt, the philosopher and educational reformer who founded the University of Berlin in 1810. Not surprisingly, the poetry of Goethe and Schiller was read aloud in the Munk home.[28] Looking back, Peter would later recognize the impact of his parents and Munk grandparents, and implicitly of *Bildung*, when he described his background as "partly medicine, partly art, partly law," noting that he grew up in the constant presence of literature and music.[29] He attributed his love of music, especially chamber music, to his father, a devotee of the form.[30] Peter's artistic propensities derived from his mother, who, like her mother, was an artist, working in oil, watercolor, and pastel.[31] According to Marie Munk, Gertrud had attended the school of the Verein der Künstlerinnen zu Berlin (Berlin Women Artists' Association), where she took classes with an artist named "Moser"; she also apparently studied in Paris, "particularly with Matisse," though Marie does not provide any dates.[32]

In 1911 Gertrud became involved with the Sera-Kreis (Sera-Circle), an independent group loosely affiliated with the broader Wandervögel, the turn-of-the-century reformist youth movement that protested against the constricting conventions of Wilhelmine society; it was characterized by a romantic, utopian yearning to return to the German past, epitomized by the wandering scholars of the Middle Ages.[33] The Sera-Kreis was one of the movements that arose at this time out of dissatisfaction with the urban, industrial, and technological transformations in Wilhelmine Germany and a desire for an intense emotional commitment to a larger community of purpose.[34] Karl Brügmann, a member close to

FIG. 3
Franz Müller, c. 1912

Eugen Diederichs, the publisher who founded the Sera-Kreis in 1908, introduced Gertrud to the group in February 1911.[35] Gertrud became a generous patron of the Sera-Kreis, and the Müller home functioned as a meeting place.[36] Activities included social evenings discussing philosophical issues, reading current authors, singing and dancing, and long day hikes through the landscape. Members eschewed alcohol and tobacco, and were committed to the equal treatment of the sexes.[37] Although Peter was only a child, he would have been aware of the milieu and his mother's central role in it. Gertrud attended the historic youth rally that took place on the Hohe Meissner, a mountain near Kassel, in October 1913, and she was the only older contributor included in Brügmann's *Sonnwendbriefe* (Summer Solstice Letters), published in 1914.[38] Her two-and-a-half-page essay, titled "Paris," is a travel meditation that contrasted the character of the French with that of the Germans and the English.[39] In it, she expresses doubts that the German people (*Volk*) are "thinkers" and concludes by declaring that whereas the French placed Rodin's sculpture of *The Thinker* in a position of honor in front of the Pantheon, a monument to the Kaiser would be what the Germans would choose, suggesting her admiration for the Republican character of France in contrast to Germany's imperial monarchy. World War I quashed the momentum of the Sera-Kreis and precipitated its dissolution after the war. The group suffered the loss of many members in battle, including Brügmann, an early casualty in 1914.

The comfortable, cultured life of the Munk and Müller families was disrupted by the advent of World War I. Ernst Munk, who had recently been appointed magistrate at the Central Berlin District Court, enlisted as a volunteer in the artillery and fell on the Russian front in 1915; for his bravery he was posthumously awarded the Iron Cross and elevated to the rank of officer.[40] Only ten years old at the outset of the war, Peter entered adolescence in the midst of the fighting, and was fourteen when the Armistice was signed in November 1918. During these years, he was educated in a typical Berlin gymnasium, a secondary school for boys that he later described as "a kind of German Eton."[41] He later recalled that he had "a very rough time in math, liked languages, did alright in history that kind of thing"; and he confessed that he "barely managed to graduate."[42] Peter's wish to "do something with my hands" and to see the concrete results, combined with the realization that "the purely abstract" in academics did not move him, led to his becoming a silversmith.[43] Fortuitously, at a fancy dress ball sometime around 1923, Gertrud met the accomplished German sculptor and silversmith Waldemar Raemisch, a professor at the Vereinigte Staatsschulen für freie und angewandte Kunst (Unified State Schools for Fine and Applied Art) in Berlin. Peter later emphasized the importance of this chance meeting: "This masquerade still ranks as one of

the most eventful and determining factors in my life."[44] With the approval of his parents, Peter was happily apprenticed to Raemisch.[45]

The predecessor to the Vereinigte Staatsschulen, the Unterrichtsanstalt des Königlichen Kunstgewerbemuseums (School of the Royal Museum of Applied Arts), was led from 1907 by Bruno Paul, a force for reform in artistic education and the elevation of standards in design. Because of Paul's involvement in contemporary developments in art and industry, especially through his activity in the Werkbund, students not only became technically proficient but also gained exposure to the avant-garde. Moreover, Paul collapsed the distinction between fine art and applied art, and, influenced by the English Arts and Crafts movement, he embraced the notion that "the process of creating an object with one's own hands was the root of artistic expression."[46] Yet he was realistic when it came to the need for standardization in serial production, and he sought a balance between it and individuality. In 1924, on the advice of Paul, the Prussian governments merged the School of the Royal Museum of Applied Arts with the Academy of Fine Arts and divided the combined units into three departments: architecture, fine arts, and applied art.[47] The newly christened Unified State Schools for Fine and Applied Art was ranked as a powerful proponent of modernism in the 1920s, equal in stature to the Bauhaus.[48] The direction of the combined schools set by Paul would be consequential for Peter's foundation as a craftsman and designer. Although Peter would state that he graduated from the "Academy of Fine and Industrial Arts," archival records list a "P. Müller" as enrolled only in an evening class of figure drawing from 1922 to 1923.[49] Because professors at the school also maintained private practices in tandem with the official workshops, this suggests that Peter was privately apprenticed to Raemisch for the three years he studied with him at the school.[50]

A transformative early experience in the studio tested him and deflated his youthful grandiosity. As Peter recalled vividly years later, this experience greatly influenced him both as a designer and as a person:

> I came in there as a budding genius—I was sure I was a genius, because I knew it. And I was going to "out Cellini" Cellini. And the second or third job that I got was a little piece of steel, and a couple of files, and a vise, and I was supposed to file this steel into a perfect cube. This didn't seem to be quite as creative as what I had been cut out to be. I decided that it was such a foolish thing, I'd be through with it that afternoon. I was at that job for about three weeks. And it almost cracked me—I went home one night and I said "Look—I'm through, I'm leaving the shop, this is not for me." And my parents said "well, if

you're really serious about that, alright." And that got my back up. I think if they would've said "no you go back," I would've said "Oh, I won't." And within the next three days, I did it … after that, nobody had to teach me what precision was anymore. And nobody's had to ever since.[51]

Although the artistic and technical influence of Raemisch was formidable, Peter also would have known the work of other distinguished Berlin silversmiths, including Emil Lettré, established on Unter den Linden; Emmy Roth, who had a workshop in Berlin-Charlottenburg; and Herbert Zeitner, a gifted young teacher at the Vereinigte Staatsschulen. He likely knew the work of Christian Dell, head of the Bauhaus metal workshop from 1922 to 1925, and possibly the work of Marianne Brandt, an apprentice at the Bauhaus beginning in 1924.

The progressive environment under Paul's leadership and Peter's interaction with other students exposed him to modernist concepts. An exhibition supported by Paul at the Vereinigte Staatsschulen that debuted in January 1926 introduced students to contemporary American architecture. *Ausstellung neuer amerikanischer Baukunst* (Exhibition of New American Building), the first exhibition of its kind in central Europe, featured contemporary works in New York City, among them, a rendering of McKenzie, Voorhees, and Gmelin's Barclay-Vesey Building under construction (designed by Ralph T. Walker); a model of Buchman and Kahn's projected Insurance Center Building for 80 John Street; and the visionary drawings of Hugh Ferriss.[52]

Peter entered the Friedrich-Wilhelms-Universität in the summer of 1923, in the School of Philosophy, and studied there through the winter of 1925–26.[53] In addition to taking a wide range of art history courses that included German, Dutch, French, Italian, and Asian painting, sculpture, and architecture, he elected courses in logic, philosophy, psychology, politics, French literature, and exercises in writing and speaking.[54] Whether courses were offered at that time in modern and contemporary art is uncertain, but none appear in his records.[55] A decade later Peter recalled "these grand years" with pleasure and revealed a bon vivant dimension to his personality: "I spent three pretty lazy and joyous years in Waldemar's shop, for when I wasn't flirting on the lawn in the court of the Academy, I was studying at the University or dancing my heels off in the homes of the bourgeoisie and the better hotels."[56] Peter claimed to have received a Bachelor of Arts degree from the University of Berlin, but official records show that he did not. Nor was he awarded the equivalent degree in German university education. Nonetheless, he pursued a full liberal arts curriculum that provided depth and broadened his worldview. The experience with Raemisch would technically and emotionally benefit his professional life [FIG. 4]. His subsequent success and accomplishments were furthermore enhanced by the culture and polish he had acquired from his family, not to mention his own elegance and personal magnetism.

New York: Silver to Industrial Design

JEWEL STERN

———

"In doing the designs and all the important work myself, in considering every line in its necessity I am trying to make out of silver real individual and modern pieces for everyday use. But only then, when the scope of my work embraces all possible techniques of the silversmith ... shall I be able to show how, based on old traditions, a modern spirit can create a new art which may last as did the masterpieces of the past."[1]

Achieving Distinction in Silver

The humiliating German defeat in World War I, the subsequent dissolution of the Wilhelmine Empire, the ensuing political turmoil that accompanied the launch of the Weimar Republic, and the economic hyperinflation, which climaxed in November 1923, resulted in much societal upheaval. In these uncertain and unsettling times, there was a paucity of customers for luxury silverware, leading Peter to immigrate to America in search of economic stability and creative independence.[2] He boarded the SS *Veendam*, a Holland-America ocean liner, at Boulogne-sur-Mer, on the north coast of France, on August 4, 1926, traveling as a second-class passenger, and arrived ten days later in the port of New York. The ship's manifest noted that Peter was a six-foot-tall "student" with brown hair and eyes.[3] He declared his nearest relative to be his father at Kastanienallee 39, his destination New York City, and his contact person a "Mr. Kleiberger" [*sic*] at 725 Fifth Avenue. The latter was Francis Kleinberger, head of the F. Kleinberger Galleries, a venerable Parisian art establishment located at 725 Fifth Avenue, which had specialized since 1909 in the sale of rare European old master paintings to wealthy Americans.[4] Of Peter's or his family's relationship to Kleinberger, nothing more is known. Less than two weeks after Peter arrived in New York, he found work at Tiffany & Co.[5] According to his recollections, he walked into Tiffany's and introduced himself with his "journeyman's certificate," photographs of his silver pieces, and a few references from teachers. To his amazement—having experienced the scarcity of jobs in Berlin—he was hired immediately and sent to the New Jersey factory in the Forest Hill district of Newark, where he worked at the bench in the silversmithing and repair department for $25 per day until December 16, 1926, when he received a raise to $27.[6] Dissatisfied with the lack of creative initiative and the opportunity to "widen [his] artistic scope," he left the firm at the end of July 1927.[7] With financial assistance from his father, Peter soon opened his own metalworking studio in Greenwich Village at 148 West Fourth Street.[8] At this same time, he began a correspondence with Katherine Dreier, the artist and influential founder of the avant-garde Société Anonyme, whom he courted as a patron.[9]

The earliest surviving commentary by Peter on his work is an essay enclosed in a letter to Dreier at the end of 1927. The purpose of this "short synopsis of my ideas for my work as a silversmith," he said, was to provide Dreier with a basis for a published article on his work. Form, he wrote, was primary, and ornament, secondary. He criticized "concessions to the broad masses of the buying public" that rendered the work in silver "an amusing momentary product that looses [*sic*] its attraction in time," and distanced himself from the novelties of art moderne, then in vogue. He equated the work of

a silversmith with that of "a sculptor and an architect," and furthermore declared that the owner of a silver creation should value it with the same joy as the possessor of a Picasso. Beyond silver in the domestic realm he envisioned portraiture and sculpture as realistic pursuits for a silversmith, a nod to his mentor Raemisch, whose oeuvre included such formidable objects. Addressing industrial silver, he opined that the most detailed copy "could never show the warmth and vitality of the hand made product."[10]

Yet, an early, undated promotional pamphlet modestly featured a small photograph of a chaste ovoid bowl—a far cry from the hyperbole in the missive to Dreier—and bears his hyphenated and anglicized professional name: "Peter Mueller-Munk." William E. Kant, identified as his "business representative," signed the page of content heaping praise on Mueller-Munk's hand-wrought pieces, "none of which will be duplicated."[11] Despite this claim, Peter evidently did repeat a few pieces in limited numbers, probably no more than two or three.[12] Although he was credited solely with conceiving the designs, the execution of the pieces was said to be "by the artist himself with the assistance of the finest craftsmen."[13]

Peter's independent silver work debuted on December 4, 1927, in the Dudensing Galleries at 5 East Fifty-Seventh Street, which was under the direction of F. Valentine Dudensing in partnership with the Paris-based art dealer Pierre Matisse. It is surprising that Peter, as an unknown and untested silversmith, secured an exhibition at this prestigious gallery. His contact at the nearby F. Kleinberger Galleries may have been a factor. The exhibition was covered by the *New York Times* on Christmas day: "Mr. Mueller-Munk, who is only 23 years old, reveals himself an artist of vision and taste. The few pieces now on view—bowls of various shapes, cracker or bon-bon boxes, an after-dinner coffee service—are highly individual and, while modern, not extreme or … bizarre."[14] Two pieces were described, a small dish fashioned with a tulip design, enhanced with applied "pale gold of a pinkish hue," and a larger covered dish on which "a landscape design is traced, the lines bold and free."[15]

Critics often commented on the individuality of his silver creations and on his toned-down modern idiom at a time when American design was awash in versions of the jazzy, cubistic art moderne popularized after the 1925 Exposition des Arts Décoratifs et Industriels Modernes in Paris. Peter was eclectic. He held his mentor Raemisch in the highest esteem while drawing freely from historical motifs and contemporary German and Scandinavian work, reinterpreting them through a personal and studied modernist lens. He was not intimidated by Bauhaus functionalist theories, and independently retained applied and chased ornament. He professed a profound respect for traditionally wrought metalwork, yet accepted machine work if it did not imitate handwork.[16]

Peter's success in the luxury market was meteoric. Early in 1928 he was so overwhelmed with orders from department stores and others that he could not honor Dreier's invitation to attend the Société Anonyme exhibition held at the Barbizon Hotel.[17] In March a hand-wrought silver candy box with chased decoration was illustrated in *Arts and Decoration*, and his hollowware was lauded for its "originality and simple beauty."[18] A month later, the candy box and a bowl were illustrated in *The Arts*: "No praise can be too great for the hand-wrought silver of Peter Mueller-Munk."[19] In *Town and Country* he was prominently paired with the distinguished Danish émigré silversmith Erik Magnussen. The patrician character of Peter's work was portrayed as similar to that of "the artist-craftsman who was established in special quarters in a great man's palace, to exploit his social stature through those refinements of silver and gold which are acquired with much ceremony by the J. P. Morgans and Otto H. Kahns of our own generation."[20] In a rare reference, an affluent client was named: Mrs. Jay Gould, for whom he had designed a hand mirror, the back of which was etched with a "modern woman's head in Picasso-classic style."[21]

A coffee service, perhaps the one exhibited earlier with Dudensing, was illustrated in the *Town and Country* article [FIG. 2]. An unusual border in a leaf pattern, described

frontispiece

FIG. 1
Detail of centerpiece,
c. 1929–30 (Fig. 20)

above

FIG. 2
Coffee service, 1927, silver,
gold, and ebony, private
collection

FIG. 3
Silver display, *An International Exposition of Art in Industry*, R. H. Macy & Co., 1928

as "appliqué on silver" in "eighteen-carat gold," encircles the vessels.[22] Peter's use of gold may have been inspired by the American master silversmith Arthur J. Stone. In a 1928 published article he cited Stone and the Society of Arts and Crafts, Boston, for their use of gold in combination with silver to create "a more colorful effect."[23] There would have been opportunities for Peter to view Stone's work earlier in New York, at the shop of the Society of Arts and Crafts, Boston, and at the Little Gallery, 29 West Fifty-Sixth Street, which held an exhibition that included Stone and other American and Swedish craftsmen.[24]

The stylized, abstract naturalism of the border bears a compelling resemblance to the serial motif on the conical lid of a cylindrical silver and gilt pyxis, a small box of the Hellenistic period, on exhibit at the time in the Metropolitan Museum of Art.[25] The quarter-round, upward-curved handles on the sugar bowl of the set emulate a shape that occurred in contemporaneous Swedish and German metalwork and other mediums.[26] Peter's use of different creamer and sugar handles was a device also employed by the well-known Swedish silversmiths Nils Fougstedt and Jacob Angman.[27] The angled

and tapered upright spout is similar to one on the coffeepot in Marianne Brandt's celebrated Bauhaus service, a type of pouring spout favored by German makers of modern silver in the 1920s. Peter was assimilating and distilling aspects of modern German and Swedish silverware into his own work.

Peter developed a relationship with Bamberger's department store in Newark, where his silver was offered; he even published an essay, "Handwrought Silver: Modern Styles and Their Creators," in the store's magazine, *Charm*, in April 1928 **[FIG. 4]**.[28] His art historical studies came into play as he analyzed the work of others and articulated his idealistic goals as a silversmith. He extolled Georg Jensen of Copenhagen as "perhaps the most famous silver-smith on the continent for the last twenty years"; recognized Dagobert Peche of Vienna for his "daring elegance"; and declared that the "modish appearance" of silver by Puiforcat of Paris was "in harmony with the modern spirit." His greatest accolade was reserved for Raemisch, whom he ranked as "the greatest modern silver-smith in Europe." Lastly, he introduced the readers to his own works—the only ones illustrated and all for sale at Bamberger's—including the coffee service with foliate borders in gold.[29]

Hand Wrought Silver

Individual pieces or sets designed, reproduced or made to order

Teapot, ebony top and ebony in handle

The best traditions of the silversmith's art are mirrored in the work produced under my personal supervision. Here are designed and manufactured candlesticks, tea and coffee sets, tea caddies, bowls, vases, trays, goblets, pitchers, boudoir sets, hand mirrors, perfume bottles, loving cups, brushes, combs and many other miscellaneous items.

Correspondence is invited or call personally

The Peter Mueller-Munk Studio
148 West Fourth St.   New York
(Spring 3376)

left to right

FIG. 4
Peter Muller-Munk portrait in
Charm **(April 1928)**

FIG. 5
Advertisement for
Peter Mueller-Munk Studio,
The Antiquarian **(May 1928)**

The planning of R. H. Macy's groundbreaking *International Exposition of Art in Industry*, to which Peter was invited to exhibit, was underway during the early months of 1928. Emboldened, Peter sought entrée to another retail establishment through Siegmund Warburg of the prominent German-Jewish banking family. Warburg wrote a letter of introduction for Peter to the head of the Abraham & Straus department store in Brooklyn, a relative, informing him that Siegmund had met Peter "several times" in New York and that Peter was a "personal friend of Lola," a reference to their cousin Lola Hahn-Warburg.[30] Peter must have met her in Germany, before he immigrated, because she did not travel to the United States in the 1920s. Admired for her exceptional beauty in those years, Lola was known as a glamorous Berlin hostess, and one susceptible to "bright, fiery, intellectual men."[31] Although nothing appears to have come of it, the letter and its inception exemplify (not unlike his courtship of Katherine Dreier) Peter's savoir faire when it came to navigating the financial and intellectual upper echelons of society to advance himself professionally.

Anticipating the exposure he would receive from the Macy's exposition, Peter placed the first of many advertisements in *The Antiquarian*, a periodical addressed to connoisseurs [FIG. 5].[32] The illustrated teapot was part of a three-piece tea set later highlighted in *Vogue*.[33] The ad listed the available objects: "candlesticks, tea and coffee sets, tea caddies, bowls, vases, trays, goblets, pitchers, boudoir sets, hand mirrors, perfume bottles, loving cups, brushes, combs and many other miscellaneous items." According to the accompanying text, "individual pieces or sets designed, reproduced or made to order" were offered.[34]

The pacesetting *International Exposition of Art in Industry* held at Macy's in May of 1928 drew an unprecedented number of spectators, said to have totaled more than 250,000. The central focus of the angular, modernistic installation designed by Lee Simonson was the striking Court of Honor lined with shop-window display cases around its perimeter.[35] Peter was awarded a coveted window to display his silver in the United States section [FIG. 3]. Two of the eight objects, previously illustrated in publications, can be discerned in the foreground of the window, and were listed in the exposition catalogue as "Tea set, silver with gold appliqué, ebony tray" and "Mirror, braided handle, chiseled design."[36] In addition to his solo exhibit, Peter's silver was prominently displayed in the elegant living room designed by Eugene Schoen and situated in the arcade behind the Court of Honor [FIG. 6].[37] The graceful, unornamented bowl on the desk has a profile favored by Peter and is an example of his experimentation in pure form [FIG. 7]. Placed on the hexagonal table near the piano were a coffeepot, a shallow covered dish, and a round covered container on a tray, each vessel embellished with a similar spherical finial.

Bruno Paul, the director of the Vereinigte Staatsschulen, was the designer of the German section and a member of the German advisory committee for the exposition. He traveled to New York to open the German exhibits and was feted at a luncheon at which he spoke prior to the opening.[38] Peter, as a former student of the Berlin school and known to its director, was enlisted by Katherine Dreier to arrange a meeting with Paul.[39] He may also have served as an interpreter for Paul, who did not speak English.

top to bottom

FIG. 6
**Silver, in the living room
designed by Eugene Schoen,
*An International Exposition
of Art in Industry*, R. H. Macy
& Co., 1928**

FIG. 7
**Bowl, c. 1928, silver, Carnegie
Museum of Art, Pittsburgh,
Decorative Arts Purchase
Fund, 87.11.1**

top to bottom

FIG. 8
Tea set, c. 1928, silver,
Newport Art Association
exhibition, 1928

FIG. 9
Prize cups, c. 1928, silver,
Newport Art Association
exhibition, 1928

The Macy's exposition marked a turning point in Peter's career. The enormous exposure swiftly led to exhibitions and greater coverage in the press. It also led to an opportunity to redirect his creativity into product design through a commission from Macy's in the category of "pottery,"[40] his earliest industrial design.[41] The exposition raised the awareness of manufacturers to the benefits of art in industry. Consequently, Macy's announced an "atelier of design" program in which the store would act as a liaison between a staff of skilled designers and manufacturers of home furnishings. Austin M. Purves Jr., an artist and art educator, was appointed the program director.[42] Peter may have designed under the aegis of this program. Although he did not mention the date of the overture from Macy's, he later recalled that it came when he was "becoming a little dissatisfied with the very exclusivity of the handmade work," and when, despite the clientele he attracted, the business was losing money: "At a very important juncture when I was sort of breaking my head, how do I get … into some broader applications to useful things that aren't just … [made] in a quantity of one or two or three, R. H. Macy's gave me a chance to design some products…. I'd never done design for industry, and I told them so. I enjoyed doing that and it was successful. And one learns by doing."[43]

Even if Peter was experiencing doubts about his future as a silversmith following the Macy's exposition, his reputation in the medium was accelerating and spreading beyond New York. In the remaining months of 1928, his silverwork traveled to exhibits in Newport, Rhode Island, and Detroit, Michigan. The Newport Art Association's exhibit opened early in August. Of special interest are the images illustrated in the *Newport Bulletin*, several of which constitute the only record of these works. One image, captioned "Three Prize Cups," demonstrates Peter's use of the stepped motif for the bases of two cups—a rare effect in his work—and of pointed applied strips as a decorative motif [FIG. 9].[44] A tea set with ebony knobs is another of his works that has not been published elsewhere [FIG. 8].[45] The vertical columnar and splayed elements, naturalistic in character, resemble an encircling arcade; the curves of the slender handles allude to contemporaneous German and Scandinavian sources.

In October 1928 Peter contributed to a decorative arts group exhibition organized by the Detroit Society of Arts and Crafts that included notable metalsmiths Oscar Bach and Marie Zimmerman. The reception to his work was resounding. *The Detroit News* pronounced him "brilliant," remarking that his "modern silver is very much the vogue among the smart people of the East" and that "his work has received enthusiastic recognition from the leading Eastern critics."[46] More significant were the favorable impressions of W. R. (Wilhelm Rheinhold) Valentiner, the German émigré director of the Detroit Institute of Arts and an eminent art historian, who had seen the exhibition, and of the mayoral-appointed Arts Commission that governed the museum. At a meeting of the commission on November 19, 1928, the architect Albert Kahn, a member, offered a gift of $500 for the purchase of an object of "metal, furniture or other industrial art," and he and Valentiner were appointed to select a "suitable object."[47] Valentiner asked Peter to submit a proposal sketch for a "special piece of rather large size."[48] Initially a sizable bowl was requested for the commission, but Peter later changed the design to a pair of candelabra, perhaps after a February 1929 meeting with Valentiner and Kahn in Detroit.[49] When Valentiner received the candelabra in the

summer of 1929, he expressed his delight in the "design and execution," deeming them "a fine example of modern German silver work."[50]

Peter's innovative design derives from an amalgam of sources [FIG. 10]. The elongated, tapered, and pointed applied strips that resemble pilasters were revived from his earlier prize cup exhibited in Newport and were utilized effectively to express movement. In various lengths, they articulate the division of the base and the upward thrust of the stem and center branch, and also snake across the outstretched branches. The Detroit commission may have been inspired by Raemisch. Candelabra by Raemisch had

previous spread

**FIG. 10
Candelabra, 1929, silver,
Detroit Institute of Arts,
Gift of Mr. Albert Kahn,
29.454.1–.2**

above

**FIG. 11
Dominikus Böhm, four-light
lamp, c. 1927**

been published in 1927 in *Deutsche Kunst und Dekoration* [SEE P. 21, FIG. 4] and displayed on a sideboard in the Bruno Paul dining room at the 1928 Macy's exposition.[51] In choosing the same form, Peter might have been seeking to measure up to or even surpass his mentor. Like Raemisch, Peter employed a quatrefoil division of the candelabra stem and unified the composition by keeping the shape of the base and the bobeches the same, though round here instead of the rectangular ones in Raemisch's candelabra; both used wrapped wire for strength and accent in their work.[52] The striking form of the branches in Peter's candelabra, with their quarter-round steps, have an uncanny resemblance to the four-light lamp by Dominikus Böhm, an architect and professor under Richard Riemerschmid at the Werkschulen in Cologne, which was illustrated in the same issue of *Deutsche Kunst und Dekoration* as the Raemisch candelabra [FIG. 11].[53] Peter's reconfiguration and refinement of influences, blended with his independent visual language, and the meticulous execution make the candelabra the acme of his silver work from the 1920s.

After the Detroit Society of Arts and Crafts exhibit, Peter was invited to participate in the inaugural exhibition of the American Designers' Gallery, a coterie of fifteen designers, including émigrés Wolfgang Hoffmann, Ilonka Karasz, Winold Reiss, and Joseph Urban, organized for the purpose of promoting their indigenous modern work. The exhibition opened in New York early in November 1928 and showed eight objects by Peter, including two cocktail shakers, a child's cup, and a cast-iron fireback (none of which have yet come to light), and a three-piece coffee set on a tray that may have been the service with gold foliate borders [SEE FIG. 2].[54]

Peter's work continued to appear in publications throughout 1928. In July, Helen Appleton Read, the *Brooklyn Daily Eagle* art critic and outspoken proponent of modernism, illustrated three of his pieces in an essay she wrote for *Vogue*, applauding the "unusual ornamentation of etched designs," which gave them "an added touch of individuality and distinction," as well as the "sturdy rationalism of his forms," which she equated with German *Sachlichkeit*.[55] And in a sly promotion, she mentioned that the pieces she chose to illustrate were currently on exhibit at Bamberger's department store in Newark. Peter was promoted less subtly in *Harper's Bazaar*: "Another excellent craftsman in silver is the charming young German, Peter Mueller-Munk.... If you have enough courage to invade the Village down to Fourth Street and Sixth Avenue (Number 148 West 4th, to be exact)—having made your appointment beforehand—you will be graciously received at his studio, where you may make your own selections to the muffled accompaniment of silver hammering, as in the old days of the gilds [*sic*]."[56] A charming endorsement, indeed. Before the end of 1928 he was recognized in *House Beautiful*, and the *New Yorker* paired him with Georg Jensen, calling them "two silversmiths worth remembering."[57]

The Architect and the Industrial Arts: An Exhibition of Contemporary American Design, the eleventh in a series organized by the Metropolitan Museum of Art, which presented individual room installations by architects, opened on February 12, 1929. The exhibition was the first of several opportunities over the years for Peter to exhibit at the museum. His silver was displayed in the Backyard Garden, a setting designed by architect Ely Jacques Kahn, who had a vital role in the realization of the exhibition. A corner of the installation was enlivened with a curvaceous built-in garden seat decorated in mosaic that had been designed by Kahn and Austin Purves, the director of Macy's atelier of design program.[58] Placed on a Formica-laminated table close to the seating were a coffee pot, teapot, and creamer, components of Peter's elaborate six-piece tea and coffee service [FIG. 12]. Centered and graduated relief panels rise from the recessed bases of the swelling rectilinear vessels, and the paneled, domed lids visually continue the flow from side to side. The dramatic curved and scored ivory handles are anchored at two points, and spherical ivory finials punctuate the service. This landmark exhibition—the first major showing of modern design in a New York museum—was enormously popular, but Peter's service did not receive press coverage.[59]

In March 1929 the Newark Museum mounted *Modern American Design in Metal*, which included an array of Peter's silver, some pieces on loan from L. Bamberger & Company.[60] On view were more than a hundred objects, by about thirty artists, which ranged from table silver to a grand piano designed by Lee Simonson and an elevator door designed by Ely Jacques Kahn.[61] Among the other exhibitors were Hunt Diederich, Ilonka Karasz, Winold Reiss, Walter von Nessen, and Kem Weber. The only object to be acquired from the exhibition by John Cotton Dana, the museum's founding director and champion of modern German applied arts, was Peter's bowl [FIG. 13]. No doubt, Peter's German training and aesthetic resonated with Dana.[62] The dominant decorative treatment of this shallow bowl—a slightly flared, applied arcade in relief—creates a scalloped edge that has architectonic connotations and evokes the rhythmic triforium story in medieval European churches and exterior corbelled arcades. The rectilinear, evenly segmented base reflects the rhythm of the edge and furnishes contrast. The arch motif is a hallmark of other works by Peter, including a compartmented tray, the matchbox of a smoking set, a notepad cover [FIG. 14], and, subtly, the tea set exhibited in Newport [SEE FIG. 8]. Peter likely adopted the medieval arch and arcade motifs in Raemisch's atelier in the early 1920s, when his mentor was an exponent of a revival of medieval German crafts in Berlin.[63]

FIG. 12
Tea and coffee service, c. 1928, silver and ivory, exhibited in *The Architect and the Industrial Arts*, Metropolitan Museum of Art, 1929

FIG. 13
Bowl, c. 1928, silver, Collection
of the Newark Museum, 29.472

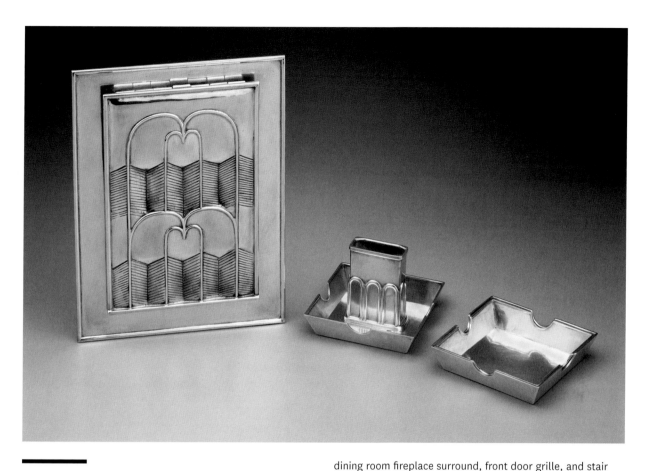

FIG. 14
Telephone pad cover and ashtray set, c. 1928–31, silver, Museum of Fine Arts, Boston, The John Axelrod Collection, 2014.1416, 2014.1417.1–4

Peter's relationship with Bamberger's yielded a unique silver commission from Louis Bamberger, the co-owner of the store, for the Bamberger Trophy cup, awarded, beginning in 1929, to the Barnegat Bay Fleet winner of the yachting race held annually by New Jersey's Seaside Park Yacht Club [FIG. 15]. The shape of the spherical and conical components of the cup together bear a resemblance to a 1922 wine jug by Christian Dell at the Bauhaus.[64] The stacked, stepped, and cantilevered disks on each side of the cup echo the graduated circular elements of the base and stem, unifying the composition. The elongated finial adds elegance, but the incised decoration, often favored by Peter, seems superfluous here.

Around this time Peter received an important metalwork commission for a princely five-story townhouse, one of the earliest single-family modernist homes in New York City. Located at 49 East Eightieth Street, the townhouse was designed by the architect Harry Allan Jacobs for Lionello Perera, a wealthy Italian-born banker.[65] It is not known how Peter secured the commission, which consisted of a dining room fireplace surround, front door grille, and stair rail. The stepped shape of the fireplace surround, made of "silver-plated copper sheet metal with repoussé leaves in polished copper," was a nod to the city's new skyscrapers [FIG. 16].[66] On the bottom right side, the surround was stamped "Peter Müller-Munk" and dated 1930. A "fecit" was added to certify Peter as the maker. A highly abstract naturalism dominates the relief through rigid, leafed branching in an espalier formation on each side of the fireplace and connected horizontally by a row of individual upright branches. The stylized design evokes earlier Viennese modernism, as do the spirals and other elements in the entrance door grille [FIG. 17]. Although somewhat unusual in his work, the wavy lines introduced in the door grille also occur in a silver bowl from around this same time [FIG. 18] and in the earlier coffee service with gold foliate borders [SEE FIG. 2]. The bilateral symmetry of the grille was in line with current interior architectural metalwork, such as the elevator doors in Kahn's commercial skyscrapers.[67] The stair rail was admired by one writer for "the clean-cut delicacy of the design and its continuing horizontal motion, that gives it the character of a running border."[68] The entrance door and stair rail, both of forged Monel metal, were executed by Renner & Maras, Inc., a well-regarded Long Island fabricator of commercial

THE BAMBERGER TROPHY
PRESENTED BY
L. BAMBERGER & Co.
TO THE
BARNEGAT BAY FLEET
I. S. C. Y. R. A.
AUGUST 1928.

WON BY
ISCYRA II
G. W ELDER
AND
E. T. EVANION
WESTERN L. I. SOUND

and residential architectural metalwork.[69] The house was completed early in 1930, and the stair rail was included in the 1931 Annual Exhibition of the Architectural League of New York in April.[70]

Peter had prevailed on Dreier to use her influence to publish his work.[71] Finally, in October 1929, a piece by him appeared in the combined issue of *Creative Art* and the London-based art periodical *The Studio* (see reprint, p. 160). The crux of the essay, "Machine—Hand," can be interpreted as a coming to terms with and balancing of the conflict between craftsmanship and manufacture: "In keeping alive the craft of the handworker, I am not afraid of the machine's rivalry. The pieces which leave my hands should have the virtues of the slow and calculating process of design and execution with which they grew. On the other side, the factory product should reflect the exactness and mathematical economy of the machine that created it."[72] Peter did not disdain machine work; what he decried was the fake emulation of handwork by silver manufacturers: "it is a fallacy to believe that [the machine] can replace or copy the work of the craftsman." Peter respected and praised the machine for achieving the qualities for which it was best suited: "The clearness of shape and neatness of surface of a spun bowl is equal in aesthetic value to any hand-made piece and superior to its hand-wrought copy." To emphasize this point he illustrated two examples of machine-made hollowware with smooth spun surfaces by the architect Fritz August Breuhaus for WMF (Württembergische Metallwarenfabrik), which had been published in *Deutsche Kunst und Dekoration*. Acknowledging the competition between the two, and implying the conquest by the machine, he held out for the handmade object: "I still have the outmodish confidence that there will always remain a sufficient number of people who want the pleasure of owning a

opposite

FIG. 15
Bamberger Trophy cup, 1929, silver and enamel (replaced), Dallas Museum of Art, Gift of Sherry Hayslip Smith, Cole Smith, and Jewel Stern, 2009.51.A-B

above, left to right

FIG. 16
Fireplace surround, 1930, Lionello Perera townhouse, New York City

FIG. 17
Exterior door, c. 1929–30, Lionello Perera townhouse, New York City

centre piece without being forced to share their joy of ownership with a few thousand other beings." To demonstrate that prospective "pleasure," he chose two illustrations of his own work, one of the candelabra in the Detroit Institute of Arts, photographed with candles inserted, and a three-piece coffee service, published for the first time. In the latter, the boxy, rectangular form of the vessels and the horizontal applied corner strips that resemble architectural quoins bring to mind a pewter vase from 1927 by the French jeweler Jean Després as well as other examples of his cubistic work featuring narrow applied strips.[73] A rigid, angled, and tapered spout, favored by Peter, was employed for the coffeepot. New in his work were the angled handles that spring from the walls of the vessels and rest on narrow, attached plinths, a treatment adapted from French silver, especially the work of Jean Puiforcat.[74] A bolder sculptural approach informs a three-piece cubist-inspired tea set of octagonal-shaped vessels, a singular example, which appears to have been experimental in its construction **[FIG. 19]**.[75]

In mid-August 1929 Peter returned to Europe for six weeks. It would have been a sad family reunion; his grandfather Wilhelm Munk had died in January, and the 1930 divorce of his parents may already have been in process. Although Peter had added his mother's family name to his surname as early as 1923 when he enrolled in the University of Berlin, he would not officially change his surname to Müller-Munk in Germany until October 1930.[76] The altered familial situation and the emotionally close relationship he had with his mother, which persisted throughout his life, must have motivated him to legally recognize his Munk heritage in the place of his birth.

Transitioning to Industrial Design

In less than a month after his return to New York, Peter faced the shock of "Black Tuesday," October 29, 1929, the day of the stock market collapse. The long financial downturn was devastating to those dependent on the demand for non-essential luxury items. Symptomatic of the situation were advertisements and notices published as early as the spring of 1930 in *The Antiquarian* of private collections offered at auction and dealer inventories sacrificed at previously unimaginable discounts.[77]

A boon at the beginning of the Depression was a private commission for a centerpiece and matching garniture that Peter received from Mr. and Mrs. Alfred L. Rose for their Park Avenue apartment, remodeled by Ely Jacques Kahn. The originality of the forms, the cohesiveness of the ensemble, and the precision of execution rank the Rose three-piece suite

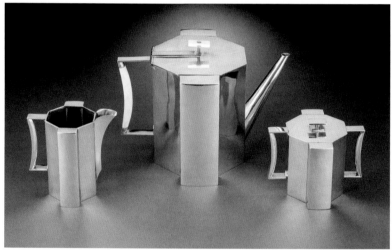

top to bottom

FIG. 18
Bowl, c. 1930–34, silver, The
Museum of Fine Arts, Houston,
Gift of William J. Hill,
2004.1489

FIG. 19
Tea set, c. 1928–29, silver and
ivory, Collection of Jacqueline
Loewe Fowler

top to bottom

FIG. 20
Centerpiece and garniture,
c. 1929–30, silver, Collection
of Jacqueline Loewe Fowler

FIG. 21
Centerpiece and garniture
in dining room, apartment of
Mr. and Mrs. Alfred L. Rose,
c. 1930

a masterwork in Peter's oeuvre [FIG. 20]. The commission doubtless originated with Kahn, who had included Peter's service in his Backyard Garden at the Metropolitan Museum of Art early in 1929. The centerpiece and garniture on the Roses' dining room table, adorned with flowers and fruit, appeared in a 1930 *Home and Field* article acclaiming Kahn's redecoration of the apartment [FIG. 21].[78] Using a flared leaflike form for the three components, Peter created stylized, naturalistic holders that harmonize with flowers and fruit. Applied ribs, alluding to botanical veins, articulate the form and add a strong decorative accent. Peter utilized this treatment in other works from this period, for example, a cylindrical sugar shaker and cream pitcher set, and a cocktail shaker.[79] And on a graceful boat-shaped centerpiece, a vertical section of four applied ribs serves as a decorative element that contributes contrast while unifying the base with the outstretched body [FIG. 22]. The base, a platform that adds stability, reverses and accentuates the curves of the bowl.[80]

Even though the forecast was dark during the deepening financial crisis, several bright notes sounded for Peter in 1931. A silver bowl and his Detroit candelabra appeared in the traveling exhibition *Decorative Metalwork and Cotton Textiles: The Third International Exhibition of Contemporary Industrial Art*, organized by the American Federation of Arts, which opened in October 1930 at the Museum of Fine Arts, Boston. It subsequently traveled to the Metropolitan Museum of Art, the Art Institute of Chicago, and the Cleveland Museum of Art. The candelabra in the Chicago venue excited the French art reviewer C. De Cordis to such a degree that he featured Peter in a generously illustrated spread in *La Revue Moderne Illustrée des Arts et de la Vie*.[81] He rated Peter the top modern silversmith and praised his work for its purity of form, links to nature, simplicity, beauty, and harmony of proportion.[82]

At the invitation of Dreier, Peter gave his first known lectures early in 1931, at the Rand School of Social Science, an institution associated with the Socialist Party of America. Dreier had taken charge of the Rand School art department as a means of perpetuating the Société Anonyme, and she organized a lecture series that opened with the visionary architect-inventor Buckminster Fuller, who presented his futuristic Dymaxion House. In his first lecture, Peter addressed "Metals and Their Applications," and a month later, concurrent with a display of his work in the gallery of the Société Anonyme at the school, he spoke on "Proportions in Machine Production."[83]

A young Russian émigré illustrator named Nina Novinska sought Peter out for one of her original covers for the *Jewelers' Circular*. Novinska imagined a soignée dinner for two set exclusively with silver hollowware by Peter [FIG. 23]. Some of the pieces depicted in the October 1931 color cover had already been published, such as the services plates, water goblets, and centerpiece fruit bowl.

FIG. 23
Nina Novinska, cover,
The Jewelers' Circular
(October 1931)

Previously unpublished were the ribbed salt and pepper set and a dramatically positioned and lighted candlestick closely resembling the Detroit Institute of Arts candelabra, a design assumed to be unique [SEE FIG. 10].[84]

Two exhibitions in the fall of 1931 gave Peter additional exposure in New York. The *12th Exhibition of American Industrial Art* at the Metropolitan Museum of Art is notable for its inclusion of several otherwise unknown works designed by Peter but fabricated and loaned by the Roman Bronze Works, a subsidiary of the General Bronze Corporation: an eight-piece silver desk set, a seven-piece bronze smoking set, and four floral vases.[85] Loaned directly from Peter were a three-piece silver coffee service and a silver sugar shaker and creamer set.[86] In time for Christmas shopping, Greenleaf & Crosby, a carriage-trade jeweler located on the twentieth floor of the new Squibb Building at 745 Fifth Avenue, designed by Kahn, mounted an exhibition exclusively of Peter's work. Formal invitations were mailed, and an extensive selection of his silver was on view. In a rare instance the selling price of two works was published: a silver and ivory tea service consisting of five pieces and a stand with alcohol burner at $1,200 (the equivalent today of $17,500), and a smoking tray with a nest of small removable trays and a lighter at $450 (the equivalent today of $6,500).[87] Photographs of the Perera door, stair rail, and fireplace surround were also exhibited.[88]

Peter met the photographer Margaret Bourke-White [FIG. 28] in 1931 at the home of Alfred de Liagre, an affluent textile manufacturer. Frida and Alfred de Liagre had a son, Alfred Jr., the same age as Peter, and it may have been through him that Peter was invited to their home in Byrdcliffe, a hamlet near Woodstock, New York. Afterward, Peter sent Bourke-White an invitation to the Greenleaf & Crosby opening, adding a handwritten note: "Do come, won't you?"[89] A long relationship between them ensued that initially appears to have been romantic. A communication from Bourke-White a year later conveys a lover's plea: "I cant [sic] stand it we will have to tango soon. Peggy."[90]

The year 1931 also marked Peter's completion of a private commission from Mr. and Mrs. Herbert R. Isenburger for a distinguished five-piece tea and coffee service [FIG. 24]. The couple had chosen Peter to make it after seeing his silver exhibited at the Metropolitan Museum of Art "around 1930" when he was "fresh from Germany."[91] This must have been the service with ivory handles in the Backyard Garden of the *Architect and the Industrial Arts* exhibition in 1929 [SEE FIG. 12]. Like the earlier service, the Isenburger set consists of rectangular vessels with a matching tray and has distinctive, curved ivory handles and spherical finials. Mrs. Isenburger, an interior decorator known by her professional name, Anne Landsman, sacrificed her silver wedding gifts, which were melted down for the service.[92] One writer reported that "the design and details were worked out jointly by Anne Landsman, interior decorator of New York, and Peter Muller-Munk."[93] At a later date, Landsman remarked that the service had been "exhibited at a Fifth Ave. jewelers," and it may have been the one at Greenleaf & Crosby referenced above and priced in the *New Yorker* article.[94] Making a full circle, the Isenburgers would give the unusual service, a tour de force in Peter's oeuvre, to the Metropolitan Museum of Art in 1978.

Soon after its completion, the service was illustrated in *Town and Country*, and in the accompanying article Peter commented on the appearance of Chinese influence: "Mr. Müller-Munk says frankly that his inspiration may have been Chinese though he had no consciousness of this when making his design."[95] For the incised geometric patterning Peter had employed the Greek key fret, a motif that also occurs in Chinese bronzes. He positioned two identical fret sections back-to-back to create the dominant surface decoration, which appears again in a dresser set of the same period **[FIG. 25]**.[96] Whether Peter's inspiration for the tea service was ancient Greek or Chinese bronzes or the result of collaboration with the client is an open question. Nevertheless, *New York Times* art critic Walter Rendell Storey mused in 1931 that the latest handmade silver objects, in addition to utilizing new forms inspired by modern techniques, "go back to the *basic principles* underlying the metal forms of ancient Greek and Chinese bronzes," and he cited Peter's work exclusively as demonstrating the two tendencies.[97] More recently, a small bowl in the collection of the Yale University Art Gallery, one of two known examples, has been singled out for its affinity with Chinese bronzes **[FIG. 26]**.[98] This object, however, is not a copy of a particular historical form; rather, it demonstrates Peter's ability to filter and synthesize various visual cues into a handsome, modern object. The panel detail on this bowl was used similarly by Peter for his tea and coffee service exhibited in the Backyard Garden in 1929.[99]

A signal event for Peter's career occurred in May 1932 when he gave a speech at the symposium organized by the New York Regional Art Council and the National Alliance of Art in Industry on the subject "Choosing a Life Career in the Design Arts." His responses to a prior questionnaire posed by the organizers reveal that Peter had seriously studied current design instruction, which he criticized fiercely, and that he was already positioning himself to be a leader in reforming industrial design education (see reprint, p. 164). His cover letter to the completed questionnaire is telling:

> The topic as a whole interests me profoundly and I believe a solution of the problems involved is of paramount importance to the entire future of American industry. If there is any way in which I might be of assistance to the Art Council in its present efforts please do not hesitate to call me. I cannot stress the pitiful inadequacy of the present system of instruction in the applied arts too strongly. As it is it is simply money wasted and it were far better nothing were done at all than the *leaderless* fumbling practiced now.[100]

The recipient of the letter and questionnaire, with Peter's added in-depth analysis and proposed remedies, including

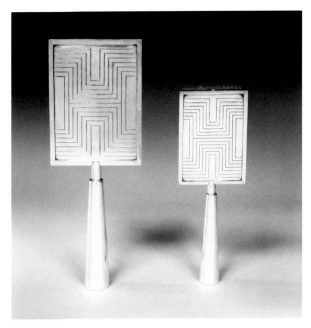

opposite

FIG. 24
Tea service with tray, 1931, nickel-plated silver and ivory, The Metropolitan Museum of Art, New York, Gift of Mr. & Mrs. Herbert R. Isenburger, 1978, 1978.439.1–.5

above, top to bottom

FIG. 25
Dresser set, c. 1931–34, silver and mirrored glass, private collection, Baltimore, Maryland

FIG. 26
Bowl, c. 1930, silver, Yale University Art Gallery, Gift of William Core Duffy, Mus.B. 1952, Mus.M. 1954, and Mrs. Duffy, 1980.101

left to right

FIG. 27
**Volupté hand mirror, 1934, chrome, mirrored glass, and enamel,
Carnegie Museum of Art, Gift of Jewel Stern, 2015.5.8**

FIG. 28
**Margaret Bourke-White, *Self-Portrait with Camera*, c. 1933,
gelatin silver print, toned, Los Angeles County Museum of Art,
AC1992.197.18**

the creation of an academy "attached to a college or university," was Florence N. Levy, the influential founder and director of the American Federation of Arts and the supervisor of the vocational service of the National Association of Art Education. Levy may have been the person who recommended Peter to the Carnegie Institute of Technology when it was developing its industrial design department. His lecture alone would have brought him to the attention of others in the field.

Peter traveled abroad in 1932; all that is known of this voyage is that he sailed tourist class from Liverpool back to New York in September 1932 aboard the White Star Line's MV *Georgic*.[101] What prompted this trip may have been changes in his immediate family. In 1931 Peter's father had remarried. Franz's second wife, Susanne Bruck, was thirty-three years his junior, the same age as Peter. Gertrud, who never remarried, studied with Helmut Ruhlemann, the chief art restorer of paintings at the Kaiser-Friedrich-Museum (now the Bode Museum) in Berlin.[102] Her training with Ruhlemann would enable her to support herself in the future. She also continued to produce her own paintings. Two were included in the *Große Berliner Kunst-Ausstellung* held May–September 1932 in the Bellevue Palace in the Tiergarten district.[103] Peter likely attended the exhibition with his mother.

Early in 1933 Peter learned of a new program sponsored by the New York–based Liturgical Arts Society, named the Craftsmen Service, to "provide liturgically correct sacramental vessels for small churches with limited means."[104] He jumped at the chance to increase his earnings during this

bleak period of the financial recession and quickly submitted drawings for ciboria and chalices, of which three survive, priced from $75 to $125.[105] He received two commissions, each for a chalice and paten. No detailed documentation survives of the first, but the second, destined for the college of the De La Salle Christian Brothers in Washington, DC, was photographed without the paten and published in *Liturgical Arts* early in 1934 [FIG. 29].[106] The potter Edwin Scheier recalled to an interviewer that early in his career he had studied silversmithing and worked for Peter, as a "low-level apprentice" doing "manual work" and "roughing out church chalices and other pieces" designed by Peter.[107] The arrangement with the Craftsmen Service ended on a sour note in September 1934 over payment of his fee for the De La Salle commission.[108] The Liturgical Arts Society terminated the program shortly afterward.

On June 23, 1933, Peter's aunt and godmother Marie Munk, a pioneer for women's rights in Germany and the first female judge in Berlin, arrived in New York on her first trip to the United States.[109] The International Federation of Business and Professional Women had invited Marie to attend as a delegate to the International Congress of Women, held in conjunction with the 1933 A Century of Progress International Exposition in Chicago.[110] Peter greeted her at the pier where the SS *Bremen* arrived from Germany, and that evening they dined together with a friend and strolled along "Broadway's milky way."[111]

Marie's trip to America coincided with the rise to power early in 1933 of Adolf Hitler and the National Socialist party. With the enactment of the *Berufsbeamtengesetz*, the Law for the Restoration of the Professional Civil Service, on April 7, 1933, conditions altered irrevocably for German Jews and Christians of Jewish descent. Both Marie Munk and Franz Müller, who held government positions, were fired. The situation for Peter's closest relatives became dire, leading them to flee Germany. The perilous turn of events might have been the catalyst for Peter's becoming an American citizen. On June 27, 1933, less than a week after Marie's arrival, he declared his intention (the first of two steps toward citizenship).[112] Peter's precarious financial situation at this time meant that Marie could not enlist his support for the assurance of work she needed to secure an immigration visa: "My nephew was struggling himself and could not have given me a guarantee."[113] To help make ends meet, Peter accepted a summer teaching position in "Metalcraft" at the Oswego State Normal School in upstate New York.[114] In a letter to Bourke-White on October 14, 1933, he wrote: "Give me a ring sometime—and perhaps I'll have the money to go to the movies."[115] To keep himself afloat he cobbled together teaching positions at the newly formed Craft Students League and at the New York School of Fine and Applied Art and the New York Evening School of Industrial Art.[116]

Early in 1934 Peter's mother, Gertrud, visited him for the first time. He was living in a bare-bones, four-story walk-up at 154 East Thirty-Ninth Street.[117] By that time, Peter was probably romantically involved with his future wife, Ilona Marion Loewenthal Tallmer, whom he would marry in October 1934. Their courtship was scandalous, as Ilona was married at the time to Albert F. Tallmer and was the mother of two young sons, Jerry and Jonathan. Peter's family, too, had concerns about his impending marriage.[118] Ilona was the older daughter of the Hungarian-born former Helen Kohut and German-born Max Loewenthal, and the granddaughter of the prominent rabbi Alexander Kohut.[119] Max Loewenthal prospered in the United States; in the 1900 census he was listed as a rubber manufacturer, and had three servants living with the family. Records show that Ilona traveled abroad several times before the age of eighteen, beginning at eight years old.[120] In New York she attended the progressive and civically liberal Jacobi School, founded in 1896 by German émigré Laura Jacobi, before entering Vassar College in 1916, where she focused on economics, history, and English.[121] Ilona dropped out of Vassar in her senior year, before her marriage, and did not

top to bottom

FIG. 29
Chalice, 1934, silver and ivory

FIG. 30
Creamer and sugar bowl, c. 1934, silver and wood, Collection of Ken and Debra Hamlett

graduate.[122] She and Albert Tallmer, a grandson of a rabbi, were married in a lavish wedding at the Ritz Carlton Hotel in March 1920.[123] The ensuing years were filled with a variety of activities. She worked in the theatrical office of Norman Bel Geddes as a secretary for about six months during the winter of 1922–23, attended classes in philosophy and playwriting at Columbia University in 1924, and helped organize a preschool program at Hamilton House, a division of the Henry Street

Settlement, from 1924 to 1926.[124] Parallel with these endeavors were the perks of affluence, trips abroad in 1926, 1929, 1930, and 1931, some with Albert and the boys.[125] In the early 1930s Ilona became involved in left-wing, so-called radical intellectual politics and served as a volunteer in 1933 on the National Committee for the Defense of Political Prisoners, and later, in relation to the Spanish Civil War, on the North American Committee to Aid Democratic Spain.[126]

As recalled by Edith H. and James A. Fisher, a couple whom Peter and Ilona later befriended in Pittsburgh, Peter met the family through a letter of introduction to Ilona's parents and became friends with Ilona and Albert. During a weekend visit, or perhaps several, to the Tallmers' summer place in New England, where Ilona stayed with the boys while Albert commuted back and forth to New York, Ilona and Peter began a passionate love affair that led her to leave her husband and move in with Peter.[127] With Jerry and Jonathan in tow, she traveled to Las Palmas, Spain, in September 1933 to secure funds from her parents for a divorce.[128] The divorce, which was granted in Reno, Nevada, in mid-October 1934, was exceedingly bitter, and Albert was awarded sole custody of the children.[129] Peter and Ilona were married in New York on October 26, 1934.[130]

When Peter's sister, Margit, married Franz Mombert, a political scientist and a son of the esteemed German-Jewish theoretical economist Dr. Paul Mombert, on December 4, 1934, Peter and Ilona did not travel to Europe to attend the wedding. Alert to the ominous situation brewing in Germany, the young couple, together with Franz's younger brother Ernst, an educated agriculturist, had established themselves as farmers in the south of France at the Propriété Banégon in Fayence, and were married there.[131] In a few years the farm would become a hiding place for other family members, including Peter's father and his second wife, Susanne.

In the fall of 1934, the American Guild of Craftsmen, an independent organization recently formed to promote the work of its members and stimulate sales, announced the opening of a shop on the main floor of the posh Bonwit Teller store on Fifth Avenue.[132] Peter was on the guild's founding board of governors.[133] The guild later negotiated an arrangement with the prestigious Jacques Seligmann Galleries at 3 East Fifty-First Street.[134] The first exhibition at the Seligmann Galleries opened in April 1935, and two works by Peter in the show, a previously unpublished water pitcher and a centerpiece, possibly the one for the Roses or a duplicate, were illustrated in the *New York Sun*.[135] The venture was unsuccessful, however, and the contract with Seligmann was not renewed in January 1936, signaling the demise of the guild.[136]

The mid-1930s witnessed an uptick in the economy and the advent of new product commissions for Peter. He was

FIG. 31
Desk set and bookends for Laura Lee Linder, Inc., New York, 1934, gold-tooled leather

becoming associated with industry through the publication of his product designs. Macy's advertised his three-piece dresser set for Volupté early in November 1934, and named him the designer [FIG. 27].[137] The outlining of form in the dresser set recalls that treatment in earlier Austrian modernism, and whereas the geometric and stepped motifs echo late-1920s popular modernism, the curved form reflects 1930s streamlining. Volupté was a manufacturer with whom the American Guild of Craftsmen had an active relationship, and Peter likely secured this commission through the auspices of the guild.[138] Late in 1934 he wrote a biographical sketch for *Creative Design* in which he sized up his current situation: "lately some of the manufacturers, who I have been bombarding for years, surrendered, so that I have been doing quite a bit of work in the industrial field."[139] Orders also trickled in from a loyal "private clientele" for "bench work" in metals, and he reported that teaching metalwork and industrial design were rounding out his labors.[140] A coffee service with ebony handles and finials, illustrated in the *New York Herald Tribune* and captioned "Unusual," has odd-shaped

clockwise

FIG. 32
Bowl, prototype for Silvermode, c. 1934, silver, Collection of James P. Karlen and Elaine K. Crawshaw

FIG. 33
Mary Ryan advertisement, "Silvermode by Mueller-Munk," *Gift and Art Buyer* (January 1934)

FIG. 34
Silvermode vase, Poole Silver Company, c. 1934, silver plate Collection of John C. Waddell

MARY RYAN PRESENTS
Silvermode
by MUELLER-MUNK

Manufactured by
POOLE SILVER CO.
Taunton, Mass.
Exclusively sold by
MARY RYAN
5 FIFTH AVENUE   New York, N. Y.
74 MERCHANDISE MART Chicago, Ill.

47

vessels and cruciform feet that recall period furniture pedestals, and may have been one of the private commissions referred to by Peter [FIG. 30].[141]

The Metropolitan Museum of Art's *Contemporary American Industrial Art* exhibition, which opened on November 5, 1934, provided a public platform for two of Peter's industrial commissions. Leather desk accessories—a pair of bookends and a desk set composed of an ink well, a letter opener, and a blotter, which he designed for the New York leather goods company Laura Lee Linder [FIG. 31]—were on view in the General Group, designed by Ely Jacques Kahn and Joseph Lotto. The accessories were well publicized in several popular magazines.[142] The other commission, which he considered to be his "most ambitious project so far," was the only production-line hollowware he designed; it was briefly manufactured in silver plate by the Poole Silver Company of Taunton, Massachusetts.[143] Silvermode, the signature line stamped with his name, was introduced in January 1934 by the firm of Mary Ryan, a leading giftware representative [FIG. 33].[144] Examples were exhibited in architect Paul Philippe Cret's East Gallery General Group in the only exclusively silver showcase in the exhibition.[145] Although Jean Puiforcat and Marianne Brandt had used the hemispheric shape for vessels in the 1920s, it was infrequent in American silver before the mid-1930s. Ponytail handles, a distinctive feature of the line, recall those on vessels by Josef Hoffmann and the Wiener Werkstätte.[146] Less than a week after the exhibition opened, Silvermode was lauded in the *New York Times*: "A dignified silver tea set by Peter Mueller-Munk follows the modern usage of gaining distinction through unusual form, the ebony handles and a tiny beading forming the only accents."[147] The line was hailed in *Arts and Decoration* for causing "a good deal of stir because of its obvious originality," and it was singled out by the reviewer as one of "the bright spots of the silver season."[148] Silvermode received further coverage after the spectacular opening on April 15, 1935, of the Industrial Arts Exposition (in which it was included), organized by the National Alliance of Art and Industry and held in the Rockefeller Center Forum. From the White House in Washington, President Franklin Delano Roosevelt telegraphically inaugurated the event, which was optimistically subtitled "A Preview of Prosperity."[149] The decorative treatment of the Silvermode water service as well as vases [FIG. 34], with pointed applied strips derived from Peter's earlier work, had a functional purpose, too, as he explained: "A goblet has to feel right in the hands. There should be no slippery surfaces. Hence spikes, because they help you grip the cup."[150] Another design for Silvermode evolved from a silver bowl wrought previously by Peter [FIG. 32]. The construction of the manufactured bowl and related pieces piqued interest: "Müller-Munk says he designed this bowl on the counter-point

movement…. By reversing the swirl of the foot, this bowl, nut dishes and candlesticks were made from two dyes [*sic*]."[151] Peter told another reporter that the "base of the bowl is the bon bon dish in reverse."[152] Although appreciated by professionals, the rarity of surviving Silvermode pieces suggests that the line was not popular with consumers.[153]

A casual style of home entertaining emerged in the 1930s, and high-styled tableware in chromium-plated metal, more affordable and easier to care for than silver, became fashionable. Revere Copper and Brass, Incorporated of Rome, New York, initiated a metal giftware line in 1935, and Peter, along with Norman Bel Geddes and others, was engaged to design for it.[154] The result for Peter was one striking object, a water pitcher in chromium-plated metal named for the new French ocean liner SS *Normandie* [FIG. 35]. Both the name and the aerodynamic teardrop shape of the pitcher sought to capitalize on the excitement generated by the arrival in New York City on June 3, 1935, of the luxury ship on its maiden transatlantic voyage. More than 200,000 people lined the harbor front and thousands "thronged rooftops, skyscrapers and observation towers from Coney Island to midtown Manhattan … for a glimpse of the majestic steamer."[155] The Normandie pitcher was introduced less than three months later, in August 1935.[156] The canted pitcher was fabricated from a single sheet of brass, held together at the sharply pointed and angled front by a rolled edge. The Revere catalogue claimed that "the Normandie was inspired by the leaning streamlined stacks of the famous French Liner bearing this name."[157] The design was a departure from Peter's eclectic modernism, and a giant leap into the future. By utilizing the streamlined, teardrop shape, championed by Bel Geddes in his groundbreaking 1932 book *Horizons*, Peter positioned himself in the vanguard. For curator Christopher Wilk, writing half a century later, the Normandie pitcher eloquently embodied "the aspirations of its time."[158] The pitcher became an iconic symbol of 1930s streamlining and was included in a United States Postal Service stamp set issued in 2011 honoring "Pioneers of American Industrial Design."

Peter's conviction grew that industrial design for mass production was the wave of the future. An opportunity fortuitously arose that profoundly altered his professional life when he was called to Pittsburgh early in the summer of 1935 to teach industrial design as an assistant professor in the newly formed program at the Carnegie Institute of Technology, the first of its kind in the country.[159]

──────────

FIG. 35

Normandie pitcher, Revere Copper and Brass, Incorporated, 1935, chromium-plated brass, Carnegie Museum of Art, Decorative Arts Purchase Fund, 87.29.1

Professor Muller-Munk, Industrial Designer

RACHEL DELPHIA

——

"Pittsburgh needs good industrial designers. I can't think of any city in which it could be more adequately taught…. You design in steel alloys; you go to a steel mill. You design in aluminum, glass and pottery; you go to aluminum, glass and pottery plants. I'm very glad to come here for that reason."[1]

In the summer of 1935, Peter and Ilona Muller-Munk, wed less than a year, embarked on a new chapter together. His appointment as assistant professor of industrial design at Pittsburgh's Carnegie Institute of Technology (now Carnegie Mellon University) offered a fresh start in more ways than one. The position lifted the financial burden of a luxury craftsman operating in the midst of economic depression and presented an opportunity to tackle the educational reforms in which Muller-Munk so fervently believed. And, although he moved to Pittsburgh to teach, the relocation would prove to be a critical step in his development as a designer. Within the next few years he would found an industrial design consultancy, and over the course of three decades he would develop it into a thriving enterprise of more than forty employees that ranked among the top ten such firms in the nation.

The Pittsburgh that the Muller-Munks encountered in the mid-1930s was a large city in the process of maturation **[FIG. 1]**. With a population nearing 700,000 (1.4 million in the metropolitan area), it was the tenth-largest city in the United States, in the same echelon as Cleveland, Baltimore, and St. Louis. During its boom years between 1870 and 1910, Pittsburgh experienced unchecked manufacturing and population growth. As the city emerged from this turbulence at the turn of the century, it underwent a more calculated phase of development. The consolidation of major industries—steel, aluminum, and glass—led to concentrations of wealth that flowed back into the community.[2] A symphony, a museum, and public parks were born. Industrialists caught up in the urban planning efforts of the City Beautiful movement sponsored major building projects downtown and, more emphatically, in the less-developed neighborhood of Oakland, some three miles away. There, civic-minded Pittsburghers saw the opportunity to shape a new cultural center. By the 1930s industrial production in the region slowed to a steady, rather than frenetic, pace. At the same time, new industries blossomed that would prove to be the backbone of continued economic success: electricity, radio, mechanical refrigeration, aluminum, and stainless steel—all areas in which Muller-Munk ultimately found design work.[3]

The Muller-Munks took up short-term residence at The Aberdeen.[4] New but not modern, the Georgian-style apartment building sat in the heart of Oakland. It was within easy walking distance to Carnegie Institute of Technology and the University of Pittsburgh; Carnegie Institute, which included the public library, the opulent Music Hall, and the Museum with sections dedicated to art and natural history; Phipps Conservatory; the 450-acre Schenley Park; and numerous private clubs, civic halls, and institutions. Each, by its very presence, proclaimed that Pittsburgh's elite were as committed to culture as they were to business. The cosmopolitan Muller-Munks surely missed New York, but their new home

frontispiece

frontispiece

FIG. 1
Aerial view of downtown Pittsburgh with Oakland in the background, c. 1935–36

above

FIG. 2
Architect Henry Hornbostel created a grand Beaux-Arts master plan for Carnegie Tech. The College of Fine Arts, completed in 1916, housed the Department of Painting and Design in which Muller-Munk taught.

was more civilized than they might have anticipated. As Peter later recalled, "Pittsburgh ... seemed very far away ... particularly to my wife who was a born New Yorker and was working with me, [but] it was a chance you couldn't let go."[5]

Muller-Munk's new employer, known as Carnegie Tech, was an institution with aspirations beyond its technical school roots. The school's founder, Andrew Carnegie, was the son of a Scottish handloom weaver who had emigrated in 1848 when industrialization took away his livelihood. The younger Carnegie, who excelled in the industrial milieu, later acknowledged the opportunities for self-improvement that had enabled his meteoric rise, and he sought to provide them to the next generation. Having observed technical schools emerging in the United States and abroad, Carnegie decided to create his own, eventually sited on thirty-two acres across the ravine from Carnegie's museums and library **[FIG. 2]**.[6]

Historically, Muller-Munk's role at Carnegie Tech has been exaggerated. It is often stated that he founded or directed the first university course in industrial design in the country. In fact, the school had established the program in 1934, the year before he arrived, after a long flirtation with design curriculum development. Indeed, Carnegie administrators had applied arts education in mind from the outset. One of the four original divisions was the School of Applied

Design (1905–1918). Furthermore, in 1906 Carnegie's president, Arthur Hamerschlag, was among a handful of academic administrators and business leaders across the country to publically endorse "the growing need for artisan training" with the "formation of a society to promote industrial education."[7] By the early 1920s, the broader College of Fine Arts, successor to the School of Applied Design, including classes in crafts, costume design, art education, advertising and printing design, and interior decoration/furniture design.[8] The course bulletin described the offerings as "a variety of strong practical courses, open to both men and women in the fields of commercial and industrial art."[9] Four-year degrees were awarded as Bachelors of Arts.[10]

Four Carnegie Tech faculty members who preceded Muller-Munk deserve mention here: Frederick Clayter, Donald Dohner, Alexander Kostellow, and Robert Lepper.[11] All but Dohner remained to teach alongside Muller-Munk. Clayter was hired as assistant professor in 1921 and taught crafts, industrial arts, and model making.[12] Like Muller-Munk, he was a silversmith, but there is no indication that the two men knew each other prior to Muller-Munk's arrival in Pittsburgh.[13] Dohner joined the faculty as a part-time instructor in 1923.[14] By all available accounts, he was the first Carnegie Tech professor who also practiced industrial design. A night class he taught for Westinghouse engineers may well have led to his appointment in 1929 as that company's art director and his associated resignation from the school.[15] Kostellow arrived in 1929 with an impressive résumé.[16] He was noted for his artistic talent, intensity, and intellectual depth, characteristics that earned him Muller-Munk's highest esteem.[17] Despite his skill as a painter, Kostellow increasingly dedicated himself to design education.[18] Like Dohner, Kostellow practiced as a design consultant in Pittsburgh, though the extent of his work is unknown.[19] In 1930 the university hired Lepper, a recent graduate of the school, as an instructor in design. Lepper taught foundational design and visualization exercises and was best known for his sculptures, paintings, and murals incorporating industrial imagery or materials.[20]

These men, together with a small cohort that concentrated on painting, drawing, illustration, and art education, composed the Painting and Design Department faculty prior to Muller-Munk's arrival. Although the department offered no major in industrial design, the faculty demonstrated serious interest in the subject. In April 1932 they featured the designs of Dohner's Westinghouse art-engineering department in the college's art gallery.[21] The professors elected to discontinue one of the department's three majors, Interior Decoration, and expressed a desire to replace it with a broader "Decorative Design" option that would "open for the student far wider fields of professional endeavor."[22] Course bulletins also show Kostellow, Clayter, and others collaborating on numerous classes in two- and three-dimensional design.[23]

At this point, previous histories of design education have variously ascribed credit for originating Carnegie Tech's industrial design degree program to Dohner, Kostellow, and/or Muller-Munk (the last of which is incorrect, as he was not yet on the faculty). Design historian Sarah Johnson recently discovered documentation that points to a student-led effort in the spring of 1933, which finally spurred the faculty into definitive action.[24] In May of that year, Glendenning Keeble, professor and College of Fine Arts faculty chair, wrote to Thomas Baker, president of Carnegie Tech:

I have felt for some time that [the department] should look forward to developing an option in Design, and that this should especially consider the problems of Industrial Design. I am therefore prepared to recommend to your attention the accompanying petition, which originated spontaneously, as far as I can learn, among the students.

The student petitions reads:

In view of the fact that manufacturers and large industrial concerns are employing highly paid officials for the purpose of improving the artistic quality of their products; and because the necessity of well trained designers and artists in nearly all industries is being realized all over the world; we, the undersigned, would like if possible to have the new Industrial Design course developed still further as an advanced course continuing through our junior and senior years.

As many of us would prefer development in design rather than teaching as our professional activity, we suggest that Industrial Design might be added to the present curriculum as an independent option.[25]

Keeble laid out three options for the president concerning how quickly such a program could be instituted. Plan 1 suggested spending the academic year 1933–34 planning the curriculum with the intention of hiring a new professor for the fall of 1934. Plan 2 proposed hiring immediately so that the rising junior class could complete the two-year major in time for its graduation. The third option, the one recommended by the faculty, was to set up a transitional curriculum for 1933–34 and to hire a new professor for the fall of 1934. This meant that some of the upperclassmen petitioners, such as Anton Parisson, later a principal with Muller-Munk's firm, left prior to the availability of the industrial design degree.

Electing option three, the faculty embarked on a transitional year, which required both internal reorganization and outside assistance. Keeble wrote that Kostellow would give up a freshman studio to teach a new course in industrial design, and that they would appeal to the College of

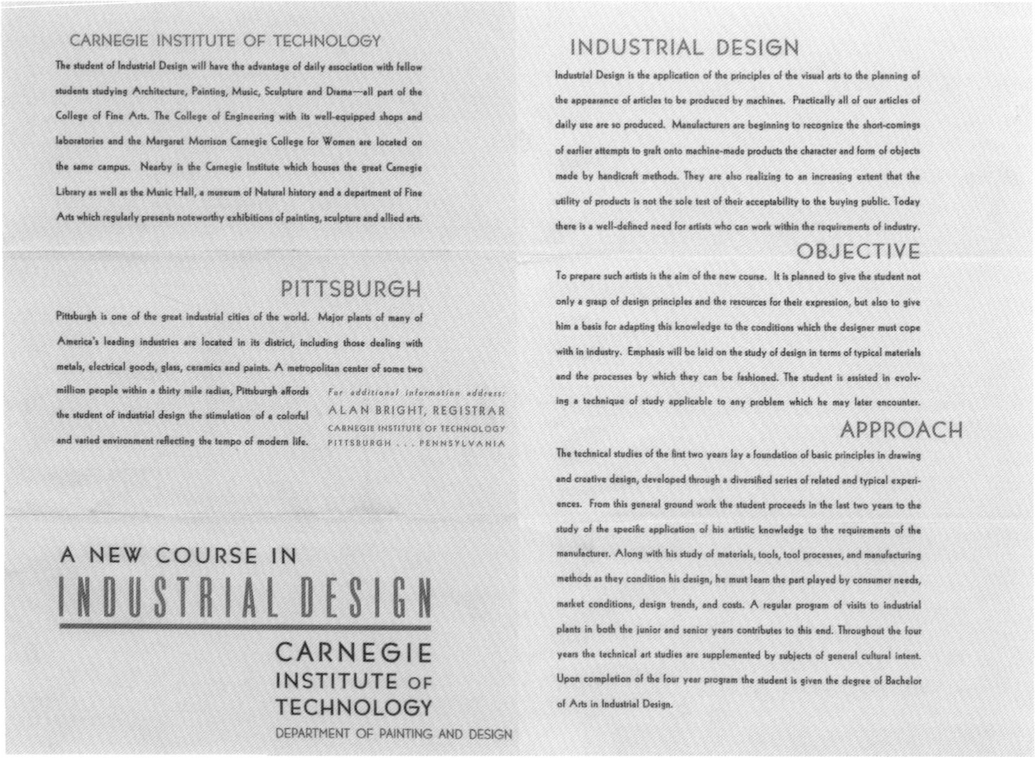

FIG. 3
Flyer announcing the new
Industrial Design program at
Carnegie Tech, probably 1934,
likely designed by Dohner and
Kostellow

Industries for a course in mechanical drawing. There are no formal records of the transitional curriculum, so it is unclear whether changes were in fact implemented. Most significantly, Keeble acknowledged that by 1934 they would "need a man with more industrial experience than Mr. Kostellow" and that "a designer of the type we wish to have might be pretty expensive even in these days."[26] For this, Carnegie Tech turned again to Dohner, whose most recent work for Westinghouse had been a highlight of Chicago's 1933 World's Fair, titled *A Century of Progress*. Dohner contributed to curriculum development and promotion of the program, as evidenced in a recently discovered pamphlet entitled "A New Course in Industrial Design" [FIG. 3].[27] Though undated, it surely came about during the winter/spring of 1934 to promote the program for fall enrollment. The flyer describes the industrial design field and the demand for practitioners, outlines the goals and structure of the program, and touts the unique context of the school in Pittsburgh, "one of the great industrial cities of the world."[28] The new program and Dohner's faculty appointment were formally announced by the university on August 5, 1934.[29]

The first full curriculum for the Industrial Design degree at Carnegie Tech was published in December 1934 for the 1935–36 year.[30] The freshman and sophomore coursework was nearly identical for students in all three majors (Painting and Illustration, Art Education, and Industrial Design). In the junior year, the Industrial Design majors were to take Industrial Design I (Dohner and Kostellow), Production Methods I (Dohner), Industrial Processes (Clayter), Drawing III, English II, and Economics. The senior coursework consisted of Industrial Design II (Dohner and Kostellow), Model Making (Clayter), Production Methods II (Dohner), Drawing IV, History of Painting and Sculpture, and electives.

Dohner gave the newly congealed faculty a shock when he resigned in late 1934 or 1935, accepting a position at the Pratt Institute in New York to create an industrial design program there.[31] No records survive of the search for Dohner's replacement, but it must have been a predicament, given that Keeble had made such a compelling argument to President Baker some two years prior that the Industrial Design program required a dedicated faculty member with significant industrial experience, which none of the other staff possessed.

It has been suggested that Muller-Munk, a formally trained silversmith, was an odd selection to replace Dohner.[32] In truth, all practicing industrial designers of the era emerged from alternative backgrounds—such as theater design, illustration, or advertising—because formal degree programs did not yet exist. Many shared Muller-Munk's opinion that the training situation was dire, but few were willing to step away from their practice in order to teach for an extended period of time.[33] On a conference panel with Muller-Munk in 1936, industrial designer Walter Dorwin Teague noted, "there is practically no education in design in this country." In his session-opening monologue Teague complained, "We [designers] are all asked constantly what to study, how to prepare for this work. The questions are so hard to answer that we would far rather deal with the problems of design than to try to tell others how to attack them."[34] Twenty years younger than Teague and far less entrenched in his practice, Muller-Munk was eager to try.

Muller-Munk also distinguished himself as a professorial candidate with his eloquence and outspokenness. He was a natural wordsmith who displayed a marked talent for persuasive composition, in English no less, which was not his native tongue. Consciously or not, years before the faculty opening at Carnegie Tech, he was positioning himself as an educator by taking a public stance on the need for reform. As early as 1929 he lamented, "if we could have designers who knew the machines which were to turn out their designs, and if these men would give the machine what it most longs for, we would really have achieved a new art resulting from the harmony of technique and object."[35] Muller-Munk found a perfect platform for his ideas in May 1932, at a seminar conducted by the New York Regional Art Council and the National Alliance of Art and Industry titled "Choosing a Life Career in the Design Arts: A Discussion of Vocational Guidance Problems." The transcript of his talk as well as his preseminar survey responses to organizer Florence N. Levy shed light on his impressive command of the subject, his conviction, and his zeal (see reprint, p. 164).[36]

In order to succeed as a designer, he suggested, one must possess: "1. Ability to present and develop [one's] own ideas so that they can be realized with the technical and human equipment of the particular client. 2. Thoroughness ... 3. Selfassurance [sic]. 4. Logical thinking. 5. Ability to deal and work with people opposed to ones [sic] own ideas. 6. Salesmanship." In terms of training, the designer should have "practical knowledge of tools and machinery"; factory, selling, and merchandising experience; "full knowledge of styles and periods"; and experience in mechanical drawing and modeling.[37] On the subject of the ad hoc educational system for three-dimensional applied arts Muller-Munk became critical, even irate. His frustrations included the lack of standards for teacher qualifications: "Almost anybody is allowed to teach, if he can promise a certain number of pupils."[38] "They are rarely even outstanding men in the professions they teach."[39] Furthermore, Muller-Munk took issue with the sharp division between practice and teaching. In his view, many a teacher has "never been required to do original creative work,"[40] and even one who has is "not allowed to have his own studio in the school nor is he encouraged to continue creative or professional work after he has been admitted to the faculty."[41] How can an instructor stay in touch with "modern tendencies and requirements for industrial design"[42]

if he does not practice? All of this, he argued, was in the best interest of students, who would observe the teacher's professional endeavors and therefore "come into contact with work which bears some relation to their own life, instead of having to listen to verbal instruction or being bored with ridiculous reproductions and Christmas presents."[43]

Despite his obvious admiration for the master–pupil relationship, he was in no way advocating a return to trade-specific apprenticeship. On the contrary, he suggested that courses should be divided "not according to materials but different techniques, which in turn are applicable to a variety of materials.... Instruction should give the pupil an understanding of the interrelationship between the tool, the material, and the desired function of the article."[44] In short, he argued that industrial design required a new and distinct skill set that should be systematized and taught: "Just as banking and medicine require a definite type of knowledge, so does Industrial Design. Yet, while there are many institutions where one can acquire the fundamental knowledge indispensable to a career as a lawyer or doctor, there are none for the Industrial Designer."[45]

There is no known extant record of the symposium's attendees, but any number of designers, educators, or administrators hearing Muller-Munk's address might have recommended him for the Carnegie Tech position.[46] Early in the fall of 1935, the university announced his appointment:

For some years [Peter Muller-Munk] has conducted a studio in New York where he has executed commissions for well-known firms in metal, leather, and pottery. He has taught at the New York School of Fine and Industrial Arts and at the New York evening School of Industrial Art.... He has lectured before numerous art groups on modern design and articles by him on this subject have appeared in many magazines and newspapers.... Examples of his work have been exhibited at the Metropolitan Museum in New York, Cleveland, [etc.].... He will have the rank of assistant professor and will teach industrial design at Tech.[47]

Coverage ran locally in Pittsburgh and in the *New York Times*, *New York American*, *New York Mirror*, and *New York Post*.[48] The press reported that Muller-Munk would "direct the course in industrial design," but the nascent program, with only nine majors enrolled across the junior and senior years, had no clear "director" or "head," according to school records.[49] Despite the program's more nuanced beginnings, by midcentury, many in the field regarded Muller-Munk as its primary founder.[50]

Upon arrival at Carnegie Tech, Muller-Munk picked up where Dohner had left off, filling the voids in each of his courses rather than shaping a whole new curriculum. He undoubtedly adapted his methods and projects from year to year, but without his notes, syllabi, or any other detailed records of content to refer to, it is impossible to trace his personal evolution as teacher. From the outset, Muller-Munk paired with Kostellow in teaching Advanced Design, the sophomore introductory studio in three-dimensional design; Industrial Design I, the junior-level studio; and Industrial Design II, the senior-level studio.[51] Additionally, Muller-Munk picked up both the junior- and senior-level courses Production Methods I and Production Methods II. The latter were among the most innovative and important courses in the curriculum, consisting of weekly visits to factories in the region and associated design projects in the materials studied, as Muller-Munk described in June 1936:

> The designing of a new chinaware pattern for hotel service, for instance, is supplemented by a visit to the Homer Laughlin Chinaware Plant—one of the largest and most modern of its kind. The opportunities for first hand observation of mass production methods are, of course, infinitely larger and more varied in Pittsburgh than in New York. The co-operation of such companies as the Aluminum Company of America, Fostoria Glass Company ... etc., are vital assets to our studies.[52]

His reference to "our studies" is revealing. These courses were as beneficial to the professor as they were to his pupils, both for learning the latest methods of manufacture and in establishing crucial client connections as he developed his professional practice in Pittsburgh. Muller-Munk acknowledged as much, calling the factory visits "a rare opportunity open to no other designer."[53]

Muller-Munk's course load and the larger Industrial Design curriculum remained unchanged until 1938, when Kostellow and his wife, the artist and designer Rowena Reed Kostellow, left Carnegie Tech to join Dohner at Pratt Institute. Lepper, who had previously concentrated on design drawing courses, stepped up to fill the void, co-teaching with Muller-Munk three classes a year for the next six years. The two professors collaborated on a pair of articles in *Art Instruction*, which give insight into their teaching interests and methods. In contrast to Lepper, who emphasized the foundational study of visual perception (line, area, volume, space, value, color, and texture), Muller-Munk emerged as the pragmatist (the practicing industrial designer), revealing how the abstract compositional exercises translated to specific purposes— "radios, refrigerators, furniture, etc."[54]

Muller-Munk's various writings provide glimpses of his students' work. His article in *Art Instruction* had included half a dozen illustrations, including a turntable by Raymond Smith, who would later become a partner in Muller-Munk's firm. Smith was one of seven seniors who produced a streamlined train interior for their thesis project. Starting with standard specifications for a club car for the Philadelphia-based Budd Company—the industry leader in stainless steel train car production—the students created a modern interior that included a vestibule, kitchen, bar, cocktail lounge, partition, reading-writing section, and observation area **[FIG. 5]**.[55] Other intriguing student work from the period includes an aviation advertising display for Pennsylvania Air Lines. Five seniors created a curved plaster relief map of the Eastern United States, showing detailed miniature cityscapes of the locations serviced by the airline: Pittsburgh, Washington, DC, and Chicago.[56] Pennsylvania Air Lines, with service at Pittsburgh's

FIG. 4
Muller-Munk's student Ruth Catherine Amrhein (class of 1938) undoubtedly rendered these glassware designs, dated March 1937, in connection with a visit to a regional factory such as Fostoria Glass

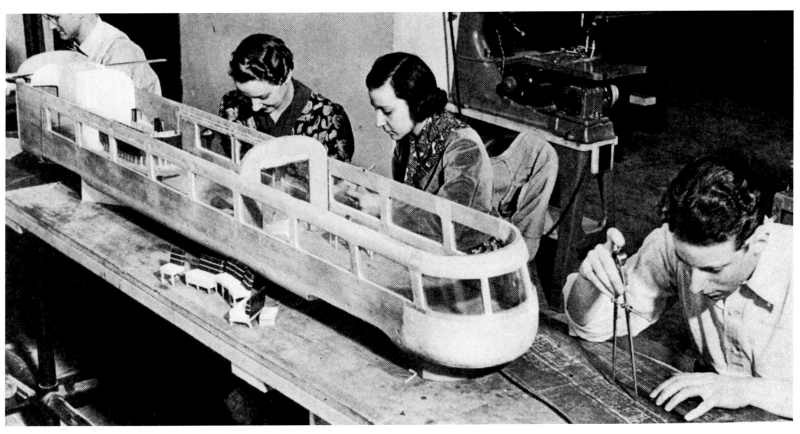

top to bottom

FIG. 5
Raymond Smith (far left)
and classmates at work on
a scale model of their senior
thesis project—a modern
train interior—which they
completed prior to graduating
in June 1938

FIG. 6
Muller-Munk (left) and industrial design seniors Paul Perrin
and Maud Bowers examine a
scale model of a modern living
room (possibly Perrin's work),
June 1936

Comb, mirror, brush

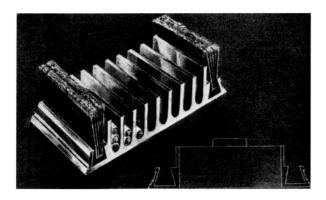

opposite

FIG. 7
From an article in *Modern Plastics* (April 1936) by Muller-Munk about his students' work, top: photograph of a model wall clock by Paul Perrin, designed to be manufactured in translucent plastic and metal; bottom: design for a plastic comb, mirror, and brush set, drawn by Isabel Shelton

above

FIG. 8
Maud Bowers's design for a cigarette box, made of a single extruded piece of aluminum, was hailed by *Architectural Forum* (July 1936) as "a brilliant solution, since extrusion is an ideal process for aluminum and means that the boxes can be turned out by the mile." Although it was reported that Alcoa would produce them, no examples have ever surfaced.

new Allegheny Airport (1931), was so pleased with the display that they arranged to have it go on view downtown at Gimbels department store, which, Muller-Munk noted, gave students firsthand experience with the window display department (in a period in which department stores and their windows were fashionable venues for modern design).[57] In another example, an individual capstone project, each student designed a modern room that he or she would wish to inhabit [FIG. 6]. Pleased with the results, Muller-Munk called them "beautiful, livable, and worthy of the most finished labor of any specialist in the field."[58]

The faculty established student design competitions, which brought students cash prizes and prestige, and, most important, practical experience through contact with industry. Maud Bowers won a competition sponsored by the Aluminum Company of America [FIG. 8] and another by the Pittsburgh Water Heater Company.[59] For her aluminum candlestick, Isabel Shelton won a Kensington Ware competition.[60] Muller-Munk secured a vanity set design competition in 1937 from his former client Volupté, and in 1940 the students enjoyed a contest sponsored by Plaskon Company of Toledo, Ohio.[61]

The only surviving indication of Muller-Munk's development as a design professor is his catalogue description of the graduate course GA-582, Structural Analysis, which he created between 1938 and 1939:

An investigation of the extent to which society nourishes and develops the language of the arts. A study of creative expression as a vital force in society and as a contributor of positive and primary values thereto. Supplementary research to develop a more complete realization of the unity of all creative endeavor and its stabilizing influence with the community.[62]

The course description presented Muller-Munk's personal and professional manifesto—indeed, his mission statement. The interrelationships across the arts and the practical benefits of creative practice to society were themes he expounded upon throughout his career.

Between 1935 and 1944 Muller-Munk taught sixty-two industrial design graduates (thirty men, thirty-two women) and dozens of students from other majors, including Arthur Pulos, class of 1939 in Art Education, who later led a major industrial design program at Syracuse University and published some of the earliest histories of the profession.[63] Muller-Munk's greatest contribution to Carnegie Tech was arguably his outspoken support and promotion of the place, the program, and the people. He championed Pittsburgh and the school from the moment he arrived, proclaiming the city to be an ideal location for training the designers of tomorrow. "The geographical situation of Carnegie Institute of Technology makes it the logical center of education in a topic whose purpose and value are so closely interwoven with industry."[64] He considered his colleagues to be leaders in the field of design education,[65] and raved about the natural aptitudes of his students:

Where do they come from? Not from Park Avenue, not from Greenwich Village, or any of the usual sources of fashion in art movements.... The most talented and daring designers in this school come from the mining and mill communities of this state, from Ohio farms, West Virginia mountains and the villages of the South and Midwest. Industrial designing, with its thoughts in terms of mass production, is in the truest sense an American art impulse springing direct from the American soil.[66]

When the inaugural class of five industrial design students graduated in the spring of 1936, no one praised their accomplishments more adamantly than Muller-Munk [FIG. 7].

Somewhere in the midst of teaching, learning, networking, and endlessly promoting industrial design, Muller-Munk fell under the sway of his own proclamations. Practice, not teaching, held the utmost allure: "I think our modern industrial apparatus offers the greatest opportunity artists ever had. They have a chance to help in the propagation of art to millions of people from designing ink bottles to airplanes."[67]

above

FIG. 9
**Ilona and Peter Muller-Munk
feted in the local paper upon
their return from Europe,**
Pittsburgh Press, **October 12,
1936**

opposite

FIG. 10
**Muller-Munk's designs for
Lektrolite (front row), photo-
graphed by Margaret Bourke-
White, 1935**

Having remained true to his conviction that teachers were at their best only when practicing, Muller-Munk had secured permission from Carnegie Tech to operate independently as an industrial designer throughout his teaching career.[68] He exerted considerable energy to building his profile as an industrial design consultant, and during his academic tenure, his design practice grew from a makeshift shop to a solid business with a downtown office. In 1944–45 Muller-Munk took a yearlong leave of absence without salary for "reasons of ill health."[69] Whether or not he was ailing, the leave proved to be the death knell of his professorial career. The following fall, he resigned to devote himself full-time to industrial design practice and his firm: Peter Muller-Munk Associates.[70]

Professional Practice

Muller-Munk launched his industrial design consulting efforts from his academic quarters at Carnegie Tech. He described the university as "very generous" for allowing him to keep his clients.[71] He found an invaluable partner in Ilona, who acted as "secretary, telephone operator, errand boy, and office manager," and whose business acumen Peter greatly admired.[72] Teaching left summers open, and prior to the war the Muller-Munks enjoyed extended periods abroad, both for pleasure, sightseeing and mountain climbing in Salzburg, for example, and for professional development, such as visiting the second Milan Triennial, the major international exhibition of modern design and architecture, in 1936 **[FIG. 9]**.[73]

Little is known about Muller-Munk's design output during his first two years in Pittsburgh.[74] Recent designs in production—the Normandie pitcher, the Volupté vanity set, and his Silvermode hollowware—enjoyed continued media coverage, especially during the holiday buying season.[75] And at least one product came to fruition in late 1935: the Quarterly cigarette lighter for the fashionable Lektrolite brand of Platinum Products Corporation. Dubbed the company's "exclusive model" in 1936 sales literature, the Quarterly was available in three finishes: smooth nickel for $5.00, rhodium engine-turn for $7.50, and Chinese-type lacquer and rhodium for $15.00. Muller-Munk's contribution was likely the modern black and multicolored lacquer patterns on the top-of-the-line models rather than their three-dimensional form. Margaret Bourke-White may have introduced him to Platinum Products head Archie Moulton Andrews, a photography client. In November 1935 she wrote to Muller-Munk, "I have just come up from seeing Andrews and two of your lighters are complete. They look marvelous and I am about to photograph them" **[FIG. 10]**.[76]

Sometime before the end of 1936, the Muller-Munks moved to the Bellefonte apartments at 5508 Elmer Street, a pair of three-story brick buildings overlooking a central garden. Between their former and new residences lived a Mr. and Mrs. Roy and Rachel Hunt. Rachel McMasters Miller Hunt was

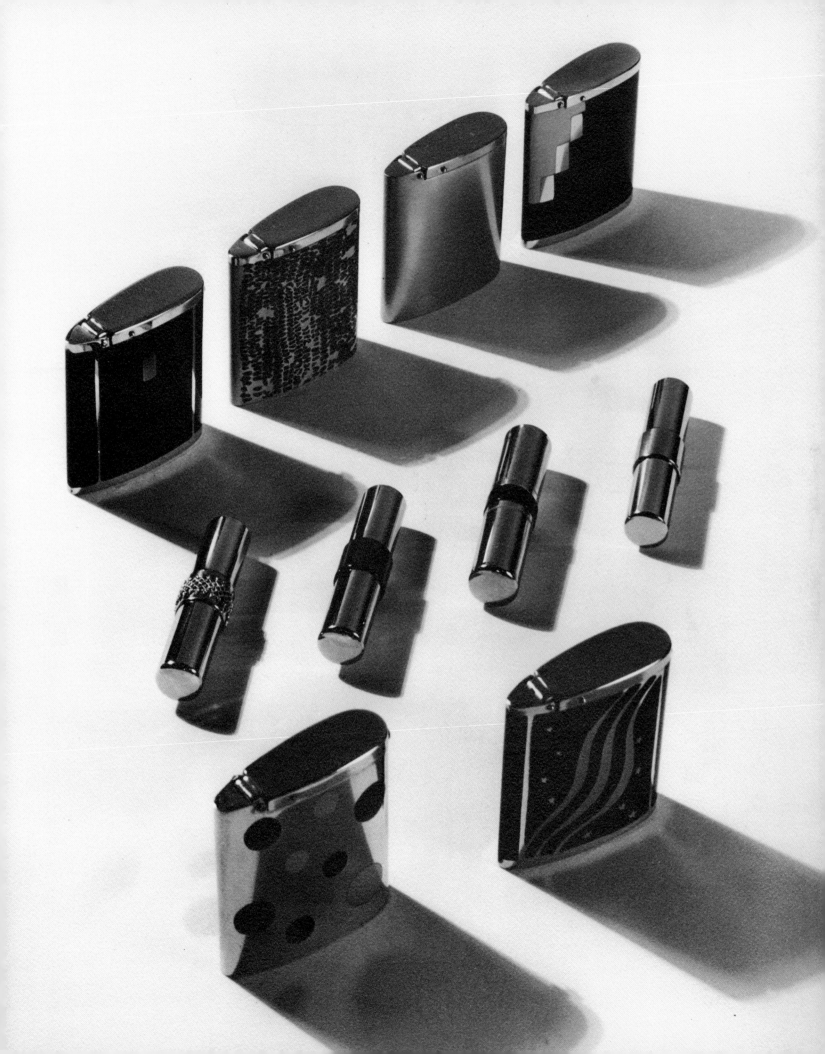

a noted artistic bookbinder and bibliophile who had exhibited extensively in New York.[77] She and her husband, Roy A. Hunt, president of the Aluminum Company of America, would be excellent connections socially and professionally. Writing to Bourke-White in October 1935, Muller-Munk mentioned a desire to meet Mrs. Hunt: "from your description and from what people tell me here I am very anxious to do so. We don't know a soul yet." By December he urgently solicited Bourke-White: "I am telling you now that I shall park myself in your handsome studio until you have given me your long promised introduction to Mrs. Roy Hunt."[78] It is unclear whether Muller-Munk managed to meet the Hunts during this early period, but his persistence was characteristic.

Muller-Munk's engagement for a lecture series in early 1936 demonstrates his rapid success in connecting with the business community. The program was coordinated by the Research Bureau for Retail Training at the University of Pittsburgh with top-shelf local department stores including Gimbel Brothers, Joseph Horne's, and Kaufmann's. Muller-Munk's course, titled "Design—The New Sales Factor," was addressed to executives of home furnishings departments to help them "explain and analyze the role which appearance play[ed] in the buying and selling of merchandise … and give them a guide toward the proper evaluation of the modern versus the modernistic." Delivered over six evenings in February and March, the course covered modern design in kitchenware; table accessories; furniture; lamps, lighting fixtures, and rugs; and packaging.[79] This program may have introduced Muller-Munk to Edgar J. Kaufmann Sr. and his son. Having returned from Frank Lloyd Wright's Taliesin Fellowship in 1935, Edgar J. Kaufmann Jr. was actively involved in the home furnishings department of his father's flagship store in Pittsburgh, which

he oversaw until he departed for New York in 1940.[80] The Muller-Munks befriended both generations of Kaufmanns and enjoyed visiting Fallingwater, the father's new country house outside of Pittsburgh, an iconic design by Wright.

In 1936 Muller-Munk wrote several articles targeted to particular industries. Ostensibly these essays celebrated the graduation of Carnegie Tech's first industrial design class, but they also gave Muller-Munk a platform to position himself as a knowledgeable emerging practitioner. Writing for *Modern Plastics*, he suggested that designers needed a handbook for the material that would enable them to design for specific inherent capabilities to minimize costs and increase visual appeal. "We believe that the plastics industry as a whole has much to gain from the success of our [academic] undertaking, just as we need their support to expand and complete our studies. It seems almost daring at times to promote plastics in a city where 'steel is king' but I hope those whose cause we are defending will not forsake us."[81] Two months later, he published a similarly obsequious missive to the glass and pottery trades: "It is only natural that we look to the Pottery, China, and Glass manufacturers with particular eagerness. They, even more than others, are our natural neighbors and we hope they will come to us for ideas and personnel, just as we go to them to learn about their problems and requirements."[82]

Muller-Munk's immersion in modern industrial materials coincided with his farewell to the medium that had launched his career.[83] It is not known when precisely he stopped making silver objects; his hands-on production surely tapered off significantly after 1935 in Pittsburgh. Nonetheless, his celebrated silver works were in demand for exhibitions until at least 1941. In 1937 he was represented in three major silver exhibitions: *Contemporary Industrial and Handwrought Silver*

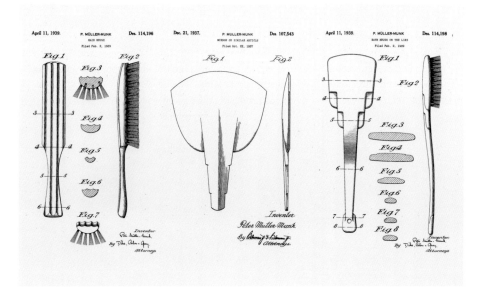

FIG. 11
Peter Muller-Munk, three US Design Patents, left to right: Design for a hair brush, Pro-phy-lac-tic Brush Company, 1939; Design for a mirror or similar article, Illinois Watch Case Company, 1937; Design for a bath brush, Pro-phy-lac-tic Brush Company 1939

1937 at the Brooklyn Museum; the Exposition Internationale des Arts et des Techniques dans la Vie Moderne in Paris; and *Silver: An Exhibition of Contemporary American Design by Manufacturers, Designers, and Craftsmen* at the Metropolitan Museum of Art, New York. He sent a "steak platter" to the Brooklyn Museum, and a client loaned "three piece silver hors d'oeuvres dishes."[84] His only object at the Paris exposition, a large silver bowl (*Coupe argent massif*), was displayed in the American silver section.[85] Critics lauded his two contributions to the Metropolitan Museum exhibit. In the *New York Times* Walter Rendell Storey wrote that Muller-Munk's chalice embodied "the clean-cut lines and perfection of technique characteristic of contemporary design."[86] Another critic humorously described his asymmetrical meat platter as extreme, "with a silhouette distorted in behalf of exciting design," and appropriate for "dining-rooms with modern paintings."[87] Also in 1937, as part of the juried Annual Exhibition of Associated Artists of Pittsburgh, held in the galleries of the Carnegie Institute, Muller-Munk's entry—his candelabra for the Detroit Institute of Arts [SEE PP. 30–31, FIG. 10]—received the Grogan Company Prize of $50 for silversmithing, marking the first time that crafts were so recognized.[88]

In each of the following years, 1938 through 1941, his silver was featured in an exhibition. His tea service for Mr. and Mrs. Isenburger [SEE P. 42, FIG. 24] shared the Mrs. Roy Arthur Hunt Crafts Prize of $50 with a ceramics entrant in the 1938 Annual Exhibition of the Associated Artists of Pittsburgh.[89] To the 1939 Golden Gate International Exposition in San Francisco he sent an "oval fruit bowl with handles" and a "silver platter."[90] These may have been the same pieces exhibited the following year in *An Exhibition of Silver: French, British, American, Modern* at the Virginia Museum of Fine Arts, where his "two-handled bowl" and "meat platter" were displayed in the "Modern Gallery."[91] Muller-Munk did not exhibit silver at the 1939–40 New York World's Fair, though he had attempted to secure a commission for a new "modern and striking" piece from the Liturgical Arts Society, an earlier client and anticipated contributor to the Fair, who ultimately declined to participate.[92] Although Carnegie Tech possessed metalworking facilities, it is doubtful that Muller-Munk continued in the craft at all after the last documented exhibition of his silver in 1941, *With Hammer and Tongs: Malleable Metals in Diverse Designs*, at the Cooper Union Museum for the Arts of Decoration in New York.[93]

By the spring of his second academic year, Muller-Munk was overrun with activity. In a letter to Bourke-White in March 1937, he described being "swamped with work for various exhibits—lectures and out side [*sic*] design orders—all in addition to my college schedule."[94] One of the projects diverting his attention, if briefly, would have been the redesign

of the Waring Blendor—a revolutionary new device for making pureed beverages—which fell into his lap quite unexpectedly (see "The Waring Blendor," pp. 74–79). The Blendor made its public debut in early October, just after the Muller-Munks had returned from a lengthy European trip.[95] That month, Muller-Munk also filed his first known applications to the US Patent Office. Granted on December 21, the design patents featured a vanity brush and mirror (though not a matched set) for the Illinois Watch Case Company [FIG. 11, CENTER]. It is unclear whether the products were ever produced. Nevertheless, he closed out the year with momentum and with the taste of success.

By early the following year, Muller-Munk's design workload necessitated hiring help, and he looked to his former students. In February 1938 he contracted Arnold L'Heureux Proellochs (class of 1937) for renderings of an electric shaver and four brushes.[96] The most important appointment occurred in March, when Muller-Munk hired his talented former student Robert (Paul) Karlen as his first true employee. The move would prompt Muller-Munk to cite 1938 as the year of his first formal design office.[97] Karlen had entered Carnegie Tech in 1934 and made a favorable impression on Muller-Munk, but when Karlen's father died in 1937 he withdrew from school to help support his mother and siblings. He worked for less than a year as a designer for the United States Glass Company before accepting Muller-Munk's offer.[98] The two men had an exceptional working relationship, described as "a stimulating and harmonious working together of two personalities and talents."[99] Muller-Munk's gift of a personally handwrought silver bowl to Karlen and his wife upon their marriage reflects the esteem and affection he had for his young colleague [SEE P. 47, FIG. 32].[100]

The two designers and Ilona crammed into the tiny office at Carnegie Tech, handling in the early years clients such as the Adams Manufacturing Company, the Automatic Canteen Company of America, the Automatic Sprinkler Corporation of America, the Pro-phy-lac-tic Brush Company, and E. A. Myers and Sons. The addition of the Catalin Corporation, the Dow Chemical Company, and the Elgin National Watch Company as clients prompted the relocation of the burgeoning practice to more comfortable quarters at the Muller-Munks' new home at 6615 Darlington Road.[101] During 1938 Muller-Munk was awarded a three-year tenure that secured his position at Carnegie Tech through 1941; in 1940 he was also promoted to associate professor.[102]

The work of Muller-Munk's fledgling office included products, appliances, graphic design and technical literature, and, increasingly, speculative designs for manufacturers of materials demonstrating creative new uses for stainless steel or plastic. Building on his prior experience with vanity products, Muller-Munk designed a number of brushes and mirrors

FIG. 12
Swank clock for the Pennwood
Company, 1940

for the Massachusetts-based Pro-phy-lac-tic Brush Company. In February 1939 he filed at least six design patents for Pro-phy-lac-tic, including one for a brush with a fluted handle and head that became a postwar success in transparent Lucite as part of a line of vanity sets named Jewelite, and another patent for an elongated bath brush **[FIG. 11]**.

Muller-Munk's agility with electromechanical devices was demonstrated by designs for a clock and vending machines. Since 1934 the Pittsburgh-based Pennwood and Lawson companies had been producing notably modernist "cyclome-ter" clocks using a digital-style display mechanism patented by Frederick Greenawalt.[103] Muller-Munk designed the ribbed and streamlined Swank model that became a popular main-stay **[FIG. 12]**. Most likely conceived in 1939—the patent was applied for on January 4, 1940—the Swank was offered in ivory, rose, or walnut Tenite plastic (cellulose acetate), with a die-cast metal base; it remained in production as late as 1958.[104]

Muller-Munk illustrated his cigarette machine for the U-Need-A-Pak Products Corporation (designed in 1938) in an up-tempo article for *Modern Plastics* in February 1940, titled "Vending Machine Glamour" **[FIG. 13]**. His design showed sensitivity to the plight of the passive machine, with red plastic darts on a pale background that would catch the eye of passersby and direct their attention to the merchandise. Absent a salesperson, he noted, "the coin machine must per-suade and ingratiate itself alone." He furthermore wrote with authority on the growing use of plastics: "The very pace and daring that motivates the manufacture of vending machine

has in itself a good deal in common with the inventiveness of the plastic producers. Here then is a case in which by the temperament and actual need, the plastics and the product quickly combine for the greater glory of both.... I believe the cast phenolics, cellulose acetates, and casein plastics play perhaps the most significant part."[105] Elsewhere, Muller-Munk's design, which was displayed at the annual convention of the Coin Machine Industries in Chicago in December 1938, was admired for its split central mirror, angled outward in each direction such that one customer "powdering her nose ... cannot rob the machine of its sales" to another.[106]

One of the most long-lasting client relationships forged in this early period was with E. A. Myers and Sons, a national leader in the development of hearing aids. As a Pittsburgher, company founder Edward A. Myers had been exposed to the very early radio broadcasts of local station KDKA (a famous collaboration with Westinghouse), yet had been unable to hear them because of significant hearing loss. In 1924 Myers and his son Edwin formed a company, and, with Westinghouse engineer George F. Harrington, developed their first hearing aid, a vacuum tube amplifier that occupied a six-foot-long cabinet and weighed a daunting 185 pounds. A revised version made the following year was dubbed "the Radioear," which the company adopted as its trade name. With the help of Myers's son-in-law Samuel F. Lybarger, an engineer who joined the business in 1930, E. A. Myers made multiple contributions to the development of life-altering personal products for the hearing impaired.[107]

The first product that arose from Muller-Munk's relationship with E. A. Myers was the Radioear 45, which debuted in January 1942 **[FIG. 14]**. The device introduced the company's first magnetic receiver technology. Product literature highlighted the skill of "nationally famous industrial designer, Peter Muller-Munk," who "brought a pleasing functional beauty" to the device whose "every streamlined curve has a meaning in relation to beauty, utility, and efficiency." On the product itself, Myers proclaimed:

New Streamlined Case: Designed by Peter Muller-Munk to make every bit of space usable and practical. Styled for comfort and convenience. Small … light … thin … durable … beautiful. Like earlier Radioear models it is cased in high-impact-strength Durez. Accidental breakage is almost impossible.[108]

Developed during the war years, the next two Radioear models—the Permo-Magnetic Multipower and the Permo-Magnetic Uniphone—were market-ready in late 1946 and early 1947. Muller-Munk continued designing for E. A. Myers and Sons until at least 1957, successively producing innovative hearing aids and eventually updating the corporate identity.

Like his fellow industrial designers, Muller-Munk was captivated by plans for the 1939 New York World's Fair. Unlike more established professionals, though, he had not received a commission. Undaunted, he dreamt up a host of civic design improvements—including fire hydrants, mailboxes, and traffic lights—and, overly confident, he attempted to present them to Mayor LaGuardia in person without an appointment. Although he did not gain an audience with the mayor, he happened to meet in the hall members of the Municipal Art Committee, who "expressed approval of the designs," according to the *New York Times*.[109] Although none of the concepts came to fruition, a flurry of press coverage suggests that Muller-Munk actively promoted his ideas.[110] While the reportage of the *New York Times* was straightforward in tone, others poked fun at his proposals, with headings such as "And How About Putting Murals on Manholes?" and "I'll Show New York City How." The former ran in the *New York Post*, which commented, "Modernistic fireplugs—mailboxes painted a flashy robins' egg blue—traffic lights redesigned to be things of beauty and with soul—these New York may have in time for the Word's [*sic*] Fair if somebody doesn't get after Professor Peter Muller-Munk in a hurry."[111] Although his combination of bravado and naïveté was cause for amusement on the part of some, Muller-Munk was undoubtedly serious about his proposals.

During the late 1930s Muller-Munk was fully cognizant of the uncertainty and opportunity for industrial designers in the face of increasing political agitation in Europe. His interest in the war effort was of course personal as well as professional.

FIG. 13
Cigarette vending machine for the U-Need-A-Pak Products Corporation, *Modern Plastics* (February 1940)

Although he left no commentary on the turmoil experienced by members of his immediate family in Nazi Germany because of their Jewish roots, we know that his European relatives were forced to take drastic actions. While his sister, Margit, and her husband, Franz Mombert, were initially safe on their farm in Fayence, France (see p. 46), his father, Franz Müller, sold the family home in Charlottenburg and in 1936 fled Germany with his second wife, Susanne, to Fiesole, Italy.[112] After the enactment of the Italian racial laws in September 1938, Franz and Susanne Müller sought refuge with the family in Fayence.[113] As conditions for Jews in Germany grew worse, Peter's aunt and mother moved permanently to the United States in 1938 and 1939 respectively.[114] Peter's father, sister, and brother-in-law survived the war in Fayence, where Franz Müller would die of natural causes in October 1945; Susanne perished at Auschwitz.[115]

As early as May 1939, Muller-Munk began thinking about the possibility of wartime contracts, particularly in the camouflage division or the designing of war equipment.[116] Although there is no documentation of his engagement, the "War Department" appears in his 1948 client list, and in a 1943 interview he alluded to having undertaken confidential war work.[117] At Carnegie Tech, Muller-Munk joined an extended cohort of faculty in teaching camouflage classes to potential soldiers within the student body.[118]

By July 1943, tired of "rubber cement paper coming down the front stairs" and "no privacy at any hour of the day or night," Muller-Munk "moved boards and airbrush to quarters on Murray Avenue"—the main commercial street between his house and Carnegie Tech.[119] That month an interview for the *Bulletin Index*, Pittsburgh's weekly newsmagazine, provided a lively snapshot of the business, headed by Muller-Munk and Karlen with four full-time assistants. The firm was presented as being invested in the postwar materials race and the retooling of American industries for a peacetime economy:

> If the stock piles are not to rot into the ground, if the machines are not to rust, U.S. industry must spend many a weary wartime night preparing for the bright morning of peace. Behind the manufacturer's postwar schemes are a tight little group of men … the industrial designers. Most of the best men, Norman Bel Geddes, Raymond Loewy, Henry Dreyfus [*sic*], etc. are centered in New York; one of the best is in Pittsburgh. The one is Peter Muller-Munk.[120]

Muller-Munk's biggest client in the postwar-planning milieu was the specialty steel manufacturer Allegheny Ludlum, which engaged him in the midst of a boom. During the war years, sales rose from $37 million to $114 million, and personnel tripled to 17,000. Flush with success, Allegheny Ludlum underwent an $80 million expansion and modernization program in 1946.[121] This escalation provided fertile ground for Muller-Munk's inventive concepts, including stainless steel giftware (1941); the Passenger Travel Center of the Future (1942); the Milk-O-Mat milkshake dispenser (1943); and the efficient, executive-class Victory Cabin for a modern postwar ocean liner (1944) **[FIGS. 15–18]**.[122] Although most were not produced as envisioned by Muller-Munk (they were not meant to be), several proved their worth as sources of inspiration for the client's clients. In 1946 Allegheny Ludlum's public relations representative confirmed that the National Dairy Products Corporation in New York would produce a version of the Milk-O-Mat, and that the Baltimore Arnot Company would make the Victory Cabin's folding berth.[123] Unfortunately, the evolution resulted in little recognition of Muller-Munk's original designs.[124]

Forging ahead in another area, Muller-Munk undertook the design of technical literature, including brochures with modern sans serif typefaces, meticulous diagrams, and atmospheric airbrushing characteristic of the period. In addition to unspecified "graphic booklets for war training," Muller-Munk designed *Welding Stainless Steels* (1943) and *Magnetic Materials* (1947), both for Allegheny Ludlum. The firm produced a brochure promoting magnesium in aviation for Dow Chemical's magnesium line, known as Dowmetal.[125] They also created for Dow some speculative products in the material, as published in "The Coming Battle of Materials: Magnesium," one of J. Gordon Lippincott's industrial design features for

Interiors. Lippincott illustrated two Muller-Munk designs in magnesium: a portable typewriter and a patio chaise.[126]

On the plastics front, Muller-Munk was engaged by both Dow and Durez Plastics and Chemicals. Recognizing that "originality and soundness" in the application of plastics' material properties were essential in capturing the postwar market, Dow hired Muller-Munk to create "thought provoking products in cooperation with company engineers, research and sales specialists."[127] Numerous Muller-Munk concepts for Dow were published in *Modern Plastics* and elsewhere, and included developmental designs for a space-saving office; desk sets; kitchen counters, built-ins, and appliances; lighting devices; and even an electrical meter.[128] The campaign for Durez was more targeted, and focused on a single aspirational though unrealized design: a sewing machine **[FIG. 20]**.[129] Muller-Munk provided not only a rendering of the device, but also expert commentary. (Indeed, he had used Durez earlier in his designs for Radioear.) According to Durez advertising manager H. S. Spencer, the ad was a great success, sending "all but one of the leading sewing machine manufacturers" clamoring to Durez for more information. Spencer also noted the potential pitfall of such speculative product design advertising: "the public, who read carelessly, began to inquire where they could secure such a machine." Regardless, the favorable response to the Muller-Munk campaign led to additional Durez ads with concepts by Egmont Arens, Raymond Loewy, Brooks Stevens, and Harold Van Doren, among others.[130]

The continued growth and success of his office, coupled with the anticipation of a postwar boom, induced Muller-Munk to step away from academia. He took a twelve-month leave of absence—without pay—in the fall of 1944, ironically

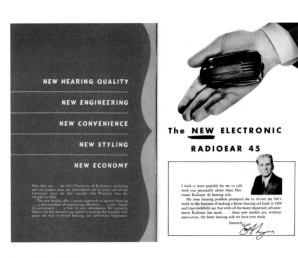

FIG. 14
Radioear, *The Dawn of a New Day for Better Hearing*, brochure, 1942

ASH TRAY NEST

Indispensable item for parties or bridge. Four stainless ash trays are held in a stainless base between two spheres of polished wood. The projecting cigarette-rests on each ash tray fit into a groove in the base, which holds them upright and in order.

POKER CHIP HOLDER

Double rows of poker chips are encased in this stainless stand. The top is hinged for easy access to the chips but will hold them firmly when not in use. The wooden handle at the side opens a compartment holding two packs of cards.

HORS D'OEUVRE TRAY

The resistance of stainless to foods and its easy cleaning properties make the metal ideal for an attractive tray to serve snacks and tid-bits. The graceful curves of this shallow tray are set off by the wooden handles at each end.

STAINLESS
Giftware
DESIGNED FOR THE FUTURE
by
PETER MULLER-MUNK

In the almost boundless field of giftware, the beauty and permanence of stainless steel place it high among the precious metals. The pieces on these pages, while entirely workable, do not now exist in fact. We merely commend them to you as smart, appealing designs, provocative of ideas. ● For further information on the designs, materials, or the designer's services . . . address STEEL HORIZONS, c/o Allegheny Ludlum Steel Corporation, Pittsburgh, Pa.

BRIDGE SCORE PAD

Gleaming stainless houses a roll of score paper, and a push on the wooden guard at the back releases fresh paper. The entire top lifts by the wooden knob at the front, revealing room for cards and pencils. The wooden base keeps table tops free of scratches, and adds its own note of beauty.

CENTERPIECE AND CANDLESTICKS

A novel and necessary gift for the party table. A shallow stainless bowl rests in a wooden base over a 4-arm candlestick arrangement. Either unit can be used separately, but the combination provides a really new, practical, and engaging table decoration.

It's designed in lines of coldly arresting beauty, this stainless iced drink pitcher. The handle, with its rubbed-finish wooden grip, prevents the hand from touching the cold metal. A small band over the spout retains the ice.

at the very moment he was awarded five-year tenure. In 1945 he elected not to return and submitted his resignation to Carnegie Tech. Although peers continued to view him as an authority on design education, his formal relationship with the school was over.

Professional practice was the future for Muller-Munk, and 1945 proved to be a pivotal year. On March 12 the Society of Industrial Designers (SID) granted him coveted recognition by voting unanimously to admit him as a member.[131] SID had formally incorporated in New York the previous year with fifteen original directors, called fellows, and Muller-Munk had just missed the cut. A select group led by chairman pro tem Walter Dorwin Teague discussed the organization's founding resolution in February and July 1944. At a July meeting Brooks Stevens and Muller-Munk were suggested as additional fellows, and whereas the former was accepted, the latter's nomination was tabled "pending a report to be made by Egmont Arens, one of the initial fellows."[132] When SID held its first annual meeting on October 11, 1944, Muller-Munk was not included.[133] It is not clear if he knew the backstory, but he lamented not being part of the initial set. His ultimate business success and leadership within SID led many to assume he had been a founder. It was an impression he did not rush to correct.

FIG. 15
"Over the Horizon: Stainless Giftware, Designed for the Future," *Steel Horizons* **(1941)**

PASSENGER
TRAVEL CENTER
of the
FUTURE

DOCKS

RAILROAD STATION
(2-LEVEL TRACKAGE)

BUS TERMINAL

BUS TERMINAL
(SUBWAY STATION BELOW)

INTERURBAN

OUTDOOR PARKING

AIRPORT

FIG. 16
In the Passenger Travel Center
of the Future, Muller-Munk
boldly suggested a multivalent
travel hub for the postwar
world in which rail, bus, plane,
ship, subway, and highway
"traffic could converge at a
single convenient interchange.

FIG. 17
Publishing a series of "pie in the sky" ideas, including the Milk-O-Mat, a stainless steel and plastic milkshake machine by Muller-Munk, *Interiors* **(November 1943) claimed that such advanced concepts soothed the public by assuring consumers that postwar products would be worth the wait.**

For the first time, he listed himself in the Pittsburgh city directory as "Peter Muller-Munk, Industrial Designs" in 1945, concurrent with moving the office to the prominent Clark Building downtown, a space befitting a rising professional.[134] Karlen's official standing as an associate was recorded on the firm's new stationery.[135] Other records indicate multiple new employees, among them recent Carnegie Tech design graduates Marion L. Costa, Eloise J. Nettleton, Mark E. Sink, and Irene Waichler, and a renderer, Robert C. Ward.[136]

Also fortuitous that year was an invitation from Henry Allman, chairman of the Industrial Design Committee of the Philadelphia Art Alliance, to participate in one of a series of solo exhibitions. Although he was eager to contribute, Muller-Munk was preoccupied by urgent work for the War Department, then underway in his office, and he asked for a later slot, in the spring of 1946.[137] The monthlong exhibition was well received by Alliance members and by Philadelphia industrial designer Harold Van Doren.[138] No images of the installation are known to exist, but correspondence suggests that about fifty photographs of both concepts and produced designs were shown. These included packaging, glassware, compact and cigarette cases, a postal scale, a bicycle, gas pumps, lighting, office equipment, stainless interiors for Allegheny Ludlum, and more.[139] Dorothy Grafly of the Art Alliance provided additional insight into the exhibition's contents in an article for *Design* in May 1946, in which she illustrated Muller-Munk's Swank clock for Pennwood, a

Radioear 45 hearing aid for E. A. Myers, a Waring Blendor, and a canteen for Industrial Food Service [FIG. 19].[140]

In what must have been a dizzying confluence of events, Karlen was drafted into the armed services just as the firm relocated.[141] Muller-Munk and Karlen undoubtedly hoped for a swift and safe return; nevertheless, Muller-Munk was compelled to recruit a replacement to maintain the existing level of operation. He reached out to former student Raymond A. Smith.[142] After graduation Smith had pursued his dream of designing cars in the General Motors' styling division until 1941 [FIG. 21]. when he enlisted in the Army Air Corps. Smith's skill set would be a tremendous asset to Muller-Munk in the product-design heyday of the late 1940s and 1950s.[143] He appealed to Smith's predilections in a letter of August 13, 1945, citing the extensive postwar retooling projects contracted to the firm and noting that "electrical appliances, office equipment, mechanical devices of all types" would be impossible to complete in a timely fashion in Karlen's absence.[144] Muller-Munk needed an experienced designer with Smith's qualifications. The younger man's reply conveyed genuine interest but also indicated that other postwar offers

FIG. 18
Muller-Munk described his
Victory Cabin (1944) as a
"design for a four-passenger
cabin for a one-class boat, not
a final solution, but an invitation to controversy. Stainless
steel is used for ladders and
supports of uppers, in sheet
form for the washing section,
for sliding doors to toilet and
closets."

were on the table, including one from General Motors. The opportunity to work with his friend Karlen (upon the completion of his military service) and the potential to be on the ground floor of a new organization were likely critical factors in Smith's decision to accept Muller-Munk's offer.[145] By October the two men had come to an agreement, and they appealed to the Armed Forces for Smith's release from service, which took place in February 1946.[146] Events did not unfurl in the order that Muller-Munk anticipated: Karlen returned from Japan about six months later (beating Smith to Pittsburgh), and Smith officially joined the firm in December 1946. With two trusted deputies secured, Peter Muller-Munk, Product Design, formally became Peter Muller-Munk Associates (PMMA).[147]

Work in the new office continued along earlier lines, with an uptick in products that surged throughout the 1950s. Advertisements for Jewelite brushes, combs, and vanity mirrors—some new PMMA designs, others designed before the war—dotted popular magazines in 1946 and 1947 [FIG. 23].

Another ladies' product, patented by Muller-Munk in 1945, hit the market in 1946: a sleek, asymmetrical compact for Elgin American [FIG. 22]. Given the longevity of their production and availability in today's vintage market, the plastic and metal vanity objects were evidently very popular.

Muller-Munk's most important early postwar product was the Cafex percolator for Hartford Products Corporation [FIG. 24].[148] The intelligence and attractiveness of the percolator design stemmed from the inventive treatment of the handle. Whereas typical rivet-joined handles accentuated the separateness of vessel and appendage, the Cafex handle appeared integral to the body and lid. Three pieces of glossy, heat-resistant Durez phenolic plastic were held tight to the body of the vessel by a stainless steel band. The cantilevered handle minimized heat transfer to the hand by avoiding contact with the lower portion of the pot. Another noteworthy design detail is the clear glass percolator knob that provided a view of the percolating action.[149] Despite a relatively high retail price

clockwise

FIG. 19
This super-efficient canteen for Industrial Food Service from 1946, was designed as a building-within-a-building, meant to be installed within existing mills and factories.

FIG. 20
Durez advertisement, July 1943

FIG. 21
Raymond A. Smith with a model car, probably 1938–41, during his tenure at General Motors

PETER MÜLLER-MUNK
Industrial Designer

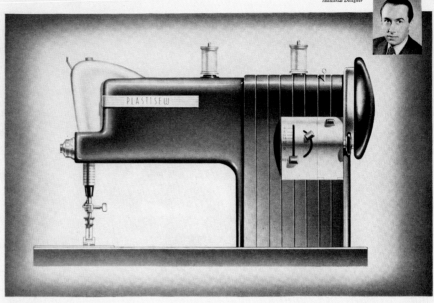

PLASTISEW

Why are men interested in this sewing machine?

Do you ever think about the vast industrial success that has been enjoyed by the manufacturers of sewing machines? What will be the position of their market in the *post*-war era?

Pursuing this thought, Mr. Müller-Munk has re-engineered the sewing machine in the above design for the future ... incorporating both functional improvements and greater sales-appeal through the use of Durez plastics. As he says ...

"Even before I ever put pencil to paper, I could visualize what scope Durez plastics would give me in re-designing the conventional machine. First of all, their molding versatility permits the use of complex shapes and sections without adding to production costs. Second, plastics give desirable lightness in weight to the finished product. Third, they have high impact strength, durability, high dielectric resistance. And eye-appeal, of course, in their lustrous finish and handsome colors—a sales advantage exploited in the contrasting-colored housings above."

Here is still another example of how Durez plastics will have a leading position in the re-shaping of America's post-war products. Today, they belong to the men at the war fronts. Tomorrow, they will give physical expression to the way of life we fought for.

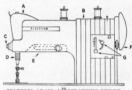

FEATURES OF MR. MÜLLER-MUNK'S DESIGN

A End Plate, molded separately of Durez to facilitate assembly
B Molded Durez Motor Housing
C Tension Regulator—shifted to center of End Plate
D Molded Durez Bearing Housing—bearings housed separately to reduce bulk of main molding ... to provide better visibility
E Light concealed in main molding will always be in correct position for proper illumination of work
F Molded Durez Shaft Disengaging Wheel
G Molded Durez Lever Knobs—redesigned for better grips; better visibility and accuracy in making stitch selection

DUREZ PLASTICS & CHEMICALS, INC.
487 WALCK ROAD   NORTH TONAWANDA, N. Y.

DUREZ
PLASTICS THAT FIT THE JOB

top to bottom

FIG. 22
Elgin American compacts,
c. 1946–49. The model on
the right was published in
Harper's Bazaar in 1949 as
the "Golden Slipper," but the
company was inconsistent
with nomenclature.

FIG. 23
Jewelite advertisement,
October 1946

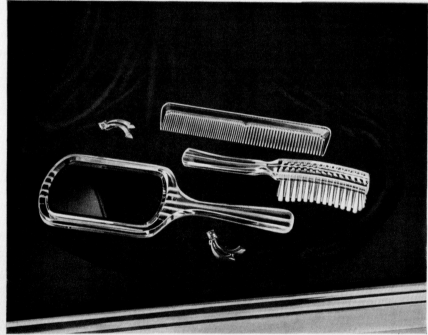

Lovely as the rarest of precious gems . . .

Jewelite

Jewelite Roll-Wave Brush, Comb and Mirror in Crystal.

● Jewelite for men, too! A club brush and comb set that's as rugged and practical as it is handsome. Available in garnet or crystal.

*H*ere, in all its entrancing new beauty, is the aristocrat of plastics—Jewelite by Pro-phy-lac-tic. Supreme creation of America's finest brush craftsmen, Jewelite brushes are backed by more than 60 years' experience in the art of brush design. Each Jewelite brush is bristled with long, resilient Prolon that reaches right down to your scalp . . . stimulates healthful circulation . . . brings shining new loveliness to your hair. Brushes, combs and dresser sets of Jewelite are now available in translucent shades of ruby or sapphire, or in diamond-clear crystal. Ask at any good brush department for Jewelite, aristocrat of plastics . . . made by Pro-phy-lac-tic, the brand name that is your best guide to quality in brushes. Look for the name Jewelite on the box! PRO-PHY-LAC-TIC BRUSH CO., *Florence, Mass.*

JEWELITE BY PRO-PHY-LAC-TIC

of $4.95, the percolator "so caught public fancy that its sale exceeded all expectations, justifying company retention of design service [Muller-Munk] to develop an entire line of products."[150] In October 1946 Muller-Munk offered Edgar Kaufmann Jr., then director of the department of industrial design at the Museum of Modern Art, New York, an example of the percolator for the museum's next focus on good design. Some 50,000 units reportedly had been sold, and Kaufmann was assured that Gimbel Brothers department store was stocking it in New York.[151] When the exhibition *Useful Objects, 1946* debuted at MoMA, the Cafex percolator was itemized on the checklist as: "Aluminum percolator, $4.95, Des. Peter Muller-Munk, Mfr. Hartford Products Corp., Ret. Gimbel Bros."[152] Exhibiting a design product at MoMA was no small triumph for Muller-Munk, yet he was equally interested in developing better industrial design exhibition opportunities at home.

As his business grew in the 1930s and 1940s, so did his engagement in Pittsburgh's cultural sector. Like many faculty members, Muller-Munk joined the Associated Artists of Pittsburgh, and he exhibited his handwrought silver and tooled leatherwork in annual exhibitions at the Carnegie Institute (now Carnegie Museum of Art).[153] Although he won several awards for his silver, he would ultimately tire of the group's fine art and craft priorities. Far more enticing to Muller-Munk, however, was Outlines, the first modern art gallery in Pittsburgh, founded in 1941 by a young woman of exceptional vision, Elizabeth (Betty) Rockwell, the daughter of a local industrialist who had studied at Sarah Lawrence College. The gallery's innovative program included painting, sculpture, jewelry, industrial design, architecture, music, theater, and film. Although it failed financially—she recalled selling only three pieces of art in six years—the model of a combined gallery, performance space, and reading library was extraordinary at the time.[154]

Rockwell's first show in October 1941 featured important artists such as Alexander Calder, Paul Klee, Pablo Picasso, Henri Matisse, Wassily Kandinsky, and others, all displayed in a gallery furnished with flat-pack plywood furniture by local architect Crombie Taylor.[155] Muller-Munk was involved in the second exhibition, *Industrial Design—A New Approach*, which opened in December, and showed student work from Carnegie Tech, including texture studies from the wartime camouflage course, alongside work from the New School of Design in Chicago and Black Mountain College in North Carolina, which sent textiles by Anni Albers.[156] László Moholy-Nagy later traveled from Chicago to lecture at the gallery.[157] Outlines held another industrial design exhibition the following spring, *Design: Today and Tomorrow*. By late 1943 Muller-Munk was a gallery director and, subsequently, a lecturer on modern design.[158] Edgar Kaufmann Sr. and Henry J. Heinz II, president of the Heinz Company and a major art collector and philan-

FIG. 24
Cafex percolator, 1946

thropist, later served on the board with Muller-Munk.[159] Ahead of its time, Outlines ceased operation in 1947. Muller-Munk's involvement demonstrated his commitment to broad-minded cultural reform and progressive ideals.

Bolstered by the success of his 1946 solo industrial design show in Philadelphia and the inclusion of his Cafex percolator in the MoMA exhibition, Muller-Munk submitted the percolator to the 1947 Associated Artists of Pittsburgh annual.[160] When it was rejected on the basis of being an industrially produced product—not conceived and made by the same hands—Muller-Munk withdrew from the organization, declaring that in order "to make the public more aware of good design, the Associated Artists and all fine arts museums should open their doors to the 'practicing arts' ... Pittsburgh should not seem to belittle the very thing that made it big and would keep it big."[161] He was vindicated when MoMA accepted into its permanent collection his gift of the Cafex percolator.[162]

Muller-Munk's design ability was by now widely acknowledged, and he had a trusted and talented team in place. Between the mid-1940s and the mid-1950s, the staff quadrupled as the client list expanded. From the helm of his consultancy, Muller-Munk secured important projects for his team to execute while simultaneously rising to national and international leadership in his field.

The Waring Blendor

JEWEL STERN

HOUSEWARES

SIXTH FLOOR

$29.75

$29.75

$29.75

$29.75

$29.75

$29.75

$29.75

$29.75

BLENDING

WARING BLENDOR

Waring
BLENDOR
$29.75
See Demonstration
Sixth Floor

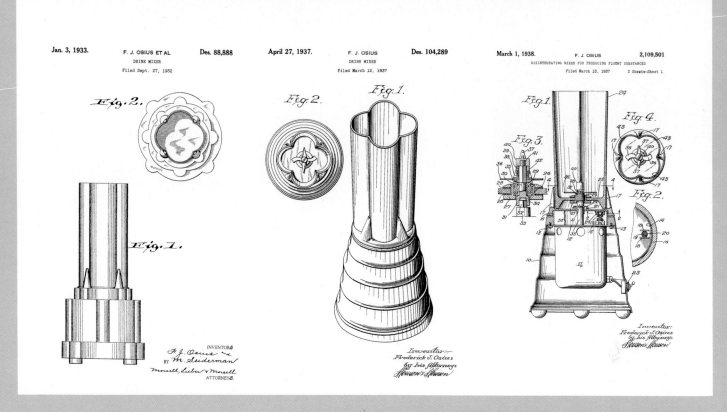

Jan. 3, 1933.   F. J. OSIUS ET AL   Des. 88,888
DRINK MIXER
Filed Sept. 27, 1932

April 27, 1937.   F. J. OSIUS   Des. 104,289
DRINK MIXER
Filed March 12, 1937

March 1, 1938.   F. J. OSIUS   2,109,501
DISINTEGRATING MIXER FOR PRODUCING FLUENT SUBSTANCES
Filed March 13, 1937   2 Sheets-Sheet 1

The Waring Blendor, which was released for commercial sale in 1938, is one of Peter Muller-Munk's most dynamic designs [FIG. 3]. Its dramatic height and stepped-back form evoked contemporary skyscrapers, generating excitement for its advanced functions and style. Yet its genesis and Muller-Munk's role in its development are anything but straightforward.

The blender evolved from a design for a food and beverage mixer created by semiretired inventor Frederick J. Osius, the founder of the Hamilton Beach Manufacturing Company, a producer of electrical motors and home appliances. He pitched his design to the popular bandleader Fred Waring, who had been a mechanical engineering student at Pennsylvania State College (now Penn State University) prior to embarking on a musical career, and was known to have an interest in "gadgets." Lore has it that in the summer of 1936 Osius arrived unannounced and flamboyantly dressed backstage at the Vanderbilt Theatre in New York City, where Waring broadcast his radio program sponsored by the Ford Motor Company. Although the prototype mixer Osius showed Waring (probably based on his copatented "Drink Mixer" from 1933) did not function properly, Waring was sold on the potential of the device and invested in its production. According to another version of the story, published in 1940 in *American Business*, Osius had visited Waring at his home in Shawnee, Pennsylvania, and had shown "only an idea—a sketchily conceived picture of a motor-driven device which, in addition to mixing liquids, would shred and liquefy solids."[1] In either case, Waring did in fact enter into an agreement with Osius in the fall of 1936, whereby he sold to Waring his half interest in the design patent 88,888 [FIG. 2, LEFT].[2] But within a few months, it became apparent that Osius was unable to deliver a fully working model based on the patent.[3] Waring's "business associate" Edward J. Lee was enlisted to solve the mechanical issues, especially leak proofing the mixer, as well as the manufacture of the glass container.[4] Although no

documentation survives to pinpoint the exact date, it appears to have been in early 1937 that Muller-Munk was called upon to redesign the mixer. He later described his intervention: "A man came barging into my home one Sunday morning with a mammoth machine. He said he had just a few days to get it together and wanted my help because Fred Waring promised to back him on it." Muller-Munk asked a high price for his assistance, whereupon "the man peeled off the bills in cash" and the "job was done" by the Wednesday deadline.[5] On March 12, 1937, Osius filed a revised design patent for a "Drink Mixer" and the next day a utility patent for a "Disintegrating Mixer for Producing Fluent Substances" [FIG. 2, CENTER AND RIGHT]. Both describe the final produced design, named the Model B, which strongly suggests that the Osius patents were in fact Muller-Munk's design. Furthermore, the drawing for the utility patent is identical to the blueprint drawing used by the Air-Way Electric Appliance Corporation to manufacture the Model B mixer.[6]

Introduced as the "Miracle Mixer" at the National Restaurant Association's convention in Chicago in early October 1937, the blender was in production by the end of the year.[7] Early in 1938 Waring negotiated a contract with the Air-Way Electric Appliance Corporation of Toledo, Ohio, to manufacture the mixer [FIG. 4].[8] At the same time, Waring teamed up with the Ronrico Corporation to jointly promote the mixer for concocting alcoholic beverages in commercial settings.[9] Originally destined for commercial use in bars and restaurants, the mixer was soon offered to retail consumers by Waring and through an arrangement with Martin W. Pretorius, a Dutch South African health-food guru in Hollywood, California, who sold the mixers under his own label as a "liquifier" for fruits and vegetables.[10] Waring's celebrity as a bandleader and his indefatigable personal promotion of the new device contributed to its phenomenal success. As his band, the Pennsylvanians, crisscrossed the country, Waring would often demonstrate the mixer using a theatrical trunk customized into a full-service bar [FIG. 5].

Muller-Munk's stunning redesign, with its stepped-back layers not present in Osius's original patent, also contributed to the blender's success. The *Chicago Tribune* raved that it was "Built Like a Skyscraper."[11] By the spring of 1938, the company dubbed the introductory two-speed Model B mixer the "Waring-Go-Round."[12] The media loved it, though it soon became apparent that for most consumers the price of $34.25 was too high.[13] Waring reduced the price to $29.75 [FIG. 1], renamed the Model B mixer the DeLuxe model, and then introduced a smaller, one-speed machine at $19.95, differentiated as the Standard model.[14] In 1939 the company issued a brochure titled *Recipes to Make Your Waring-Go-Round*, in which both models are referred to as "Waring Blendors," with the unique, registered spelling of the name. Although the Standard model was based on its predecessor, there is no indication that Muller-Munk was involved in the modification.

Spurred by the excitement generated by the Waring mixer, Muller-Munk asserted his claim to the design at the beginning of 1939; in a published newspaper photograph of him, the caption read: "He's shown with his drink and vegetable mixer which is already a best-seller."[15] A day before the article appeared on January 6, 1939, the ailing Osius died. Whether he would have challenged Muller-Munk for recognition will never be known. Muller-Munk's credit for the design was firmly established in October 1940 when the DeLuxe model was illustrated in the Design Decade special issue of *Architectural Forum* and he was named the designer.[16] Although production of Muller-Munk's blender was relatively brief and likely ceased soon after World War II, the appliance has remained an iconic object of streamlined industrial design.[17]

FIG. 4
Factory production of the Model B,
Waring mixer, c. 1938

FIG. 5
Fred Waring demonstrating the Waring
Blendor, c. 1938

The Postwar "Do-It-Yourself" Movement

CATHERINE WALWORTH

Time magazine's cover for August 2, 1954, presented a plaid-shirted American male with chiseled features, sculpted hair, and the multiple powers of a Hindu god. Using each of his eight arms, he "repairs" the journal's masthead, paints a wall, buffs a car, saws lumber, cuts a tree limb, and rides a lawnmower matched to the journal's famous red border [FIG. 2]. The surrealistic image by Boris Zybasheff—a vision of the suburban homeowner as a confident whir of activity with a tool for each task—announced the feature article inside: "Do-It-Yourself: The New Billion-Dollar Hobby."

According to historian Steven M. Gelber, the term "do-it-yourself" (today popularly condensed to DIY) dates to at least 1912; *Business Week* resalvaged the term in its issue for June 2, 1952, when it announced: "This is the age of do-it-yourself."[1] The postwar hobbyist phenomenon led to a related term—the "shoulder trade"—connoting the growing number of do-it-yourselfers carrying wooden planks out of lumber stores. Construction industry branches adjusted their materials to meet the needs of a lucrative amateur market: US Plywood Corporation offered new 16-inch-wide sheets (rather than the standard 48-inch), and rubber companies produced new foam rubber materials for at-home furniture makers and upholsterers encouraged by simpler modern styles.[2] Paint companies developed latex paint and paint rollers in addition to the professional-grade oil-based paints, thus creating one of the most affordable ways to spruce up a home. Reynolds produced easy-to-cut aluminum in sheets, tubes, and rods and suggested a host of projects for it, from spice shelves to contemporary "Eamesian" aluminum tables, referring to the midcentury furniture design of Charles and Ray Eames.[3]

New construction began on nearly two million single-family homes in 1950, a massive increase after a wartime low of 139,000 and the "largest number of housing starts in American history."[4] Meanwhile, the 1938 Fair Labor Standards Act had initiated a five-day, forty-hour workweek, creating more leisure time than ever before. These conditions, combined with a spate of manual and industrial skills acquired during the Great Depression and World War II, formulated the ideal conditions for a do-it-yourself revolution [FIG. 3]. Home repair and handicraft emerged as satisfying brands of work that crossed socioeconomic borders. By the mid-1950s, only reading and watching television ranked as more popular forms of recreation.[5]

Time's feature article spotlighted the passions of actual hobbyists across the country, including vice president of US Steel David Austin's $5,000 woodworking shop, and singer Perry Como's and movie star Jane Russell's love of handicraft. Russell was in no way an anomaly either. Even though advertisements commonly depicted women pointing out what needed to be done to men standing at the ready to fix it, US Plywood learned from its dealers that husbands and wives were shopping in lumberyards together and that a large number of women were shopping alone.[6]

Power tools were a $25 million market in 1940 and rose nearly tenfold to $200 million by 1954.[7] Even as manufacturers scaled their tool lines down to portable versions, they made them powerful enough to meet the needs of a growing class of semi-professionals. This field of product development drew the attention of *Industrial Design* magazine's editors, who devoted a lengthy feature to the subject's popularity titled "Power Tools: The Newest Home Appliance."[8] The article discussed methods for restyling portable power tools for eye appeal—both "fashion color" treatments (such as Henry Dreyfuss's yellow DeWalt lathe) and dynamic new shapes that conveyed a sense of power. Rockwell Manufacturing, DeWalt (a subsidiary of American Machine and Foundry Company), and Black & Decker all introduced new portable

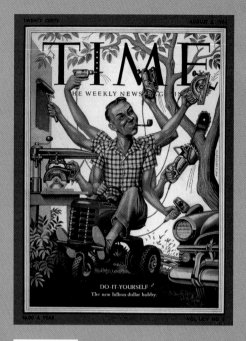

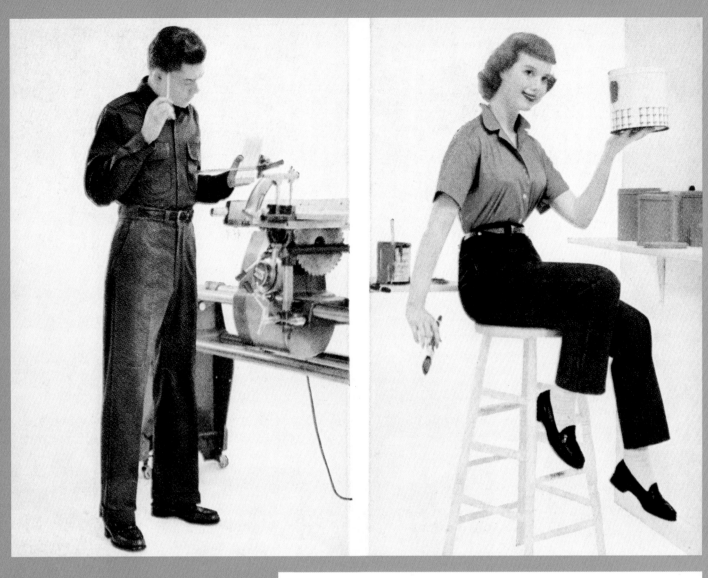

FIG. 3
Detail of an advertisement for Blue Bell casual wear, for "practical folks who do-it-them-selves," *Life*, September 5, 1955

FIG. 4
PMMA's design concept for Stanley sander, 1960s

FIG. 5
PMMA-designed tools for Porter-Cable: finishing
sander, Guild model 106, with carefully calculated
handle angle and knob for two-handed use; portable
electric saw, model 108; router, model 150, with flat
plastic top to enable easy changing of bits; portable
electric saw, Guild model A-6; and portable belt
sander, model 500, a well-balanced tool, styled like
a locomotive

electric tools on the market. PMMA worked for most of these firms on various
projects, but their first and most extensive relationship was with Syracuse-
based toolmaker Porter-Cable Machine Company.

Porter-Cable first engaged PMMA in 1948 or 1949 to design a low-cost,
lightweight 6-inch portable electric saw for nonprofessionals. Having the
current 8-inch saw and preliminary engineering specs for the smaller version
(prepared under Porter-Cable's chief engineer Art Emmons) from which to
work, PMMA applied their design skills to a new tool that could be sold at a
retail price of just $65. Designers chose more economical die-cast (rather than
sand-cast) aluminum to reduce weight (and cost) and to provide high tensile
strength, and eliminated the miter adjustment commonly found on 8-inch
saws to further reduce production costs.[9] Aluminum die castings also allowed
for "the freedom of the designer in arriving at a pleasing external form" with
complex curves.[10] The resulting Guild-6 power saw could cut two inches deep
through lumber, plywood, and aluminum siding [FIG. 5]. Weighing a mere
twelve pounds and with a newly styled blade guard, handle, and depth
adjusting knob, the PMMA-designed tool was described by *Industrial Design*
as having a "more massive appearance" while its distinctive lean provided
an "intimation of speed."[11]

With Porter-Cable in their portfolio, PMMA went on to design tools for
other major companies in both small and large industry, including a portable
line for Stanley Tools [FIG. 4] and a much-lauded milling machine for Kearney
& Trecker.[12] PMMA's major redesign in 1957 of DeWalt's radial arm saw, introduced as the new "Imperial" and designed for medium to heavy industry,
is typical of the firm's concern with human engineering (ergonomics).[13]
Designers relocated the tool's controls to the front of the arm, for example,
so the operator no longer had to reach over the spinning blade to stop the
machine.[14] From portable tools for the expanding market of handicraftsmen
to machines for large industry, PMMA was designing with the end user
foremost in mind.

PMMA: Product Design

RACHEL DELPHIA

——

"No single individual, of course, is able to solve the many complex problems of product design … minute analysis of its construction, price, marketing problem and performance. To accomplish this, different members of the designer's staff are responsible for different phases of the vivisection of the old product and the growth of the new one. Researchers, designers, draftsmen, and model makers all work in unison."[1]

The Growth of PMMA

Peter Muller-Munk brought to his developing industrial design business the same fastidiousness that characterized his nature and impeccable dress [FIG. 1]. Having established himself and his firm by the end of the war, he expanded his personnel in the late 1940s and early 1950s to execute a growing list of products for both consumers and industry. Promotional literature portrayed an advanced consultancy able to serve clients across the board, from market research to three-dimensional models. With a professional staff overseeing operations, Muller-Munk matured as a visionary leader and a spokesperson in the field, roles that he clearly enjoyed and at which he excelled. He wrote, lectured, and traveled to international conferences and exhibitions. Always a strident promoter, he talked up the profession, PMMA, and his latest pet topics, from "product styling versus product planning" to the integration of lighting design and architecture. He drummed up new clients along the way but kept growth in check, never taking on more work than he and the principals could oversee. Muller-Munk entered client meetings with a flourish and commanded conversations over drawings or mockups. He delegated the execution of details to his team,

frontispiece

FIG. 1
Muller-Munk (center) and Anton Parisson (right) review designs for Westinghouse appliances, 1957

above

FIG. 2
Muller-Munk, Paul Karlen, and Raymond Smith (last three on the right) discuss products with a client, probably Silex, 1946–47, published in *Machine Design* (1954)

but kept a watchful eye over the whole enterprise, assuring clients that "no project, no matter how small or large, ever [left] the premises without the personal inspection and supervision of Peter Muller-Munk."[2] At the same time, he ascended to leadership in the professional design community, serving successively as chairman of the Allegheny Chapter of the Society of Industrial Designers (SID), as national president of SID, and president of the International Council of Societies of Industrial Design (ICSID), an organization that he cofounded. In this bustling, optimistic era of American prosperity, Muller-Munk and his firm thrived, proudly advertising themselves as the largest design-consulting outfit between Chicago and New York City.[3]

With Muller-Munk, Paul Karlen, and Raymond Smith **[FIG. 2]**, PMMA had a talented triumvirate in place by 1946, supported by a staff of a half dozen or more. In 1948 it added a key player in Anton Parisson, a former Carnegie Tech student who had been chief designer at Phoenix Glass Company during the previous twelve years. Later PMMA literature described Parisson as an exceptional design talent with a deep knowledge of industry.[4] In 1953 Muller-Munk announced the formation of a partnership including himself, Karlen, Smith, and Ilona (Parisson was named an associate in 1952 and would become the fifth partner in 1957).[5] Little is known of Ilona's continued role in the firm. She was listed separately in the city directories of 1947 and 1949 as office manager of PMMA, and was frequently cited in the press as her husband's business partner **[FIG. 3]**.[6] Between 1949 and 1959 Muller-Munk hired eight additional designers who would become associates within his lifetime: Ernst Budke III (joined 1949), Robert J. Renaud (1950), Donald J. Behnk (1952), Howard A. Anderson (1953), Roger I. Protas (1954), Leonard Levitan (1956), Glenn W. Monigle (1957), and Paul R. Wiedmann (1959).[7] Five of those would be named partners in 1966.[8] Countless other designers passed through the firm before moving on to independent careers, leading some to call the incubating Pittsburgh firm "Mother-Munk."[9]

In the spring of 1952, PMMA moved offices nearby to the Gamble Building at 725 Liberty Avenue.[10] For the new space Pittsburgh architect Walter Roberts, a former student of Muller-Munk's, was hired to design some 5,600 square feet from scratch in collaboration with the firm **[FIG. 5]**.[11] PMMA occupied the entire sixth and seventh floors. The lower level housed executive, administrative, and accounting offices, a client office, a conference and presentation room, and a research center. Design activity centered on the seventh floor, with a bull pen of drafting boards, a conference room for team discussion, and space for model making, assembly, and display **[FIG. 4]**. By 1955 PMMA staff numbered twenty-five, including designers as well as "technical personnel trained in market research, industrial engineering, budgetary

FIG. 3
Ilona and Peter Muller-Munk
on the *Ile de France*, probably
September 1953

top to bottom

FIG. 4
The designers' drafting room at PMMA's offices at 725 Liberty Avenue, as photographed in 1957

FIG. 5
PMMA's office reception area at 725 Liberty Avenue with grasscloth walls by the New York firm of Charles R. Gracie and a light-diffusing ceiling of corrugated Plexiglas and aluminum, published in *Domus* (1955)

control, manufacturing methods, graphics and drafting, and rendering."[12] The *Wall Street Journal* reported PMMA's staff expansion as "reflecting such client additions as Caloric Appliance Corp., Perfection Stove Co., Lionel Corp., and Westinghouse Electric Corp.'s lighting division."[13] By 1958 the staff had grown to thirty-two.[14]

The firm emphasized the team approach to its clients: "PMMA believes that to give the Client the best possible product, each assignment undertaken must become the concern of the whole organization.... [B]efore a design project has been completed, not only the three associates, but the entire organization has played a part in its solution."[15] PMMA operated as a unit, and as a matter of policy, individuals did not take credit for designs. Of course, in the field at large, many credited Muller-Munk alone for the products of his namesake firm, a common practice at the time.

From the earliest known promotional literature, Muller-Munk espoused a balanced design philosophy that weighed aesthetics alongside function and that served both client and consumer. The work of the firm was stylish, inventive, and original, to be sure, but it was never, claimed PMMA, "just a handsome picture."[16] PMMA prided itself on its ability to meet

LIGHT WEIGHT is big selling point for new Porter-Cable saw, designed by Peter Müller-Munk. Use of die castings instead of sand castings, care in specifying section thicknesses slices cost as well as weight.

FIG. 6
A photograph of PMMA's model for a Porter-Cable saw, printed in *Modern Industry* (August 1949), elucidated the potential pitfall of impeccable craftsmanship: a mock-up was mistaken for the real thing. In a November letter to the editor, Muller-Munk clarified that the photograph depicted their mock-up and not the final Porter-Cable Guild model A-6 saw as put into production.

a client's desired retail price point, saving money in materials and manufacturing, while at the same time delivering useful products to the public. Muller-Munk valued the opinion of his clients' customers: "It is the people that decide whether they like or dislike, buy or not buy something. And the advice they give you with that, that is reliable advice."[17] He had little patience for artificial styling and ephemeral fashions: "Advanced design that fills no existing need to me is an experimental thing that may be very interesting and stimulating *to the profession* but fails in its function as design."[18] A well-designed object, aside from looking good, should move people to purchase it because they feel they have use for it and can afford it. To produce the best possible products a designer had to function as "a planner ... a coordinator of skills of many other experts." Further defining his role, Muller-Munk continued, "[the designer] is a non-specialist in the middle of specialists, who has to integrate the work of the specialists ... into a tangible, useful end. He has to respect the specialties of the experts ... and he has to be respected by them."[19] Rather than projecting his personal preferences onto the market, a designer also had to intuit the broad needs and tastes of the "total public" his products would eventually serve.

To prospective clients Muller-Munk emphasized the benefits of his mid-sized organization in Pittsburgh. PMMA was small enough to offer individualized services and direct contact with the associates, yet large and diverse enough to tackle the full scope of potential projects. Situated halfway between New York and Chicago, the firm was positioned to serve clients from a wide geographic area.[20] By 1955 PMMA reported that the firm had completed work for more than seventy American and European organizations, resulting in some 1,200 marketed products.[21]

PMMA's design procedure began with a dissection of the existing product to understand its construction, materials, use, and buying public. The Client Services department conducted market and design research, gathering relevant statistics, looking at comparative products, and interpreting broad trends, often with input from the client's sales department. Research informed the initial creative work of the designers, who brought to bear their own awareness of style, materials, and production processes to suggest a general direction. With consensus from the client on the overall scheme, the designers produced new sketches in volume to demonstrate the breadth of possibilities. These were presented to the executive, sales, and production branches of the client, who, together with PMMA, identified strengths and preferences from the many ideas, often culling various elements into one new concept (for example, using the handle from one sketch with the body from another). Revised and refined designs were then shared with the client. From this point on, the firm preferred three-dimensional mock-ups to drawings so that the client could better appreciate the actual appearance and construction details [FIG. 6]. Such mock-ups took into account materials, engineering, and production specifications to ensure the plausibility of the concepts presented. PMMA then checked and rechecked the design against the original goals and specifications before presenting the final design to the client, often in the form of a quasi-functional model. With full accord between designer and client, PMMA's technical staff took over, resolving engineering and construction details and remaining on the project until the product was ready for market, or as long at the client desired.[22] Client engagements ranged from single products to long-term retainers with consulting fees anywhere from $1,000 to $75,000.[23]

Although PMMA's output would diversify greatly from the mid-1950s onward, the firm skyrocketed to early success with product design. This included consumer goods from kitchenware to cameras, and industrial and commercial equipment such as lathes, milling machines, and gas pumps. Products for cooking or for serving food and beverages were pillars of the PMMA portfolio. Following the tremendously successful Cafex percolator, Hartford Products engaged PMMA for additional designs. The most notable is the Cafex Kwik-Cup, a stepped and flanged funnel for drip-brewing a single serving of coffee directly into one's cup. Designed by February 1947, the device was on the market by the end of the year.[24] Available in black

above

FIG. 7
Cafex Kwik-Cup coffee makers
1947

opposite

FIG. 8
Silex Constellation carafe
on Silex Candlelight coffee
warmer, 1948–49

or red plastic with an aluminum core, it perched on top of a coffee cup like a mini rocket booster **[FIG. 7]**. Around the same time, the H. J. Heinz Company hired PMMA to modernize its commercial countertop "soup kitchen" **[FIG. 10]**, and the Silex Company engaged PMMA for a full range of coffee-related products. Among the first to appear was the brilliantly low-tech Candlelight coffee warmer: a pressed-glass cylinder with a perforated metal lid, which enclosed a votive candle.[25] PMMA also designed a ubiquitous diner staple, the Constellation carafe, which could sit atop the Candlelight warmer **[FIG. 8]** or any of the single (1947), double, or quad (both 1950) electric burners that the firm also tackled **[FIG. 9]**. For the endless preparation of this caffeinated "rocket fuel," which surged in popularity in this era, PMMA also redesigned Silex's commercial coffee mill and vacuum coffeemaker.[26] The new line had packaging designed by PMMA as well, one of the earliest documented examples of this type of work by the firm **[FIG. 11]**.

Modeling the glass portions of the Silex redesigns gave PMMA an early opportunity to collaborate with the Corning Glass Works, while knobs and handles carried forth

clockwise

FIG. 9
Silex double-burner electric range, 1950

FIG. 10
Soup kitchen for the H. J. Heinz Company, c. 1950

FIG. 11
Silex packaging, 1949–50

Muller-Munk's established relationships with plastics manufacturers.[27] Another PMMA redesign of 1949 was the Silex
Air-Lift steam iron **[FIG. 12]**. The improved iron was celebrated
for its lighter weight (2.75 lbs.) and increased water capacity
(16 oz. as compared to 8 oz.).[28] At a time when ergonomic
research was in its infancy (the term had barely been minted),
Modern Industry commended the range of intelligent handle
solutions developed by PMMA. In the carafe, they noted, where
"firm grasp is important and pressure is concentrated at the top
of the handle ... finger ridges were provided." The handle of the
iron was smooth and comfortable for extended use, protected
fingers from the hot metal, and created a stable platform when
set on end. Handles on saucepans for Ekco Products enabled
"balance and sure grip," and the undercutting of the knob on
the lid provided "fingertip clearance" **[FIG. 13]**.[29]

Nuances of function and user safety were also para-
mount in PMMA's designs for tools and industrial equipment.
One of the firm's earliest clients in this area was the Mine
Safety Appliances Company (MSA), for which it designed the
Dustfoe respirator and, later, ear protection, hard hats, and
the company's entire scope of packaging. The straightforward
V-Gard safety helmet, designed for MSA in 1962, is still in
production in its original form and remains an industry leader
[FIG. 14]. Another early client was the Porter-Cable Machine
Company. Working closely with the client's chief engineer,
Arthur Emmons, an impressive innovator in his own right,
PMMA redesigned more than half a dozen portable electric
tools for Porter-Cable beginning in 1948 or 1949 **[SEE P. 81,
FIG. 5]**. The designers' task across the entire product line
was to economize production and assembly and to improve
usability and consumer appeal. They uniformly replaced sand
castings with die castings, enabling even cross sections to
minimize material and weight. Die casting also allowed for
greater precision in molding components, which contributed
to easier assemblage of the individual parts. Usability and
style were assessed on a tool-by-tool basis (see "The Postwar
'Do-It-Yourself' Movement," pp. 78–81).

PMMA added other lasting clients for tools, industrial products, and major appliances, including the Jacobs
Manufacturing Company, the Wayne Pump Company
(later Symington-Wayne), and the Westinghouse Electric
Corporation. The relationship with Jacobs began in 1948 and
gave rise to beautifully refined and user-friendly machine
components in aluminum and steel: namely, collet chucks
for lathes and drills **[FIG. 16]**. PMMA also designed Lodge
& Shipley lathes, Kearney & Trecker milling machines, and
a radial arm saw for DeWalt, to name just a few of their
contributions to large-scale tools.[30] Muller-Munk and Karlen
claimed to be at work on a gas pump as early as 1943, but the
first documented pump by the firm—the start of many fruitful
contracts in that industry—was the distinctive Wayne 500

top to bottom

FIG. 12
Silex Air-Lift steam iron, 1949

FIG. 13
Ekco Flint-Ware saucepan, 1950

FIG. 14
V-Gard safety helmets for
Mine Safety Appliances,
modern examples of a product
designed in 1962

FIG. 15
PMMA received accolades
for this scalable mechanical
counter designed for Veeder-
Root, 1953. The assignment
may have stemmed from
PMMA's relationship with
Wayne Pump, which used
Veeder-Root computing
elements in its gas pumps.

FIG. 16
Spindle-nose lathe chuck
for Jacobs Manufacturing
Company, 1949

opposite

FIG. 17
Wayne 500 series gasoline
pump, 1950 (restored)

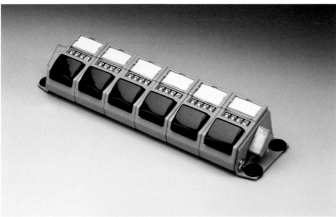

series computing pump, designed in 1950 [FIG. 17].[31] PMMA's design offered convenient access for the station operator as well as easy customization with panels that could be repainted, an inset ad glass on the upper face that could be changed out, and the latest computational components by Veeder-Root [FIG. 15]. The top could be solid or outfitted with an illuminated globe, and the lighted "cove set" dials gleamed within their stainless-steel bezels. Wayne's promotional literature proclaimed, "Day or night, Wayne 500 has that look of modern efficiency which motorists can't resist in choosing a station." PMMA exhibited photographs of the Wayne 500 at the 1951 Milan Triennial along with its Jacobs lathe chuck, Porter-Cable belt sander, and another new design: a Westinghouse refrigerator [FIG. 18].[32]

At midcentury, the Westinghouse Electric Corporation was a research and manufacturing behemoth, a pioneer in multiple industries: electricity, lighting, radio, television, and more. Landing them as a client represented an immeasurable achievement for PMMA. Their association began in late 1949 with the ambitious redesign and retooling of Westinghouse's 1951 line of refrigerators and freezers, and grew to include all major appliances (see "The 1950s 'Kitchen Revolution,'" pp. 110–13), exhibition design for trade fairs, and even an experimental system combining ambient lighting, heating/cooling, and abstract sculptural décor (see "The Color Explosion," pp. 114–17). In the mid-1950s PMMA was responsible for the new "square look" on Westinghouse's entire appliance line, and innovated further with the 1960 Center Drawer Refrigerator.

CONVERTIBLE? IT'S A SNAP! To convert your Radioear from glasses to the other attractive ways you may wear it, a single snap-in motion does it in an instant.

IT'S A MAN'S HEARING AID TOO! All the advantages of the new Radioear are available in the men's version, the handsome Model "840". They wear this tiny, light and efficient Radioear under a tie, clipped to the shirt or coat lapel, as a tie clip or as a smart pair of glasses.

opposite

FIG. 18
Westinghouse DFC-10 Frost Free refrigerator, 1951

above, left to right

FIG. 19
Anton Parisson (left) and Peter Muller-Munk (standing) reviewing designs for corporate identity with Radioear's Samuel Lybarger (center) and E. J. Myers (right), c. 1956–57

FIG. 20
Advertisement showing Lady America and Radioear 840 hearing aids integrated into eyeglasses, published in *Life* (1956)

PMMA also continued to develop its repertoire of small consumer products. For E. A. Myers, designers contributed to biannual, if not annual, changes to hearing aids—updating styles and materials and also improving function and human factors. Upon exhibiting the Radioear 830, at the Milan Triennial in 1954 ("the only American hearing aid so displayed"), Muller-Munk reported back to Samuel F. Lybarger, Myers's son-in-law, that "without any exaggeration, the Radioear product put [the Swiss, English, French, and Belgian manufacturers] all to shame, and they acknowledged this to me during my contacts with them."[33] Another noteworthy series was the Lady America and corresponding Radioear 840 for men, both 1956. To minimize the stigma of wearing hearing aids, this convertible line masqueraded as fashion accessories by snapping onto scarf clips, barrettes, or headbands (available in day and jewel-encrusted evening styles) and onto twenty-five different styles of eyeglasses for men and women

[FIG. 20]. Men could also disguise the apparatus as a tie clip or lapel pin.[34] At the same time, PMMA modernized the Radioear graphic identity, which was in use by 1957 [FIG. 19].

PMMA designed at least one of Westinghouse's popular radios for 1951. Intended to be carried like a purse, the PMMA radio was advertised as "outdoor-styled" and "super-portable," with the ability to run on AC, DC, or battery power. At least four two-tone polystyrene color variations were offered: black and red, brown and tan, maroon and tan, and teal and tan [FIGS. 21, 23]. The bold, modern design of the Westinghouse radio featured a speaker and station indicator integrated into a central circular motif. At the same moment, PMMA achieved a more traditional radio look for the Colonial Radio and Television Division of Sylvania Electric Products [FIG. 22]. These "first models in a new line" by the client featured a phenolic resin shell by Chicago Molded Plastics, available in ivory, walnut, or black. The company reportedly released a portable version and a clock radio within months, but it is unclear whether PMMA designed those as well.[35]

Schick, Incorporated, the inventor (in 1929) and industry leader in electric shavers, engaged PMMA to redesign their entire line in 1957. The company had recently experimented with market segmentation with the introduction of the Lady Schick, hinting to its male customers: "give her one of these and she'll never borrow yours again."[36] PMMA revised the top men's and lady's models and helped Schick introduce a new one for the young men in the family, who, market research had shown, tended to borrow shavers from their fathers. Wanting

FIG. 21
Nancy Lou Burress and Ann Thomas, students at the
Pennsylvania College for Women (Chatham University), pose
with a Bell & Howell Filmosound projector, Westinghouse radio,
and Porter-Cable belt sander to promote an exhibition of PMMA
designs at the college's Berry Hall Art Gallery, March 2–28, 1952

FIG. 22
Radio for Sylvania, model 510B, 1950

opposite

FIG. 23
Westinghouse portable radio, model H-349P5, 1951

to tap the eleven-million-man-strong market of students, servicemen, and young workers (dubbed the "peach fuzz" crowd), Schick and PMMA created the "world's first and only electric shaver especially engineered and designed for young men."[37] The Varsity model was shaped to "virtually force" the inexperienced user to shave correctly, featured a "collegiate" insignia, and came with a preppy plaid travel tote. The new Powershave for dad replaced the former "bellwether," the Schick 25, and channeled the vogue for muscle cars and all things powerful. When packaged as the "Auto-Home," the model included both car and household power adapters for the man on the move.[38] By the following year, PMMA had also completed the new Futura model for Lady Schick. Like the Varsity it stood on end to save space on the vanity or in the medicine cabinet (a feature enabled by moving the power cord input to the side), and it introduced the first on-off switch for those who wanted to leave the device plugged in.[39] Retailers reported that customers moved more quickly to pick up devices that stood on end rather than lying on their sides [FIG. 24].

Photographic equipment for still images, motion picture recordings, and projection provided another fertile field for PMMA designers. Their first (and longest-running) client in this arena was Bell & Howell, which sought a formal indus-trial design partnership to help it tap the potential postwar market for home movies. Though aiming to appeal to a broad consumer base that included "the average housewife" and even children, Bell & Howell did not want to sacrifice its "tradition of quality—the product would not be cheapened; it would only be simplified."[40] PMMA took to heart the quality engineering of the client's products and their simultaneous charge to make them unintimidating and easy to use—all while maintaining a unified look across their product line. In 1952–53 PMMA undertook redesign of three projectors and their carrying cases: the Filmosound [FIG. 21], the model 273, and the model 221. The last was an entirely new 8 mm projector intended for the family audience [FIG. 28]. Its all-aluminum base and Tenite plastic housing made it light-weight (12 pounds total). Only one side of the shell lifted off, allowing the other side to serve as the fixed housing for the mechanism. With a retail price of $100, the 221 represented a 40 percent reduction in price from Bell & Howell's previous 8 mm model, which greatly aided in its accessibility to con-sumers.[41] Paired with the 8 mm projector on the market was the new 8 mm camera, model 252, on which PMMA and Bell & Howell gave considerable attention to the viewfinder and the lens settings to reassure users that the camera was easy to operate [FIG. 26]. One of the most technically challenging designs presented itself in the lens mounts. As Muller-Munk recalled, "This was a study of pure precision in which we had to organize finishes, knurls, and proportions into clean

previous spread

FIG. 24
Electric shavers for the whole family: the Schick Power-shave, 1957; the Lady Schick Futura, 1958; and the Schick Varsity, 1957

clockwise

FIG. 25
Graflex Super Graphic 45 camera, 1958

FIG. 26
Bell & Howell 8 mm movie camera, model 252, 1953, paired with another PMMA design, the Sun Gun movie lamp for Sylvania, 1960

FIG. 27
Bell & Howell 16 mm movie camera, model 240, 1957

opposite

FIG. 28
A family enjoys Bell & Howell's new 8 mm movie projector, model 221, *Modern Plastics* (January 1953)

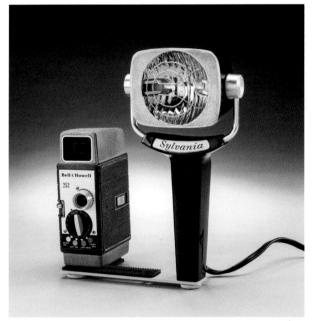

left

FIG. 29
Graflex Strobomite portable
electronic flash unit, 1957

opposite

FIG. 30
Advertisement for Bausch &
Lomb's Balomatic slide pro-
jector, published in *National*
Geographic **(1957)**

and convincing forms which would express effortlessly the function and spirit of optical equipment."[42] At the same time, PMMA tackled for Bell & Howell the Microtwin microfilm recorder and reader, a portable archiving device that astonishingly photographed both sides of documents passed into its slot. The other half of the machine provided a screen for viewing completed reels of microfilm.[43] Later in the decade, PMMA developed the 16 mm model 240 movie camera, which was selected by *Fortune* in 1959 as one of 100 "best designed mass produced products of modern times" **[FIG. 27]**.[44] PMMA also designed the Bausch & Lomb Balomatic series of slide projectors, 1957 **[FIG. 30]**. Its merits included automatic focus, automatic slide advancing (by setting an easy timer) or remote-control advance, and quiet operation. Although the product was well received, it had the misfortune of debuting only a few years before all straight-tray slide projectors were swept aside by the revolutionary Kodak Carousel, which made its debut in 1961.

PMMA's greatest contribution to still photography was unequivocally the Super Graphic 45 press camera, redesigned for Graflex in 1956–57 to hit the market in February 1958 **[FIG. 25]**. Like Bell & Howell, Graflex was a long-established industry leader among professionals. Yet the company recognized the appeal of the press camera to the ever-growing ranks of amateur photographers. To succeed in that market, they needed to improve usability. PMMA was hired to simplify "festoons of range fingers, view finders, light meters, wires and solenoids" as well as to design "new features including a revolving back and lens board that could tilt, swing, rise and drop."[45] Over nearly two years, PMMA switched out the

expensive dovetailed mahogany case for modern extruded aluminum, devised an elegant two-tone style, and reconfigured and reduced the number of locks, pivots, stops, and switches. In the words of one reviewer, PMMA had done away with all the "ungainly, studded protuberances, which ... threatened in a short while to make the instrument resemble a mechanical porcupine."[46] All this amounted to "a modern dream camera," with production costs no higher than the previous models (the Pacemaker Speed Graphic and the Crown Graphic) despite the many improvements.[47] The following year, Graflex introduced the Super Speed Graphic, which was identical to the Super Graphic, save the desirable addition of the 1/1000 speed shutter. The Super Graphic was a highly successful design for PMMA; not only did they please their immediate client—Graflex—but they also developed their existing relationship with local manufacturing giant Alcoa. Indeed, Alcoa's chief designer, Sam Fahnestock, was a willing collaborator, having worked for PMMA between 1951 and 1955. Jurors of Alcoa's Industrial Design Award, granted for "imaginative and effective uses of aluminum," bestowed the honor on PMMA for the Super Graphic. PMMA also designed a Strobomite portable flash unit **[FIG. 29]** and film projectors for Graflex, but the 4x5 camera was the standout.[48] *Industrial Design* called it an "admirable demonstration of how a classic product can be improved and updated without becoming overdesigned," and noted that "the camera's impressiveness lies not in its appearance (although it is handsome) but in the simplification of its parts."[49]

Equally important to an understanding of PMMA's product output are the omissions, the areas for which they

BAUSCH & LOMB announces
the first automatic slide projector that
ALWAYS STAYS IN FOCUS

slide after slide after slide !

LOOK ! NO HANDS !

LOOK ! NO "POP" !

Slides never pop out of focus! Only Balomatic shows your slides constantly in sharp detail.

Fully Automatic! Set your own timing...the Balomatic runs itself! You watch the picture, not the projector.

Finger-tip automatic or remote control! Automatic slide change without noisy protruding levers.

Famous Bausch & Lomb lens quality: Makers of the world's finest optics give you a Balcoted f/3.5 lens.

YOUR slide showing fun will never be spoiled by constant re-focusing due to annoying slide "popping"! The new Bausch & Lomb Balomatic Projector, made by the manufacturer of CinemaScope lenses, guarantees you constant focus! At last you can have a 100% automatic projector that you don't have to touch from start to finish. See it at your photographic dealer's now.

BALOMATIC 500: Takes all 2″ x 2″ slides, including Super Slides; 500-watt, fully automatic cycling, finger-tip automatic, and optional remote control; all controls grouped on central illuminated panel; Balcoted 5″, f/3.5 lens; 40-slide tray and case. Get one at terms as low as $8.10 a month.

$149⁵⁰

BALOMATIC 300: Most advanced finger-tip automatic available. Many exclusive 500 features, including illuminated central control panel, 40-slide tray and case; 4″, f/3.5 lens; 300-watt. Easy terms as low as $5.82 a month.

$84⁵⁰

BAUSCH & LOMB

BAUSCH & LOMB OPTICAL CO.
ROCHESTER 2, NEW YORK

Balomatic
AUTOMATIC SLIDE PROJECTORS

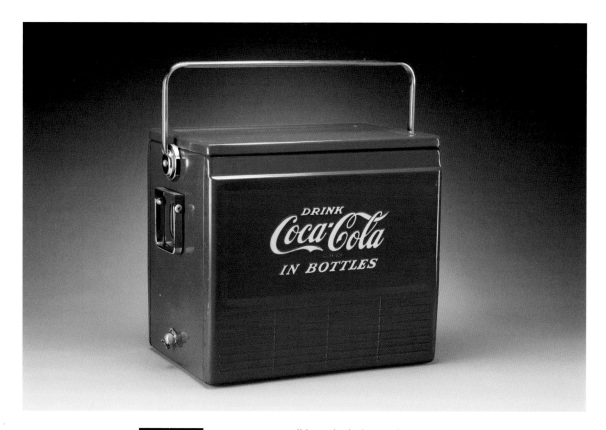

FIG. 31
The postwar leisure culture
of automobiles and speedboats
called for portable accessories
such as this fiberglass-
insulated cooler designed
by PMMA for the Progress
Refrigerator Company in 1955

did not do design work. Despite having a General Motors veteran among his top deputies, Muller-Munk veered away from vehicles. The firm would tackle accessories and components—compasses for Dinsmore and even automotive windshields developed with Pittsburgh Plate Glass—but never a full automobile, which he considered to be a high-stakes game. Muller-Munk once joked with a journalist: "A car is a natural for an industrial designer. It leads him into temptation and is more likely than not to deliver him into evil. One bad guess in the automobile industry is enough to put finis to the career of even the most successful designer, but if you guess wrong on an adding machine ... you can always try again."[50] The closest PMMA came to automotive tail fins was a range of boat hardware for Attwood Brass Works, designed between 1956 and 1959 (the latter designs under the trade name Seaflite) [FIGS. 32–33]. Available in chrome or 24-karat gold plate, the cleats (one of them shaped like an airplane), bow light, steering wheel, and flagstaff exuded the same promises of power, acceleration, and aerodynamics as the era's muscle cars.

Decorative household furnishings—dinnerware, tables, chairs, lamps, and vases—are also noticeably absent from the PMMA portfolio. This is especially curious given that Muller-Munk's silversmithing career began precisely in the realm of high-style decorative goods. The only notable exception was a line of crystal tabletop accessories designed by PMMA for the Belgian firm Val Saint Lambert in 1956. According to

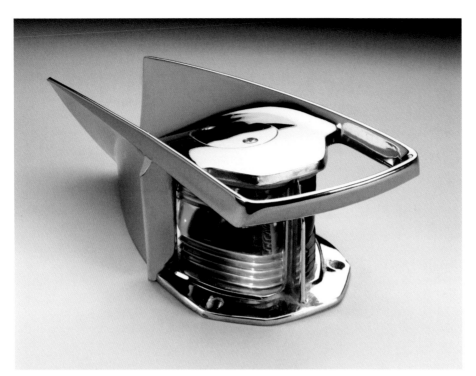

top to bottom

FIG. 32
Seaflite bow light for Attwood
Brass, 1959

FIG. 33
Marine hardware for Attwood
Brass, including a Seaflite
cleat (left), 1959, and an ear-
lier design (right), 1956

Muller-Munk, the job offer came after he had mocked the company's products within earshot of an "important official in the Belgian Export Ministry" during a somewhat raucous dinner party at the top of the Eiffel Tower. The subsequent invitation from Val Saint Lambert to design a new line revealed that the minister had relayed "an almost verbatim report of [Muller-Munk's] dinner table conversation."[51] Dinner remarks aside, Muller-Munk possessed practical insights for a Belgian firm wanting to further tap the American market. For instance, whereas a European table was set with wineglasses, Americans required water glasses for the table. Muller-Munk's decorative Tricorne line (amusingly transliterated "Tree Corn" in one American newspaper) would prove to be popular with consumers. Based on a rounded triangular cross section, the line included wasp-waisted candleholders in graduated

heights **[FIG. 34]**, centerpiece and accent bowls, and smoking accessories.[52] Evidencing the remarkable departure from the rest of the product design work of his office at the time, Muller-Munk noted how refreshing it was, after a long hiatus, "to design an article when beauty is the only requirement and there are hardly any functional limitations."[53]

A Leader in the Field

Given his natural abilities as a writer, orator, and leader, Muller-Munk perhaps inevitably donned the mantle not only of his firm but also of the industrial design profession as a whole. Despite some initial frustrations with the Society of Industrial Designers (SID)—for instance, the difficulty for members farther afield to participate in New York meetings and events[54]—he rapidly ascended the ladder of the organization, beginning with the fraternity of his regional group. The Allegheny Chapter of SID was established in 1948 (as the Cleveland Chapter) with local designer John Gordon Rideout as its first chairman; it covered western New York and Pennsylvania, Ohio, and Kentucky.[55] With Rideout's untimely passing in the spring of 1951, Muller-Munk assumed chairmanship of the chapter, which he held through the following year. Also in 1951, chapter secretary Ted Clement began to edit an irreverent regional newsletter, *The Allegheny Smog*, which faithfully reported on official activities of the membership (chapter meetings, publicity, travels, lectures etc.) while regaling readers with hyperbolic tales and sarcastic jabs at one another. The *Smog* paints a picture of a productive, good-natured, and rowdy fellowship, with Muller-Munk at the helm.[56]

By this time Muller-Munk was heavily involved in the national body (having been elected to his first three-year term on the SID Board of Directors in 1951). But he declined a nomination to be on the ballot for president, a post for which he felt neither ready nor deserving: "I have not as yet made a substantial enough contribution to the [society] nor does my standing in the profession as yet give me the right prestige for so high an office."[57] He did, however, invest himself in numerous national SID committees: Exhibits, Fellowship, Awards, and External Affairs. His activity comprised pinch-hitting on the installation of SID photographs at the 1951 Milan Triennial (which he found in disarray when he arrived in Italy six weeks prior to the opening), formally orchestrating subsequent exhibition efforts, contributing to design contract templates for use by members, and planning events such as a lecture on industrial design to be given at the Harvard Business School and SID conferences, often with considerable help from Ilona.[58] With his characteristic sarcasm, Muller-Munk complained about the demands of the professional society, telling president Russel Wright in 1952, "one of these days I really should get back to practicing industrial design, but in the meantime I guess you can expect me on Monday."[59] Joking aside, he firmly believed in the merits of the organization and took great pride in his involvement. In a "Shop Talk" article to fellow members, he remarked: "With all our faults, we still belong to a group that is progressive and that has the tremendous potential of bringing order and beauty and reason to an industrial environment which is desperately in need of it. I think we are still just at the beginning of this phase, but I also think that we are on the right track and that we have started something that is bigger and more important than any one of us can handle or realize singly."[60]

Muller-Munk was elected vice president of SID in 1953–54 under president Robert Hose of Henry Dreyfuss's office. He succeeded Hose as president of the 170-member organization in October 1954. Muller-Munk quickly discovered that his role presented numerous opportunities to act as a spokesperson for American industrial designers. It was a delicate, diplomatic task and one to which he was personally well suited.

Internally, Muller-Munk revamped the society's newsletter, giving it more gravitas (his description) through the inclusion of speeches by leading members and special reports on key issues and events. He also worked with the International Cooperation Administration of the US State Department to distribute information to membership related to "bidding on government contracts for research programs in underdeveloped areas" (see pp. 120–21), which would lead to major overseas engagements for Muller-Munk's own office and others. Perhaps the most visible result of his presidency was

the change of the organization's name, effective October 1955, to the American Society of Industrial Designers (ASID). Given the increasing scope of international design work by many members and the ongoing exhibitions of SID designs abroad, Muller-Munk felt it was essential to designate the nationality of their society.[61]

Muller-Munk was in constant contact with professional groups and educational institutions. In January 1955 he sat on a panel organized by the Industrial Designers Institute (a sister organization to SID) and held at the Museum of Modern Art in New York called "What's Cooking in the Kitchens?" Moderated by John Peter, the home-living editor of *Look Magazine*, the panel included Glenn Beyer, director of the Cornell University Housing Research Center; Josephine McCarthy, home economist and food editor, WRCA-TV; David Wheeler, General Motors stylist and designer; and designer/architect Eliot Noyes. Three months later, Muller-Munk hosted SID's own forum at MoMA, entitled "What's Happening to America's Taste?" It was an impressive panel, with a standing-room-only crowd that saw Loewy, Dreyfuss, and Teague all on the same stage, along with journalist Harriett Morrison of the *Herald Tribune* and retailing analyst Perry Meyers.[62] SID also worked with the Philadelphia Museum School of Art in the organization of its Design Council, and Muller-Munk himself would be elected to their Board of Governors the following year. He spearheaded conversations with groups such as the National Industrial Conference Board, with which SID explored "Increasing Profits Through Better Product Design" at a roundtable conference held at the Waldorf Astoria in New York; the American Management Association; the Association of Consulting Management Engineers; and the American Institute of Architects, from which SID hoped to gain insight into the pros and cons of incorporating architectural offices (a subject of some contention among designers at the time following Loewy's incorporation in Chicago). Muller-Munk also worked toward the unification of SID and IDI, the Industrial Designers Institute, a separate professional organization with roots in the design of home furnishings. The two organizations were at odds with each other for decades over the definition of industrial design practice, among other minutiae.[63] Muller-Munk made it a point to include Robert Gruen, president of IDI, in the annual SID meeting in October 1955 and acknowledged his presence from the podium.[64]

Muller-Munk believed not only in national unity and standards for industrial designers, but also in the development of an international industrial design community. As president of SID, he played host to prominent international

FIG. 34
Tricorne candleholders for
Val Saint Lambert, 1956

visitors who wanted to learn about the American systems of design and manufacturing. The society organized and led tours (sponsored by the federal government) for Danish and German designers and industrialists. The Danish delegation paid a visit not only to New York but also to Pittsburgh. Privately, Muller-Munk and PMMA also hosted Austrian industrial designer Karl Schwanzer and Swedish industrialist Thure Öberg. The latter was head of Husqvarna Vapenfabrik, one of the largest manufacturers in Sweden, which had recently contracted PMMA as a design consultant for corporate identity and product design.[65] That so many international designers deemed Pittsburgh worthy of a visit was a tribute to the city's manufacturing prowess and to Muller-Munk's establishing a solid reputation for industrial design.

As they were leading foreign designers on tours through the United States, the SID also undertook major efforts to share their work abroad. During Muller-Munk's presidency alone, the society sent photographic exhibits of their designers' work to Austria, France, England, India, and Australia.[66] Through a collaboration with the US Department of Commerce and its International Fair Program, the SID mounted an exhibition of their designed products, which traveled to Liège, Barcelona, Paris, and Milan to reach a total audience of more than one million [FIG. 35].[67] Muller-Munk reported with pride that the SID was awarded a special diploma in recognition of its services by the president of the Tenth Milan Triennial (August–November, 1954). An accompanying letter described their participation as "not only intrinsically excellent, but worthy as a step in the internationalization of design effort, and a forwarding of cultural rapport among the nations."[68]

Such cultural rapport was of utmost importance to Muller-Munk, who played a pivotal role in the development of an international professional design society over the course of the 1950s. In formal terms, it began in 1953, when he was appointed the SID representative to the International Design Congress, a meeting organized in Paris by the French Institut d'Esthétique Industrielle. Muller-Munk developed close friendships with British designer Misha Black, Swedish designer Count Sigvard Bernadotte, and French designer Jacques Viénot; the latter would present some obstacles in the formation of the international society because a number of American industrial designers did not think highly of him.[69] Always the consummate diplomat, Muller-Munk rose above the fray, assuring SID that the international partnerships would be between the societies, not between individuals.[70] By 1955 Muller-Munk and his English and French counterparts had proposed the founding of the International Coordinating Committee of Industrial Design Societies, which would work to develop a formal international organization. With the supporting vote of SID, Muller-Munk forged ahead.[71] Meeting in Paris in April 1956, he, Black, and Frenchman Pierre Vago

began to develop a constitution. In June 1957, in London, the provisional organization was founded as the International Council of Societies of Industrial Design (ICSID), and included the professional organizations of Denmark, France, West Germany, Italy, Norway, Sweden, the United Kingdom, and the United States [FIG. 36]. Muller-Munk was elected as the first president.[72]

The international group aimed to act as a clearinghouse for industrial design activities in member nations, with the goals of informing each other and avoiding duplication. They would also facilitate exchanges of information on ethics and rules of conduct, and assist in the development of design education. Through the publication of a biannual summary of activities and an annual conference (to rotate among member nations), the ICSID provided platforms for international exchange among peers.[73] Like the ASID domestically, the international body also promoted the profession by "informing the general public and industries about the value of industrial design."[74] By 1959 the ICSID had twenty-three societal memberships from seventeen countries, which collectively represented more than 6,500 designers.[75] It was a far cry from the exclusive fellowship of fifteen American industrial designers, which had incorporated as SID fifteen years earlier. This virtual explosion of design as a worldwide profession worried some, but Muller-Munk found it invigorating and necessary. Such organizations set "worthwhile status and tone" to the activities of his field.[76]

All told, this was a rollicking decade of professional success for Muller-Munk. He entered the 1950s as a small business owner and product designer and exited as a senior statesman and a self-styled design philosopher. His lectures and writings throughout the era shed light on the transition. In the early 1950s he penned articles on concrete issues such as material substitutions in wartime and the importance of functional design over styling.[77] He compared and contrasted the designs of European and American tools: "Americans build a workhorse, Europeans build a racehorse."[78] And he extolled the virtues of engineers and industrial designers working together to resolve products.[79] In the latter half of the decade, Muller-Munk's published musings began to reflect the expansion of PMMA, and of American industrial design in general, beyond stand-alone products and into systems, and from production-focused problem solving to marketing considerations.[80] His designers' primary contacts were now the clients' marketing executives rather than their engineers.[81] Muller-Munk increasingly opined on broad topics such as city planning and modernization, the integration of design and architecture, and adapting the American design business model for use in Europe.[82] It was a remarkable shift over a short period, reflecting a decade of rapid evolution in the field. Muller-Munk appeared to shoulder it all with aplomb,

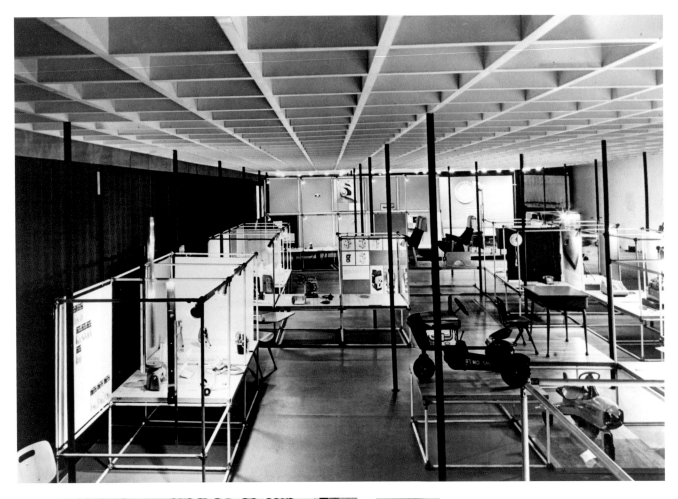

FIG. 35
**American industrial design exhibition in Liège, Belgium,
organized by Muller-Munk and William Winterbottom, 1955;
PMMA designs for Bell & Howell are visible in the center**

FIG. 36
**Muller-Munk (far right) with fellow members of ICSID, includ-
ing (from the left) Misha Black of Great Britain, Pierre Vago of
France, and Count Sigvard Bernadotte of Sweden, 1959**

even enthusiasm, yet the decline of traditional product design
rankled a man who had dedicated so much energy to its
development. It was unpleasant to conclude, as Muller-Munk
soon would, that "we [industrial designers] are the guys who
have designed most of the gadgets that rust in our garages,
that clutter our cellars, that fill our neighborhood and the
air above it with shattering noise and with noxious fumes."[83]
Designers' contributions to the development of products had
been significant, but the world demanded problem solving on
a higher level. Muller-Munk marched onward, determined to
conquer the amorphous design challenges of the next decade.

The 1950s "Kitchen Revolution"

CATHERINE WALWORTH

opposite

FIG. 1
Detail of Westinghouse's DFC-10 refrigerator
with chrome-finished three-way door handle, 1951

above, left to right

FIG. 2
Lucille Ball and Vivian Vance in "Pioneer
Women," *I Love Lucy*, season 1, episode 25, first
broadcast March 31, 1952, by CBS

FIG. 3
Freez-File featured in a Westinghouse
advertisement, *Life*, April 27, 1953

Few objects are as iconic of 1950s American homes as the streamlined,
porcelain-enameled refrigerator filled with jingling Coca-Cola bottles and
colorful Jell-O mold desserts. A signature of the American dream, this modern
appliance was the domestic interior's complement to a shining new
automobile in the garage.

In the 1950s General Electric and Westinghouse Electric Corporation
were sales leaders among a sea of Hotpoints, Admirals, and Frigidaires.
To help create a distinctive image, Westinghouse maintained celebrity
endorsements, including former 1930s film actress Betty Furness, who was the
company's refined pitchwoman from 1948 until 1960. The superstar television
couple Lucille Ball and Desi Arnaz appeared in Westinghouse commercials,
and *I Love Lucy* offered a prominent backdrop to showcase new appliance
designs until 1957. In the episode "Pioneer Women," Lucy Ricardo and Ethel
Mertz attempt to bake homemade bread and churn butter in the manner of
their turn-of-the-century forebears [FIG. 2]. Having lost prewar home economic
skills, however, the comically inept food scientists blow up their laboratory
with a behemoth yeast-fueled bread loaf. Nearby stands the symbol of their
modernity—a Westinghouse refrigerator with three-way door handle designed
by Peter Muller-Munk Associates.

Handles were often the most significant features of refrigerators, with their
spare lines and a general absence of exterior details. The chrome triple-action
handle on PMMA's 1951 Westinghouse design conveniently tilted left, right,
or backward, allowing one to open the door with an elbow when hands were
full [FIG. 1]. Muller-Munk retained the traditional white porcelain exterior and
rounded curves, as if the appliance were generously bulging with food. For the
interior, he stated it was important to "flatter the food, to make the appearance
not only visually attractive, but to carry a feeling of cleanliness"; to that effect,
color styling in blue and gold was meant to underscore the refrigerator's icy
cold environment.[1] The design was the culmination of technical and market
research that began in December 1949, and the beginning of a longstanding
relationship between PMMA and Westinghouse.[2] The manner in which
Americans shopped, stored, and prepared food was undergoing a radical shift
and influencing 1950s appliance design. Tin rationing during World War II had
motivated production of frozen foods in paperboard, and Birds Eye continued

FIG. 4
"The Shape of Tomorrow," Westinghouse advertisement, *Saturday Evening Post*, September 28, 1957

to promote the liberating advantages of frozen food for busy housewives. The TV dinner phenomenon would ignite in 1954, and refrigerator freezer compartments grew in size along with the market for stand-alone home freezers. Although aiming to make domestic life easier, appliance manufacturers also needed to free housewives from the burdens—scraping, chipping, thawing, and mopping—of freezing itself. The 1951 line that PMMA designed for Westinghouse introduced three revolutionary "Frost-Free" models, based on a decade of technological research.[3]

Throughout the 1950s, PMMA continued to create innovations for Westinghouse refrigerators. In 1953, for example, PMMA patented an index file that attached to the freezer's exterior to track storage of various types and amounts of foods. Marketed as a "Freez-File," the device was a favorite feature of both Lizabeth Scott and Edward G. Robinson at the star-studded Westinghouse "Freedom Fair," as imagined in a double-page color spread in *Life* magazine [FIG. 3]. PMMA's 1954 "Food File" refrigerator offered nine different storage temperatures and individualized units for everything from beverages to butter. On the exterior, a new gold-colored push-button pad—"the first electrically operated door-opening device for a domestic refrigerator"—opened the appliance with a gentle touch.[4]

Following a crippling 156-day strike in 1955–56, Westinghouse launched an optimistic comeback in 1956 with a bold advertising strategy, new management structure, and renewed emphasis on consumer appliances and radios.[5] PMMA, a key weapon in the appliance giant's image arsenal, was to be their sole design consultant. The firm was tasked with developing *all* major Westinghouse appliances as a unified "family."[6] The result was a comprehensive "square look" that would help define a new era.

Muller-Munk described what he saw as a pervasive "kitchen revolution" underway in 1957: "Kitchen walls are tumbling down. Kitchen appliances are building up—into one synchronized unit."[7] Beginning in 1954, Muller-Munk and his team began developing a line of built-in appliances for Westinghouse: "To the designer and to the engineer, the problem is no longer one of the specific appliance but now that of the total design of the integrated kitchen in which all appliances are related. The entire kitchen will now, in effect, become one appliance."[8] With the square look promoted (by Westinghouse's advertising agency, McCann-Erickson) as "The Shape of Tomorrow," the fully developed 1958 line of appliances was the new face of Westinghouse and interchangeable modularity a burgeoning concept [FIG. 4].

In August 1954 *Industrial Design* posed the question: "Is the kitchen disintegrating?"[9] It would seem the answer was decidedly "yes," as manufacturers engaged designers to rethink available space in all areas of the house. PMMA's 1958 portable Westinghouse dishwasher, for example, allowed one to wheel the appliance to the table to clear the dishes, then back to the kitchen for washing, and finally to the china cabinet for unloading. Muller-Munk described this ease of mobility in 1960:

> The "working furniture" thus envisioned by the designer will no longer be confined in one single area, namely the kitchen, but will be stationed at strategic points all over the house. Space is far too expensive to waste; separate kitchens and dining rooms, as we have known them, are on their way out. I can see a sideboard containing heating units and a refrigerator as being far more efficient for today's cooks-hostess than the conventional kitchen is [FIG. 5].[10]

PMMA also developed a complete kitchen environment for Westinghouse that could be installed to fit any room and simultaneously open out onto multiple spaces. In this "Kitchen-of-the-Future," what appeared to be traditional cabinets and drawers in fact opened to reveal small freezers and refrigerated compartments at various locations throughout the kitchen, including an under-the-counter freezer drawer.[11]

PMMA had already made this drawer concept the signature feature of its 1960 Center Drawer Refrigerator [FIG. 6]. A central pull-out compartment for easy access to food staples, the drawer held storage units to keep meats and vegetables fresh for a full week. The Center Drawer Refrigerator was also decoratively adaptable—vinyl-coated steel panels were available in a range of colors and textures to personalize the exterior. PMMA's space-age ballet of transformable appliances also included a Westinghouse range that rotated outward to reveal a circular grouping of additional burners.

The 1964 New York World's Fair featured "Dorothy Draper's Westinghouse Dream Home"—a 3,000-square-foot single-level house installed on the first floor of the Better Living Building, designed to showcase Westinghouse's modern lighting and entertainment products. The kitchen included PMMA's split-level Terrace Top Range as well as a Center Drawer Refrigerator model. Noticeably, the 1950s' confection colors were turning into the autumnal shades of the late 1960s, and the dream home felt less optimistic. PMMA's lengthy relationship with Westinghouse reflected important changes occurring within the industrial design profession itself. The monolithic nature of individual products was giving way to integrated and transformable systems of physical space as a design challenge for the 1960s and beyond.

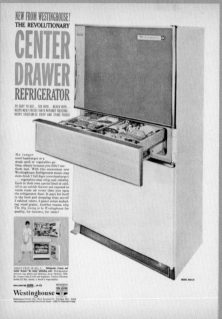

top to bottom

FIG. 5
Westinghouse room-divider refrigerator, c. 1959

FIG. 6
Advertisement, Westinghouse Center Drawer Refrigerator, 1960

The Color Explosion

CATHERINE WALWORTH

By the mid-1950s, the war era's somber hues had thoroughly dissipated, and designers were bringing exuberance to everyday objects, from pink telephones to aquamarine automobiles. *Industrial Design* magazine, in their annual design review of 1955, acknowledged the pervasive and newly uninhibited use of color.[1] American kitchens in particular, the review noted, were breaking out of their formerly sterile conditions and into pastel palettes, with appliances now resembling edible pastries in soft yellows, greens, and pinks.

Now that so many colors were available for everyday products, manufacturers were faced with having to choose. A special field of study devoted to the psychological responses to and cultural associations of color paralleled the rise of industrial design in the postwar era. In order to actively engage with the subject, the Society of Industrial Designers (SID) joined the Inter-Society Color Council in 1949.[2] Muller-Munk was among SID's representatives, with Egmont Arens as chairman.[3] From their organization's perspective, industrial designers had a potentially powerful role to play in influencing consumer behavior through the astute use of color.[4]

It was at this moment that Caloric Appliance Corporation, based in Topton, Pennsylvania, engaged PMMA to devise a design concept for its new 1955 line of gas ranges and ovens.[5] The result was a successful product that remained largely unchanged until decade's end [FIG. 1]. Caloric's marketing feted the "brilliant years-ahead styling" of PMMA and the stoves' "tasteful use of color."[6] Consumers had their choice not only of various range sizes and modular configurations of doors, burners, and ovens, but also of colors—the stamped steel body came in traditional white and five different colors.[7] PMMA's design also featured incandescent "colortone" lighting options in the illuminated backguard, with bulbs available in "frosty blue," "minty green," "rosy pink," and (for the perennially conservative) "cool white."[8]

opposite

FIG. 1
Caloric White Sands 4-burner range, 1955

below

FIG. 2
Lady Schick Futura electric shaver in multiple shades, 1958

FIG. 3
Sylva-Lume brochure, 1957

Typical Design Illustrations of Sylvania's

New **SYLVA-LUME** Lighting System

A DYNAMIC CONCEPT FOR UNLIMITED FLEXIBILITY IN WALL-TO-WALL LIGHTING

SYLVANIA ELECTRIC PRODUCTS INC.   FLUORESCENT LIGHTING FIXTURES   WHEELING, WEST VIRGINIA

PRINTED IN U.S.A.

Small-scale goods, too, owed much of their consumer appeal to up-to-date color choices. In 1958 Schick, Incorporated, a national company based in Lancaster, Pennsylvania, introduced the Futura model to its line of Lady Schick electric shavers. PMMA brought restrained elegance and refinement to a product that was intended to be both feminine and functional. The firm's model makers experimented with clay forms, ultimately settling on a compact, faceted shape that was centrally weighted and easy to grip. While previous Lady Schick models relied heavily on surface decoration, Futura's form resembled an exquisite gemstone.[9]

The luxurious new Lady Schick benefitted from the best consultants in the field. PMMA teamed up with package designer Francis Blod, who created the miniature hatbox-shaped carrying case, and commercial color expert Faber Birren, who selected four personalized shades—"frost white," "blush rose," "flame red," and "turquoise" [FIG. 2].[10] Birren was a luminary among a growing number of professional color consultants working in concert with architects, industrial designers, and manufacturers.[11] By 1960 every new Caloric stove included a kitchen color plan by home color stylist Beatrice West, while at Westinghouse, Melanie Kahane created fabrics and wallpapers coordinated to the company's Confection Color appliances in shades such as "Frosting Pink" and "Lemon Yellow."[12]

Understanding the behavioral impact of color not only served to boost sales for individual products, but also offered an opportunity to improve daily environments. PMMA's Sylva-Lume luminescent ceiling for Sylvania is a case in point, designed to soften modernist interiors through colored lighting because, as Muller-Munk said, "lumens alone do not make for happiness."[13] In February 1957 Muller-Munk presented the new architectural product to his client with the following challenge: "The Sylvania Sylva-Lume system was developed by a creative group for a creative profession ... it is up to you to follow through where we left off."[14] Composed of a suspension grid with three-by-three-foot modular units of colored vinyl [FIG. 3], Sylva-Lume offered architects and businesses a customizable lighting palette of pastel colors that broke up the large light-diffusing plastic ceilings that were "as monotonous and standardized as if they had been invented for a race of robots."[15]

PMMA built upon the Sylva-Lume experience in a related project with Westinghouse engineers who were developing the technology to create "bulb-less" lighting systems—luminous panels of glowing phosphor encased between sheets of coated, electrically conductive glass. Branded Rayescent, this "thermoelectric electro-luminescent" technology produced a "cool, shadow-less light which can be varied in brightness and in color" and be used not only as a ceiling, but also as walls and flooring for a total environment with a full spectrum of color options.[16] PMMA designed room environments showcasing these panels, as well as the sculptural anodized aluminum "mobiles" used to pass electric currents and alternatively cool and heat the room [FIG. 4].[17] With the touch of a dial, inhabitants could adjust color, light intensity, and temperature, altering a room's mood with these "chameleon-like, color changing panels."[18] Ambitious projects such as these anticipated the light environments soon to emerge in 1960s avant-garde art, and positioned PMMA at the cutting edge of color as a design tool.

FIG. 4
PMMA's prototype Rayescent panels for a full-scale dining room environment. Options shown were for blue to blue-green to green, but a full spectrum of color combinations was possible.

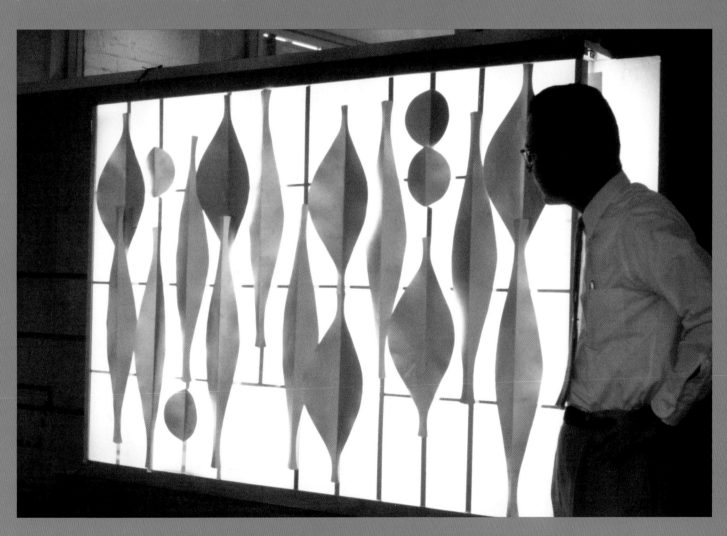

New Frontiers

RACHEL DELPHIA AND CATHERINE WALWORTH

———

"The look of tomorrow is based on the supposition that everything is technically or scientifically feasible.... The industrial revolution is over. You name it—we'll find the brains and techniques to do it. Our challenge is no longer one of production, of manufacturing, or of building; but one of inventing, of scientific problem-solving, of research, and of creative conceptualizing."[1]

From the time he entered the profession until the mid-1950s, Peter Muller-Munk experienced industrial design as an object-centric practice. He gave products a competitive edge through functional and visual improvements, new materials, or more efficient production; and he took great pride in creating tangible things that served real needs. But when the postwar hunger was satiated, industrial designers and their clients had to reconsider their tactics. A surfeit of goods meant that product redesign was no longer enough: it was not sufficient to sell the clients' merchandise nor to sustain a large design consulting firm. Amid cultural upheaval, designers and others also recognized pressing new needs that went far beyond individual consumer products. Accordingly, the design field expanded into systems and infrastructure. Changes weighed heavily on the cerebral Muller-Munk, and he grappled in lectures and writings with the shifting nature of design practice and with designers' ultimate responsibilities to the culture at large (see "Think Small," p. 170). Privately he admitted that he was "fundamentally a very traditional professional with pleasantly antiquated loyalties and sentimentalities [that are] not very fashionable these days."[2] Some new ways of working, especially the creation of markets where none existed, challenged his personal tenets.[3] Yet, as a businessman, he accepted that his firm must adapt to survive, and he began to explore new frontiers that would carry PMMA into the next century. Product specialists no more, PMMA designers increasingly applied their problem-solving skills and aesthetic acumen to long-range planning; market research, analysis, and development; corporate identity; interiors; exhibitions; civic planning; mass-transit vehicles; and architectural and wayfinding graphics. They went so far as to reimagine basic utilities—the electricity grid and water towers—as sculptural fixtures of the landscape or communal centers of the urban environment **[P. 8 AND FIG. 1]**.[4]

International Expansion

Ironically, just as the domestic design scene began a dramatic evolution, new demand emerged for exporting traditional American industrial design know-how abroad. Beginning in 1955 Muller-Munk secured for his firm some of the first US federal government contracts for design assistance in underdeveloped nations and for the design of trade fair exhibitions behind the Iron Curtain. Both programs were efforts of Cold War containment strategy.[5] The collective US policy impetus that led to the involvement of industrial designers was the desire to rebuild the postwar world with stable capitalist economies and comfortable living standards that would fortify "uncommitted" nations against the communist threat.[6] To accomplish this, President Truman's foreign policy laid the groundwork for "not only direct financial

frontispiece

FIG. 1
One of a series of concepts for US Steel's Power Styling program, 1964, a campaign to promote the imaginative redesign of electrical utility structures

above

FIG. 2
Marshal Tito (left) greets Carole and Paul R. Wiedmann at the opening of a trade fair in Zagreb, Yugoslavia, 1964. Wiedmann, a PMMA designer, oversaw the "Farm to Table"–themed US display, which included photographs of his wife, Carole, shopping at a modern American outdoor mall.

assistance, but also the transfer of some technical knowledge and skills ... through programs and consultancy work."[7] The first programs to materialize for American designers were technical assistance contracts with an arm of the State Department, followed by Department of Commerce contracts for its trade fair program **[FIG. 2]**.

As early as 1950 the Society of Industrial Designers (SID) approached Dean Acheson, secretary of state, to offer help in stimulating foreign economies.[8] In the ensuing years, Muller-Munk and Chicago designer Dave Chapman were two stalwart champions of the international cause. In the spring of 1955 the pair reached an agreement with James M. Silberman of the Foreign Operations Administration to draft a request for proposals to SID members.[9] On May 4, Silberman provided the brief outlining the government's desire to contract "several competent American industrial design consultant firms to assist in improving products and increasing production among countries participating with the United States in industrial technical cooperation programs."[10] These included countries in the Near East, Far East, and Latin America where manual industries and crafts predominated, and which often underutilized local resources while producing little to satisfy needs for basic consumer goods. By August SID and the newly minted International Cooperation Administration (ICA) announced awards to five firms: Dave Chapman; Peter Muller-Munk; Smith, Scherr, McDermott; Walter Dorwin Teague; and Russel Wright.[11] The designers were to survey their countries and report back with recommendations. The array of suggestions and subsequent implementations constituted a fascinating and unprecedented program of official American diplomacy through industrial design.[12]

Muller-Munk was awarded an initial contract for three countries: Turkey, India, and Israel.[13] Paul Karlen headed the tripartite program with assistance from fellow PMMA designer Robert Renaud. In the fall of 1955 the men embarked on a four-month study tour, meeting with government officials, chambers of commerce, industrial groups, small manufacturers, and individual craftspeople. They covered more than 4,000 miles in Turkey alone. In India they focused on New Delhi, Calcutta, Madras, and Bombay, including the surrounding backcountries. In Israel, Tel Aviv served as home base, with side trips to Haifa, Jerusalem, and "as far south as restrictions permitted."[14] Muller-Munk personally met with Turkish, Indian, and Israeli officials, although he did not undertake the entire tour.[15] Back stateside by early 1956, Karlen and Renaud prepared action plans for each country

FIG. 3
Left to right: Natanel Cohen
(probably), Paul Karlen, and
Mort Rothenberg in the Israel
Product Design Office, likely in
the Tel Aviv location, 1958–59.
PMMA products, sketches, and
photographs, visible behind
the group, served as teaching
examples for the IPDO staff.

to be submitted to ICA. Ultimately, PMMA passed on the execution stage of the Indian project, electing to devote their time and resources to Israel and Turkey.[16]

In the minds of the designers, Israel was a plum contract.[17] The country had a significant business and manufacturing base, an educated and Western-oriented populace, a high standard of living, and discerning consumers.[18] On the down side, tiny Israel had limited natural resources and an unfavorable trade balance.[19] PMMA's goals for Israel included the design of better domestic products (to cut down on imports), an increase in the design and production of exportable goods, and the building of a local cohort of practicing designers.[20] Muller-Munk saw the potential for Israel to become "the Switzerland of the Middle East," that is, a respected leader in specific niche markets.[21] Thanks in large part to the underlying advantages, PMMA executed a program in Israel that was unique across all ICA contracts: they launched and operated an industrial design consulting office that served domestic clients.[22]

In May 1956, with ICA funds and Israeli matching funds, PMMA founded the Israel Product Design Office, or IPDO, in Haifa. As a government-funded enterprise, it was not a branch office per se; yet, for the duration, PMMA folded IPDO into the overall identity and promotion of the Pittsburgh-based firm. PMMA's Karlen and Mort Rothenberg were appointed director and chief designer, while two Israelis who were born and educated in America—Natanel Cohen and Aryeh Lavi—became Israeli counterpart director and Israeli counterpart chief designer.[23] IPDO's first project was a three-day seminar on the principles of industrial design for Israeli manufacturers, held in June in Herzliya, just north of Tel Aviv. Some seventy-five representatives of industrial sectors attended, and the event served as a brainstorming session for potential IPDO projects. Several attendees signed on as IPDO's first clients and enabled the formal establishment of an office in July.[24]

Simultaneously, IPDO recruited available staff with backgrounds in graphics, engineering, and advertising.[25] Even Cohen's experience was not in industrial design but in public relations, reflecting the absence of trained designers in Israel at the time. IPDO operated with a model of learning by doing and growth commensurate to need (not unlike Muller-Munk's own fledgling office in the 1930s). It charged clients a fee— because Muller-Munk felt that paying for service increased the perceived value to the buyer—but the rate was reduced to one half the cost and was subsidized by the government project funds.[26] The office tackled design assignments by day, and Karlen and Rothenberg conducted evening seminars on professional practice [FIG. 3].

Despite a six-month disruption because of the Suez Canal crisis (the US government forced the Americans to evacuate),[27] IPDO completed thirty-three assignments for Israeli clients during its first eighteen months of operation. Items designed in this early period included metal giftware, olive wood products, silver flatware, glass bottles, radio components, pressure cookers, commercial bakery ovens, and a variety of packaging and labeling.[28] In 1958 the office relocated to Tel Aviv, to the Maariv Building, home of a newspaper of the same name. Major clients and projects included Thermoil Ltd. (space heaters), Amron Ltd. (hi-fi speaker enclosure), and Amcor Ltd. (air conditioner and washing machine).[29] The office also designed door and cabinet hardware, graphics and in-flight accessories for the airline El Al, the first tractor designed and produced in Israel, and another original: an Israeli espresso machine. The latter was remarked upon by a Maariv reporter, Moshe Dor, who visited the office in 1959: "I don't know whether Hatzkel's clients notice his espresso machine … but it might give them the satisfaction of knowing that the machine was designed and manufactured in Israel and not in Italy" [FIG. 4].[30] Other projects included faucets and fixtures for Hamat, and food packaging for Froumine and Tnuva. By far the most extensive campaign was the complete design service performed for Supersol, the first chain of supermarkets in Israel, which opened in 1958. IPDO consulted on the layout of the store, display design, equipment, and all aspects of corporate identity including signage, store-brand packaging, stationery, and labels [FIGS. 5–6].[31]

By the fall of 1959 the American team was observing rather than practicing and had begun to plan its withdrawal. Karlen reported enthusiastically that IPDO had worked on 160 projects for sixty-five clients and had trained eighteen

Israeli designers on the job.[32] When the Americans departed in early 1960, they left behind an active staff of nine under the direction of Cohen and an office facing greater demand for its services than it could meet.[33]

Implementation of PMMA's Turkish ICA project began in earnest about a year after IPDO.[34] Turkey presented a very different set of challenges. In contrast to Israel, it was an immense and established nation with a largely agrarian population and a widespread craft economy. Yet the ruling liberal political party was interested in "trade-driven growth policy" and openly allied itself with Western Europe and the United States.[35] The country was rich in resources, including copper, wood, and minerals suitable for carving, yet PMMA found little international interest in existing Turkish craft products. PMMA recommended modernizing crafts and giftware based on Turkish motifs, skills, and materials, but with greater international market appeal.[36]

The designers launched their effort with the formation of an advisory group, the Turkish Handicraft Development Board, consisting of representatives from the Turkish government's Ministries of Economy and Commerce, the Confederation of Turkish Tradesmen, individual artisans, and Turkish banking interests.[37] They opened the Turkish Handicraft Development Office (THDO) on Ankara's Gazi Mustafa Kemal Boulevard with three main action items: to organize craftspeople into cooperatives that could produce in quantity, meet delivery dates, and control quality; to design high-quality products that would find ready acceptance in world markets; and to develop international promotion and distribution systems to merchandise the goods produced.[38] Renaud served as co-director of THDO with Turkish counterpart Mehmet Ali Oksal, an industrial engineering graduate from Cornell University.[39] PMMA also contracted Robert Gabriel, a member of the design faculty at Carnegie Tech, as assistant American advisor under Renaud.[40]

The team probed Anatolia for raw materials, native skills, and traditional product ideas and reported encouraging finds: Selçuk motifs could be applied to assorted products; woodworking in Caucasian walnut could be adapted to more modern tastes, as could woven mats and basketry; copper, then exported as ore, was ripe for the development of finished products that could be exported for greater profit than could the raw material; and minerals unique to Turkey such

FIG. 4
Promotional photograph for the Amcor espresso machine. Although the photograph dates from 1969, the machine was designed by IPDO more than a decade earlier.

clockwise

FIG. 5
Supersol grocery store,
Tel Aviv, c. 1958

FIG. 6
Supersol packaging, c. 1958

FIG. 7
Each of the objects seen in
this 1957 image (save the
radiator) was designed by
PMMA's Turkish Handicraft
Development Office in Ankara
and executed by native craftspeople repurposing traditional
materials such as copper and
Kütahya ceramics as modern
pendant lights and tile-topped
coffee tables.

FIG. 8
Leylâ Özön and Mehmet
Ali Oksal of the Turkish
Handicraft Development
Office review meerschaum
and wooden products with
Muller-Munk (far right)
during his fall 1957 visit.

as meerschaum could be carved in modern designs with international appeal.[41] Renaud also took a junket to Italy, Switzerland, and Scandinavia in search of internationally successful craft products that could inspire Turkish creations.

Renaud, Gabriel, and a Turkish staff of about six to eight set about designing some one hundred products in the fall and winter of 1957–58.[42] Fifteen newly formed collaboratives located in craft centers such as Kütahya, Konya, Antep, and Eskişehir executed the designs: some entirely new, others based on tradition. Still other products combined media, and thus the labors of previously unassociated artisans [FIGS. 7–8].[43] THDO planned to exhibit the finished goods for international merchandizing agents in the summer of 1958 in Ankara, Istanbul, and Izmir.[44]

All told, PMMA spent three years in Turkey and four in Israel. The designers treated IPDO and THDO as fully realized satellite offices, going so far as to coordinate the letterhead for all three "branches" of their operations and to include Israeli and Turkish products in PMMA's promotional literature back in the United States. Yet continuation of the programs from year to year was far from guaranteed. Muller-Munk personally defended ICA initiatives to Congress when it revisited the Mutual Security/Mutual Aid programs and federal budgets in 1957 and 1958. In August 1957, Pennsylvania representative James G. Fulton submitted a statement from the designer; and the following spring Muller-Munk took the

top to bottom

FIG. 9
Interior of the American
pavilion at the trade fair in
Poznan, Poland, 1962

FIG. 10
American pavilion at the trade
fair in Izmir, Turkey, 1957

FIG. 11
Exterior portion of the American pavilion at the trade fair in
Poznan, Poland, 1962

floor and addressed the House Foreign Affairs Committee at length (see reprint, p. 168).[45] His testimony undoubtedly reflected his firm's stake in the continuation of contracts (they requested $138,000 for Turkey for 1958–59), but also a fervent belief in the importance of the program. "Weaker ... needy" nations, Muller-Munk reminded Congress, "[had] only two places to look for such [technical] help—to the Soviets and to us. Very bluntly, if we abandon them now, there is no such thing as our getting a second chance." Muller-Munk shared similar thoughts with the American public as a guest of Dave Garroway on NBC's *Today Show* in November 1957.[46]

The ICA legacy was complicated and perhaps not as grand as its architects envisioned. It is not clear to what extent THDO succeeded in merchandizing its products abroad. Craft journalists cautioned Muller-Munk about the complexities of the task he set for himself, yet news outlets enthusiastically reported THDO products hitting the market.[47] PMMA could claim unequivocal success in Israel. IPDO was unique among the ICA projects as a fully operational domestic design office, and the country continued to develop its industrial design practice after PMMA's withdrawal. Historians have noted that although most ICA projects fell short of their broad political objectives, Taiwan, South Korea, and Israel "did grow close to the U.S. in political and economic ideology as well as in technology."[48]

In late 1959 Muller-Munk assumed further responsibility for sharing the American industrial design method abroad. Together with Karlen, he agreed to "initiate and establish product development programs for the European Productivity Agency of the Organization for European Economic Cooperation (OEEC)." The ambitious new program would take the PMMA men on a fourteen-month tour of seventeen OEEC countries for "seminars and workshops in industrial design

techniques."[49] Muller-Munk reflected on the magnitude of the commitment, which, he came to realize, was "really quite a job."[50] This was a somewhat surprising comment from a man who had always relished the opportunity to travel, especially with Ilona by his side. But his movements were increasingly complicated in the 1960s by problems with his wife's health. Concern for her well-being and disappointment over her inability to accompany him as extensively as in the past must have cast a pall over travel plans.[51] Nevertheless, Muller-Munk kicked off his leg of the OEEC tour on March 5 in Paris and returned in mid-August following stops in Belgium, Norway, Denmark, Austria, and Ireland.[52] Karlen took over in September upon the return of Muller-Munk, who published two lengthy synopses of lectures given on the tour in *Industrial Design*.[53]

Beginning in 1957 PMMA also began a long relationship with the US Department of Commerce's Office of International Trade Fairs (OITF). American involvement in the fairs had begun in 1954 following the realization that "Russia had participated in more than 130 international trade fairs since 1950, not so much to display export products as to promote communism."[54] Not wanting to concede any ground to the Russians, the United States upped its participation and welcomed "some 12 million people" to its first exhibits in fifteen countries in 1954 alone.[55] OITF initially used its own design teams, but program chairman Harold C. McClellan lamented that the results did not represent the best of American design. Beginning in 1956 OITF began a bidding process with the American Society of Industrial Designers.[56]

PMMA designers Leonard Levitan, Paul Wiedmann, and Kenneth Love recall the trade fair programs they oversaw with a mixture of pride in the aesthetic and technical execution and astonishment at the propaganda of the period.[57] The government-set themes of the American exhibitions ranged from "Free Men Build the Future" (Izmir, Turkey, 1957) and "Expanding Industry Serving the Consumer" (Poznan, Poland, 1961), to "Allied in Progress" (Rio de Janeiro, 1963) and "Farm to Table" (Zagreb, Yugoslavia, 1964) **[FIGS. 9–11]**. Once the Departments of State, Commerce, and later Agriculture sorted out the overarching message and the products that would be shown, PMMA had mere months to design the exhibits (a complex amalgam of space planning, graphics, and architectural components) and to oversee their implementation with OITF teams and building crews in the host countries. The scale was immense. American pavilions covered anywhere from several thousand to more than one hundred thousand square feet and showcased the products of fifty to two thousand manufacturers, all visually integrated into a cohesive, entertaining, and informative whole. PMMA's designs competed for visitation with those of other nations, and they often confronted communist displays head-on: in

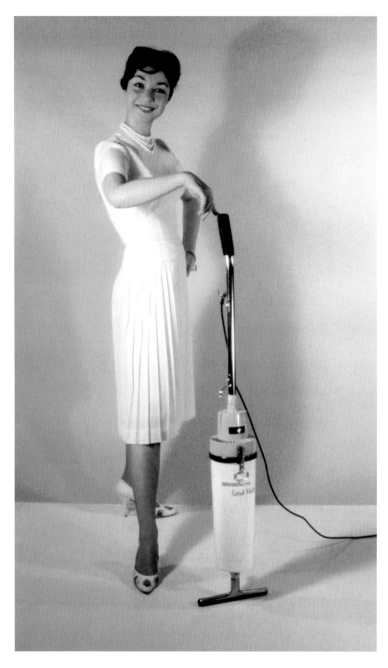

left to right

FIG. 12
Bissell Scrub Master, 1960

FIG. 13
PMMA's color-coded packaging system for Bissell, c. 1963, not only appealed to consumers but also streamlined the inventory process: blue denoted carpet sweepers; green, electric products; yellow, rug shampoo applicators, and so forth.

Poznan, in 1966, they were "directly adjacent" to Russia's exhibit, and "Red China's [was] just across the way."[58] Muller-Munk seems to have used the trade fair program as a proving ground for young designers, many of whom recall being handed the command of an entire fair, a task far beyond their experience levels. Deliberately or not, it was a sink or swim assignment; those who handled the projects skillfully continued to rise within PMMA.[59]

It is easy to dismiss the trade fairs as a forum for Cold War indoctrination. Yet regardless of the messages delivered, the PMMA designers firmly committed themselves to their roles as visual communicators.[60] Together with work on domestic trade fairs, for clients such as Aluminum Company of America (Alcoa), Bissell, Pittsburgh Plate Glass, United States Steel, and Westinghouse Electric Corporation, the OITF program solidified PMMA's reputation as a leader in exhibition design, architectural graphics, and wayfinding systems.

Changes on the Home Front

While Muller-Munk and select staff juggled demanding schedules overseas, the PMMA office in Pittsburgh continued to evolve. In March 1964 PMMA announced a new long-term lease in Four Gateway Center, the distinguished twenty-two-story glass and steel office tower designed by Max Abramovitz of Harrison & Abramovitz and completed just four years earlier. In addition to the 8,355 square feet in Gateway Four, as it was colloquially known, PMMA announced that it would occupy an entire floor across the street with an immense model shop where staff could execute something as large as a concept train car at full scale **[SEE P. 141, FIG. 32]**.

PMMA reported the move as part of an expansion program. Indeed, the staff and the client portfolio were growing quickly, though not without some pains. Waves of hiring in

FIG. 14
Concept sketch for Bissell's
display at the Housewares
Show, 1962

the late 1950s gave way to at least one economic layoff in 1963; yet by 1965 the staff had swelled to nearly fifty (up from thirty-two in 1958).[61] Muller-Munk himself was stretched thin at the time by supporting his aging mother in New York (and by his lifelong penchant for luxurious living and travel). There is no indication that his financial concerns affected personnel at the office, but they may have contributed to his decision to incorporate the firm, in July 1965.[62] One major blow to PMMA was the loss, around 1964, of the Westinghouse appliance account, parts of which it had held continuously since 1949. The threat was systemic, reflecting the period trend among large corporations to pull design in-house. But spirits at PMMA were bolstered by an ever increasing portfolio of projects for US Steel, and new relationships with American Standard, Bayer AG, Fisher Scientific, and Texaco, among others. Clients came from around the nation, but the immediate environs were ripe with potential: Pittsburgh in this period ranked third in the country in its number of corporate headquarters.[63]

For PMMA one of the most logical ways to expand its design scope was to broaden the range of services performed for a single client, as it did with well-known sweeper company Bissell Incorporated. PMMA had been one of several consultants to design products for Bissell in the late 1950s, including a self-wringing Sponge Master mop and updated Grand Rapids floor sweeper. When Bissell found its market share slipping with purely mechanical devices, president Melville Bissell III reenvisioned the company to compete with modern electrics and stationed PMMA at the creative helm.[64] The consultant's exclusive engagement, beginning in 1960, led to a concert of product development and corporate identity

design that extended throughout the home cleaning products, associated packaging, store displays, printed materials, and domestic trade exhibitions.

Bissell placed PMMA unequivocally at the root of its product development system, despite retaining in-house designers as well. "From the very first stage," wrote Bissell's head of product planning, Henry T. Lathrop, "industrial design has had a hand in the product development and—as is often the case—the original suggestion for the product came from Muller-Munk."[65] As ideas moved through Lathrop's twenty-stage process, they returned to PMMA designers for refinement. From Muller-Munk's perspective, Bissell was a poster child for consulting design success. He stressed that consultants' naïveté was their greatest asset. Unburdened with preconceived notions about management's expectations, consultants could overturn an entire concept. And as outside experts paid for their opinions, they could push management to take a more daring new path.[66]

One of the most groundbreaking new products to be developed under PMMA's aegis was the multitasking Sweep Master/Scrub Master, with electric vacuum cleaner and floor scrubber components that snapped onto an interchangeable power unit. This much-celebrated tool represented Bissell's first foray into electric vacuums, but with a dynamic twist. Initially, two different products were considered—one for scrubbing hard surface floors and the other a vacuum—until PMMA suggested a single combination unit.[67] Bissell promoted the new household tool as "the world's first appliance for all household cleaning." Released in 1960, this product contributed to a five-fold sales increase for Bissell in just three years [FIG. 12].[68]

PMMA also addressed the entire scope of Bissell's corporate identity, reflecting the era's growing reliance on the marketing side (rather than the production side) of the design equation. Muller-Munk advanced the idea that "every time we mail a letter, send an invoice, present a calling card, stick a label on an envelope or print a report, we reveal a little bit of our true face."[69] PMMA modernized and refined Bissell's logotype and generated a graphics standards manual to govern correct usage. The designers also improved the packaging scheme. They chose white boxes with bold illustrations topped by the Bissell logo in a designated band of color [FIG. 13].[70] Rounding out their concept-to-market approach, PMMA helped Bissell showcase its products in stores and at tradeshows [FIG. 14]. The firm also designed Bissell's new executive offices as part of its extension into space planning and interior design.[71] According to PMMA, this was a logical extension of corporate identity, "a medium for projecting a desired personality."[72]

"Total corporate service" became a catchphrase at PMMA, and it offered clients a full menu of choices. Companies such as Mine Safety Appliances, a product design partner since the 1940s, expanded their collaboration with PMMA on extensive new packaging. Mellon Bank approached PMMA for the first time for a corporate identity treatment. Still others, including local engineering leader Dravo Corporation, signed up first for corporate identity and soon after for space planning and interior design of their 85,000-square-foot headquarters in downtown Pittsburgh.[73]

In a city of materials manufacturers, market development design provided another growth area for PMMA. Reviving the strategies they had honed on plastics and metals promotion in the 1930s and 1940s, PMMA helped clients bridge the "serious gap ... between technological developments and their commercial realization."[74] According to Karlen, market development was a natural outgrowth of classic industrial design, with research and development campaigns to expand existing markets, to break into new markets with existing or new materials, to protect against competition, or simply to enhance the overall prestige and image of a material.[75] PMMA's slogan in this period, "We exist to help our clients lead their markets," seems to have been crafted precisely to lure this kind of work. Local businesses turned to PMMA in droves, but the firm also fielded new bids with the Budd Company, DuPont, Griswold Manufacturing Company, and others [FIG. 15]. No single association better exemplifies PMMA's market development capabilities than its relationship with US Steel, which began in the mid-1950s with PMMA's recommendations to promote vinyl-clad steel, a colorful heat-cured sheet material that could be die stamped with any number of textures and used in products or as architectural elements [FIG. 16].[76]

FIG. 15
The Symbol line of cast aluminum cookware (porcelain-enameled steel lids), 1962, was designed by PMMA to help client Griswold, a leader in cast iron cookware since 1865, meet the demands of the contemporary hostess for informal yet stylish oven-to-table entertaining.

'Strong as steel'

YOU MAY SOON be using in your home a new "strong as steel" material which looks like leather, linen or almost any other surface you can think of.

It has all of the desirable characteristics of not-so-strong plastics and was developed in a Pittsburgh laboratory.

In the near future there is a good possibility it will be appearing in varied forms, colors and textures as radio and television cabinets, wall panels, furniture and the finest of interior trimmings.

The new material is "strong as steel" because its base actually is thin steel sheet, but its visible surface is vinyl plastic.

By a new process the two materials have been "wedded" instead of laminated.

The result is a product which can be shaped and formed like thin sheet steel without materially changing its finely-finished surface texture.

Decorative sheets of vinyl plastic steel may have a range in surface texture from the warm pleasantness of fine leather to the color, feel and appearance of linen or almost any other material.

Whatever color or surface finish, it is practically scratch proof and actually it can be buffed without damage.

These vinyl steel sheets already are in semi-commercial production at the Irvin Works of United States Steel.

Such internationally eminent designers

as Pittsburgh's Peter Muller-Munk are studying its utilization and design value. Mr. Muller-Munk is the design artist who is presently consultant on planning for the American exhibits in the 1958 Brussels Worlds Fair.

The idea of combining steel's durability with the beauty and texture of plastics was accomplished by bonding liquid plastic to cold reduced sheets. The plastic is solidified to a permanent, tough surface by heat treatment.

(In this photograph Mr. Muller-Munk and Gloria Rodgers, secretary to the superintendent of tin finishing, Irvin Works, are looking over some of the colorful, new material.)

FIG. 16
Advertisement for US Steel's vinyl-clad steel, 1957. PMMA designed at least four prototypical textures to be die rolled into the sheet and modeled dozens of interiors to showcase and promote the material.

In 1960 US Steel announced the results of an extensive research and development collaboration with PMMA. Their experimental work, packaged as "A Study in Steel," was exhibited with much fanfare at New York City's Biltmore Hotel and went on to make a nationwide tour. On September 22, 1960, US Steel's vice president of marketing, Bay E. Estes Jr., announced that the momentous initiative represented a concerted effort to combat steel's waning impact on American progress.[77] Estes made it clear what the project was intended to do: they had hired PMMA to "probe the secrets of our raw material" as a substance with a host of uncharted uses. Estes did not state it publicly, but the company faced unprecedented competition from foreign trade and new materials. Plastics and metals, developed significantly through the war years and beyond, now felt modern and fresh compared to the old mainstays of iron and steel. US Steel executives could not help but notice Alcoa's enviously hip Forecast program, launched in 1956, which had made a significant splash with public advertising campaigns and trade-specific promotions.[78] So great was US Steel's concern regarding head-to-head competition that PMMA limited its engagement with Alcoa during this period to appease its major client.[79]

For the Study in Steel campaigns, PMMA was tasked with devising engaging prototypes for a range of new end uses. Each design had to express the mechanical principles of tension, compression, and cantilevering, thereby illustrating steel's "personality" and physical strength beyond the architectural I-beam. After spending two years on research and development, studying existing applications from fire escapes and bicycle wheels to bridges and crane booms, PMMA produced the first suite of concept designs for Estes's 1960 announcement.[80] Estes proclaimed: "U.S. Steel is offering its design ideas to manufacturers and fabricators with no strings attached. We want anyone who is interested to take all or any part of our design ideas."[81] PMMA forecasted a host of lively new uses for steel, including patio furniture, playground equipment, restaurant and stadium seating, and a collapsible camping trailer.[82]

The 1961 campaign focused on executive office designs. PMMA's concept desks were symphonies of steel: vinyl-clad steel sides, a steel desktop thinly veneered in oiled wood laminate, and a punch-patterned stainless steel modesty panel in front. By injecting thin boxes of sheet steel with urethane foam, the designers banished the tinny sound associated with steel furniture, and enabled strong, modular components that were 25 percent lighter than plywood.[83] The foam-filled steel floated over slim steel legs in an arcing C shape, a support replicated on office chairs [FIG. 17]. Such cantilevered prototypes presaged Herman Miller's 1964 Action Office furniture.[84] Convincing executives to do away with their wooden desks proved to be more difficult than wooing

clockwise

FIG. 17
Study in Steel, 1961

FIG. 18
Study in Steel, 1962

FIG. 19
Study in Steel, 1962

the press or manufacturers.[85] Muller-Munk himself publicly lamented that the heads of US Steel still used wooden desks rather than steel versions.[86] Nevertheless, by 1962 US Steel could boast that three different steel furniture manufacturers were using their design suggestions.[87]

    The 1962 campaign was themed "Indoor-Outdoor Living," and featured design concepts in both image and prototype form.[88] Indoors, the kitchen was broken down into a hanging modular grid of cubical storage units [FIG. 18]. Each facet of storage and work surfaces hung from F-shaped wall supports or tension-fixed floor-to-ceiling posts, prompting the forecast: "It may be that the future homemaker will take her kitchen with her from house to house."[89] The "most revolutionary" of 1962's designs was the interlocking modular steel patio with posts that adjusted in height to mitigate sloping yards [FIG. 19].[90] Where the colorful steel sections met, postholes (some with electric wiring) allowed for chair stems, conical grills, and tables to stand as inserts. Following its New York launch at the Drake Hotel on March 7, the exhibit went on tour to thirteen more cities, including Boston, Philadelphia, Cleveland, Detroit, Seattle, San Francisco, and Los Angeles.

FIG. 20
Concepts in Steel, 1961–63, consisted of dozens of PMMA renderings assembled as a brochure for US Steel to promote innovative ideas to architects and developers

PMMA's series of steel design programs reached an exuberant pitch in the early 1960s brochure *Concepts in Steel*, assembling the firm's colorful concept renderings of a world of architectural facades. After surveying architectural needs on US Steel's behalf, PMMA created a series of load-bearing curtain wall concepts in various geometric shapes [**FIG. 20**].[91] This concept was employed in IBM's new thirteen-floor corporate tower at Pittsburgh's Gateway Center, built between 1961 and 1963 [**FIG. 21**]. Designed by Curtis & Davis of New Orleans, the building was a marvel that inverted architectural conventions—it was supported by a central core and load-bearing steel facade of geometric facets rather than by internal structural columns.[92] The architects originally conceived the building in prestressed concrete, but were "reminded that [they] were building in the steel town of Pittsburgh—there was no question that it should be done in steel."[93] Interlocking steel diamonds filled by clear and opaque glass spread across the building as an architectural skin that also acted uniquely as a support truss. Rising at the same moment was the stainless steel Unisphere, the landmark centerpiece of the 1964–65 New York World's Fair, which US Steel sponsored and executed. Not surprisingly, the company asked PMMA to help them complete the colossal task (see "The Unisphere," pp. 144–47).

PMMA also reenvisioned Pittsburgh Corning's architectural glass block (nondescriptly ubiquitous in construction since the Great Depression) and made it a modern product for architects and interior designers [**FIG. 22**]. PMMA's first line for Corning was Intaglio, introduced in 1962. Dramatically different from the traditional glass brick, Intaglio had a border of opaque concrete-gray ceramic frit fused to a textured surface, creating the impression of masonry with "cutouts" of mix-and-match clear glass shapes—hourglass, oval, circle, and the charmingly named nugget.[94] The designers' second round of innovative redesign, originally called Cameo (in reference to its raised surfaces) and then Chiaro (Italian for both "clear" and "light"), appeared on the market in 1967 to great accolades in both the architectural and the design communities.[95] With a sleek, glossy black surface design and two shaped variations—a semicircle (Chiaro I) and a boomerang (Chiaro II)—the line offered dramatic graphic possibilities akin to geometric abstraction. Chiaro blocks won an International Design Award from the American Institute of Interior Designers among a sea of design finalists that included Italy's Gio Ponti and Emilio Pucci.[96]

While PMMA breathed new life into the historic regional industries of steel and glass, it also tackled the promotion of new synthetic materials, particularly those of Mobay Chemical Company, a joint venture between Monsanto Company and the German Farbenfabriken Bayer AG, headquartered in Pittsburgh from 1958. PMMA had first engaged with Mobay

FIG. 21
IBM tower during construction, 1961–63, later known as the United Steelworkers building. US Steel supplied materials for the structure and worked closely with the architects, Curtis & Davis.

Glass blocks ...windows you don't clean, walls you don't paint, beauty you can't match.

More than ever, architects are discovering the functional beauty of glass blocks by Pittsburgh Corning.
Functional, because each glass block contains a hermetically-sealed partial vacuum. Keeps out the winter cold and that blistering summer heat. Heating and air conditioning costs are significantly lower. So are maintenance costs

—glass blocks are virtually self-cleaning!
Beautiful, because of the look and the feel you can achieve using ten different patterns, individually or in combination.
Our catalog will start you thinking. Write for it: Pittsburgh Corning Corporation, Dept. PA-30G, One Gateway Center, Pittsburgh, Pennsylvania 15222.

This advertisement appears in: ARCHITECTURAL RECORD, and PROGRESSIVE ARCHITECTURE.

**FIG. 22
Advertisement for Pittsburgh Corning Intaglio and Chiaro glass blocks, 1967**

around 1961, when the firm deployed urethane foam as a rigidizing and soundproofing filler in the Study in Steel office furniture conceived for US Steel.[97] Later, PMMA consulted on the application of Mobay's polymers to snowmobile parts for the Canadian manufacturer Bombardier.[98] But the most alluring project for Mobay was a range of seventeen pieces of concept furniture keyed to three "schools of design": "traditional, contemporary, and free-form."[99] Designed by PMMA in 1969 for promotion by Mobay in 1970, the objects were intended to inspire the furniture trades to employ urethane foam materials and techniques.

Mobay asked PMMA to focus on two materials: the self-skinning rigid Duromer foam, developed by the German Bayer office in 1968, and a new, flexible cold-cure foam. Duromer required a clamped metal mold and moderate heat to develop its signature hard skin (which could then be stained or painted). Its high strength-to-weight ratio compared to a soft coniferous wood. The cold-cure foam, described as "rising like bread" within its mold, demanded very little pressure to contain it. It could even be molded within an impermeable textile shell such as vinyl. Designers called the combination of the two materials "a dream

marriage" to be limited only by imagination.[100] PMMA put its imagination to greatest use in the biomorphic, space-age ensemble of the free-form furniture line [FIG. 23]. For the stimulation of the middle market, the designers created modern rectilinear forms, and to whet conservative appetites, they prototyped cabriole-legged furniture in faux wood-grained Duromer. The resulting market development message was multilayered: urethane furniture could implement cutting-edge style, but it could also reduce the number of parts and cut labor costs. In one example, a traditionally styled credenza built in wood required ninety components as compared to just twelve in Duromer. Mobay undoubtedly appreciated upticks in material sales from all ranges of taste, whereas the PMMA designers, less than enamored with the Queen Anne lowboy in urethane (part of the "traditional" line), stressed that the material was "best when used for its own sake rather than as a substitute."[101]

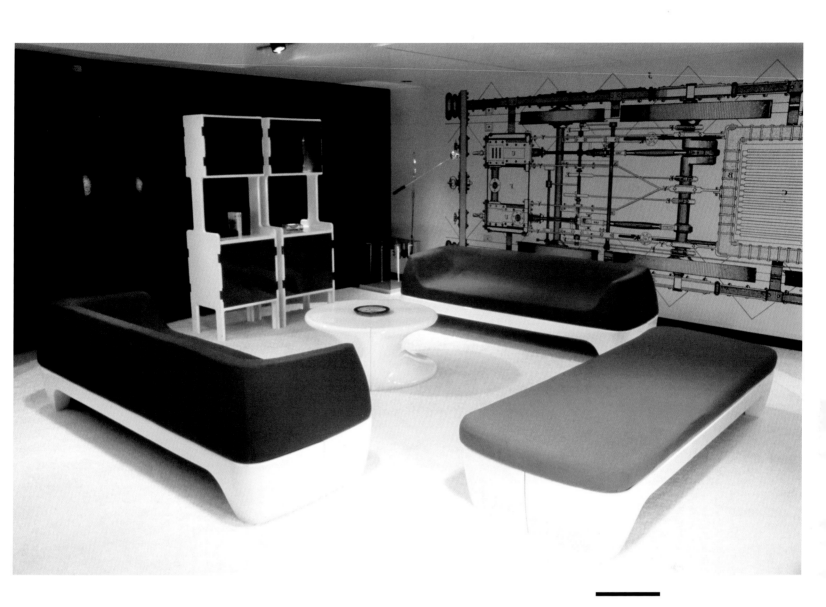

FIG. 23
Suite of polyurethane concept
furniture designed by PMMA
for Mobay; photographed for
promotional purposes, 1969–70

top to bottom

FIG. 24
Model of Sohio gas station, 1961–62

FIG. 25
In 1963 PMMA significantly reworked the Texaco logotype, replacing the famous star incribed within a circle with an elongated hexagonal reserve. The company name in bold black type took visual precedence over the star and green T, which were imbedded below. One design aim was to mitigate any unwanted association consumers might make with the famous red star of communism.

Space planning constituted another important new frontier for PMMA. The firm's procedure started with detailed analysis "of the people and their tasks in an organization, determination of space needs by function, circulation patterns, adjacency priorities, determination of space standards, analysis of the organization's growth potential and … future space need projections."[102] With these complex needs in mind, the designers moved on to floor plans and interior treatments, designating and designing spaces to meet the requisite functions, both quantitatively and qualitatively. Muller-Munk recognized such holistic thinking about human environments as one of the great design challenges of the era (see "Think Small," p. 170), and PMMA heeded the call for more humane urbanization and architectural standardization.

One of the firm's early forays into space planning occurred in the redesign of gas stations. Traditionally, filling station attendants had greeted drivers at their cars, and station interiors were reserved as offices and workspaces. Postwar stations shifted to self-service modes, and station attendants became obsolete. Without that personal touch, and with cultural critics at their heels over the reckless spread of billboards, junkyards, and other "detritus" that flourished along American highways, petroleum companies aimed to refurbish their images and to better serve their customers.[103] They sought station designs to complement suburban aesthetics and changed their marketing paradigm, coaxing motorists out of their cars and into pleasant gas stations offering new services, comfortable waiting lounges, and appealing food, drink, and merchandise.

In 1961 regional petroleum company Standard Oil of Ohio (Sohio) approached PMMA with an architectural design challenge: develop a flexible system of retail gas stations that could range in size from 700 to 1,450 square feet, be economical to build, and include "new merchandising and identity features."[104] PMMA devised a modular steel system for a Sohio service station that was adaptable in size and allowed options for either front or side access [FIG. 24].[105] The following year, PMMA launched a major corporate identity and planning project with Texaco, including the development of a new logotype and three service station prototypes [FIG. 25]. Identified by their respective locations, the stations were test-marketed in Garden City, New York; Matawan, New Jersey; and Tulsa,

top to bottom

FIG. 26
Texaco Station, sketch of
Matawan, New Jersey, version,
c. 1963

FIG. 27
Prototype Texaco Station,
erected at Roosevelt Field,
Garden City, New York, 1964

Oklahoma.[106] Each version had distinctive features. The Garden City model offered convenience products and automotive repair in two separate building units connected by winglike hexagonal roofs [FIG. 27].[107] Tulsa featured the same rooflines with a different orientation of the buildings. The Matawan station was a single structure that greeted visitors with an expansive fifty-two-foot show window of product displays in front and entrances to service bays on the sides. Fieldstone facades recalled American vernacular architecture. Its signature feature, however, was a sloping mansard roof made from green vinyl-covered aluminum over steel girding [FIG. 26].[108] The raised mansard roof visually differentiated the service bay from the store.

FIG. 28
View of the US Steel Tower,
Pittsburgh, completed 1971

Fluorescent illumination of the buildings and pump islands made the businesses visible from a distance. Designed to encourage drivers to enter the stores, pumps stood close to glass-curtain walls revealing well-lit display areas, while overhead canopies facilitated motorists' trips inside even in inclement weather.[109] Having test-marketed PMMA's three prototypes in their respective geographical areas, Texaco announced its choice of a new primary service station design in 1967: the mansard-roofed "Matawan."[110] A confirmed success, this station design was emulated by other American companies set on building better "community relations," including PMMA's client Ashland Oil and Refining Company.[111]

PMMA's intense market development relationship with US Steel, coupled with its growing expertise in space planning and interior design, positioned the firm as a natural partner in "Big Steel's" new corporate headquarters, built between 1967 and 1971 by Harrison, Abramovitz & Abbe [FIG. 28]. Muller-Munk himself sat on the cross-disciplinary Innovations Committee, formed in May 1965 and tasked with consolidating the steel giant's existing functions from twelve buildings into one proud showpiece. The building was also to demonstrate innovative uses of steel throughout while offering ultimate operational ease and flexibility for future change and growth. In addition to the utilization of Cor-Ten weathering steel for the structural columns and curtain wall, the most notable recommendation of the committee was the triangular footprint, which aided in the stability and wind resistance of the 64-story, 841-foot tower while also alluding to downtown Pittsburgh's moniker, "The Golden Triangle."[112]

PMMA served as the space planners and interior designers of record, with primary responsibility for the overall conceptual design for the sixty-first-floor executive level and the concourse-level auditorium [FIG. 29]. Considerable energies went into devising a modular planning grid, situating offices within a triangular floor plan around a central service-elevator core, designing completely demountable steel office partitioning systems and hidden ceiling- or floor-fed electrical cord management. On the executive level, PMMA laid out eleven executive office suites and an executive apartment, which were decorated by Maria Bergson Associates, an interior design company out of New York. The executive conference room was a tour de force of the latest technology. The parabolic conference table (measuring 43 by 13 feet) was custom-designed to maximize the "man-to-man" and "man-to-screen" sightlines. The walnut surface floated on twelve stainless steel cantilevered legs—an extension of Studies in Steel—which also hid the power cords to twenty-two strategically located microphones. Triple, rear-screen projection and commodious soundproofing assured the ultimate executive conference experience.[113] PMMA continued modular office planning with US Steel and Hauserman [FIG. 30], as well as with new clients such as Bank Building Corporation, for which

PMMA designed expandable banks to help the client quickly establish a presence in new suburban developments while providing for easy growth as a neighborhood boomed, and Sheraton Corporation, for which PMMA designed completely prefabricated hotel bathrooms in steel.[114]

Space planning and office partition design experience lent themselves to other modular applications. In 1964 Fisher Scientific, a company long known for outfitting scientific laboratories with furniture and equipment, engaged PMMA to develop a new line of their "unitized" furniture. James A. Fisher, son of the company's founder Chester G. Fisher, had been tasked with bringing in a new line of product. He and his wife, Edith H. Fisher, were good friends with the Muller-Munks, and he was pleased to engage PMMA for the project. Years later, Fisher fondly recalled, "It was a wonderful assignment. I had a ball. A *ball*. And we had little tiny things … you know, you'd open the cabinet and there … [would be] a split shelf so that if you had a tall piece of apparatus, you could take out half…. There were a dozen or more little gimmicks like that that we built into the line."[115]

As Fisher highlighted, PMMA improved upon existing modular elements. They also keyed the system to an utterly revolutionary color palette **[FIG. 31]**. Designers recommended converting the traditionally drab scientific lab settings of Fisher's 1930s "brown line" and 1940s "gray line" to a bold modern array with functional implications—color variation not only made for a more pleasant work environment but also lent itself to categorized equipment storage. The Contempra line offered fifty-five different modules with bright cupboard interiors of "shell white" with slate gray doors and black worktops that tilted into position for simple installation.[116] Interchangeable drawer fronts in orange, yellow, green, and beige enabled endless reconfiguration. The company's in-house literature compared the effect of the storage grids to a Mondrian painting. Touted as "the most important advance in laboratory furniture in 30 years," the Contempra line remained a best seller for decades.[117]

Exhibiting market prescience in yet another field, PMMA was hard at work with US Steel on mass-transit research and development well in advance of the High-Speed Ground Transportation Act, which President Lyndon B. Johnson signed into law on September 30, 1965. One month prior, in August 1965, they unveiled the Steel Car of Tomorrow (SCOT) in New York City to both transit officials and the press, positioning US Steel as a purveyor of materials for national mass-transit initiatives **[FIG. 32]**. SCOT was a 300-passenger modular car, adaptable as conveyance on either bus chassis or rails, that illustrated how to make commuting safe, appealing, and more economical through the use of steel.[118] A structural steel "honeycomb" pattern sandwiched between thin sheets of steel reduced weight, thereby competing with aluminum concept cars. PMMA had creative control over SCOT's interior

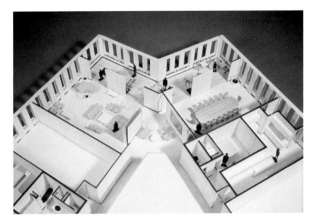

top to bottom

FIG. 29
PMMA scale model of the executive level, US Steel Tower, c. 1967

FIG. 30
Concept rendering for a prefabricated modular office system designed by PMMA for US Steel and its partner Cleveland-based Hauserman, Inc., specialists in movable wall partitions

139

environment: seating design, spacing, and arrangement; passenger flow; lighting; and material and color selections. The design, with its modern lines and generous proportions, carefully considered the masses. Yet it also accounted for every rider's individual comfort (and therefore competed with automobiles) by providing lamps, ashtrays, trash receptacles, package racks, armrests, and seat dividers—and even large windows and a skydome.[119] For climate control, windows were heat and glare absorbent.[120] Steel cantilevered seats removed the forest of floor-to-ceiling support poles typical in commuter trains and created more open space.[121] The SCOT prototype and PMMA's related infrastructure designs for terminal stations, tunnels, and power structures illustrated what US Steel had to offer the transportation field on a massive scale [FIG. 33].

While his designers forayed into new areas of transportation and urban design, Muller-Munk assumed his usual role as promoter. At the First International Conference on Urban Transportation, held in Pittsburgh, February 1–3, 1966, he represented industrial design alongside experts in business, engineering, industry, and architecture. The panel on which he sat—"Transportation and the Balanced City in the Year 2000"—featured associates from national architecture and civil engineering firms, including Max Abramovitz. Muller-Munk's speech encouraged experimental thinking and exploration, but tempered ambition with an understanding of a total picture:

> Since everything is *possible*, it now becomes our responsibility to develop the methods for deciding what is *desirable*. Perhaps this is what this panel is meant to illuminate, not so much what transportation and the city might be like 34 years hence, but what we *want* them to be like.... There comes a point where the *qualities* of life are strangled by the overwhelming impact of *quantities*. There are just so many vehicles, so many architectural or engineering monuments, and so many concentrations of people which we can accommodate with any decency before their numbers and the scale of their proportions strangle the individual.[122]

With his personal cocktail of everyman's wit and cosmopolitan charm, Muller-Munk expressed the need for humane controls on unbridled urban and transportation design, offering anecdotes about his elderly mother navigating New York City's labyrinthine airports and subways, and a PMMA associate on crutches after disembarking from a bus under perilous conditions for pedestrians. His beliefs about passenger travel—that it should be safer, more attractive and spacious, cleaner for the environment, and quieter, and that it should provide views of more beautiful scenery—were all present in his firm's work.

opposite

FIG. 31
Advertisement for Fisher Scientific Contempra laboratory furniture, 1965

above, top to bottom

FIG. 32
Anton Parisson examines a full-scale model of the SCOT Car interior in PMMA's model shop, 1964–65

FIG. 33
Sketch depicting an elevated SCOT train and its station fully integrated within a modern urban environment, 1964–65

The End of an Era

While PMMA's portfolio blossomed across new frontiers, Muller-Munk's personal life began to unravel, though no one outside of his inner circle would have suspected. In 1959 his sister, Margit Mombert, committed suicide, possibly related to her health issues.[123] Two years later, his mother, Gertrud, had an apparent heart attack or stroke.[124] By 1965 the pillars of his personal life all seemed to be crumbling. Muller-Munk, always the dutiful son, helped Gertrud as she moved from her Brooklyn apartment to one retirement home and then another. Her expenses totaled $7,000–8,000 a year, straining the coffers of a man who managed to save little despite his success.[125] From her home in Boston, his aunt Marie Munk helped logistically and financially with her sister's care, and chided her "overworked" nephew to take care of himself and his wife.[126] At the same time, Marie began to pass her own end-of-life instructions to Muller-Munk: details regarding her pension from the German courts where she had worked before the war, her burial preferences, and so on.[127]

Ilona was suffering from her own health issues at this time. A chronic malady (phlebitis it was said) had for many years caused her foot to swell.[128] Now she was plagued by troubles with her eyes, which made it difficult to read. In January 1965 she had eye surgery. Family papers mention another, unspecified surgery as well.[129] Marie fretted over Ilona to her nephew, and suggested he hire a reader or find audio-recorded books to help her pass the time.[130] The destabilization of Muller-Munk's family coupled with the endlessly changing demands of the business left him unsettled. In his Christmas letter to his dear "Tante" Marie he divulged, "this has been just about the hardest year of my life. I would erase 1965 if I could. It has taken its toll. Let's hope 1966 will be a little easier, at least some of the time."[131]

The following year brought continued professional success if not personal respite. Muller-Munk spoke at the Urban Transportation conference in February. He promoted five new partners in the firm, and a host of new associates.[132] In June 1966 *Industrial Design* featured PMMA generously within an issue dedicated to the nation's top consultancies.[133] In September the Muller-Munks were honored to attend a state dinner at the White House for Chancellor and Mrs. Ludwig Erhard of the Federal Republic of Germany.[134] Muller-Munk also joined several of his peers as a volunteer consultant for Project Earning Power, an initiative backed by President Johnson and the First Lady and intended to "create new jobs and better earnings for the disabled."[135]

The early months of 1967 brought great tragedy. On February 12, Muller-Munk left on a business trip, perhaps to meet with colleagues regarding Project Earning Power in advance of the luncheon that Lady Bird Johnson was hosting at the White House two days later.[136] In Pittsburgh, Ilona had made plans to dine with James and Edith Fisher. When Edith Fisher arrived to pick Ilona up, no one answered the door. Thinking that her husband must have given their guest a ride, Edith returned home, but it soon became clear that something was wrong. The Fishers returned to the Muller-Munks' house, where James found Ilona on the floor of the garage, having succumbed to carbon monoxide poisoning. The Fishers gathered the Muller-Munks' other closest friends, J. Craig and Sally Kuhn, to await Peter's return that evening and break the news.[137]

Ilona Muller-Munk's funeral service was held two days later, on Valentine's Day, in the Muller-Munks' living room.[138] Edgar Kaufmann Jr. delivered the eulogy for the small gathering. At Peter's request Jim Fisher played a recording of Ilona's favorite piece of music, a Brahms quintet.[139] Ilona's motive was never made clear, even to the closest family members.[140] By some accounts, there was a note, which Muller-Munk did not allow anyone else to see.[141] There were speculations about her physical health, although her physician told her son Jerry Tallmer that she did not suffer from any life-threatening condition.[142]

Peter's devastation greatly concerned his friends. The Fishers recalled the Muller-Munks once saying that when one of them died, the other would too.[143] Dreading the worst, friends tried to keep him busy. Within a week he made an attempt at suicide, but was discovered and hospitalized.[144] Marie Munk wrote to her nephew pleading with him to take her into his confidence, but he kept her at bay.[145] His secretary of many years, Ann Radion, wrote to Marie and assured her that he was back at work but not ready for company.[146] Senior associates at the firm, equally worried about their boss, made concerted efforts to involve him at the office.[147] Everyone remained vigilant. Peter's aunt Marie called him the morning of March 12, and the Kuhns checked on him as well.[148] On March 13, 1967, Peter Muller-Munk, who had remained inconsolable, followed precisely in Ilona's footsteps. Friends and family gathered to pay their respects at the residence on March 14, and a small service was held at the house the following morning.[149]

The obituaries that emerged in professional journals in the subsequent months captured a sophisticated and principled man who held everyone, including himself, to the highest standards of comportment and achievement. "Abrasive he certainly could be, and charming as well," wrote editor-in-chief James R. Mellow in *Industrial Design*. "There were those who found him opinionated; others who admired his energy and expertise." Mellow called for special remembrance not of Muller-Munk's designs, but of his unwavering dedication to the collective good. "He was a man who knew the worth of his profession. For a lifetime he devoted himself to impressing its importance upon others."[150] British designer Misha Black, cofounder with Muller-Munk of ICSID, praised his friend's service to the international community: "He showed the world that, in the field of industrial design, the US [had] much to contribute and [gave] generously of its knowledge and experience."[151] Muller-Munk made a life and a career out of sharing his expertise, furthering the cause of industrial design as an agent of positive change and an "indispensable component of economic health," observed Arthur Pulos.[152] Charged with a "philosophy of cultural responsibility," he inspired others to join the battle, mused Raymond Spilman, a friend and colleague of many years, who aptly lamented Muller-Munk's passing: "respected advisor ... our understanding friend, this cultured human being was tragically driven ... by some private call to destiny, to follow his wife Ilona, in search for other, more ethereal worlds to conquer."[153]

Equipped with artistic talent, quick wit, and the personal force and charisma to propel his ideas, Peter Muller-Munk had ascended to great heights in the terrestrial realm. He excelled first as an artisan and then set an example of industrial design as both an idealistic and a practical discipline—concerned as much with improving quality of life as with the bottom line. Along his path from silversmith, to professor, to designer, to businessman, and to global advisor and industry advocate, he found his niche in assessing the landscape of modern life and pointing the way to the parcels where he and his staff could make a difference. He took an early leave, while at the very summit of his accomplishments. But it left those around him without a denouement.

The Unisphere

RACHEL DELPHIA

US Steel's twelve-story stainless steel Unisphere, symbol of
the 1964 World's Fair, was designed by Peter Muller-Munk
Associates. The base will be encircied by fountain displays.

One of the most visible landmarks in Queens, New York, is the towering Unisphere, the thematic centerpiece and grand remnant of the 1964–65 New York World's Fair [FIG. 4]. As the public nostalgically celebrates the icon's fiftieth birthday, it can be difficult to recall the widespread ridicule that shrouded the project prior to its realization. It is also challenging to uncover the exact origins of a structure that was chronicled primarily by the corporate sponsor and the fair organizers for promotional purposes. The role of Peter Muller-Munk Associates was almost lost to history because Muller-Munk shrewdly distanced his firm from the controversy surrounding the Unisphere's design and, as result, from recognition of their work on it.

The Unisphere was developed at the behest of Robert Moses, the president of the Fair Corporation, which organized the event. The concept of an armillary sphere originated with Gilmore Clarke, partner of Clarke and Rapuano, one of Moses's most trusted landscape architects from his longstanding post as New York City Parks Commissioner.[1] But according to several sources, Clarke was "simply the one to put down on paper what was in the mind of Mr. Moses."[2] The design of the Unisphere was derided from the moment it was published, in February 1961, with a rendering by Hugh Ferriss [FIG. 2].[3] Of chief concern was the sheer lack of originality. Coming on the heels of the Atomium in Brussels (1958) and in anticipation of Seattle's Space Needle (1962), the Unisphere was more literal (a gargantuan globe) and less inspired than creative professionals would have liked in representing their nation on the world's stage. "Surely in 1964 we should come up with something that hasn't been done a thousand times before," wrote Walter Dorwin Teague.[4]

Design critic Ralph Caplan penned an editorial, "Fair Is (So Far) Foul," that challenged designers and architects to oppose Moses and his larger plans for the fair, which he regarded as insufficiently visionary. The Unisphere itself, this "symbol of man's achievements on a shrinking globe," Caplan continued, "has been received with mingled horror and nausea by designers."[5] Leon Gordon Miller, president of the Industrial Designers Institute, wrote a scathing open letter to Moses in defense of American designers' international reputation.[6] Even the Design Committee of the fair (composed of Gordon Bunshaft, Henry Dreyfuss, and Edward Durell Stone) resigned in dismay when it became clear that Moses would budge on neither the fair's footprint nor its symbol.[7]

This was the environment that ungraciously unfolded around PMMA and one of their most important clients, US Steel, which had agreed to sponsor, engineer, and fabricate the twelve-story landmark with PMMA as its consultants.[8] From the outset, Muller-Munk thus found himself in an unenviable position: his major client needed his firm's expertise to resolve and execute a highly visible concept derided by his peers. His choice was to keep the client happy. Prior to PMMA's and US Steel's involvement, the Unisphere had undergone a variety of revisions, yet practical considerations were unresolved. Muller-Munk acknowledged the challenge of realizing a concept that had been made public prior to sorting out such details: "U.S. Steel ... was given the task of designing a feasible Unisphere," *Industrial Design* paraphrased Muller-Munk, "one that would really stand up when fabricated in steel to a height of 12 stories (and which would look, of course, as much like the already published design as possible)."[9]

In 1961 and 1962 PMMA and their partners in US Steel's American Bridge Division tackled a host of design details and engineering decisions. The designers discarded the original idea of stainless steel mesh for the continents: it would have reduced wind loads (a great concern in Flushing Meadows), but the perforated material virtually disappeared when backlit, underscoring Muller-Munk's observation that the Unisphere was "a piece

opposite

FIG. 1
Industrial Design's March 1964 illustration with caption ascribing sole credit for the Unisphere to PMMA

above

FIG. 2
US Steel chairman Roger M. Blough (left) with fair president Robert Moses posed in front of Hugh Ferriss's rendering to publically announce their partnership on the Unisphere, February 14, 1961

of open sculpture ... the most demanding of all art forms."[10] Solid sheets of stainless steel were equally problematic: they went dark under floodlights, with only individual high points illuminated. PMMA's solution was an irregularly textured sheet, which they custom designed.[11] Rigidizing the material with stamped texture also added critical strength and stability. Rather than stamping the landmasses in relief, as originally suggested, PMMA designed mountains as built-in topographical tiers of textured steel [FIGS. 3, 5]. The firm also addressed problems of scale—altitude had to be magnified some forty-four times lest the Unisphere's mountains stand just half an inch tall—and of geography, devising subtle shifts to support tiny islands that fell in between the parallels and meridians. The steel beams would taper to provide critical support at the bottom while minimizing visual clutter above. PMMA also designed a sculptural, three-point base out of weathering Cor-Ten steel. *Industrial Design* reported, in 1962, that after a year of work, "esthetically speaking," Muller-Munk "thinks he has improved considerably on the original conception."[12]

Yet criticisms of the design lingered, and Muller-Munk was sensitive to the opinion of his colleagues. Rumor had it that he was particularly stung by criticism from Bunshaft, who reportedly likened the monument to a jungle gym for King Kong.[13] When, on the eve of the fair's opening, *Industrial Design* published an article in which PMMA was given sole credit for the Unisphere [FIG. 1], Muller-Munk resolved to distance the firm from the design.[14] In a letter to the editor published the following month, he wrote, "The statement is incorrect. Our office did not design the Unisphere.... What we did do at the request of our client, United States Steel Corporation, was to collaborate with their American Bridge Division in the solution of the many complicated structural and design details of the Unisphere."[15] Muller-Munk's calculated statement was meant to protect his firm's reputation among its peers, but it had the unfortunate effect, until now, of almost entirely writing out of the historical record PMMA's substantial role in the realization of the iconic landmark.[16]

top to bottom

FIG. 4
The Unisphere as it stands in 2015

FIG. 5
**PMMA's layer cake–style continents denote the
mountains of North America, photographed in 2015**

Epilogue

RACHEL DELPHIA AND CATHERINE WALWORTH

———

"Peter Muller-Munk Associates, one of the nation's better known design firms, will continue in spite of the sudden death of its founder."[1]

The untimely passing of Peter Muller-Munk in March 1967 left personal and professional voids. The field had lost a titan and a senior statesman. PMMA, Inc. had lost its eponymous leader, which presented a distinct public relations challenge regarding the future of the firm. Muller-Munk had been the visionary figurehead, the one who sat on panels at national conferences, socialized with political and business leaders, and gave the press pithy quotes—all of which translated into visibility, prestige, and new business for the firm. Nevertheless, the senior managers of PMMA knew that they could carry on without Muller-Munk. Operations were secure: Paul Karlen had previously emerged as Muller-Munk's logical successor. Many a client already knew him as the day-to-day face of the organization. Raymond Smith remained the consummate senior product designer who oversaw the three-dimensional work of the office. And, for more than a decade, the partners and associates had project managed individual client accounts. All of this could continue within the new concentrations that Muller-Munk had helped to forge.

Just one week after Muller-Munk's death, Karlen assured the public—most importantly their current and potential clients—that the forty-six-member "firm would continue, just like any other corporation which loses a leader."[2] PMMA

frontispiece

FIG. 1
SCOT concept drawings for
US Steel, pinned up in PMMA
conference room, c. 1965

above

FIG. 2
Senior staff, left to right: Paul
Karlen, Anton Parisson, and
Raymond Smith

issued a press release announcing new officers: Karlen was elected chairman of the Board of Directors; Raymond Smith, president; and Anton Parisson, senior vice president [FIG. 2]. A new slate of vice presidents included Howard A. Anderson, Donald J. Behnk, Ernst Budke, Glenn W. Monigle, and Roger I. Protas.[3] Not surprisingly, staff continued to shuffle in the ensuing months. Some saw the opportunity to move up in the organization; others saw it as the moment to retire or move on. Parisson left in 1968, and in 1970, Protas, Behnk, and Anderson announced the formation of their own firm.[4] Three years later, in 1971, though Karlen and Smith retained the same posts, all but one of the vice presidents were new appointees. Budke was joined at the VP level by Robert Gaylor Jr., Kenneth Love, and Paul Wiedmann. Each of the four headed one of PMMA's primary design areas: corporate identity (including packaging and print collateral), market development design, design for the urban environment, and space planning and interior design. Meanwhile, Karlen and Smith together supervised transportation design. New staff came on board as well, particularly graphic design specialists and a marketing writer to focus on the critical area of promoting PMMA and its services.[5]

Work continued within each of the concentrations. PMMA completed a wild market development project for Mobay [SEE P. 135, FIG. 23] with space-age furniture made of polyurethane. When Corning developed photochromic glass (which changed color in UV light), it was PMMA that suggested its application in eyeglasses.[6] Through its American Bridge Division, long-term client US Steel hired PMMA to develop steel highway bridge designs utilizing a new computerized flame-cutting technology. One of these proliferated throughout the country and remains in use to this day.[7] But it was an amalgam of four areas—identity design, the urban environment, space planning, and transportation—that began to congeal into a unique new specialization at PMMA, one concerned with moving and situating people within the complex web of modern public spaces.

Building on the vehicle-design success of US Steel's SCOT program [SEE P. 141, FIGS. 32–33], PMMA joined Philadelphia engineers Louis T. Klauder and Associates in redesigning San Francisco's Municipal, or "Muni," system of buses, trolleys, and cable cars.[8] The ambitious program aimed to transform a city known for its quaint cable cars and trolleys into one admired for modern subway-to-surface streetcars. The consultants collaborated on seventy-eight new passenger rail cars.[9] Keeping the historic streetcar concept (steel wheels on rail lines) but modernizing it, the Muni design team borrowed a unique feature they had seen on European rail cars—articulation that allowed them to bend in the middle. It was an ideal solution for San Francisco's steep grades, subway tunnels, and surface lines.[10] Electrically powered, the Muni car increased passenger capacity, while upgrading comfort, speed, and economy.

PMMA's nationally recognized transportation experience culminated in yet another futuristic project design—the Advanced Concept Train (ACT-1)—an urban rapid-transit train made for no city in particular but designed to attract the interest of multiple cities. Whereas PMMA's SCOT car had been aimed at selling steel to mass-transit programs [FIG. 1], ACT represented an attempt by the US Department of Transportation (USDOT), through the Urban Rapid Rail Improvement Program, to increase mass-transit ridership by improving the experience that high-speed, frequent-stop, urban rail systems offered.[11] As part of a multistage project, the end goal was to have a well-tested, newly standardized transit railcar system in place by the early 1980s.[12] PMMA joined one of four competitive cross-disciplinary research teams, each composed of designers, engineers, and train car manufacturers.[13] The competition included the design offices of Raymond Loewy, Sundberg-Ferar, and Walter Dorwin Teague.[14] Work began in 1972 with each team preparing and submitting initial proposals. In January 1974 USDOT chose PMMA's version of ACT-1 as the winning design for the opportunity to develop and test two prototype trains [FIG. 4].[15]

PMMA realized that mass-transit developers had neglected a central marketing principle: riders had been treated as statistics rather than as consumers who wanted choices.[16] Meeting this need, ACT-1 approached design "from the inside out," starting with user comfort.[17] Departing from the typical design with rows of identical seating, PMMA divided the car into three distinct compartments and let that concept (and an ideal number of riders for each human-engineered seating area) determine the train car's exterior dimensions. Passengers could choose among zones with different color schemes and seating configurations, each area providing privacy, individuality, and visual interest, including swiveling seats for adjustable facing views [FIG. 3].[18] The modular compartment concept was flexible enough to respond to passenger and operator needs nationwide, including the requirements of the elderly or disabled.[19]

Vehicle design was only part of the urban-planning challenge of the era. Karlen mused, "We are also active in a relatively new area, which we find fascinating, which we call public graphics ... the development of visual communication systems for public areas."[20] In effect, PMMA was developing wayfinding systems before the field even had a name. A complex network of symbols and text, PMMA's wayfinding programs were researched, designed, and situated to move people efficiently through complicated spaces (stadiums, airports, convention centers, and even cities), while projecting the venue's identity through color, type, and imagery. A wayfinding program began at a site's exterior boundaries,

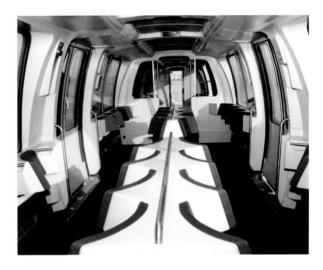

above

FIG. 3
High-density standee car
in the ACT-1 train prototype,
c. 1977

following spread

FIG. 4
Rendering of the Advanced
Concept Train (ACT-1), c. 1973

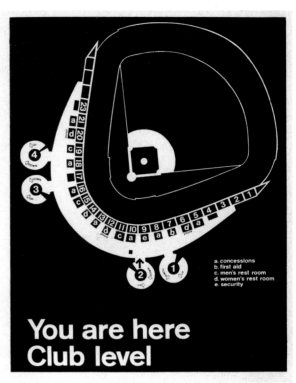

THREE SIGNS for different stadia by Peter Muller-Munk Associates (PMMA) illustrate how the amount of information increases as a person reaches points of greater decision. Trail blazer (left) to Pittsburgh's stadium uses only symbols that can be quickly recognized by the motorist.

Entrance sign for Philadelphia's stadium (above) will show only its eight basic sections but, once inside the Kansas City stadium (right) all seating sections and other major places of interest will be indicated.

top to bottom

FIG. 5
Assorted wayfinding graphics for Three Rivers Stadium, Philadelphia Stadium, and Kansas City Stadium demonstrate the increasing level of visual detail provided for viewers as they progress deeper into the stadium

FIG. 6
Rendering of proposed uniforms for employees of Three Rivers Stadium, utilizing the spoked stadium logo, 1967–69

such as roadway approaches, with "trail blazers," or bold signage that was intelligible to motorists. Signage in the parking lot and at building entrances provided visitors with greater detail as they progressed into the structure [FIG. 5]. PMMA complemented wayfinding with visual communications programs for institutional literature, employee uniforms, or service vehicles. By 1969 the firm had embarked on programs for four sports stadiums, each distinctive to their respective cities: Three Rivers Stadium (Pittsburgh), the Philadelphia Stadium, Louisiana Stadium (New Orleans's Superdome), and Arrowhead Stadium (Kansas City).

Pittsburgh's Stadium Authority retained PMMA in 1967 to design an entire corporate identity program for the new Three Rivers Stadium, slated to open in 1970, and to house both football and baseball teams. PMMA's four-spoked circle logo, based on an aerial image of the stadium, became easy visual shorthand that appeared on all city and corporate signage [FIG. 5, LEFT]. Indeed, Pittsburgh's Department of City Planning contracted the designers for a broad traffic signage and wayfinding program to direct residents to all sorts of cultural attractions. Besides creating the stadium's graphics system, PMMA provided interior design for private lounge boxes, as well as the Allegheny Club overlooking the playing field.[21] As part of a total visual identity package, PMMA also designed uniforms for stadium employees and for the Pirates baseball team [FIG. 6].[22]

PMMA created one of their most distinctive corporate identity and wayfinding programs for Louisiana's Superdome, which opened in January 1975.[23] In concert with New Orleans-based architects Curtis & Davis, PMMA's designers created signage that integrated with the stadium's architecture. Color-coded tickets and elevators, for example, directed visitors to proper seating levels. PMMA's unifying program of colorful banners, abstract and psychedelic super graphics, event tickets, and signage combined images of jazz musicians and sports figures in a bright palette that captured the exuberance of Mardi Gras [FIGS. 7–8].

top to bottom

FIG. 7
PMMA's color-coded tickets referring to one of six seating levels at the Louisiana Superdome, c. 1975

FIG. 8
Concept drawing for the Louisiana Superdome's interior concourse supergraphics, c. 1974

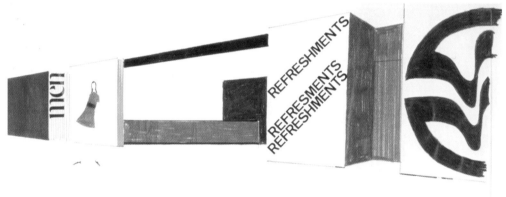

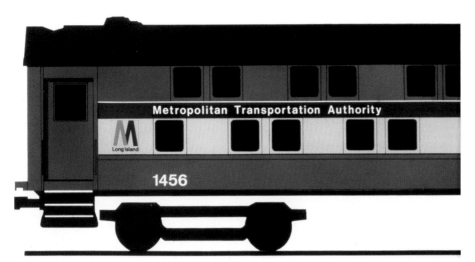

left

FIG. 9
**PMMA's new graphics program
updated New York's old train
stock, c. 1968**

opposite

FIG. 10
**Pittsburgh's "Mod Trolley"
with PMMA's psychedelic
design, 1972**

PMMA's comprehensive graphics could also be applied to far-flung transit systems. In 1968 the Metropolitan Commuter Transportation Authority (MCTA) of New York State changed its name to Metropolitan Transportation Authority (MTA). The shorter name reflected a broader network of transit systems, encompassing not only the Long Island Rail Road, but also New York City's bus and subway transit systems. MTA hired PMMA to develop a unifying graphics program for the newly centralized entity, and one that would also accommodate future acquisitions. The resulting standardized two-tone "M"—designed "to reflect the heretofore separate transportation systems"—remained in use until the mid-1990s.[24] PMMA's new graphics blanketed MTA's disparate subway trains, buses, and railroad cars, unifying both new stainless steel train cars and old stock [FIG. 9].[25]

In a related program back home, PMMA created a spirited new visual identity for Pittsburgh's Port Authority Transit (PAT), with its fleet of streamlined circa-1935 trolley cars still in use. PAT's Early Action Program was a public relations move meant to offset "financial problems, court battles and public disinterest" by boldly signaling to the public its recently improved transit service.[26] With the first examples rolling out in 1972, PMMA enveloped twenty-five trolleys in a spectacularly colorful scheme, thus updating their appearance until the fleet's ultimate replacement by buses in seven years' time.[27] There were eight trolleys each in red, orange, yellow, and white color-blocked designs, but the most memorable was the twenty-fifth, known as the "Mod Trolley," with its psychedelic sunburst [FIG. 10].[28]

Despite its diversification and the success of individual projects, PMMA struggled to advance its overall program in the years after Muller-Munk's death. Karlen pointed to a shifting field that required the designers to join elaborate

consortia of architects and engineers. Relegated to subcontractor status and "without the resources to tackle the whole job," Karlen described the firm's standing as "mainly just staying even."[29] By this point, in late 1973, Karlen and Wiedmann were the only remaining officers of PMMA, and the staff was down to a mere twenty employees. Recognizing the potential to continue in space planning and wayfinding systems, and the corresponding need to get in on the ground floor of their projects, the PMMA officers decided to merge with a larger organization: Wilbur Smith Associates, Inc. (WSA). Founded in 1952 by South Carolina's first state traffic engineer, the Columbia-based engineering consultancy focused on urban development projects for national and international clients.[30] Karlen and Wiedmann sold the business to WSA, and effective January 1, 1974, it became Peter Muller-Munk Associates, a Division of Wilbur Smith Associates.[31] The designers retained the right to independent operations under Karlen, as division manager, and Wiedmann, as director of division operations.[32] Karlen expressed the advantages of building "full-service organizations to handle the transportation and community design projects of the future."[33] The new arrangement proved to be mutually beneficial, and the partnership lasted more than four decades, until the PMMA brand ceased to resonate and was ultimately phased out by the mid-2000s. Throughout the 1970s, 1980s, and 1990s, however, PMMA was internationally noted for its expertise in wayfinding. With their understated aesthetics and clear functionality, the graphics produced by PMMA made invaluable contributions to the visual order of the urban environment. Some of the most demanding airport, ground transit, and stadium designs of the era crossed the designers' desks, and they addressed graphics for hospitals, universities, municipalities, and more.[34]

An Inspiring Legacy

Recounting the life and career of Peter Muller-Munk, one arrives at the unmistakable conclusion that he was a rare individual, charged with an electric combination of artistic talent, confidence, verbal acuity, charisma, and deep-seated humanistic values. A natural leader, he inspired clients, students, staff, and peers alike. For forty years he seized and tackled the diverse opportunities and challenges of modern America and its burgeoning status as a superpower. Sixteen months after landing in the United States as a twenty-two-year-old silversmith, Muller-Munk achieved a solo silver exhibition in a prominent Manhattan gallery. With his multivalent talents, he propelled his silver into the era's avant-garde industrial art exhibitions and into the prestigious halls of the Metropolitan Museum of Art, the Newark Museum, and the Detroit Institute of Arts—all before his twenty-sixth birthday. Then, with a fire ignited to contribute to the nascent field of industrial design education, he headed to Carnegie Tech, where he spent a decade as a professor, rousing students who would go on to illustrious careers as designers and educators. Pivoting into professional design practice himself, he launched his namesake consultancy—the first major effort of its kind in the ripe industrial city of Pittsburgh—which grew into a landmark enterprise, regionally, nationally, and internationally.

Muller-Munk struck an ideal balance between the personas of cosmopolitan visionary, friend of business, and consumer advocate. A sophisticated world citizen, fluent in German, French, and English, he operated with ease on any continent and inspired the confidence of business leaders worldwide.[35] He peppered his writings and speeches with literary and art historical references that complimented the cognoscenti within his audiences, while also deploying colloquialisms and delightful sarcasm that reassured and entertained ordinary folk. Despite his highly refined personal tastes—his tailored suits, his love of fine wine, his erudition, and his penchant for sending staff to the theater to cleanse their palates—his commitment to better design for the masses was genuine. He was highly attuned to the needs of clients and consumers, and spent his career promoting the idea that good design both stimulated the economy and provided for better living. When the luster of the postwar consumer promise started to fall away, Muller-Munk reached higher still, to an improved, total urban environment.

A compilation of great objects—great as they are, across many indices—does not sufficiently capture the essence of Peter Muller-Munk's contribution. For this one must go back to the young professor's graduate course in Structural Analysis, which exhorted pupils to examine the common artistic elements across all structures—from the grandest architecture to the small articles of daily use—and to recognize therein the essential, interconnected benefits of creative endeavor to society. Thus analyzed, such seemingly disparate objects as a handwrought silver bowl and candelabra, a portable power saw, a home movie projector, a water tower refashioned as a soaring observation deck, and color-coded laboratory cabinets are part of an overarching vision to bring order, reason, and elegance to the daily rituals of life. In Muller-Munk's view, good design was that basic, and that essential. In February 1967, just weeks before his death, Muller-Munk summed up his beautifully practical philosophy: "Design is an attitude. It is not just an aphrodisiac. It's bread and butter, and sometimes, jam."[36]

FIG. 11
Peter Muller-Munk, mid-1960s

CREATIVE·ART

A Magazine of Fine and Applied Art

Incorporating "The Studio" of London

MACHINE—HAND

By Peter Mueller-Munk

EVER since the silver industries and their associates in the fields of similar metals and merchandise have developed their mediums for production, to meet the standards of mass production, their only aim has been to copy the looks and finesse of the hand-made piece with one of their machines. They are proudest if they can show a bowl or a pair of candle-sticks and convince the customer that it has all the attributes of a hand-wrought article. With the disappearance of the connoisseur who knew the qualities of his purchase, this artful practice became increasingly prevalent. Elaborate ornamentations applied by hand to a spun or stamped object are supposed to take the last sting from the mark "machinework" and greedy buyers

An example of machinework. Designed by Professor F. A. Breuhaus for Württ, Metallwaren-Fabrik, Geisslingen. (By courtesy of Deutsche Kunst u. Dekoration)

An example of machinework. Designed by Professor F. A. Breuhaus,
executed by Württ Metallwaren-Fabrik, Geisslingen. (By courtesy
of Deutsche Kunst u. Dekoration)

delight in wares with a hammered surface, carefully cut into the silent die.

With our modern passion for analysis, why does nobody ever try to define the process of the machine in action and to deduct the forms and decorations most closely related to it? Why, in other words, do not our manufacturers try to improve upon their merchandise by adapting it to their machines, instead of doing the contrary?

We have heard and seen enough of the beauty of power houses, steel structures and all the implements of motors and furnaces to know that the machine is able to turn out a piece of beauty, but it is a fallacy to believe that it can replace or copy the work of the craftsman. The clearness of shape and neatness of surface of a spun bowl is equal in æsthetic value to any hand-made piece and superior to its hand-wrought copy. If we could have designers who knew the machines which were to turn out their designs, and if these men would give the machine what it most longs for, we would really have achieved a new art resulting from the harmony of technique and object. The sharpness and chastity of the forms most easily spun or stamped in a die would take on a new impressive character, and we would discover that the frank admission of the machine's power surpasses by far the faked and childish semblance of the would-be home-made product.

This would by no means be the end of the silversmith who continues to fashion his wares with his own hands, for his problems lie where the factory's possibilities end. The host of shapes which defy the machine (for example, the lustre of the surface of a hand-wrought tea kettle), the greater resources of time which allow the experimenting in the proportions and the decoration, and the resulting subtle variety of the craftsman's work, leave to him the worries and triumphs of the sculptor. And I still have the outmodish confidence that there will always remain a sufficient number of people who want the pleasure of owning a centre piece without being forced to share their joy of ownership with a few thousand other beings.

In keeping alive the craft of the hand-worker, I am not afraid of the machine's rivalry. The pieces which leave my hands should have the virtues of the slow and calculating process of design and execution with which they grew. On the other side, the factory product should reflect the exactness and mathematical economy of the machine that created it.

An example of handwork. Designed and executed by Peter Mueller-Munk

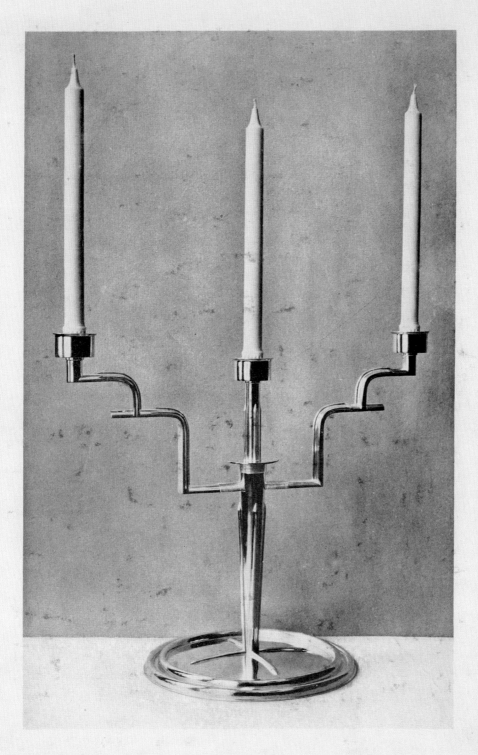

An example of handwork. Candlesticks designed and executed by Peter Mueller-Munk

CHOOSING A LIFE CAREER IN THE DESIGN ARTS

a symposium conducted by the

NEW YORK REGIONAL ART COUNCIL and the NATIONAL ALLIANCE OF ART AND INDUSTRY
Art Center Building, 65 East 56th Street, New York, N. Y.

PLEASE FILL OUT AND RETURN BY APRIL 15th: Additional remarks may be put on back

1. What is the nature of work required from the designers in your field? *Architectural*

    1.Sketches-working drawings and actual models for new articles in *Hardware Lighting Fixtures etc.*
the fields of: Hardware-Silverware-Clocks-Pottery-Electrical Appliances-
Kitchenware-Hollowware in Copper,Brass,Aluminum,Watches etc.
2.Surveys and development of detailed merchandsg.plans regardg. distribution and promotion of new articles created.3.Supervision of design
departmt. in factories.4.Advisry. capacity in all matters regarding
design,style and other promotional activities.

2. What personal qualities are most important for success?
    ·1.Ability to present and develop own ideas so that they can be realized
with the technical and human equipment of the particular client.
2. Thoroughness,i.e. ability to work out a problem from angles not
directly partaining to ones work. 3. Selfassurance.4.Logical thinking
5.Ability to deal and work with people opposed to ones own ideas.
6. Salesmanship.

3. What training and experience are required?
    1. Practical knowledge of tools and machinery employed in the manufacture
of the article to be designed. 2. Factory experience.3.Selling experce.
4. Merchandsg. experience. 5.Full knowledge of styles and periods.
6.Mechanical drawing.7.Modeling.8.High school or college degree.
9.Training at Art school.

4. How is employment secured?

    1. Direct contact.2.Recommendation by placement bureaus.3.Personal
publicity 4.Exhibitions of own work.5.Advertsg.Agencies. 6.Magazines

5. What is the range of compensation and prospect for advancement?
    From $ 50 to $ 500 for single design.
From $ 2000 upward for yearly contracts
Advancement depends on success of work rendered in either sales
or prestige.

(Over)

Name *Peter Müller-Munk* Address *148 West 4 Street N. Y. C'y*

6. Do you consider that young people are being adequately prepared
   for your field?
   Most emphatically: No.
   I know of no instance whatsoever where the training given the
   young people is in any way adequate to the requirements of a
   designer in the industries I associate with.

7. What further training do you think they ought to have?
   I would have to change this question. It is not so much a problem
   of what " further " training they ought to have, but of what kind
   of training alltogether. The present system of training is not so
   much incomplete as regards details but entirely inadequate and
   obsolete throughout.
   This would necessitate a reorganization of the agencies which now
   dispense vocational guidance.
   ~~In the enclosed~~ I have attempted to give a short resume of the
   reasons for the failure of the present system and suggestions
   for remedies. My list is of necessity incomplete as space forbids
   a more detailed analysis.
Whereas the training in the two dimensional fields(Wallpaper,Fabrics,
Packaging,Lay out etc.) is steadily improving,instruction in the field
of the three dimensional applied arts is conspicously inefficient.
Proof: Compare the number of good designs in two dimensional merchdse.
with the rest.
Causes and Alternatives: Teachers are licensed according to formulas
which in no way embody the requirements for modern industrial design.
They have never been required to do original creative work, they are
rarely even outstanding men in the/profe sions they teach..They are in
consequence teachers, not industrial designers. 2.Division between shop
and art work. 3. Teachers have no opportunity for nor are required to
do creative and professional work after they have joined the faculty.
They do not have to exhibit their work to a competent jury in regular
intervals.Their own interest in and contact with the modern tendencies
and requirements for industrial design ceases very soon. 4. The pupil
cannot see the teacher at work as he is rarely allowed to do his own
work in school and his instruction therefore has to be mainly verbal.
5.Work required of pupil has no relation to their every day life and
its/necessities.6.Creation of a public high school for Industrial Art
or an Academy for Applied Arts attached to a college or university.
7.Present classes in apllied art should be reorganized.8.New requirements for teachers on the basis outlined above.9.Division of classes
not according to materials but different techniques, which in turn are
applicable to a variety of materials.10.Instruction should give the
pupil an understanding of the interrelationship between the tool, the
material and the desired function of the article.11.Close contact between
the school, or class and the industry.

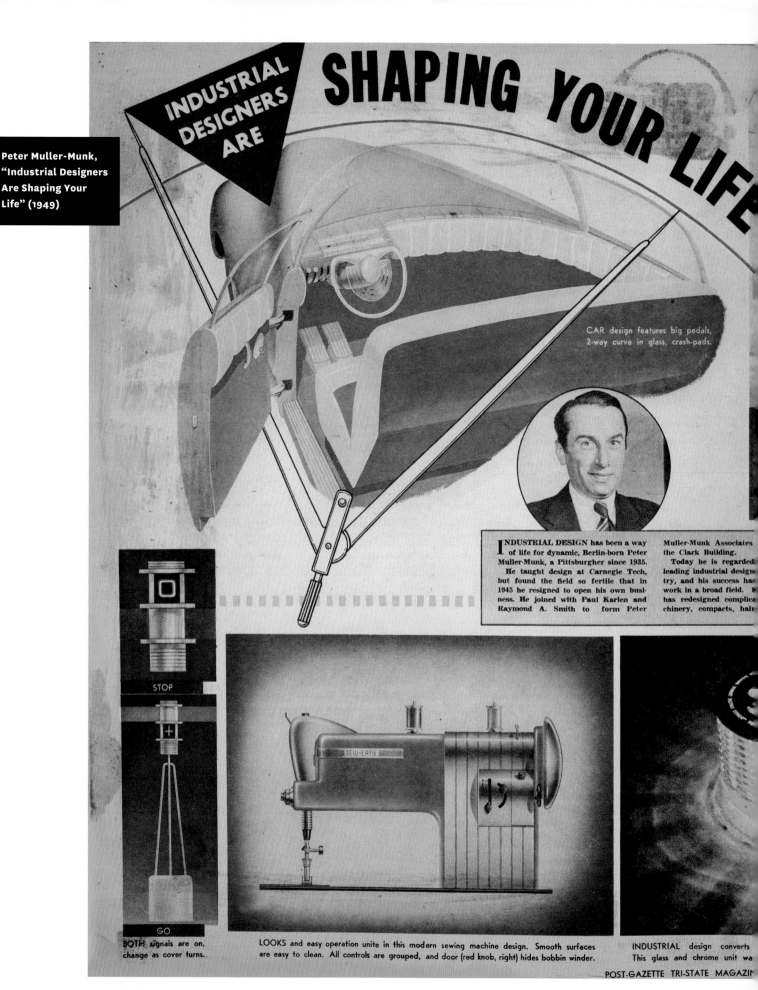

INDUSTRIAL DESIGNERS ARE

SHAPING YOUR LIFE

CAR design features big pedals, 2-way curve in glass, crash-pads.

INDUSTRIAL DESIGN has been a way of life for dynamic, Berlin-born Peter Muller-Munk, a Pittsburgher since 1935.

He taught design at Carnegie Tech, but found the field so fertile that in 1945 he resigned to open his own business. He joined with Paul Karlen and Raymond A. Smith to form Peter Muller-Munk Associates the Clark Building.

Today he is regarded leading industrial design try, and his success ha work in a broad field. has redesigned complic chinery, compacts, hair

STOP

GO

BOTH signals are on, change as cover turns.

LOOKS and easy operation unite in this modern sewing machine design. Smooth surfaces are easy to clean. All controls are grouped, and door (red knob, right) hides bobbin winder.

INDUSTRIAL design converts This glass and chrome unit wa

POST-GAZETTE TRI-STATE MAGAZIN

Peter Muller-Munk, "Industrial Designers Are Shaping Your Life," *Pittsburgh Post-Gazette Tri-State Magazine*
(April 24, 1949).

LIGHTS are concealed in ceiling of this modern room, can be switched on in various patterns from one central point.

...mple candle into a handsome coffee warmer. ...around a large candle, which supplies proper heat.

...ffices in ...e of the ...he coun- ...through ...anization ...avy ma- ...es, drill

chucks, and household wares from the kitchen sink to the lowly coffee pot. Every design attempts a blending of the functional and the esthetically pleasing.

Mr. Muller-Munk has written "Industrial Designers Are Shaping Your Life" to explain some of the philosophies behind his rapidly growing profession.

By PETER MULLER-MUNK

WHETHER YOU WORK or whether you play, whether you are rich or whether you are poor, there is an invisible hand that shapes your life—the hand of the industrial designer.

Are you held spellbound by the svelte lines and eye catching colors of a new car? Do you marvel at the roomy interior and mechanical perfection of your shiny new refrigerator?

Does your hand feel comfortable, remain untired and seem to "belong" on the smooth, cool handle of your new electric iron?

There you are—you are under his spell!

Who is this sculptor in mass production, this artist who anticipates your wants to bring beauty and usefulness within the reach of everyone? What is this magic he wields?

BEHIND THE CLICHES of streamlining and "imagineering" is a new profession spawned by American industry and the Arts, and equally indebted to each.

Its beginnings go back no more than 20 or 30 years, but its members already have made a bridge with the great periods of the past. Recruits who were once engineers, stage designers, craftsmen, artists and architects have joined together to shape your life.

For the designer it's a fascinating work, with surprises and stimulations in infinite number. Within the same month our office may be designing a new case for a lipstick—a new model for a gasoline pump—a sparkling, plastic hairbrush— a 1950 bathtub.

Each job in its own way is a new challenge— to refine, to simplify and to improve not only the product's appearance, but its usefulness.

NO SINGLE INDIVIDUAL, of course, is able to solve the many complex problems of product design, hence the need for the varied backgrounds found in industrial designing. A product must be subjected to a minute analysis of its construction, price, marketing problem and performance.

To accomplish this, different members of the designer's staff are responsible for different phases of the vivisection of the old product and the growth of the new one. Researchers, designers, draftsmen, and model makers all work in unison with the more specialized experts.

Even today many Pittsburghers are prone to think of the industrial designer—if they are aware of him at all—as a long-haired artist who sketches fanciful pipe dreams of the future in solitary confinement.

There are even some manufacturers who consider the industrial designer a fascinating luxury, to be indulged in only when all other business stimulants have failed.

THE TRUTH IS FAR from this distorted picture. Industrial design is not just the superficial, last minute slicking up of some product ready to go on the market.

It is a sincere and laborious effort to express inherent qualities of engineering and performance in their most economical and convincing forms.

Small mistakes can no longer be tolerated in this new and growing profession; any mistake at today's prices becomes a major one.

It may ruin the sales acceptance of a whole line of products and thereby the financial position of the producer. On the other hand, good design judgment can enable a slow product to take the lead, and can give you, the consumer, more service and value for your money.

WHAT'S MORE, the industrial designer is really responsible for the world of tomorrow.

It takes serious thinking and a knowledge of public demand to start to work on a product, one to two years ahead of the date when the finished product will be offered for your approval. In this sense, the industrial designer is indeed responsible for the world of tomorrow.

It's on his drawing boards and in his model shops today.

Peter Muller-Munk,
Statement to the House
of Representatives on
the Mutual Security
Act (1958)

Peter Muller-Munk, Statement to the House of Representatives on the Mutual Security Act (1958)

Mutual Security Act of 1958: Hearings before the Committee on Foreign Affairs, House of Representatives, Eighty-Fifth Congress, Second Session on Draft Legislation to Amend Further the Mutual Security Act of 1954, as Amended, and for Other Purposes, March 13 (Afternoon Session) and 14, 1958, Part VII (Washington, DC: United States Government Printing Office, 1958), 925-29.

Statement of Peter Muller-Munk, Peter Muller-Munk Associates, Industrial Designers, Pittsburgh 22, PA.

Mr. Muller-Munk. With your permission, I would like to give you a summary of my statement, and if you and the members of the committee would care to ask me any questions, the answers to which would lie within the realm of my competence, I would be happy to answer them.

Members of the House Foreign Affairs Committee, I appear before you as an American businessman who has had the privilege of participating in the program involving the spending of American foreign-aid moneys. Because of my direct experience in this spending, I may be able to share with you some observations and insights I have gained. And, because I gained them on the spot, where the dollars are spent, and because as an industrial designer I apply a somewhat unusual perspective to this work, these observations may be of some value to you in your most important deliberations.

To help you judge my remarks properly, let me identify myself—I am the managing partner of Peter Muller-Munk Associates, industrial designers with home offices in Pittsburgh, Pa. We render design services to such clients as United States Steel Co., Westinghouse Electric Corp., Sylvania Electric Corp., Schick, Inc., Graflex, Inc., and the Aluminum Company of America, to name but a few.

Recently, I was elected first president of the International Council of Societies of Industrial Designers, which includes leaders of industrial design from some 15 foreign countries and the United States. Also, as past president and chairman of the board of the American Society of Industrial Designers, I now serve as chairman of that society's foreign relations committee. Thus my remarks here today should be considered as the collective opinion of all American industrial designers who are working abroad for our Government.

Like other colleagues of mine, the firm of Peter Muller-Munk Associates has contracts for projects in selected Near East and Asian countries—countries that are critical areas in our entire foreign policy picture. They are also identified as countries most

in need, and most able to assimilate and implement this kind of technical aid. These contracts have been processed through ICA—the International Cooperation Administration of the Department of State. We have been called upon for the same service we perform for American industry—services involving a considered analysis to help determine what kind of products industry should manufacture. In approaching this work, we find the answers to questions like: "Is the product needed?" "Who will buy it?" "What should it do—how should it function?" "Whose skills shall we use to make it?" "What will it look like?" and "How will we sell it?"

Now then, how does the industrial designer fit into the American foreign-aid picture? Of the three main thrusts to our foreign-aid program—(1) military aid, (2) public projects, (3) the exporting of know-how, the last category is the one in which we work.

To us, exporting this "know-how" to the host country is of prime importance—and it seems the most self-perpetuating and self-rewarding. For this program produces capital within other countries, and it does not go on and on as a never-ending drain on American resources. This is the kind of project in which we American industrial designers participate. Our firm, for instance, has contracts in both Turkey and Israel.

Let me explain how we work.

Under our contract ICA funds do not get paid to any foreign nation. Its moneys go to Americans only—American exports working on selected foreign-aid projects. In a way, therefore, we are being paid out of our own tax dollars. Foreign nations with whom we work must provide manpower to match ours, and they must also provide at least matching sums of money. Actually, both Turkey and Israel, where we work, are spending more on these projects than our own Government is spending. In other words, our dollar investment is automatically multiplied—at no expense to ourselves.

These are not projects which depend on transient teams of experts who fly into a foreign land one day, give advice, and fly out the next, without hardly having touched land—or reality.

To be successful, these projects call for Americans living with their foreign counterparts, and training them in daily contact. Thus, today we have offices in Ankara, Turkey, and Tel Aviv, Israel, as well as in Pittsburgh, Pa., in the United States. And my colleagues working in this program have staffs in such countries as Pakistan, Indonesia, Thailand, Southern Korea, Formosa.

Now, what are we trying to accomplish? It is no secret that the economies of our foreign friends are weak. Giving them mere dollars only helps until the dollars are spent. Then, too often, they are back where they started. On the other hand, educating them, as we are doing, in the manufacture of salable products will enable them to build industries which in turn will provide them with worthwhile business activity—and capital. In addition, as each country can produce more of its basic needs, it can become less dependent on imports, and save more of its precious capital for reinvestment. As it builds its production to a high enough point, it can begin to export and it gains more capital. With growth in capital comes a rise in its standard of living—and, incidentally, a growth for America of a good customer for our own products and services.

Let's take Turkey for an example and see how this works. Our work in Turkey is jointly supervised by the ICA and by the Ministry of Economy and Commerce of the Government of Turkey. In Turkey we have two young Americans, an associate of ours, Robert Renaud, who is chief American adviser, and Robert Gabriel as assistant American adviser. These men, incidentally, receive no bonus for overseas work—the Government is a hard and business-like client. Our men and their families live under conditions far less comfortable than any which they are accustomed to here.

Before beginning our work in Turkey, we surveyed that nation intensively. Because industrially speaking, Turkey is still years behind our economy, we surveyed with a particular eye to handicrafts and small industry. You will understand the problem when I tell you that Turkey is about 10 percent rural, and in many parts of the country the population harvests only one crop, and is nonproductive for the rest of the year.

The survey took 5 weeks of intensive work in Turkey by our American team. It included a 22-day tour of the country. It provided us with an analysis of raw materials, native skills, and traditional products. It recommended a course of action. When it was completed and presented to Turkey, their Government agreed to put up the money for their part of the program.

Then our staff went to work beyond Turkey. First we surveyed the markets in Italy, Switzerland, and Scandinavian countries for handicraft and other products which could be manufactured by Turkey's light industries. Second, we helped set up a development board representing financial, government, labor, commercial, and foreign trade interests in Turkey. This was the first step in building new companies around which new industries could be centered.

Only then did Peter Muller-Munk Associates begin the design of Turkey's products. And while doing this, we also began educating our counterparts whom the Turkish Government had provided. Since there are no real counterparts to industrial designers in Turkey, this means that we are training others in the designing of their own products. In both Turkey and Israel we are training 3 to 4 times the size of our staff, and imparting to them in 3 years—what it takes us 7 years to learn—the equivalent of what it takes to become an industrial designer.

I think the results are already evident. In a very few years, this part of the program should be completed. We shall be able to pull out of it, leaving behind active industries, producing new products, and with trained designers and management who can continue new-product development and flow. This is the future which Turkey is buying with its money. And we are buying a long-range insurance policy to give meaning to the important foreign defense dollars we spend through other channels. Through such a program we can see our friends abroad becoming strong enough to stand on their own feet and eventually outgrow the need for prolonged American subsidies.

I hope I have made it clear why industrial designers have been used. It is for the same reason that American business uses us. We analyze and plan, based on a knowledge of markets, products, materials, skills, production processes and sales patterns—in effect we become the conductor of a giant symphony of productivity.

Perhaps a very brief look at Israel, where our partner Paul Karlen, director of our firm's overseas operations and M. L. Rothenberg, senior designer, supervise the Israel Product Design Office, will serve to reemphasize the overwhelming profit which America derives from mutual aid programs. Israel is more sophisticated industrially than Turkey, for many of its people came from all over Europe and served their apprenticeships with European manufacturers. They do have skills, they do know how to use machinery, but they have been away from the world scene so long they cannot properly judge what the world needs in the way of products, and how its products should be designed to meet those needs.

A stable Israel, self-sufficient, providing its neighbors the fruit of its specialized production, a Switzerland of the Middle East, can be a helpful friend, indeed, for an America with vital interests in the Middle East.

Therefore, in this program, we have a true self-liquidating activity. Look what our small firm, Peter Muller-Munk Associates, is accomplishing with but 4 men, 2 in Turkey, and 2 in Israel. In less than a year, we have designed over 100 products for Turkey alone. Every product is geared into making Turkey more self-sufficient. To be specific as to costs—we are now entering the originally planned second phase of this program. To capitalize on the organizational work of the first year, the 1958–59 program calls for doubled effort involving man power, materials and backstopping from America.

For this entire program in Turkey for the 1958–59 year, dollar funds are being requested in the amount of $138,000.

Though there may be no quick-acting antibiotic for poverty and for primitive methods of foreign-government production and manufacturing, this particular phase of our Government's foreign-aid program goes a long way. The cure here involves long-range planning and long-range implementation. It requires patience, tolerance, and above all, hard work. In short, this type of foreign aid is truly a two-way street in which we are in very real personal and financial partnership with those nations who want to learn from us how to prosper in freedom.

These mutual aid programs are just beginning to produce. The Turks, the Israelis, the other peoples of the world who have lived with poverty and disaster are not people whom we court for friendship, but for our own self-interest. If these countries do not get stronger through our aid, it will not affect them greatly, for they have known little else. But it will affect us severely if they turn to pied pipers who promise them much—never to return.

The race is on for every independent weak nation in the world. To paraphrase Thomas Wolfe, "When you do business with the Soviets, you can't go home again." If, through this program, we can build internal strength in each of the countries wherein our ICA program is active; if we can build it through this process which gives self-respect with self-sufficiency; we shall provide strength for our Nation equal to many military divisions—and rich markets of incalculable value to our industries.

Gentlemen, to be quite objective and realistic, I have seen this program work. I feel I know the consequences if some of the weaker or needy nations could not benefit from it. These nations have only two places to look for such help—to the Soviets and to us. Very bluntly, if we abandon them now, there is no such thing as our getting a second chance. This is no time to quibble. We must provide this program with a budget which is equal to the protection of our interests.

This is good statesmanship. This is good business.

THINK
SMALL

BY   PETER   MULLER-MUNK,   FASID

SINCE WHAT I AM DOING as an industrial designer is so much in flux, I
have recently tried to take a look at
what I have done — what does it look
like, what does it amount to; and then
I went further and asked myself, how
about today's architecture? What does
it look like, what does it amount to?
After all, here is the proof, isn't it —

the tangible evidence of the mutual
worth of the industrial designer and the
architect to the community and to each
other.

What did I find? I found that my
profession, industrial design, is responsible for the looks and the effect — visual, technological, and sociological — of
about 75% of our industrially produced

products, systems, and components. Yes,
we are the guys who have designed most
of the gadgets that rust in our garages,
that clutter our cellars, that fill our
neighborhood and the air above it with
shattering noise and with noxious fumes.
Not a very pretty picture, but I do not
believe that I can forever rely on the
references of Cellini, of Chippendale, or

Peter Muller-Munk, "Think Small," *Charette: Pennsylvania Journal of Architecture*
(October 1965).

of William Morris to make myself look more noble than my past performance indicates.

Yes, I am afraid I as an industrial designer have to take the responsibility for much of the mess that surrounds us, because I consider this as more honest than blaming it on the other fellow, just to get out from under. No, I am not altogether happy with what industrial design has done so far, but I do believe we are slowly getting there and that we are tuned in on the right wave length. Our ultimate objectives? Order, beauty, elegance — pretty hard to come by, but we are trying.

And now when I look at the record of today's architecture, does it really look much better than the results of our work, or how do you defend the Holiday Inns, the Equitable Life Assurance monstrosities in Pittsburgh's Gateway Center, the Huntington Hartford Museum, to say nothing of the costly domestic dwellings in the block in which I live? Sure, I know there is also the Seagram Building, there is our Gateway No. 4, and some few of the great new churches and synagogues. But, by the same token, there are also some of the pure delights of industrial design — your telephone, the Boeing 707, the Buick Riviera, our computers.

Is it not interesting that in the last few months, the Museum of Modern Art in New York has had two exhibits which, at least to me, had a distinctly anti-architecture message — first, "20th Century Engineering" (a fine exhibit, by the way), and, just now, Rudofski's "Architecture without Architects." I take no position on either, but it would appear that even Philip Johnson did not have enough influence to stop the inquiry into the meaning of architectural monuments to a chaotic .urbanism. If industrial design is not always as good as it should be, perhaps you, too, share this stigma with us, for why else would a jury of architectural Brahmins find only one acceptable entry among the 350 for our North Side Piazza competition?

I believe, therefore, that we might agree that neither industrial design nor architecture has, so far, created the best of all possible worlds. The question, however, is to what extent has industrial design contributed to this unhappy state of affairs, and how can the industrial designers help to correct it?

In the absence of enough scholarly and creative definition concerning my profession and its relation to others, I had to try to do some of it myself, much as I dislike amateurism. In trying to think this thing out, I asked myself where industrial design belongs and what it can do that needs doing. I very early realized that at best it could only contribute one part to the whole and that to do even that competently was quite a job. No total environment for me —no siree. The more I looked at the perspective of me vs. the universe, the more clearly came back the message, "Think small, Peter; but damn it, try and think clearly!"

Lest any of you think that I am merely coy or unfashionably modest, have no fear. Quite on the contrary: I am really quite happy and content that I no longer parade under false auspices — and would be judged accordingly — but that, instead, I could now concentrate on fulfilling my role as a kind of 20th century nurseryman of the humus of culture without which society cannot hope to breed either dignity or grace.

Now, what are the ingredients of this topsoil for taste, for elegance, and for sensual enjoyment of our surroundings? Well, I think I know the answer to that one: the taming of the mass product by teaching it manners, a truly democratic concern with and respect for the needs of people — *needs*, not wants — and an entirely naive and indefatigable excitement about the esthetic and social potential of mass-produced precision. Industrial design has accepted the responsibilities and disciplines of quantitative reproduction, not as a soulless infringe-

Distribution poles for electric power

ment on our creative liberties, but as a way of life into which we are introducing the qualitative element of design.

With industrial design positioned as the conscience of industrial management by injecting the element of social responsibility into its products and services, it followed that industrial design has had .to jettison any philosophical or creative dependence on the craft tradition with its single-person-to-single-object relationship. Industrial design, therefore, is never concerned with the organization of one structure only, but with the esthetic, technological, operating and distribution problems of multiples.

It is perhaps here that architecture and industrial design often differ. If I understand it correctly, the character of the architect's work remains more personal than ours in that his projects, more often than ours, are concerned with single structures, projects, or situations, with the possibility—if not the requirement —for v a r i a t i o n and individuality. Standardization and multiplication, which are inherent to the industrial de-

sign process, make our position much more difficult because we are hardly ever dealing with one specific individual or group but with vast scattered populations, interests, and needs that frequently, but not exclusively, also involve architecture. Our personal design signature, therefore, becomes insignificant compared to the degree to which the products and systems of our design truly and usefully serve their users and contribute to their physical and spiritual well-being, regardless of whether this be a secretary and her typewriter, a machinist and his lathe, a housewife shopping in a supermarket, or a driver in need of a tankfull of gasoline.

I realize that the design-for-people doctrine is as imperative for architecture as it is for industrial design; and, if I am correct, this would only illuminate one more affinity between our two professions.

I submit to you, however, that the craft ideology is no longer tenable and that neither you nor I can any longer assume *total* responsibility for our creations or for their impact on society. All of us — you and I, our clients and their customers, our captains of industry and heads of state, the deans of our colleges and their students, every last citizen of our unstable world — are dependent on the other and on the integrity and talent which they are willing to contribute to the solutions of our common problems. And that's why I say "think small"; because, only after we are willing to assume our limited but specific roles in the drama of our century can we ever create a fitting style for the democracy.

Let me enlarge on this point for a minute as it relates to industrial design and architecture. In my haphazard reading of the New York *Times*, of *Progressive Architecture*, the *Harvard Business Review, The New Yorker* as well as of *Domus* and *Habitas*, I continue to be subjected to a discussion of the pros and cons of prefabrication and on the vulgarities of mass production and mass consumption. I may very well have missed the point, but most of these *sometimes* learned, *occasionally* entertaining, and often *pontifical* reviews sound very academic to me. I even suspect that the current and not always *virtuous* passion for the voluptuous attractions of reinforced concrete is a kind of revolt against the restraints of industrially designed and standardized components.

As I see it, prefabrication is a fact of life, and *Sweet's Catalogue* is its well-established bible and dictionary. I challenge the architect to show me one contemporary piece of architecture — and I mean this in the literal, not in the stylistic sense — which is not prefabricated — or should I say pre-stressed? Come to think of it, maybe we industrial designers should really take the credit, instead of Gordon Bunshaft or Ed Stone, because is it not we and our clients who have designed and manufactured the steel and glass, the heating, the air conditioning and lighting systems, the elevators, the curtain-wall panels, the plumbing, the interior partitions, and equipment so that all they had to do was to dimension the elevation and floor plans and specify our components to their contractors? Perish forbid, no, I am not really serious — only half.

Be that as it may, what concerns my partners and me when we are commissioned to develop advanced functional and design concepts for the bathroom, the kitchen, for office partitioning, for water towers, or for petroleum marketing — and, as a matter of fact, these, among others, are all active projects in our office right now — what concerns us is the convergence of the problems of design with those of other specialists. A single bathtub might be a tempting experiment in pure sculpture, but *the bathroom* is part of the process of water supply, of plumbing codes, of human engineering, of space utilization; and it immediately explodes into a much more complicated string of relationships that we cannot unravel without reference to the national water table, to engineering, to architecture, and to present and future attitudes towards hygiene and birth control.

I am sure I need not tell you that the design of a chain of service stations cannot be solved with some neo-rococo blueprints of fake Yamasaki arches and without an investigation in depth of automotive speeds, driver and station attendants' attitudes, zoning ordinances, the federal highway system, etc., etc., to say nothing of maintenance problems and the economics of square-foot and gallonage revenue. If our contract were merely for one more station for the corner at Murray and Forbes, I honestly think an architect rather than we industrial designers should be commissioned to put his stamp on it. However, when it comes to designing a *system* of motoring facilities that must combine standardization of building and other components with sufficient flexibility to fit different lot sizes, traffic patterns, and regional as well as climatic conditions, then I honestly believe the industrial designer — and only the industrial designer — is the better man for the job.

Whether we like it or not, industry is not geared to manufacture custom products for one citizen, one taste, or one pocketbook, but for their nearest common denominator, and it is here that industrial design acts as their most educated and sensitive interpreter. It is psychologically tempting to strike an aristocratic stance and to pretend that the individual is all-powerful and self-sufficient; but, I ask you, where are the kings of yesteryear? With every respect for their civic pride and financial power, I hardly believe that either Adolph Schmidt or David Rockefeller would compare himself to Louis XIV; and, as a consequence, the fountains on Mellon Square and the Chase Manhattan Plaza are also somewhat less grandiose than those of Versailles.

It so happens that I have a rather intimate experience with what occurs

The Intaglio Glass Wall Unit Line

Single-lever lavatory faucet

Custom Carpet Sweeper

Applicator for Upholstery Shampoo

Lenses for 16 mm movie cameras

These new stations went into service on a test basis this year in Matawan, New Jersey, and at Roosevelt Field in Garden City, New York. (Another is under construction in Tulsa, Oklahoma.) Each is a radical departure from the rectangular structure that the company introduced more than 30 years ago and that became the model for the industry.

when a neighborhood is abandoned to the free choice of its inhabitants. In the court in which I live and which has been constructed on the fill of two magnificient former Mellon residences, there are 18 dwellings which range from *Better Homes & Gardens* Georgian to *Esquire* Neutra. My pleasantly affluent neighbors elected to forego the regimentation of the Duquesne Light Company and chose, instead, each his own personal — or, excuse me, his own "personalized" — street light. Result? Eighteen miserably inefficient and outrageously cute lanterns that would arouse the ridicule of Tom Jones and Paul Revere if they could but see, which, of course, none of we eighteen can, come nightfall. I am mentioning this little domestic experience because I think it is symptomatic of a quite serious schism in our attitude to ourselves and to our community. No matter how much freedom of action and freedom of choice I want to reserve for myself, I maintain that I must first acknowledge that my actions, my choices, and my work cannot be judged in isolation from their effect on others.

If I consider the interrelation and responsibility of people to people as a serious imperative, I very quickly also arrive at the conclusion that the same is true between objects and structures. They act upon each other, they clarify or confuse, they relate to each other. I, therefore, tell my office that, alas, we can no longer make a small mistake because not only are our errors multiplied *ad infinitum*, but they intrude upon every last bit of their surroundings. If an industrial designer may be permitted to quote Mies, "God is in the details," and, gentlemen, I claim no more than a somewhat educated competence in the design of some of the essential details of the total environment, and it is to these that I am trying to contribute some integrity and finesse.

Just as I consider the quality of building components as vital to the ultimate quality of architecture, I believe the same is true of all of the myriad other components of the city, the highway, the neighborhood, the community.

What about the traffic lights, and those hideous electrical substations? What about the whole uncoordinated and confusing graphic communication of street and highway signs, road markers, parking instructions, and billboards? What about our bulbous water towers, high on the horizon? Are they only details or are they not the weeds that smother what little healthy turf we have left?

What I am trying to get at is that the quality of our environment is very largely determined by the *quality of its components*. If the eggs aren't fresh and the butter is rancid, you might as well forget about the omelet. I realize that a good looking and efficient kitchen or some well-designed and constructed chairs do not alone make for a happier home any more than a fancy dormitory makes for better education. By the same token, I also do not believe that one more

SOM office building, one new opera house, or just another redevelopment project succeeds in improving the city. In fact, they often do quite the opposite. There is one thing, however, which they all have in common. Plans and structures of architects, just like those of the industrial designer, are also only components of much larger systems that cannot ever hope to function properly without a respectful recognition that no one profession is either capable or omnipotent enough to handle the whole ball of wax. It seems to me there is plenty to do for what architects, and only architects, can do, with quite enough left over to keep us industrial designers busy. Might it not be better to divide responsibilities and to concentrate on what one is best capable of doing, instead of insisting that it might still be possible to be all things to all men and end up by improving neither?

I think I should also mention the subject of obsolescence which, so far, I have only touched upon by innuendo. The life span of the products of industrial design is not the same as those of the Taj Mahal or of the pyramids. Is that bad? Nuclear energy may very well replace our present concept of furnaces, food preservation, and power supply. The life span of a 1965 refrigerator is about 15 years, but my banker has told me that my house, i.e., his mortgage, is not going to do much better. I submit that the original model for the Pan Am Building, Gio Ponti's Pirelli skyscraper in Milan, which is of very recent vintage, is already obsolete because it has no air conditioning. Eternity has become shorter, and I believe that this imposes a new kind of modesty on our evaluations and work attitudes. If impermanence is accepted as a permanent fact of our age, then we must become the judges of our own designing efforts, and we can no longer relax in an arrogant indifference to the present in the hope that some future century will admit us to Olympus.

Every so often, therefore, I and my partners meet as a jury on our own designs of the last five to ten years, and we have found this a quite salutary experience. I confess that far too much of our past work really shakes us up. Why didn't we do better at the time? Ignorance, pressure, lack of imagination or courage? No matter, but let's not do it again; and, thank heaven, most of those 1957 designs are no longer on the market because technology and science have made them obsolete. However, some of our work still does hold up — sometimes in appearance only and sometimes even in function and performance. The trick, or course, is to increase the percentage of this category, and we are hard at it, believe me. The point I am trying to make is that we are our own judges. We are not waiting for the future. The time is now.

As a matter of fact, one of our problems — and I would imagine one of the architect's as well — is what to do with the accumulated junk of yesterday. I have never seen an old-car dump for Rolls-Royces, but I doubt that it would

look much better than a mountain of rusty Volkswagens. Where do we throw the trolleys and buses when our rapid-transit systems have finally arrived? And what plans do *you* have for the Pan Am Building or Gateway Towers when their monumental obsolescence is assigned to the demolition crews? Perhaps they might supply the paving for some more miles of the Federal highway system which, in turn, will have to be torn up when we visit each other in hovercrafts and programmed space capsules. It is not industrial design that invented obsolescence; it is part of the concept of 20th century science and technology. There is a saying that to shake your fist against the tide is one sure way to get drowned; so, I say, it is flood control we need — control of ugliness, of mediocrity, and of civic indifference.

Is there any way to get out of this syndrome? I think so. It is for the environmental professions to get together, to stop genuflecting to the speculators and the capital-gains operators and to start tearing down the fences that divide us. If I may borrow a word that I overheard on my way to the Forum, we need a *consensus;* we need a local platform for an effective intra-professional dialog; we need a national — and we must begin to organize an international — federation of those creative professions which together control the composite shape of our physical world. We must stand up and be counted; and when that roll call comes, I can assure you the industrial designers will be standing shoulder to shoulder with you. *Think small, gentlemen, and we can be big.*

Peter Muller-Munk, FASID, is Managing Partner of Peter Muller-Munk Associates in Pittsburgh which is regarded as one of the most influential industrial-design organizations in the country. The PMMA office is retained by major United States corporations, such as American Radiator & Standard Sanitary Corporation; Bissell Inc.; E. I. du Pont de Nemours & Company, Incorporated; Pittsburgh Corning Corporation; Texaco, Inc.; United States Steel Corporation, and has completed important projects for a number of foreign companies and governments. Mr. Muller-Munk was also industrial-design consultant to the Brussels Universal and International Exhibition, and he has conducted industry seminars in many European countries for the Organization for Economic Cooperation and Development. A past president and Fellow of the American Society of Industrial Designers and currently serving on the Board of Directors of the Industrial Designers Society of America, he was one of the co-founders and first president of the International Council of Societies of Industrial Design (ICSID) whose membership includes 33 design societies from 21 countries. He is also a member of the Design Committee of The Kaufmann International Design Award and a Fellow of the Royal Society of Arts. This article is based on a talk given early this year before the Pittsburgh Chapter, AIA.

Notes

PMMA Archival Sources

Substantial portions of Peter Muller-Munk Associates' archives were lost in two major office flooding incidents (one from the river and one from a faulty HVAC system). The surviving records were dispersed over many years.

This project was informed by documents and images generously shared by Ned DeForrest, Joanne Parisson Gaus, H. Kurt Heinz, James P. Karlen, Wesley E. Lerdon, Leonard Levitan, Curtiss D. Lischer, Kenneth D. Love, Diana Riddle, George R. Scheuring, Eric Smith, Walton E. Sparks, and Paul R. Wiedmann.

The surviving PMMA archival material comprises the years 1927–c. 2000 but is particularly incomplete for the years 1937–48. Throughout, there are no client account records, no financial accounts, and no correspondence files. No complete list of clients or projects survives. The authors made substantial efforts to contact extant client firms, but in most cases their records were also lost or unavailable to scholars.

Slide cabinet

A slide cabinet of some 30,000 slides (collection of Paul R. Wiedmann) includes images of PMMA sketches, models, concepts, and finished designs and covers the period 1938–c. 1998. More than half of the contents predates the 1974 merger with Wilbur Smith Associates, but less than 2 percent of the total dates from before 1950.

Scrapbooks

Four scrapbooks (collection of Paul R. Wiedmann) include press clippings, photographs, brochures, and other print ephemera. These cover the years 1927–71, with one substantial gap, assumed to be an entire missing scrapbook or books:

Scrapbook 1: 1927–36
Scrapbook 2: 1949–58
Scrapbook 3: 1958–61
Scrapbook 4: 1961–71

Lando Binders

Lando Advertising Agency, which worked with PMMA during the 1950s, compiled binders (collection of Paul R. Wiedmann) of press releases, photographic contact sheets, and articles pertaining to PMMA from the following periods:

Binder 1: 1956–57
Binder 2: 1957–58
Binder 3: 1958–59
Binder 4: 1960

Additional Archival Sources

The Bissell Archives at the Grand Rapids Public Museum, Grand Rapids, MI

Carnegie Mellon Architecture Archives, Pittsburgh, PA

Carnegie Mellon School of Design, Pittsburgh, PA

Carnegie Mellon University Archives, Pittsburgh, PA

Fred Waring's America: A Collection of Memories, Penn State University Archives in The Eberly Family Special Collections Library, State College, PA

Industrial Designers Society of America (IDSA) Records, Special Collections Research Center, Syracuse University Libraries, Syracuse, NY

The Kenneth Berger Hearing Aid Museum and Archives, Kent State University, Kent, OH

The Museum and Archives Division of the Rivers of Steel National Heritage Area, Homestead, PA

Senator John Heinz History Center, Pittsburgh, PA

Preface

1   Peter Muller Munk, speech, "10/8/55 2nd Half Fri. PM Hose/Muller-Munk," sound recording, October 8, 1955, Industrial Designers Society of America (IDSA) Records, Special Collections Research Center, Syracuse University Libraries, Box 116.

2   The Waring Blendor is mentioned in Richard Guy Wilson, Dianne H. Pilgrim, and Dickran Tashjian, *The Machine Age in America, 1918–1941* (New York: Brooklyn Museum in association with Abrams, 1986), 308. A photograph of it is included in Victoria Kasuba Matranga with Karen Kohn, *America at Home: A Celebration of Twentieth-Century Housewares* (Rosemont, IL: National Housewares Manufacturers Association, 1997), 41.

3   However, two major early exhibition catalogues on art deco omitted Muller-Munk altogether: Judith Applegate, *Art Deco* (New York: Finch College Museum of Art, 1970); and Bevis Hillier, *The World of Art Deco: An Exhibition Organized by the Minneapolis Institute of Arts, July–September 1971* (London: Studio Vista, 1971).

4   *Antiques and the Arts Weekly*, August 10, 1979, 30. The service was illustrated in Roslyn Tunis, *Treasure House: Museums of the Empire State* (Binghamton, NY: Roberson Center for the Arts and Sciences, 1979), 77. Research by W. Scott Braznell.

5   "Art Nouveau and Art Deco," Sale 234, Phillips Fine Art Auctioneers, New York, October 24, 1979, Lot 47, and "Important Art Nouveau and Art Deco," Sale 4354, Sotheby Parke Bernet, New York, March 27, 1980, Lot 304; the three-piece coffee service was described without a named maker. Research by W. Scott Braznell.

6   Alastair Duncan, *American Art Deco* (New York: Abrams, 1986), 83. In addition to the Metropolitan's tea service, Duncan illustrated the Normandie pitcher. At the end of the decade Muller-Munk silver garnered attention in Annelies Krekel-Aalberse's *Art Nouveau and Art Deco Silver* (New York: H. N. Abrams, 1989).

7   In addition, Muller-Munk's candelabra for the Detroit Institute of Arts was featured in *The 1920s: Age of the Metropolis* (Montreal Museum of Fine Arts, 1991).

8   It was encouraging that David A. Hanks and Anne Hoy in *American Streamlined Design: The World of Tomorrow* (2005), which focused on industrial production, represented Muller-Munk as a designer for Porter-Cable Machine Company and illustrated a portable sander. This A3 model, however, was not designed by Muller-Munk. The referenced Design Patent 166,148 is actually for the Muller-Munk model 500 sander [p. 81, Fig. 5].

9   Published articles that touched on Muller-Munk as a professor include Jim Lesko, "Industrial Design at Carnegie Institute of Technology, 1934–1967," *Journal of Design History* 10, no. 3 (1997), 269–92; Carroll Gantz, "Pioneer Design Innovators from the 'Burgh," *Innovation* (Spring 2013): 10–13; and Sarah Johnson, "An Overview of Carnegie Institute of Technology's Industrial Design Program, 1920–40s," in *ID80: Celebrating 80 Years of Industrial Design Education at Carnegie Mellon, 1934–2014*, ed. Mark Baskinger (Pittsburgh: Carnegie Mellon University, 2015), 8–41.

10   Peter Muller-Munk, "Industrial Designers Can Face Today's Challenge," *Electrical Manufacturing*, June 1951, 116.

11   Peter Muller-Munk, "O Wad Some Power the Giftie Gie Us," *Art and Industry* 50, no. 298 (April 1951): 134.

12   Contributions by Stern in subsequent chapters are recognized in the endnotes.

13   Peter Muller Munk to Howard Applegate, November 23, 1965, PMMA archives.

Berlin: Family

1   Peter Müller-Munk, "The Life History of a Craftsman-Designer," *Creative Design* 1 (Winter 1934–1935): 34.

2   Klaus-Peter Wilhelm Müller, Birth Register No. 532, June 27, 1904, copy courtesy of the Standesamt, Bezirksamt Charlottenburg-Wilmersdorf von Berlin.

3   Marcel Montandon, writing in 1903, quoted in Iain Boyd Whyte and David Frisby, eds., *Metropolis Berlin: 1880–1940* (Berkeley: University of California Press, 2012), 11.

4   Whyte and Frisby, *Metropolis Berlin*, 11.

5   See, for example, Charles W. Haxthausen and Heidrun Surh, eds., *Berlin Culture and Metropolis* (Minneapolis: University of Minnesota Press, 1990).

6   The first known example of Peter adding his mother's family name, Munk, to his name is in his University of Berlin record of 1926 (see note 53). In America an anglicized version of his name appeared by 1927 as "Peter Mueller-Munk," but variations both with and without the umlaut appear in published sources throughout the 1920s and 1930s. By the mid-1950s the physical sign on the firm's office door proclaimed, "Peter Muller-Munk Associates, Industrial Design." Confusingly, the umlaut persisted in printed letterhead of the same period.

7   Oda Cordes, *Marie Munk und die Stellung der Frau im Recht: Wissenschaftliche Studie über Leben und Werk von Marie Munk in drei Teilen*, 3 vols. (Schwerin, Germany: O. Cordes, 2011), 1:12.

8   Landesarchiv Berlin, B Rep. 235-12 (Nachlass Marie Munk), MF-Nr. 3505-3509, Maschinenschriftliches Manuskript der Autobiographie Marie Munks in englischer Sprache (Teil 1), 1961, here: MF-Nr. 3505, I. "Childhood," p. 2; and Cordes, *Marie Munk und die Stellung der Frau im Recht*, 1:13.

9   Ibid., p. 15, quoted in Cordes, *Marie Munk und die Stellung der Frau im Recht*, 1:10.

10   Marie Munk, "Reminiscences of a Pioneer-Woman Judge in Pre-Hitler Germany: Rise and Fall of German Feminism," Part I, p. 2, Marie Munk Papers, Sophia Smith Collection, Smith College, Northampton, MA, Series III, Writings, Box 10: folder 2.

11   Ibid., Part I, p. 10c.

12   Landesarchiv Berlin, MF-Nr. 3505, I. "Childhood," pp. 8, 13, 10.

13   Barbara Welker, Centrum Judaicum Archiv, Berlin, e-mail message to author, January 8, 2014.

14   Gustav Karpeles, *Jews and Judaism in the Nineteenth Century* (Philadelphia: Jewish Publication Society of America, 1905), 66. Marie Munk has described herself as a "non-Aryan Christian." Munk, "Reminiscences of a Pioneer-Woman Judge," Part I, p. 4.

15   George L. Mosse, *German Jews beyond Judaism* (Bloomington: Indiana University Press; Cincinnati: Hebrew Union College Press, 1985), 43.

16   Barbara Welker, Centrum Judaicum Archiv, Berlin, e-mail message to author, January 8, 2014.

17   Ibid.

18   According to Thomas Neville Bonner, medical education at this time was "becoming a monopoly of the wealthy," indicating that the Müller family was financially secure. Thomas Neville Bonner, *Becoming a Physician: Medical Education in Britain, France, Germany, and the United States, 1750–1945* (New York: Oxford University Press, 1995), 310. At the University of Heidelberg, in 1890–92, Franz Müller completed his studies in chemistry. In 1896 he returned as "Dr. rer. nat.," a designation comparable to a PhD in natural sciences, to study medicine. In the interim he attended the University of Berlin. He most likely received his doctorate in medicine from the University of Heidelberg in 1898. Documentation from Universitätsarchiv Heidelberg, Stud. A.: Müller, Franz, 1897/98.

19 Franz Müller, "Beiträge zur Toxikologie des Ricins," *Naunyn-Schmiedeberg's Archives of Pharmacology* 42, nos. 2–4 (1899): xiv; and Hanns-Christian Gunga, *Nathan Zuntz: His Life and Work in the Fields of High Altitude Physiology and Aviation Medicine* (Amsterdam: Academic, 2009), 138–39.

20 Johannes Asen, ed., *Gesamtverzeichnis des Lehrkörpers der Universität Berlin* (Leipzig: Otto Harrassowitz, 1955), n.p. The institution was founded as the Universität zu Berlin (University of Berlin) and is currently known as the Humboldt-Universität zu Berlin (Humboldt University of Berlin). In his entry in the Berlin address books (*Berliner Adressbuch*, 1904–12), Franz Müller listed himself as "Dr. rer. nat." (abbreviation of *doctor rerum naturalium*, for German doctoral degree in the natural sciences) and "med." for medicine. It was exceedingly rare for a Jew to be named a full professor in medicine at this time, and the situation may have contributed to Franz Müller's decision to convert from Judaism. See Bonner, *Becoming a Physician*, 316.

21 Franz Müller's addresses determined from the *Berliner Adressbuch*, 1904–12.

22 My thanks to Barbara Welker, Centrum Judaicum Archiv, Berlin, for information about the death of Franz's mother; e-mail message to author, January 8, 2014.

23 Richard J. Evans, "Liberalism and Society: The Feminist Movement and Social Change," in *Society and Politics in Wilhelmine Germany*, ed. Richard J. Evans (London: Croom Helm; New York: Barnes & Noble, 1978), 197.

24 Munk, "Reminiscences of a Pioneer-Woman Judge," Part I, p. 12; and Marie Munk, "Summary of Experiences and Training," p. 1, Marie Munk Papers, Sophia Smith Collection, Smith College, Northampton, MA, Series I, Biographical Material, Box 1: folder 3. In 1924 Marie Munk became the first woman admitted to practice law in Berlin and, in 1930, the first female judge in Berlin.

25 Asen, *Gesamtverzeichnis des Lehrkörpers*, photocopy courtesy of Sabine Friedrich, Universitätsarchiv, Humboldt-Universität zu Berlin. See also Paul Weindling, "Bourgeois Values, Doctors, and the State: The Professionalization of Medicine in Germany, 1848–1933," in *The German Bourgeoisie: Essays on the Social History of the German Middle Class from the Late Eighteenth to the Early Twentieth Century*, ed. David Blackbourn and Richard J. Evans (London: Routledge, 1991), 201.

26 *Berliner Adressbuch* 1910 and 1912, and address of family residence (Kastanienallee 39), in (Claus) Peter Muller entry in List or Manifest of Alien Passengers for the United States Arriving at Port of New York, SS *Veendam*, August 14, 1926, New York Passenger Lists, 1820–1957, Ancestry.com.

27 Paul Mendes-Flohr, "The Berlin Jew as Cosmopolitan," in *Berlin Metropolis: Jews and the New Culture, 1890–1918*, ed. Emily D. Bilski (Berkeley: University of California Press; New York: Jewish Museum under the auspices of the Jewish Theological Seminary of America, 1999), 15, 23. For an enlightening and concise discussion of *Bildung*, see, for example, Klaus Vondung, *The Apocalypse in Germany*, trans. Stephen D. Ricks (Columbia: University of Missouri Press, 2000), 134–36.

28 Landesarchiv Berlin, MF-Nr. 3505, I. "Childhood," p. 6.

29 "John Peter interviews P. Muller-Munk," sound recording, 1957, Library of Congress, transcription in exhibition files, Carnegie Museum of Art, p. 1.

30 Peter Muller-Munk to Arthur J. Pulos, August 13, 1963, PMMA archives. Peter's maternal grandfather, Wilhelm Munk, was also musical and had played the violin. See Landesarchiv Berlin, MF-Nr. 3505, I. "Childhood," p. 22.

31 Landesarchiv Berlin, MF-Nr. 3505, I. "Childhood," p. 13.

32 Marie Munk to Eva Roth, November 15, 1971, Marie Munk Papers, Sophia Smith Collection, Smith College, Northampton, MA, Series II, Correspondence, Box 4: folder 21, cited in Cordes, *Marie Munk und die Stellung der Frau im Recht*, 3: Biographischer Anhang: Gertrud Müller-Munk, 1. Although Marie Munk's reference to Gertrud's study with Matisse in Paris is clear, the one to Moser is not. There is no evidence that Gertrud studied with painters Koloman Moser, Emil Moser, or Richard Moser. Marie probably meant professor George Mossen, who taught in the rooms of the Künstlerinnen Vereins between 1909 and 1922, and specifically for the Künstlerinnen Vereins in 1917 and 1918. My thanks to Oda Cordes for sharing her research and documentation at the Akademie der Künste in Berlin on the Verein der Künstlerinnen zu Berlin and for her analysis; e-mail message to author, October 3, 2014.

33 Peter D. Stachura, *The German Youth Movement, 1900–1945* (London: MacMillan, 1981), 15, 18.

34 Jerry Z. Muller, *The Other God That Failed: Hans Freyer and the Deradicalization of German Conservatism* (Princeton, NJ: Princeton University Press, 1987), 30, 44, 63. Muller's depiction of the Sera-Kreis, of which Freyer was a member, is rare in the English language.

35 Cordes, *Marie Munk und die Stellung der Frau im Recht*, 3: Gertrud Müller-Munk, 1. For Diederichs, see Meike Werner, *Moderne in der Provinz: Kulturelle Experimente im fin-de-siècle Jena* (Göttingen: Wallstein Verlag, 2003), 286.

36 The depth of Gertrud's involvement in the Sera-Kreis is documented in the fifty-eight letters she wrote to Brügmann between March 28, 1911, and October 26, 1914. The content of the letters became a key source for his nephew's dissertation: Heinrich Gerhard Brügmann, "Karl Brügmann und der Freideutsche Sera-Kreis: Untersuchung eines Modells von Jugendleben und Geist der Meissner-Generation vor 1914" (PhD diss., Johann Wolfgang Goethe University, Frankfurt am Main, 1965), 8.

37 Muller, *The Other God That Failed*, 34.

38 Gertrud's contributions were recognized with an invitation from the Sera-Kreis to attend with them the historic First Free German Youth Day (Erster Freideutscher Jugendtag), the rally that brought together the various youth groups on the Hohe Meissner. Information on Gertrud Müller and the Sera-Kreis from Cordes, *Marie Munk und die Stellung der Frau im Recht*, 3: Gertrud Müller-Munk, 1.

39 Trude Müller, "Paris," in Karl Brügmann, *Sonnwendbriefe* (Jena, Germany: F. Frommann, 1914), 15–17. My thanks to professor Oliver Gorf at the Florida International University in Miami for his translation of "Paris" and for his insights about its contents and the intellect of Gertrud "Trude" Müller.

40 Cordes, *Marie Munk und die Stellung der Frau im Recht*, 1:8; and Landesarchiv Berlin, MF-Nr. 3505, I. "Childhood," p. 14.

41 Müller-Munk, "The Life History of a Craftsman-Designer," 34.

42 John Peter interview, p. 1; and Müller-Munk, "The Life History of a Craftsman-Designer," 34.

43 John Peter interview, p. 1.

44 Müller-Munk, "The Life History of a Craftsman-Designer," 34.

45 John Peter interview, p. 1. Wilhelm Munk, who had his grandson "pegged for the law," did not approve.

46 William Owen Harrod, *Bruno Paul: The Life and Work of a Pragmatic Modernist* (Stuttgart: Edition Axel Menges, 2005), 55.

47 Angela Schönberger, "It's a Joy to Live—Spirits Are Rising," in *Berlin 1900–1933: Architecture and Design*, ed. Tilmann Buddensieg (New York: Cooper-Hewitt Museum, The Smithsonian Institution's National Museum of Design; Berlin: Gebr. Mann Verlag, 1987), 110.

48 William Owen Harrod, "The Vereinigte Staatsschulen für freie und angewandte Kunst and the Mainstem of German Modernism," *Architectural History* 52 (2009): 233. Harrod makes a cogent case for a revision. The same year as its integration, the Vereinigte Staatsschulen moved to a campus in Charlottenburg, conveniently located for Peter. Harrod, *Bruno Paul*, 55.

49 Antje Kalcher, graduate archivist, University of the Arts (Universität der Künste), Berlin, e-mail message to author, January 31, 2013.

50 For private practices of professors, see Harrod, "The Vereinigte Staatsschulen," 238–39.

51 John Peter interview, p. 2.

52 Among others included were Raymond Hood, Albert Kahn, and Kem Weber. A ninety-five-page exhibition catalogue was produced: *Ausstellung neuer amerikanischer Baukunst* (Berlin: Königliche Akademie der Künste zu Berlin, 1926). Exhibition cited in Cervin Robinson, "Buildings and Architects," in Cervin Robinson and Rosemarie Haag Bletter, *Skyscraper Style: Art Deco, New York* (New York: Oxford University Press, 1975), 12–13n23, 31; and in Harrod, *Bruno Paul*, 82; Paul was a member of the committee that planned the exhibition, so it is likely that student attendance was encouraged.

53 "Abgangszeugnis," granted to Peter Müller-Munck [*sic*], April 23, 1926, Archiv, Humboldt-Universität zu Berlin. This document is the university's leaving certificate, which confirmed the courses he had taken. It is not a diploma. Interpretation of document courtesy of Oda Cordes. Translation courtesy of Renate Reiss.

54 My thanks to Renate Reiss for her translation of the courses listed in longhand.

55 One course, different from the rest, and perhaps motivated by the prospect of immigration to America, stands out: "English Newspapers," which engaged him during the 1925 summer semester and doubtless improved his mastery of the language. It is likely that Peter had some prior knowledge of English, perhaps through private tutoring.

56 Müller-Munk, "The Life History of a Craftsman-Designer," 34.

New York: Silver to Industrial Design

1 Peter Mueller-Munk, "Handwrought Silver: Modern Styles and Their Creators," *Charm* 9 (April 1928): 83.

2 See, for example, commentary by Marie Munk in Landesarchiv Berlin, B Rep. 235-12 (Nachlass Marie Munk), MF-Nr. 3505-3509, Maschinenschriftliches Manuskript der Autobiographie Marie Munks in englischer Sprache (Teil 2), 1961, here: MF-Nr. 3505, I. "Impressions as a Visitor in 1933," p. 3; and Betty Eberhart, "Oral History," 1971, transcript, p. 20, Marie Munk Papers, Sophia Smith Collection, Smith College, Northampton, MA, Series I. Biographical Material, Box 1: folder 4.

3 List or Manifest of Alien Passengers for the United States Arriving at Port of New York, SS *Veendam*, August 14, 1926, New York Passenger Lists, 1820–1957, Ancestry.com. The class of passage provided by Martijn Verbon, Stadsarchief Rotterdam, e-mail message to author, May 22, 2014. On the ship's manifest his name was typed "Peter Muller"; "Claus" in longhand was added later.

4 See, for example, "Gets Rare Portrait Painted by Perreal," *New York Times*, March 4, 1926, 9.

5 He was hired on August 25, 1926. Tiffany & Co., Personnel Records, Newark Factory, G-M, Peter Muller-Munk, shelf G 11/6, Employee Records, Tiffany & Co. Archives.

6 "John Peter interviews P. Muller-Munk," sound recording, 1957, Library of Congress, transcription in exhibition files, Carnegie Museum of Art, p. 5. It has been variously reported that Peter received a "Masters Degree" or "journeyman's certificate" from the German Gold and Silversmith Guild in 1926, but no surviving corroboration has been found. Records also show that Peter worked in Room 18, the Silversmithing and Repair Department. Shelf G 11/6, Employee Records, Tiffany & Co. Archives.

7 Date of his departure, July 30, 1927, from Tiffany & Co. Shelf G 11/6, Employee Records, Tiffany & Co. Archives. He described his reason for leaving in a letter to Katherine Dreier: Peter Mueller-Munk to Katherine Dreier, December 1, 1927, Katherine S. Dreier Papers/Société Anonyme Archive, Yale Collection of American Literature, Beinecke Rare Book and Manuscript Library, Yale University, YCAL MSS 101, Series 1. Katherine S. Dreier Correspondence, 1906–1952, General Correspondence, Box 25, Folder 722. The address of his new studio was on the letterhead. In an undated résumé, circa 1935, in the University Archives, Carnegie Mellon University, Peter stated that he had worked for German émigré metalsmith Oscar B. Bach. It is not known when, and it has not been possible to confirm his employment, but it may have been in the interval between his exit from Tiffany and the opening of his own studio.

8 Peter Müller-Munk, "The Life History of a Craftsman-Designer," *Creative Design* 1 (Winter 1934–1935): 34. The first listing of the studio in the city's telephone directory appeared in the winter of 1927; New York City White Pages Telephone Directory, Winter 1927–Summer 1928, microfilm reel 42, New York City Public Library. Since the 1980s publications have mistakenly reported that Peter had a design practice or studio in Chicago, but no evidence for this exists. The error appears to have been originated by John Heskett in

Industrial Design (London: Thames and Hudson, 1980): "Chicago was also an important centre where many designers, such as Dave Chapman, Jack Little and Peter Muller-Munk, developed extensive practices" (p. 109). The scenario of the Chicago studio was repeated by Sarah Bodine in *Contemporary Designers*, ed. Ann Lee Morgan (Detroit: Gale Research, 1984); Lenore Newman in *Design 1935–1965: What Modern Was* (Montreal: Musée des Arts Décoratifs; New York: Harry N. Abrams, 1991); Mel Byars in *The Design Encyclopedia* (London: Laurence King; New York: Museum of Modern Art, 2004); and David A. Hanks and Anne H. Hoy in *American Streamlined Design: The World of Tomorrow* (Paris: Flammarion, 2005).

9 Peter Mueller-Munk to Katherine Dreier, December 1, 1927, Katherine S. Dreier Papers/Société Anonyme Archive, Box 25, Folder 722. The introduction to Dreier may have come through Dr. Gerhard Lütkens, a German lawyer in diplomatic circles in Washington, DC, who may have known Wilhelm Munk in the judiciary and Gertrud Müller from their earlier involvement in the German youth movements; both attended the 1913 rally on the Hohe Meissner.

10 Peter Mueller-Munk to Katherine Dreier, December 31, 1927, Katherine S. Dreier Papers/Société Anonyme Archive, Box 25, Folder 722.

11 "Peter Mueller-Munk Hand Wrought Silver," PMMA archive, Scrapbook 1. The only other reference to Kant is in a letter to Katherine Dreier, March 13, 1928, Katherine S. Dreier Papers/Société Anonyme Archive, in which he wrote, "my partner, Mr. Kant, has left for Europe recently." Nothing more has come to light on this relationship.

12 Peter referred to the limitation in making silver in a quantity of "one or two or three." See John Peter interview, p. 6.

13 "Peter Mueller-Munk Hand Wrought Silver."

14 "Garden Sculpture and Silver," *New York Times*, December 25, 1927, X13.

15 Ibid.

16 Peter Mueller-Munk, "Machine—Hand," *The Studio/Creative Art* 98 (October 1929): 710.

17 Peter Mueller-Munk to Katherine Dreier, March 13, 1928, Katherine S. Dreier Papers/Société Anonyme Archive, Box 25, Folder 722.

18 Elizabeth Lounsberry, "From the Smart Shops," *Arts and Decoration* 28 (March 1928): 20. Interestingly, reference was made to his jewelry designs, none of which have yet come to light.

19 C. Adolph Glassgold, "The Modern Note in Decorative Arts," *The Arts* 13 (April 1928): 229–30. On page 234, Glassgold stated that Peter had "exhibited in many European cities and also at the Paris Exposition." It is doubtful that Peter exhibited at the 1925 Paris Exposition. No record has been found, and Germany did not participate in the exposition. Nor has any record been found of silver exhibited in Europe prior to April 1928.

20 Augusta Owen Patterson, "The Decorative Arts," *Town and Country*, April 15, 1928, 71.

21 Ibid.

22 Ibid., 70, 118.

23 Mueller-Munk, "Handwrought Silver," 83.

24 Little Gallery advertisement, *New York Times*, November 27, 1927, X11. My thanks to W. Scott Braznell for his insights on the origin of influences for this set.

25 Gisela Richter, *Handbook of the Classical Collection* (New York: Metropolitan Museum of Art, 1927), 176 and fig. 120. The classical rooms were located just beyond the main hall on Fifth Avenue. The pyxis (accession number 03.24.6a, b) was displayed in room six, off the central hall of the classical rooms, and would have been hard to miss. Only one other set with this border is known. For this second set Peter modified the shape of the coffeepot handle and the shape of the silver finial tips, making them flat instead of spherical. For an image of the differing coffeepot handle, see Shirley Lowell, "Design in Contemporary Silver," *Home and Field*, February 1930, 35. For the flat silver-tipped finial, see the sugar bowl and cream pitcher in the Art Institute of Chicago, accession number 2003.9.1-2.

26 See, for example, the lighting designed by the architect Dominikus Böhm, Offenbach am Main, published in *Deutsche Kunst und Dekoration* 61 (December 1927): 229. Karen Davies noted the Swedish silversmith Nils Fougstedt as a source for the quarter-round shaped handles. See Karen Davies, *At Home in Manhattan* (New Haven: Yale University Art Gallery, 1983), 28. Quarter-round motifs occur in Swedish design other than metalwork, including a carpet for the SS *Kungsholm* illustrated in *Creative Art*, July 1929, 482.

27 For Fougstedt, see note 26. For Angman, see Graham Hughes, *Modern Silver Throughout the World, 1880–1967* (London: Studio Vista, 1967), 33.

28 Mueller-Munk, "Handwrought Silver," 38–39, 81–83. All quotes that follow are from this source.

29 The others illustrated were a hand mirror with a female head and braided handle, a small bowl with a tulip motif, and a round covered box with a chased pastoral motif.

30 Siegmund Warburg to Walter Rothschild, April 21, 1928, WARBURG/2/27, Warburg Papers, London School of Economics and Political Science Library.

31 Ron Chernow, *The Warburgs: The Twentieth-Century Odyssey of a Remarkable Jewish Family* (New York: Random House, 1993), 298, 297, and 303.

32 "Hand Wrought Silver: The Peter Mueller-Munk Studio," advertisement, *The Antiquarian* 10 (May 1928): 87. In this first advertisement, his silver was referred to as "manufactured." This was corrected to "Hand Wrought" in future advertisements.

33 The teapot image occurred only once. Subsequently, and through the last advertisement in *The Antiquarian* in June 1929, the figurative tea caddy was illustrated exclusively. See "Modern Tea-Sets," *Vogue*, July 6, 1929, 54. The tea set was for sale at the Lord and Taylor department store in New York. This tea set has not yet come to light.

34 "Hand Wrought Silver: The Peter Mueller-Munk Studio" advertisement. It is not clear what was meant by "reproduced." There is no evidence that Peter made and sold reproductions of earlier period styles, nor has any object surfaced with his mark that reproduces a design from a customer's existing silver. John Stuart Gordon surmises that "either he didn't copy existing designs on commission or he didn't mark those pieces." John Stuart Gordon, e-mail message to author, July 18, 2014. Gordon goes on to explain the genesis of the wording on pages 216 and 414 in his book *A Modern World: American Design from the Yale University Art Gallery, 1920–1950* (New Haven: Yale University Press, 2011), which states that the Mueller-Munk Studio sold "reproduction silver": "I interpreted the reproduced (in the Antiquarian ad) as offering to replicate a piece a customer brought in. During the severe editing process of the book, the nuance of that thought may have been over simplified to 'reproduction.'" The Mueller-Munk Studio did not sell reproduction silver.

35 For an image of the Court of Honor and floor plan of the Macy's exposition, see Marilyn F. Friedman, *Selling Good Design: Promoting the Early Modern Interior* (New York: Rizzoli, 2003), 77, 78.

36 "American Exhibitors, Silver, from Peter Mueller-Munk," in *An International Exposition of Art in Industry from May 14 to May 28, 1928 at Macy's* (New York: R. H. Macy and Company, 1928), 69. For tea set and hand mirror, see Mueller-Munk, "Handwrought Silver," 38, 39. For tea set alone, see Patterson, "The Decorative Arts," 70. Six other objects were listed: a bowl with silver ornament, a horseshoe-shaped bowl, a small bowl with gold appliqué inside, a cigarette box with horseshoe ornament, a powder box, and a candy box with a landscape design.

37 "Living Room Designed by Eugene Schoen," in *An International Exposition of Art in Industry*, 68. The only silver objects credited to Peter in the catalogue were "Bowls" and a "Candy jar." Apparently, the others were added to the Schoen living room later.

38 "Luncheon Precedes Art Show at Macy's, *New York Times*, May 13, 1928, 45.

39 Peter Mueller-Munk to Katherine Dreier, June 9, 1928, Katherine S. Dreier Papers/Société Anonyme Archive, Box 25, Folder 722.

40 Peter Müller-Munk résumé, undated (circa 1935), University Archives, Carnegie Mellon University. That a pottery commission was his earliest industrial design is corroborated in Peter Muller-Munk Associates, promotional literature, circa 1948, p. 3, PMMA archives. The document declared: "An order from R. H. Macy, therefore, to design a line of pottery was a milestone in his career." Research has yielded no other information regarding the pottery design. In the résumé, Peter also noted a commission from Macy's in "metal." For such a commission, see note 96 below.

41 John Peter interview, p. 6

42 "Would Aid Art in Industry: Macy's Plans Atelier to Furnish Designs to Manufacturers," *New York Times*, June 5, 1928, 50.

43 John Peter interview, p. 6. In one instance, the firm placed 1932 as the year Muller-Munk began work as an industrial design consultant; Peter Muller-Munk Associates, promotional literature, November 1955, p. 2, PMMA archives. That date, however, has not been corroborated by other documents, and firm histories written more than two decades after the fact may not be reliable. The dates of the Macy's commissions remain uncertain, but they likely fell at some point between 1928 and 1935.

44 "Three Prize Cups," *Newport Bulletin, Official Weekly Publication of the Newport Casino*, August 6, 1928, PMMA archives, Scrapbook 1.

45 A divided serving dish, another unpublished example, has come to light at auction. See "Modern Art & Design Auction," February 10, 2008, Los Angeles Modern Auctions, Lot 54.

46 "Modern: Silver Tea Caddy by Peter Mueller Munk," *Detroit News*, October 25, 1928.

47 Minutes of the November 19, 1928, meeting of the Arts Commission, Detroit Institute of Arts Archives.

48 W. R. Valentiner to Peter Mueller-Munk, November 20, 1928, Detroit Institute of Arts Archives.

49 Peter Mueller-Munk to W. R. Valentiner, March 1, 1929, Detroit Institute of Arts Archives.

50 Despite his requests for an advance to cover his expenses, Peter was paid in full only after the completion of the commission in August 1929. See W. R. Valentiner to Peter Mueller-Munk, April 15, 1929, and August 28, 1929, Detroit Institute of Arts Archives.

51 "Ausstellung Monza: Vitrine mit Silberarbeiten von Waldemar Raemisch-Berlin," *Deutsche Kunst und Dekoration* 61 (December 1927): 209. For an image of the Paul dining room, see Helen Appleton Read, "Twentieth-Century Decoration: A Significant Meeting of Various Modernists," *Vogue*, July 15, 1928, 75.

52 For wrapped wire treatment, see "W. Raemisch-Berlin: Handgetriebene Messingschale," *Dekorative Kunst* 30 (October 1921): 29.

53 "Dominikus Böhm," *Deutsche Kunst und Dekoration* 61 (December 1927): 229.

54 Marilyn F. Friedman, e-mail message to author, February 14, 2007, for list of objects; and Marilyn F. Friedman, "Defining Modernism at the American Designers' Gallery, New York," *Studies in the Decorative Arts* 14 (Spring–Summer 2007): 79–116. For published mention of him exhibiting, see Helen Appleton Read, "Art in Industry," *Brooklyn Daily Eagle*, November 4, 1928, 6E; and Edward Alden Jewell, "A Designer's Workshop," *New York Times*, November 11, 1928, 146.

55 Helen Appleton Read, "Twentieth-Century Decoration: The Modern Theme Finds a Distinctive Medium in American Silver," *Vogue*, July 1, 1928, 58, 98, 100.

56 Rebecca Stickney, "New York's Full of Weddings and Wedding Presents," *Harper's Bazaar*, September 1928, 134. For an illustration of a bowl and centerpiece, also published in September, see Burton Stillman, "The Modern Spirit in Silver," *The Spur*, September 15, 1928, 98.

57 M. S., "What I See in New York," *House Beautiful*, October 1928, 369; and B. B., "On and Off the Avenue: Silver," *New Yorker*, November 24, 1928, 81.

58 *The Architect and the Industrial Arts: An Exhibition of Contemporary American Design* (New York: Metropolitan Museum of Art, 1929), 34. The selection of Peter's service for display may have had a connection to Purves and the Macy's design program.

59 "Industrial Art Show So Successful It Will Be Continued All Summer," *Art Digest* 3 (March 1, 1929): 20.

60 *Modern American Design in Metal*, 1929, Newark Museum Archives, exhibition files, box 22. The objects from Bamberger's were a tea caddy, a water pitcher, a candy jar, a coffee set with tray, and a bowl. Peter also made a "breakfast set" for the store; it was not in the exhibition and may have been sold previously. Peter Mueller-Munk to Miss N. E. Winser, February 26, 1929, Newark Museum object files. In the letter Peter offered the following objects in his possession for loan:

hand mirror, cracker box, oval bowl, centerpiece, pair of candlesticks, and flower vase. From these a group of three, not identified individually, was selected for the exhibition.

61 "The Metal Exhibit," *The Museum: Science, Art, Industry* 2 (April 1929): 51–52.

62 Ulysses Grant Dietz, "Twentieth-Century Silver in The Newark Museum, Part 1," *Silver Magazine* 32 (November–December 2000): 26. The accession number of the bowl is 29.472. The price listed for the bowl was $185; the museum paid $125. Ulysses Dietz, e-mail message to author, May 22, 2014.

63 Muriel Ciolkowska, "Raemisch—Metal Worker," *International Studio* 77 (June 1923): 234; and Mueller-Munk, "Handwrought Silver," 82. See also the decorative arcade around the doorway of the first-class lounge of the Swedish ocean liner SS *Kungsholm* in Count Louis Sparre, "The Interior Decoration of a Liner," *Creative Art* 5 (July 1929): 479.

64 For an illustration of the Christian Dell wine jug, see Barry Bergdoll and Leah Dickerman, *Bauhaus 1919–1933: Workshops for Modernity* (New York: Museum of Modern Art, 2009), 108.

65 "Manhattan Private Home Plans at Low Record," *New York Times*, February 9, 1930, RE1; Laura Cameron, "Formed in Metal to Achieve Fresh Effect," *Home and Field*, July 1932, 34, 36; and *Practical Design in Monel Metal* (New York: International Nickel Company, c. 1931), 24, 44–45.

66 Cameron, "Formed in Metal to Achieve Fresh Effect," 34. The article featured a photograph of the fireplace surround and one of the stair rail.

67 Jewel Stern and John A. Stuart, *Ely Jacques Kahn, Architect: Beaux-Arts to Modernism in New York* (New York and London: W. W. Norton, 2006): 129–61.

68 Cameron, "Formed in Metal to Achieve Fresh Effect," 36.

69 *Wrought in Metal* (New York: Renner and Maras, c. 1932), n.p.; and *Practical Design in Monel Metal*, 24, 45. Jacobs was credited with the front door in *Wrought in Metal*, and for the front door and stair rail in *Practical Design in Monel Metal*. Peter was credited with the design and execution of the stair rail in Cameron, "Formed in Metal to Achieve Fresh Effect," 36.

70 "Mueller-Munk, Peter," in *Index of Exhibits, 46th Annual Exhibition of the Architectural League of New York, April 18–25, 1931* (New York: Architectural League of New York, 1931), 19. The entry, "Monel Metal Railing for Staircase in Residence, 49 East 80th Street, New York City," does not indicate if the stair rail was represented by a photograph or drawing.

71 Peter Mueller-Munk to Katherine Dreier, December 31, 1927, and March 13, 1928, Katherine S. Dreier Papers/Société Anonyme Archive, Box 25, Folder 722.

72 Mueller-Munk, "Machine—Hand," 711. All quotes below are from this source, 709–11.

73 Dedo von Kerssenbrock-Krosigk, ed., *Modern Art of Metalwork: Bröhan-Museum, State Museum of Art Nouveau, Art Deco and Functionalism (1889–1939)* (Berlin: Bröhan Museum, 2001), 401.

74 The location of this service is as yet unknown.

75 An image of the set in a 1995 Sotheby's auction catalogue shows that the outermost flat planes of the projecting elements of the vessels had a black patina. See "Important 20th Century Decorative Works of Arts," Sotheby's, December 2, 1995, Lot 200.

76 The certified change was entered into his original birth registration on October 25, 1930. Klaus-Peter Wilhelm Müller, Birth Register No. 532, June 27, 1904, copy courtesy of the Standesamt, Bezirksamt Charlottenburg-Wilmersdorf von Berlin. Munk was spelled Munck in this document, as it was in his University of Berlin record. However, his Birth Register No. 532 lists his mother's maiden name as Munk.

77 For example, "Entire Stock Sacrificed at Drastic Price Reduction, Lans, 554 Madison Avenue," *The Antiquarian*, April 1930, 79; and "Flayderman & Kaufman, Boston, Unrestricted Liquidation Sale," *The Antiquarian*, April 1930, 8–11. These two were just the tip of the iceberg.

78 Beverley Carter, "Ely Kahn and the Economy of Beauty," *Home and Field*, June 1930, 47. The centerpiece alone was illustrated in "Notes of the Month," *International Studio* 98 (January 1931): 43.

79 The sugar shaker and creamer were illustrated in "A Little Tale of Little Shops," *Harper's Bazaar*, February 1932, 96; and in "Fine Craftsmanship: Metalwork," *London Studio* 5 (June 1933): 396. The set had been exhibited in an exhibition of Peter's work at Greenleaf & Crosby, New York, and in the *12th Exhibition of American Industrial Art* at the Metropolitan Museum of Art, both 1931. The shaker was illustrated in C. De Cordis, "L'Orfevrerie," *La Revue Moderne Illustrée des Arts et de la Vie* 31 (July 1931): 27.

80 The profile of the body of the centerpiece, but not the base, recalls the Pirogue chaise longue, 1919–20, designed by Eileen Gray for a Paris apartment. See Virginia Museum of Fine Arts, accession number 85.112.

81 De Cordis, "L'Orfevrerie," 27–29. Illustrated were one of the Detroit Institute of Arts candelabra (see Fig. 10), a monogrammed service plate (see Fig. 22), a coffee set (see "Machine—Hand," reprint, p. 160), a centerpiece (see Fig. 21), a pedestal bowl (also published in "To the Victors," *Country Life*, March 1932, 44), and a cocktail shaker (the only known published image).

82 "Ce qui me séduit chez lui, c'est, avec la pureté des formes, le souci de les relier avec celles que nous offre la nature, le désir constant de tender vers la simplicité, la beauté, la harmonie des proportions tout en ne perdant pas de vue la destination de l'objet"; De Cordis, "L'Orfevrerie," 27–28.

83 Katherine S. Dreier Papers/Société Anonyme Archive, Box 89, Folder 2299. The school was located at 7 East Fifteenth Street. Peter's lectures took place on February 3 and March 3.

84 It is not known if the salt and pepper set or the candlestick were ever made. Novinska may have invented them or copied them from drawings of Peter's unrealized works.

85 Special Exhibition Object Loan Receipt: S.L. 1950, *12th Exhibition of American Industrial Art*, Registrar's File, Metropolitan Museum of Art, New York. The exhibition was on view October 12–November 22, 1931. Although the material of only two of the four vases can be documented as bronze, given the pricing, it can be assumed that all four were of bronze. Undated letter from the Roman Bronze Works, Inc., to Richard F. Bach, Metropolitan Museum of Art Archives. On the Object Loan Receipt retail prices were indicated: desk set, $1,600 (the equivalent today of $23,335); smoking set, $110 ($1,604 today); and four floral vases at $40 to $70 ($583 to $1,020 today).

86 Special Exhibition Object Loan Receipt: S.L. 1950, *12th Exhibition of American Industrial Art*, Metropolitan Museum of Art, New York. The listed retail prices on the Object Loan Receipt were $275 (the equivalent today of $4,010) for the coffee set, and $110 ($1,604 today) for the sugar shaker and creamer.

87 "On and Off the Avenue: Two Weeks Before Christmas!," *New Yorker*, December 12, 1931, 72. Other objects mentioned in publications were: a pair of fruit vases or bowls; a shallow circular bowl with long handles on a fluted column; a long, low fruit dish with a boat-shaped body, supported on a low curve; a large square sectional vegetable dish; a sugar shaker and cream pitcher; and a cocktail shaker with silver-wire appliqué and cups to match. For a photograph of the bowl on a fluted column, see "To the Victors," *Country Life*, March 1932, 44–45. For a photograph of the sugar shaker and cream pitcher, "A Little Tale of Little Shops," *Harper's Bazaar*, February 1932, 96. See also Walter Rendell Storey, "Groupings for the Modern Living Room," *New York Times*, December 6, 1931, SM16.

88 "A Little Tale of Little Shops," 96.

89 Invitation, Margaret Bourke-White Papers, Correspondence—Subject Files, Box 31, Peter Muller-Munk, Special Collections Research Center, Syracuse University Libraries. On the invitation is a handwritten memo by Bourke-White: "met de Liagre's Woodstock."

90 Postal telegraph, Peggy to Mr. Peter Mueller-Munk, December 28, 1932, Margaret Bourke-White Papers. Bourke-White was known to have had several lovers in the early 1930s. See Vicki Goldberg, *Margaret Bourke-White: A Biography* (Reading, MA: Addison-Wesley/Harper and Row, 1987), 119; also, "Margaret's ability to keep a lover as a friend never failed her," ibid., 123. The dated correspondence in the Margaret Bourke-White Papers continues through July 9, 1959.

91 Anne Landsman to Henry Geldzahler, February 1, 1973, Metropolitan Museum of Art, object file 1978.439.1-5. In this letter she and her husband offered the service as a gift to the museum.

92 "Offer of Gift or Bequest—Curator's Report," Metropolitan Museum of Art, object file 1978.439.1-5.

93 "Modern Design in Silverware," *Metal Industry* 36 (April 1938): 178. Metropolitan Museum of Art conservators confirmed the set is nickel-plated, not rhodium-plated as stated in this article.

94 Anne Landsman to Henry Geldzahler, February 1, 1973, Metropolitan Museum of Art, object file 1978.439.1-5. See also "On and Off the Avenue: Two Weeks Before Christmas!," 72.

95 Augusta Owen Patterson, "The Decorative Arts," *Town and Country*, January 15, 1932, 47. More recently, scholar W. Scott Braznell has pointed out that the bracket feet and incised ornament of the Isenburger service "recall Chinese art." W. Scott Braznell, "The Advent of Modern American Silver," *Magazine Antiques* 125 (January 1984): 237.

96 A "Sheffield plate" dresser set, sold at Macy's, that appears almost identical to this silver dresser set, but is not attributed to Peter, was illustrated in "Gifts to Adorn the House," *House and Garden*, December 1934, 40. This may have been a commission in "metal" from Macy's referred to by Peter in his undated résumé, circa 1935, in the University Archives of Carnegie Mellon University. The fret surface decoration was also employed for bases of a pair of silver-plated *torchères* (candleholders), reportedly bearing Peter's hallmark, and offered for sale about a decade ago by a New York City dealer in the decorative arts.

97 Walter Rendell Storey, "Groupings for the Modern Living Room," *New York Times*, December 6, 1931, SM16. Italics added.

98 Gordon, *A Modern World*, 216; and Ellen Paul Denker, *After the Chinese Taste: China's Influence in America, 1730–1930* (Salem, MA: Peabody Museum of Salem, 1985), 48. The second bowl is in a private collection. A similar example was sold at the Los Angeles Modern Auctions on October 17, 2010, lot 324.

99 A tea caddy engraved with figures of Asian farm workers wearing coolie hats (illustrated in "Hand Wrought Silver: The Peter Mueller-Munk Studio," advertisement, *The Antiquarian* 11 [October 1928], p. 102) has also been cited as an example of Chinese influence; Gordon, *A Modern World*, 216.

100 Peter Müller-Munk to Florence N. Levy, April 13, 1932, and questionnaire, "Choosing a Life Career in the Design Arts," Box 2, Florence Nightingale Levy Papers, 1890–1947, Manuscripts and Archives Division, New York Public Library. Italics added.

101 Peter departed Liverpool on September 24, 1932, and arrived in New York on October 2, 1932. List or Manifest of Alien Passengers for the United States Immigration Officer at Port of Arrival, New York, MV *Georgic*, October 2, 1932, New York Passenger Lists, 1820–1957, Ancestry.com. The *Georgic* was a motor ship, not a steamer.

102 Oda Cordes, *Marie Munk und die Stellung der Frau im Recht: Wissenschaftliche Studie über Leben und Werk von Marie Munk in drei Teilen*, 3 vols. (Schwerin, Germany: O. Cordes, 2011), 3: Gertrud Müller-Munk, 1. Her sister Marie wrote that Gertrud had studied in Paris, particularly with Matisse, later with Hans Hofmann: "[Gertrud] studierte in Paris, besonders bei Matisse, spaeter bei Hans Hoffmann [*sic*]." Marie Munk to Eva Roth, November 15, 1971. Marie Munk Papers, Sophia Smith Collection, Smith College, Northampton, MA, Series II. Correspondence, Box 4: folder 21.

103 Cordes, *Marie Munk und die Stellung der Frau im Recht*, 3: Gertrud Müller-Munk, 1; and *Große Berliner Kunst-Ausstellung 1932 im Schloss Bellevue* (Berlin: Kartell der Vereinigten Verbände Bildender Künstler, 1932), 23. The paintings were titled *Südfrankreich* (From the South of France) and *Fischer mit Netzen* (Fishing with Nets). Gertrud's work was exhibited the following year at the *Ausstellung des Vereins der Künstlerinnen zu Berlin*. See Kate Friedmann, "Ausstellung des Vereins der Künstlerinnen," *Die Christliche Frau*, Münster, April 1933, 123. Gertrud's *Spanische Landschaft* (Spanish Landscape) was mentioned in this article. Friedmann citation courtesy of Oda Cordes and the Archiv Bildende Kunst, Akademie der Künste, Berlin.

104 William Kevin Cawley, Senior Archivist and Curator of Manuscripts, Archives of the University of Notre Dame, e-mail message to author, May 13, 2014.

105 Peter Müller-Munk to Harry Lorin Binsse, March 28, 1933, CLIT 11/42 Folder: Mueller-Munk, Peter 1933–1938, Liturgical Arts Society Records (LIT), University of Notre Dame Archives (UNDA), Notre Dame, IN 46556. The three drawings are in CLIT 08/09 Folder: Liturgical Arts Society—craftsmen service (Pictures).

106 Brother Luke, De La Salle College, to Harry Lorin Binsse, February 22, 1934, CLIT 09/01 Folder: craftsmen service, 1933–1935, Liturgical Arts Society Records; and "Chalice in Sterling Silver with Ivory Knop Executed for the Craftsmen's Service of The Liturgical Arts Society by Peter Mueller-Munk," *Liturgical Arts* 3 (First Quarter 1934): advertising sec. An exhaustive search did not turn up the De La Salle chalice.

107 Michael K. Komanecky, *American Potters: Mary and Edwin Scheier* (Manchester, NH: Currier Gallery of Art, 1993), 34.

108 Peter Müller-Munk to Harry Lorin Binsse, September 17, 1934; and Harry Lorin Binsse to Peter Muller-Munk, September 21, 1934, CLIT 09/01 Folder: craftsmen service, 1933–1935, Liturgical Arts Society Records. Peter later wrote to inquire if the Society would participate in the New York World's Fair and to offer his services. Peter Müller-Munk to Harry Lorin Binsse, March 7, 1938. The Society did not participate.

109 Cordes, *Marie Munk und die Stellung der Frau im Recht*, 1:66.

110 Landesarchiv Berlin, MF-Nr. 3509, I. "Impressions as a Visitor in 1933," p. 1. Marie Munk and Gertrud Müller-Munk founded the German Federation of Business and Professional Women in 1931. Gertrud was responsible for proofing references on membership applications. Landesarchiv Berlin, B Rep. 235-01 Bund Deutscher Frauenvereine (BDF) MF-Nr.1486, "Deutsche Vereinigung Berufstätiger Frauen," p. 3; and Oda Cordes, e-mail message to author, December 14. 2014. See also Marie Munk, "Die Bedeutung der Internationalen Vereinigung berufstätiger Frauen und ihr erster internationaler Kongress vom 26. Juli bis 31. Juli 1931 in Wien," in *Die Frau* 39, no. 1 (October 1931): 44–45.

111 Landesarchiv Berlin, MF-Nr. 3509, I. "Impressions as a Visitor in 1933," pp. 3, 4.

112 Declaration of Intention, No. 344972, Peter Muller-Munk, State of New York, Southern District of New York, June 27, 1933. Citizenship was granted on May 4, 1936.

113 Landesarchiv Berlin, MF-Nr. 3509, I. "Impressions as a Visitor in 1933," p. 11.

114 "Public Invited to View Exhibits at State Normal School," *Oswego Palladium-Times*, August 10, 1933. For course title, Nancy Johnson, Special Collections, Penfield Library, SUNY Oswego, e-mail message to author, May 13, 2013.

115 Peter Müller-Munk to Margaret Bourke-White, October 14, 1933, Margaret Bourke-White Papers.

116 Peter Muller-Munk entry in Robert C. Cook, ed., *Who's Who in American Education*, 7th ed. (New York: Robert C. Cook Company, 1936), xxviii. Peter also listed these four schools under "Teaching Experience" in an undated,

circa 1935, résumé in the Carnegie Mellon University Archives. The only record that can be verified is from the Oswego State Normal School.

117 "Gertrude Muller," List or Manifest of Alien Passengers for the United States Immigration Officer at Port of Arrival, SS *Alaunia*, February 21, 1934, New York, Passenger Lists, 1820–1957, Ancestry.com. The person Gertrud was to join was entered: "Mr. Peter Muller Munk, 154 E. 39 St."

118 Paula Munk to Marie Munk, October 10, 1934, Marie Munk Papers, Sophia Smith Collection, Smith College, Northampton, MA, Series II. Correspondence, Box 7: folder 8. My thanks to Renate Reiss for translating the correspondence from German to English.

119 Ilona had a younger sister, Juliet.

120 Determined from New York Passenger Lists, 1820–1957, Ancestry.com.

121 Ilona L. Tallmer, Biographical Records Questionnaire, November 27, 1929, and March 20, 1950, Alumnae Association of Vassar College, Biographical Files.

122 Ilona Müller-Munk, Associate Alumnae of Vassar College, 1938 Biographical Register Questionnaire, February 27, 1938, Alumnae Association of Vassar College, Biographical Files.

123 "Miss Loewenthal Weds A. F. Tallmer," *New York Times*, March 17, 1920, 11.

124 Ilona Müller-Munk, Biographical Register Questionnaire, February 27, 1938, Alumnae Association of Vassar College.

125 Determined from New York Passenger Lists, 1820–1957, Ancestry.com.

126 Ilona Müller-Munk, Biographical Register Questionnaire, February 27, 1938, Alumnae Association of Vassar College. Though Ilona listed this group as the North American Committee for Defense of Spanish Democracy, she probably meant the North American Committee to Aid Democratic Spain.

127 Edith H. and James A. Fisher, conversation with Jason Busch and Rachel Delphia, June 2008. According to Jerry Tallmer, Ilona left Albert and began living with Peter, "who was a starving artist," in a building on the corner of Third Avenue. Jerry Tallmer, telephone interview with author, April 6, 2013.

128 Jerry Tallmer, telephone interview with author, April 18, 1996. Ship records confirm that Ilona, Jerry, and Jonathan returned from Palma, Majorca, on September 21, 1933, aboard the SS *Excambion*; New York Passenger Lists, 1820–1957, Ancestry.com.

129 "City News in Brief: Decrees Granted," *Nevada State Journal Reno, Nevada*, October 14, 1934, 8.

130 Marriage License, No. 24923, New York State Department of Health, October 24, 1934; and Certificate of Marriage Registration, City of New York, October 26, 1934. Peter was thirty, Ilona, thirty-five. Peter's close friend Ulrich Meisel was his best man and witness.

131 For Propriété Banégon, Margit Mombert, Affidavit, December 1, 1950, Marie Munk Papers, Sophia Smith Collection, Smith College, Northampton, MA, Series I. Biographical Material, Box 1: folder 7. Certificate of marriage, AR91046, Fayence, December 4, 1934, Courtesy of Richard Brook.

132 "American Guild of Craftsmen Announces the Opening of a Shop at Bonwit Teller's," advertisement, *New York Sun*, September 22, 1934, 16.

133 "Hand Craftsmen Unite in Display," *New York Sun*, October 6, 1934, 10.

134 Leon Loeb to Germain Seligmann, January 24, 1935, Archives of American Art, Jacques Seligmann & Co. Records, General Correspondence: American Guild of Craftsmen 1935–1936, Box 8, Folder 21.

135 "Craftsmen Show in New Galleries," *New York Sun*, April 20, 1935, 29; and Howard Devree, "A Reviewer's Week in the Galleries," *New York Times*, April 21, 1935, X9. An example of the pitcher illustrated in the *New York Sun* is in a private collection and reportedly has been in the family since 1929. The organization opened a branch in Provincetown, Massachusetts, for the summer of 1935; "Items in Brief," *New York Times*, May 12, 1935, X7.

136 Memo from Mr. Mosessohn to Mr. Seligmann, January 2, 1936, Archives of American Art, Jacques Seligmann & Co. Records. Seligmann had been given the option to renew the arrangement on January 1, 1936. The memo appears to have been an attempt to boost the potential of the American Guild of Craftsmen and to secure the renewal.

137 "A Distinctive Dresser Set Designed by Peter Müller Munk," *New York Sun*, November 7, 1934, 15. The price for the mirror, brush, and comb was $9.98; and "Macy's Gift Centre U.S.A.," *New York Times*, December 22, 1935, 19. The set was offered in "enameled" blue, green, black, and white.

138 Mr. Mosessohn to Mr. Seligmann, January 2, 1936, Archives of American Art, Jacques Seligmann & Co. Records.

139 Müller-Munk, "The Life History of a Craftsman-Designer," 34.

140 Ibid.

141 "Unusual," *New York Herald Tribune*, December 9, 1934.

142 "This Is News from Markets," *House and Garden*, January 1935, x; and "Window Shopping," *House Beautiful*, February 1935, 8. His Laura Lee Linder accessories were also published in "Gifts to Adorn the House," *House and Garden*, December 1934, 40; "100 Gifts: Home for Christmas," *Vogue*, December 1, 1934, 66, 67; and "100 Gifts: The Male Box," *Vogue*, December 1, 1934, 70.

143 Müller-Munk, "The Life History of a Craftsman-Designer," 34.

144 For Mary Ryan, "We Nominate for the Pioneers' Club," *Gift and Art Buyer* 33 (April 1937): 29, 110; and "Mary Ryan Presents Silvermode by Mueller-Munk," advertisement, *Gift and Art Buyer* 31 (January 1934): 57.

145 Determined from review of archival exhibition photographs and the catalogue: *Contemporary American Industrial Art 1934, Thirteenth Exhibition, November 5, 1934–January 6, 1935* (New York: Metropolitan Museum of Art, 1934), 14, 31, and "Additions and Changes," n.p.

146 "Tea Services by Famous Viennese Craftsmen," *Arts and Decoration* 32 (November 1929): 55; C. G. Holme, ed., *Decorative Art Year-Book* (London: The Studio, 1931), 158; and Annelies Krekel-Aalberse, *Silver of a New Era: International Highlights of Precious Metalware from 1880–1940* (Rotterdam: Museum Boymans-van Beuningen, 1992), 211.

147 Walter Rendell Storey, "Modern Trends in Decorative Art," *New York Times*, November 11, 1934, SM12.

148 "Original Design in Silver," *Arts and Decoration* 42 (April 1935): 29.

149 "Arts in Industry Glorified in Show," *New York Times*, April 16, 1935, 23; "Show to Feature Art in Industry," *New York Times*, April 14, 1935, N4; Blanche Naylor, "Industrial Art Exhibit," *Design* 37 (June 1935): 14–16, 43; and "At the Industrial Arts Exposition," *Jewelers' Circular—Keystone* 105 (May 1935): 65.

150 Quoted in "Use and Beauty Govern Silver Design," *Newark Evening News*, April 27, 1935. Water service illustrated in "This Is News from Markets," x. Three "beer or julep glasses" were pictured in "For Serious Students of the Pleasant," *Esquire*, December 1935, 109. For another example of the form, Gordon, *A Modern World*, 269.

151 "Short Biographies of Good Design," *Creative Design* 1 (Spring 1935): 31. Further described in the same issue: "Even the forms in this new table service are changed, although by ingenuity and reverse fitting two dyes [*sic*] have produced a center bowl, nut dishes and candlesticks." See "Sterling Plate," *Creative Design* 1 (Spring 1935): 15.

152 "Original Design in Silver," 29. Silvermode also illustrated in "Country Host," *Country Life*, August 1935, 58.

153 The price points for the pieces may have been a factor. For example, the tea set with tray cost $63 in 1935 (the equivalent today of $1,120), when the average salary was $1,500 annually, or $125 monthly.

154 Peter's referral possibly originated with the American Guild of Craftsmen, which had ties to Revere. Mr. Mosessohn to Mr. Seligmann, January 2, 1936, Archives of American Art, Jacques Seligmann & Co. Records. "At the present we are doing work for: Revere Copper & Brass Co."

155 "200,000 Line Shore for First Glimpse," *New York Times*, June 4, 1935, 2.

156 Dorothy Malone, "Table Talk," *New York American*, August 30, 1935. The pitcher was on display at the Revere exhibit at the Atlantic Coast Premium Buyers Exposition at the Hotel Pennsylvania, New York, September 23–27, 1935; Revere Copper and Brass advertisement, *Printer's Ink Monthly*, September 1935, n.p.

157 *Gifts by Revere* (Rome, NY: Revere Copper and Brass Incorporated; Home Manufacturing Company Division, 1936), n.p. In the catalogue, Peter was acknowledged as the designer. The base and prow of the pitcher were initially seamless on the exterior, but were soon modified for stability with applied edgings. Muller-Munk's input on this alteration is unknown.

158 Christopher Wilk, "Peter Müller-Munk: Normandie Pitcher," in *Design 1935–1965: What Modern Was*, ed. Martin Eidelberg (Montreal: Musée des arts décoratifs de Montréal; New York: Harry N. Abrams, 1991), 81. See also "Peter Müller-Munk," in David A. Hanks, *American Streamlined Design: The World of Tomorrow* (Paris: Flammarion, 2005), 165; and Gordon, *A Modern World*, 138.

159 Alice Hughes, "He's a 'Prof' Now," *New York American*, June 29, 1935, 6; and "In the Local Galleries," *New York Times*, August 18, 1935, X7. In the *New York Times* article, Design Associates Inc. announced his appointment. Individual announcements from "Design Associates Inc., 3 East 51st Street, New York" were printed for mailing. Design Associates Inc. appears to have been solely a title devised by Peter at this time. No other evidence has been found for it. The address in the printed announcement is the same as that of the Jacques Seligmann Galleries, but the phone number associated with it is the personal one of Germain Seligmann, the president of the gallery. For the telephone number, Marisa Bourgoin, Archives of American Art, e-mail message to author, April 27, 2015.

Professor Muller-Munk, Industrial Designer

1 "Get Most from Machine, Keep Its Looks, Teacher of Industrial Design Advises: New Associate Professor at Tech Is Graduate of Berlin School," *Pittsburgh Press*, September 25, 1935.

2 John F. Bauman and Edward K. Muller, *Before Renaissance: Planning in Pittsburgh, 1889–1943* (Pittsburgh: University of Pittsburgh Press, 2006), 8–29.

3 Glenn Everett McLaughlin, *Growth of American Manufacturing Areas: A Comparative Analysis with Special Emphasis on Trends in the Pittsburgh District* (Pittsburgh: Bureau of Business Research, University of Pittsburgh, 1938), 303.

4 *Carnegie Institute of Technology Faculty Bulletin*, series 1935–36, no. 1 (September 25, 1935): 2. The address was 4628 Bayard Street.

5 John Peter interviews P. Muller-Munk, sound recording, 1957, Library of Congress, transcription in exhibition files, Carnegie Museum of Art, p. 7.

6 Carnegie pledged $1 million in 1900 for "a technical institute to serve Pittsburgh and its workers" and another $1 million in 1901. The city of Pittsburgh provided the land. Edwin Fenton, *Carnegie Mellon, 1999–2000: A Centennial History* (Pittsburgh: Carnegie Mellon University Press, 2000), 15, 28.

7 "A Society for the Promotion of Industrial Education," *The Tartan* (Carnegie Tech student newspaper) 1, no. 3 (November 7, 1906): 4. Others included Henry S. Pritchett, Massachusetts Institute of Technology, Cambridge; M. W. Alexander, General Electric; Leslie Miller, Pennsylvania Museum and School of Industrial Art, Philadelphia; and C. R. Richards, Teachers College, Columbia University, New York.

8 "P. & D. Department Undergoing Reorganization," *The Tartan* 15, no. 22 (March 16, 1921): 1. *Bulletin of the Carnegie Institute of Technology College of Fine Arts, 1923–24*, series 18, no. 9 (May 1, 1923): 34, 66–72.

9 *Bulletin of the Carnegie Institute of Technology College of Fine Arts, 1923–24*, series 18, no. 9 (May 1, 1923): 65.

10 I am indebted to both Jim Lesko and Sarah Johnson for their published histories of the Industrial Design program at Carnegie Tech; see Jim Lesko, "Industrial Design at Carnegie Institute of Technology, 1934–1967," *Journal of Design History* 10, no. 3 (1997): 269–92; and Sarah Johnson, "An Overview of Carnegie

Institute of Technology's Industrial Design Program, 1920–40s," in *ID80: Celebrating 80 Years of Industrial Design Education at Carnegie Mellon, 1934–2014*, ed. Mark Baskinger (Pittsburgh: Carnegie Mellon University, 2015), 8–41.

11 Other significant faculty in 1934–35 included Edmund Marion Ashe, Joseph Bailey Ellis, Russell Taber Hyde, Norwood MacGilvary, and Wilfred Allen Readio. Ashe and Hyde focused on drawing and illustration, and had less overlap with Muller-Munk. Ellis taught sculpture and engaged with design students in the foundry. And Readio, as department chair, seems to have spent more time as an administrator than as an instructor.

12 Clayter's education included the Hackley Manual Training School, Muskegon, Michigan, and the Pennsylvania Museum and School of Industrial Art, Philadelphia.

13 *Bulletin of the Carnegie Institute of Technology College of Fine Arts, 1923–24*, series 18, no. 9 (May 1, 1923): 6–7, and series 29, no. 5 (December 1, 1933): 9.

14 An Indiana native, Dohner reportedly moved to Pittsburgh in 1918 to study set design at Carnegie Tech, but found work teaching industrial art in the Pittsburgh Public Schools; see "Donald R. Dohner," Industrial Designers Society of America, http://www.idsa.org/donald-r-dohner. Dohner's later faculty biography cites 1923 as his start date at Carnegie Tech: *Bulletin of the Carnegie Institute of Technology College of Fine Arts, 1926–27*, series 21, no. 3 (November 1, 1925): 13. See also *Carnegie Institute of Technology Personnel Directory 1923–1924*, 12.

15 E. B. Roberts to Glendenning Keeble, October 18, 1928, cited in Lesko, "Industrial Design at Carnegie Institute of Technology," 272. *The Carnegie Institute of Technology Faculty Bulletin*, series 1930–1931, no. 6 (December 10, 1930), notes Dohner's appointment as "director of Art" for Westinghouse. The *Carnegie Institute of Technology Faculty Bulletin*, series 1934–35, no. 1 (September 26, 1934), notes that Dohner had returned to the faculty, "having been director of art in the engineering department of Westinghouse since 1929" (p. 4). *Faculty Bulletins* did not include names of faculty for night courses, so it is unclear which course the Westinghouse engineers took with Dohner. Night courses in design were offered from the time Dohner joined the faculty; see *Bulletin of the Carnegie Institute of Technology Night Courses*, series 18, no. 9 (May 1, 1923): 134, and series 20, no. 1 (September 1, 1924): 78–86. Although Dohner is not listed as faculty for the 1933–34 school year, he is recorded as instructing A-500b, Block Printing (*Bulletin of the Carnegie Institute of Technology College of Fine Arts*, series 28, no. 4 [November 15, 1932]), and was clearly involved in curriculum development on and off between the spring of 1933 and the fall of 1934, when he resumed full-time teaching.

16 Kostellow studied in New York with modernist painter Vaclav Vytlacil at the Art Students League, and at the National Academy of Design, Columbia University, and the University of Berlin. Prior to moving to Pittsburgh with his wife, the artist and designer Rowena Reed Kostellow, he taught at the Kansas City Art Institute. *Bulletin of the Carnegie Institute of Technology College of Fine Arts*, series 28, no. 4 (November 15, 1932): 11.

17 Muller-Munk called Kostellow "probably one of the most brilliant people I have ever met. His influence on everybody he came in contact with, his magnetic enthusiasm, and his almost hypnotic effect on academic and industrial authorities have no equal"; Muller-Munk to Arthur Pulos at Syracuse University, July 23, 1963. In the same letter, Muller-Munk addresses Dohner thus, "Of course I knew him, but never intimately. You see—he was my predecessor at Carnegie Tech, and left when I came. He started the course with Kostellow in 1934 and went to the Pratt Institute in 1935…. As I knew him, he was a captivating personality full of enthusiasm and big ideas which he could project very forcibly…. But with little intellectual depth. This was supplied by Kostellow." PMMA archives.

18 Arthur Pulos, *The American Design Adventure: 1940–1975* (Cambridge, MA: MIT Press, 1988), 166.

19 Dohner and Kostellow briefly practiced industrial design together, evidenced by a surviving envelope imprinted with their joint logotype in the privately held Donald Dohner papers.

20 Lepper graduated from Carnegie Tech in 1927 and pursued education in Europe in 1928 before returning to Pittsburgh and joining Carnegie Tech's faculty. Lepper taught there longer than Kostellow and Muller-Munk combined, retiring in 1975, after a forty-five-year tenure. "Biographical Information," Robert Lepper Papers, Carnegie Mellon University (CMU) Archives, Box 1, Folder 34.

21 *Carnegie Institute of Technology Faculty Bulletin*, series 1931–1932, no. 13 (April 13, 1932): 2.

22 Minutes of Faculty Meeting, December 9, 1930, CMU Archives, Box 3, Folder 33

23 *Bulletin of the Carnegie Institute of Technology College of Fine Arts*, series 28, no. 4 (November 15, 1932): 80–81, lists: A-483-484 Composition (principles of pictorial design in monochrome); A-501-502 Pictorial and Decorative Design (basic creative course in line, value, mass, and color); and A-511-512 Advanced Design (continuation of the above with concentration on three-dimensional design involving the interrelation of function, materials, and appearance). Kostellow also taught A-174 Industrial Design (listed through the Dept. of Architecture), which focused on the design of textiles, fixtures, and utensils, and Clayter teamed up with Sculpture professor Joseph Bailey Ellis, continuing the Industrial Design Modeling course, A-1717 and A 1718, which had been offered since 1925.

24 Johnson, "An Overview of Carnegie Institute of Technology's Industrial Design Program, 1920–40s," 20.

25 Glendenning Keeble to Thomas Baker, May 19, 1933, and student petition, "Analysis for Instituting an Option in Industrial Design," not dated, but clearly 1933 from the context; both in Working Papers, College of Fine Arts, 1930–36, CMU Archives, Box 5, Folder 24. Keeble, although instrumental in shepherding the petition to President Baker, was not a design professor. He was professor of History of Music and Aesthetics; see *Bulletin of the Carnegie Institute of Technology College of Fine Arts*, series 28, no. 4 (November 15, 1932): 9.

26 Apparently Keeble also sought outside advice, as he added, "Mr. [Donald] Deskey yesterday confirmed this from his own experience. If this be true, the new course should bring the Department of Painting and Decoration a wider reputation and increased enrollment." Keeble to Baker, May 19, 1933.

27 My thanks to Sarah Johnson for drawing attention to the pamphlet, "A New Course in Industrial Design," College of Fine Arts Records, CMU Archives, Box 1, Folder 1.

28 Ibid. A recently discovered annotated typescript for the pamphlet—in the privately held personal papers of Dohner—all but confirms his authorship and deep involvement in the document. The graphic design was also by Dohner and/or Kostellow.

29 As reported the following day: "New Art Course to Aid Industry," *Pittsburgh Post-Gazette*, August 6, 1934, 4.

30 *Bulletin of the Carnegie Institute of Technology College of Fine Arts*, series 30, no. 5 (December 1, 1934): 53–56.

31 Dohner was likely lured to Pratt by his former boss at Pittsburgh Public Schools, James Boudreau, then Dean of Pratt. "Around the Campus: Former Art Instructor Dies," *Carnegie Alumnus* 29, no. 3 (March 1944): 9.

32 Lesko, "Industrial Design at Carnegie Institute of Technology," 273–74.

33 A parallel, early effort in industrial design education occurred at the School of the Art Institute of Chicago. See Barbara Jaffee, "Before the New Bauhaus: From Industrial Drawing to Art and Design Education in Chicago," *Design Issues* 21, no. 1 (Winter 2005): 58. For a broad overview on professional designers' engagement with curriculum development, see Pulos, "Training and Education," in *The American Design Adventure*, 164–93.

34 *Proceeding of the Conference on Art Occupations in Industry* (New York: Institute of Women's Professional Relations, 1936), 97, 91.

35 Peter Mueller-Munk, "Machine—Hand," *The Studio/Creative Art* 98 (October 1929): 711.

36 Muller-Munk, questionnaire and transcript for symposium "Choosing a Life Career in the Design Arts," New York Regional Art Council and the National Alliance of Art and Industry, 1932. Original in Florence Nightingale Levy Papers, Manuscripts and Archives Division, New York Public Library. My thanks to Jewel Stern for discovering Muller-Munk's role in this event.

37 "Choosing a Life Career in the Design Arts," questionnaire, 1.

38 "Choosing a Life Career in the Design Arts," transcript, 55.

39 "Choosing a Life Career in the Design Arts," questionnaire, 2.

40 Ibid.

41 "Choosing a Life Career in the Design Arts," transcript, 56.

42 "Choosing a Life Career in the Design Arts," questionnaire, 2.

43 "Choosing a Life Career in the Design Arts," transcript, 56.

44 "Choosing a Life Career in the Design Arts," questionnaire, 2.

45 "Choosing a Life Career in the Design Arts," transcript, 57.

46 There are no records of the university's hiring process and no job posting has ever been found. However, Muller-Munk's appointment was announced as early as June. See Alice Hughes, "He's a 'Prof' Now," *New York American*, June 29, 1935, 6.

47 Carnegie Institute of Technology, News Service, n.d. (but likely late September 1935), CMU Archives, Dept. of P&D, Box 14: Faculty bios, Folder: PMM. "Get Most from Machine, Keep Its Looks, Teacher of Industrial Design Advises"; News announcement, *The Tartan*, October 1, 1935; "To Carnegie Tech," *Bulletin Index*, October 3, 1935, n.p.; "New Staff Members at Carnegie," *Design* 37, no. 5 (November 1935): n.p., PMMA archives, Scrapbook 1.

48 "In the Local Galleries," *New York Times*, August 18, 1935; *New York American*, August 19, 1935; *New York Mirror*, August 19, 1935; *New York Post*, August 19, 1935. These articles were likely published in response to an earlier press release, made in New York, which erroneously reported that Muller-Munk was hired with the rank of associate professor. See Lillian Eddy, Press Representative, Design Associates, Inc., 1440 Broadway, New York, August 19, 1935; CMU Archives, Dept. of P&D, Box 14: Faculty bios, Folder: PMM.

49 At the time of his hiring, Muller-Munk and Dohner were the only two among the twelve full-time faculty members in the Painting and Design department to teach solely in the industrial design track; *Bulletin of the Carnegie Institute of Technology College of Fine Arts*, series 29, no. 5 (December 1, 1933): 78. Kostellow also referred to himself as "Head" of the program; Alexander Kostellow, "Design and Structure Program of the Pratt Institute Art School," *Design* 41, no. 9 (May 1940): 6.

50 See, for instance, Ray Spilman, letter to the editor, *Industrial Design* 2, no. 4 (August 1955): 10, "Peter Muller-Munk instituted the first bona fide school of Industrial Design in the United States at Carnegie Tech."

51 Because it took two years for the first degree class to matriculate, and because Dohner left after their junior year, Muller-Munk did instruct the first graduating class.

52 Peter Muller-Munk, "Carnegie Tech School Advances Ceramic Design," *Crockery and Glass Journal*, June 1936, 17, PMMA archives, Scrapbook 1. Other documented factory visits included Armstrong Linoleum, Westinghouse, and the Pittsburgh Reflector Company; see Peter Muller-Munk, "Industrial Design," *Design* 38, no. 7 (January 1937): 13.

53 Peter Muller-Munk Associates, promotional literature, 1948, 4, PMMA archives.

54 Compare Robert Lepper, "Apprenticeship for Industrial Design," *Art Instruction*, September 1938, 9–12, and Peter Muller-Munk, "Apprenticeship for Industrial Design," *Art Instruction*, October 1938, 8–11.

55 *See Carnegie Technical* 11, no. 4 (April 4, 1938); "The Streamlined Train," *Carnegie Technical* 11, no. 5 (May 9, 1938): 19–20; "An Industrial Design Thesis," *Design* 40, no. 5 (December 1938): 8. The May 1938 *Technical* records the seven students involved as Ruth Amrhein, Clarissa Benedik, Lorene Fairall, Kathryn S. Herpel, Robert E. Schleihauff, Raymond A. Smith, and Robert S. Zeidman, doing work "under the supervision of Kostellow and Clayter." Yet, Muller-Munk is listed as co-teaching the studio course in which the work occurred, A-563-564, Industrial Design II (see *Bulletin of the Carnegie Institute of Technology College of Fine Arts*, series 32, no. 5 [December 1, 1936]: 77). Smith, who excelled during his tenure at General Motors prior to joining Muller-Munk's firm, likely played a lead role in this project.

56 "3 Cities Seen from the Air," *Pittsburgh Sun Telegraph*, January 8, 1936.

57 Muller-Munk, "Industrial Design," 15. Students involved on the airline display were Maud Bowers, Mary Louise Hankinson, Robert Kelly, Paul Perrin, and Jane Thompson. Bowers went on to work in the display department at Kaufmann's department store in Pittsburgh.

58 Muller-Munk, "Industrial Design," 15.

59 "Forum of Events: Designers Graduate," *Architectural Forum* 65, no. 1 (July 1936): 62. "Maud Bowers Rice A'36," interview by Jim Lesko, n.d., transcript, CMU Archives.

60 Muller-Munk, "Industrial Design," 13.

61 For the Volupté competition, see Muller-Munk, "Industrial Design," 15. See also "New Designing Modernizes Toilet Sets," *Democrat Chronicle* (Rochester, NY), May 7, 1937. The Plaskon competition fielded fifty entries in three categories from thirty students. Judges included two Plaskon representatives; Dr. R. L. Wakeman, a plastics research specialist at Mellon Institute in Pittsburgh; and Muller-Munk and Lepper. A total of $250 went to seven students for designs including hardware (Frank Zavada), an airplane dining tray (Gilbert McMurtrie), a kitchen scale (William Winterbottom), stove hardware (James Winkworth), a watch package (Raymond Cyphers), a radio cabinet (Dolores Niehoff), and cosmetic packages (Louise Cruthers and Marjorie King); see "Student Design," *Modern Plastics* 17, no. 9 (May 1940): 37, 78.

62 *Carnegie Institute of Technology: General Catalogue*, vol. 34 (1940–41): 47. Notation for Muller-Munk's course says "offered in 1941–42."

63 For the gender breakdown of the students, see Carnegie Institute of Technology, commencement programs, CMU Archives. In 1936, at the Conference on Art Occupations in Industry (see note 34), Muller-Munk said, "Sex does not enter into the question of taste. Our classes are evenly divided, equal numbers of men and women. All students are employed on the same projects. On graduation, their work was put out without any names. No one could distinguish the men's work from the women's." Earlier, he had noted that the only fault he found with his women students was "that they lacked confidence," which he blamed on traditional custom; see Mary Thompson, "Want to 'Revolutionize' Your Life?: Girls Studying Industrial Design Can Almost Do Just That!," *Pittsburgh Press*, March 23, 1928. Arthur Pulos, *The American Design Ethic* (Cambridge, MA: MIT Press, 1983), and *The American Design Adventure*.

64 "Get Most from Machine, Keep Its Looks, Teacher of Industrial Design Advises"; and Muller-Munk, "Carnegie Tech School Advances Ceramic Design," 17.

65 "The faculty of the Department of Painting and Design ... were loathe [*sic*] to add just one more class in fancy rendering to those already flourishing in other 'art' schools. If industrial design was to be more than a catchword, then the manufacturer and student were entitled to get more basic understanding ... of the relation of art to machine production than had hitherto prevailed." Muller-Munk, "Design at Carnegie Tech," *Modern Plastics* 13 (April 1936): 21.

66 Muller-Munk quoted in "Five Artists to Graduate from Tech to Paying Jobs," *Pittsburgh Post-Gazette*, June 6, 1936.

67 Muller-Munk quoted in Douglas Naylor, "New Tech Teacher Finds Flaws in Pennell's Work," *Pittsburgh Press*, March 11, 1936, 36.

68 Lepper criticized Muller-Munk for his desire to practice and to hire students; see Lesko, "Industrial Design at Carnegie Institute of Technology," 284. Muller-Munk for his part disapproved of Kostellow's purportedly *unpaid* dependence on his students; see Muller-Munk to Arthur Pulos, July 23, 1963, PMMA archives.

69 Minutes of the meeting of the executive committee of the trustees of Carnegie Tech, September 25, 1944, CMU Archives.

70 "Resignations," *Carnegie Institute of Technology Faculty Bulletin*, series 1945–1946, no. 5 (October 10, 1945): 4.

71 John Peter interview, p. 7.

72 Peter Muller-Munk Associates, promotional literature, 1948, 3, PMMA archives. Muller-Munk to Arthur Pulos, August 13, 1963, PMMA archives.

73 The year 1936 was a significant one in Peter's family. His maternal grandmother, Paula Munk, died July 20, 1936; see Oda Cordes, *Marie Munk und die Stellung der Frau im Recht: Wissenschaftliche Studie über Leben und Werk von Marie Munk in drei Teilen*, 3 vols. (Schwerin, Germany: O. Cordes, 2011), 1:240. Peter's father and stepmother, Franz and Susanne Müller, sold the house at Kastanienallee 39 and moved to Fiesole, Italy. Peter chronicled his and Ilona's extensive summer travels (which included visits with his sister and brother-in-law, Margit and Franz Mombert, at their farm in Fayence, France, and with Franz and Susanne in Italy) in a postcard to Margaret Bourke-White, September 14, 1936, Margaret Bourke-White Papers, Correspondence—Subject Files, Box 31, Peter Muller-Munk, Special Collections Research Center, Syracuse University Libraries. Research by Jewel Stern.

74 The period 1936–48 is poorly documented in the Muller-Munk archives, due to a missing scrapbook, leaving scant records for work produced.

75 See ad for Volupté, *New York Times*, December 22, 1935; for Silvermode: *Esquire* 4, no. 6, December 1935, 109; for Normandie: *Gifts by Revere 1936*, promotional pamphlet, PMMA archives, Scrapbook 1.

76 Platinum Products Co., *Presenting Lektrolites*, brochure (New York: Platinum Products, 1936), Saul Zalesch Collection of American Ephemera, Winterthur Library. The utility patent for the lighter was filed by G. P. Schmitt, December 27, 1935, and granted May 30, 1939, as 2,160,002. "Smart Smokers Don't Use Matches," advertisement no. 21, R3*, PMMA archives, Scrapbook 1. Margaret Bourke-White to Peter Muller-Munk, November 21, 1935, Margaret Bourke-White Papers.

77 Mary Catherine Johnsen, "Rachel McMasters Miller Hunt as a Collector and Patron of the Arts and Crafts," *Journal of William Morris Studies* 15, no. 4 (Summer 2004): 145. Hunt was with the New York Guild of Bookworkers and the Grolier Club.

78 Peter Muller-Munk to Margaret Bourke-White, October 3, 1935, and December 16, 1935, Margaret Bourke-White Papers.

79 "Design—The New Sales Factor," Retail Institute Program, pamphlet, February 25–March 31, 1936. PMMA archives, Scrapbook 1.

80 On Edgar Kaufmann, see Obituary, *New York Times*, August 1, 1989, online at http://www.nytimes.com/1989/08/01/obituaries/edgar-kaufmann-jr-79-architecture-historian.html.

81 Muller-Munk, "Design at Carnegie Tech," 52.

82 Muller-Munk, "Carnegie Tech School Advances Ceramic Design," 17.

83 I thank my coauthor Jewel Stern for her research and description of Muller-Munk's silver career and exhibitions in this paragraph and the next.

84 Peter Muller-Munk to Louise W. Chase, Brooklyn Museum, January 11, 1938, The Brooklyn Museum Archives, *Contemporary Industrial and Handwrought Silver 1937*, Registrar's Files, Department of Decorative Arts. Mr. and Mrs. Ed Friedlander of New York City were the lenders of the hors d'oeuvres dishes. The museum published a catalogue, *Contemporary Industrial and Handwrought Silver, November 20, 1937–January 23, 1938*. According to a letter from Walter B. Snow, Poole Silver Company, to Louise W. Chase, Brooklyn Museum, October 26, 1937, also in the Brooklyn Museum Archives, the museum requested examples of Muller-Munk's Silvermode from the Poole Silver Company, but no pieces were available.

85 "Peter Muller Munk: (Coupe argent massif)," Group IX, Métiers d'Art, Classe 44, Orfèvrerie, in *"Liste des exposants États-Unis," Vol. 1, Exposition Internationale des Arts et des Techniques dans la Vie Moderne, Paris 1937, Catalogue Général Officiel* (Paris: R. Stenger, 1937), 678. Other noted silversmiths representing the United States—all, including Muller-Munk, selected by the Society of Designer Craftsmen—were Porter Blanchard, Arthur Nevill Kirk, Katherine Pratt, and James T. Wooley.

86 Walter Rendell Storey, "Old and New in the Silver Craft of Today: An Exhibition at the Metropolitan Museum Shows Both Craftsmen and Machine Technique," *New York Times*, April 18, 1937, 138.

87 Helen Johnson Keyes, "Contemporary American Silver," *Christian Science Monitor, Boston*, May 1, 1937, sec. 5, 6. For an image of the meat platter in its display case, "For This Day and Age," *Jewelers' Circular-Keystone* 107 (May 1937): 106.

88 Dorothy Kanter, "Crafts Prizes Awarded for First Time," *Pittsburgh Post-Gazette*, February 5, 1937; and Edmund Ashe, "Pittsburgh's Best," *Carnegie Magazine* 10 (February 1937): 279–80. The Grogan Company was a local silver firm.

89 The judges admired his composition and balancing of elements: "The straight lines of Mr. Müller-Munk's tea service are finely handled both in the relationship of the pieces as a group and in the simply chased design, while the practical curved bone handles set them off with modern distinction." Walter Read Hovey, "The Pittsburgh Show," *Carnegie Magazine* 11 (February 1938): 276. The $50 prize for crafts given by Mrs. Roy Arthur Hunt was divided between Muller-Munk and Wesley A. Mills.

90 *Decorative Arts: Official Catalog, Department of Fine Arts, Division of Decorative Arts, Golden Gate International Exposition, San Francisco 1939* (San Francisco: San Francisco Bay Exposition Company, 1939), 83.

91 *An Exhibition of Silver: French, British, American, Modern* (Richmond: Virginia Museum of Fine Arts, 1940), 46.

92 Peter Müller-Munk to Harry Binsse, Liturgical Arts Society, March 7, 1938, and Harry Binsse, to Peter Müller-Munk, March 21, 1938, CLIT 11/42 Folder: Mueller-Munk, Peter, 1933–1938, Liturgical Arts Society Records (LIT), University of Notre Dame Archives (UNDA), Notre Dame, IN 46556.

93 No list of his exhibited work is in the archives of Cooper Union. Muller-Munk was mentioned as one of the contributors to the exhibition in "Child Nurses with Bells On," *New York Sun*, February 20, 1941.

94 Peter Muller-Munk to Margaret Bourke-White, March. 18, 1937, Margaret Bourke-White Papers.

95 Ilona and Peter returned from Europe, September 28, 1937, aboard the SS *Berengaria*, sailing from Cherbourg. Passenger Lists of Vessels Arriving at New York, New York, 1820–1957, SS *Berengaria*, September 28, 1937, Ancestry.com.

96 Muller-Munk compensated Proellochs for five days' work with the option to continue the following week, and offered him a bonus if the shaver design were successfully sold to a manufacturer; Peter Muller-Munk to Arnold L'Heureux Proellochs, February 21, 1938, PMMA archives.

97 Peter Muller-Munk Associates, promotional literature, November 1955, 2, PMMA archives.

98 Rowena Reed Kostellow patented numerous glassware designs for the US Glass Company during this period and may have provided the link for the young student, who would have studied with her husband as well as with Muller-Munk. In April 1944 Carnegie Tech granted Karlen's Industrial Design degree on the basis of his professional accomplishments. James P. Karlen, conversation with the author, April 14, 2014. Carnegie Institute of Technology, College of Fine Arts, Commencement Program, April 30, 1944, CMU Archives.

99 Peter Muller-Munk Associates, promotional literature, 1948, 5, PMMA archives.

100 Paul Karlen wed Emily Madjaric in January 1938, per James P. Karlen (son), conversation with the author, April 14, 2014. See also Cindi Lash, News Obituary, "Robert Paul Karlen: Industrial Design Pioneer and Artist," *Pittsburgh Post Gazette*, January 8, 2000, C3.

101 Precise dates for Muller-Munk's informal early office moves are unavailable because he continued to use his university address for all business correspondence. The move to the home office occurred no earlier than April 1938, when the Muller-Munks moved to Darlington Road. *Carnegie Institute of Technology Faculty Bulletin*, series 1937–1938, no. 21 (April 27, 1938).

102 Carnegie Institute of Technology, General Faculty Meeting minutes, March 22, 1938, CMU Archives. *Carnegie Institute of Technology Faculty Bulletin*, series 1939–40, no. 32 (May 22, 1940).

103 US Patent 1,990,645, filed March 10, 1933, granted February 12, 1935.

104 Dorothy Grafly, "Peter Muller-Munk: Industrial Designer," *Design* 47, no. 9 (May 1946): 9. For an image of a Swank with a June 1958 manufacturing stamp: http://www.collectorsweekly.com/stories/110099-pennwoodtymeter-model-500-swank-june.

105 Peter Müller Munk, "Vending Machine Glamour," *Modern Plastics* 17, no. 6 (February 1940): 26–27, 66.

106 "Show in Review," *Automatic Age*, January 1939, 42.

107 Kenneth W. Berger, *The Hearing Aid: Its Operation and Development*, Part 2: *Hearing Aid Industry Directory*, 3rd ed. (Livonia, MI: National Hearing Aid Society, 1984), 275.

108 E. A. Myers, *The Dawn of a New Day for Better Hearing*, brochure for the Radioear 45 (Mount Lebanon, PA: E. A. Myers & Sons, 1942), 11, The Kenneth Berger Hearing Aid Museum and Archives, Kent State University.

109 "Art Bows to City on Financing Plan: Committee Meets Spectre of Economy at City Hall and Abandons Plea for $60,000," *New York Times*, February 3, 1939, 3.

110 Muller-Munk stayed with Mr. and Mrs. Will Yolen on his visit to New York. Yolen, a press agent for the amusement area of the fair, could have provided a connection. See Will Yolen, Obituary, *New York Times*, November 11, 1985, online at http://www.nytimes.com/1985/11/22/nyregion/will-yolen-former-executive-and-kite-enthusiast-is-dead.html. Also L. L. Stevenson, "Light of New York," *Evening Recorder* (Amsterdam, NY), January 28, 1939, 4; "Streamlined Mail Boxes Next?," *Daily Sentinel* (Rome, NY), February 25, 1939, 6; "New Model Streamlined and Called Safer: Mailbox Changes Urged," *Knickerbocker News*, February 17, 1939, 12B; "And How About Putting Murals on Manholes," *New York Post*, December 23, 1938; and "'I'll Show New York City How,' Says Design Teacher at Tech: Prof. Muller-Munk Gives Modern Note to Gadgets," *Pittsburgh Sun Telegraph*, January 6, 1939.

111 "And How About Putting Murals on Manholes."

112 I thank my coauthor Jewel Stern for her research and description of the family's situation during the war years. Data from a document provided by Lucia Nadetti, Archivio Comunale di Fiesole, to Richard Brook, March 28, 2014. The Müllers arrived from Berlin on April 30, 1936, and lived in a villa at Salviatino 14. Our thanks to Richard Brook for a copy of this document.

113 Franz and Susanne Müller left Fiesole on September 16, 1938. Data from a document provided by Lucia Nadetti, Archivio Comunale di Fiesole, to Richard Brook, March 28, 2014.

114 Marie Munk arrived in New York on September 2, 1938; see Passenger Lists of Vessels Arriving at New York, New York, 1820–1957, SS *Deutschland*, September 2, 1938, Ancestry.com. Gertrud Müller arrived on February 23, 1939, on the SS *Queen Mary* from Southampton, England; see Gertrud Muller Munk, Declaration of Intention, State of New York, Southern District of New York, US Department of Labor Immigration and Naturalization Service, No. 443866, October 11, 1939.

115 Franz Müller died in Fayence on October 1, 1945; see Frantz [*sic*] Muller, Death Certificate No. 22, 1945, Mairie de Fayence, Arrondissement de Draguignan, France. Susanne Müller and Ernst Mombert were arrested in 1942 by French police. They would not reveal where the other family members were hiding. They were first sent to the internment camp at Drancy outside of Paris and then deported to Auschwitz, where they died; see Stolpersteine for Susanne Müller at Kastanienallee 39, Berlin; and Stolpersteine for Ernst Mombert, Giessen, Germany. Courtesy of Richard Brook.

116 As described in a letter from Ilona Muller-Munk to Margaret Bourke-White, May 20, 1939, Margaret Bourke-White Papers.

117 "Post-War Design for Industry," *Bulletin Index*, July 9, 1943, 10–11.

118 "Voluntary Course in Camouflage," *Carnegie Alumnus* 27, no. 4 (June 1942): 4. See also "Art: New Arrival," *Bulletin Index*, January 1, 1942, 6.

119 John Peter interview, 7; Peter Muller-Munk Associates, promotional literature, 1948, 4, PMMA archives. The address on Murray Avenue has not been identified, as it was not listed in city directories. See note 101.

120 "Post-War Design for Industry," 10.

121 Allegheny Ludlum Company History, http://www.fundinguniverse.com/company-histories/allegheny-ludlum-corporation-history/. Source cited as *International Directory of Company Histories*, vol. 8 (St. James Press, 1994).

122 "Over the Horizon," *Steel Horizons* 3, no. 4 (1941), n.p.; "Passenger Travel Center of the Future," *Popular Mechanics*, July 1942, 78–79; "Milkshake Bar Designed for the Future by Peter Muller-Munk," *Steel Horizons* 3, no. 3 (1941): 6–7. Victory Cabin published in "Postwar Design of the Month," *Architectural Forum* 81, no. 6 (December 1944): 6.

123 M. G. van Voorhis, M. K. Mellot & Co., Public Relations, to Dorothy Grafly, Philadelphia Art Alliance, March 13, 1946. Annenberg Rare Book & Manuscript Library, University of Pennsylvania, Art Alliance files. Muller-Munk's client list includes National Dairy, suggesting that he may have been engaged in the redesign of the Milk-O-Mat for production. There is no evidence for his direct involvement with Arnot.

124 In October 1945 Stanley F. Reed submitted a utility patent for a folding "Bed or Berth Structure" for Arnot & Co., which may well be the product referenced by Van Voorhies. See US Patent 2,550,599, filed October 22, 1945, granted April 24, 1951.

125 "Post-War Design for Industry," 11; Paul Karlen, "History of Peter Muller-Munk Associates," audio recording, March 15, 1969, Raymond Spilman Papers, Special Collections Research Center, Syracuse University Libraries, Box 92, Item 120.

126 J. Gordon Lippincott, "The Coming Battle of Materials: Magnesium," *Interiors*, December 1944, n.p. The chaise is explicitly credited to Dow. The typewriter was not attributed to any manufacturer, and may or may not be for Dow.

127 "Kitchen Prototype—Designed for Plastics," *Modern Plastics* 22, no. 10 (June 1945): 97.

128 Ibid.; "Designs for Light and Lightness," *Modern Plastics* 23, no. 1 (September 1945): 119–21; "Designs by Peter Muller-Munk for the Dow Chemical Co.," in *Plastics Catalog: The 1945 Encyclopedia of Plastics* (New York: Plastics Catalog Corporation, 1945), 36–37.

129 H. S. Spencer, Advertising Manager, Durez Plastics & Chemicals, Inc., "Practical Product Predictions," *The Red Barrel* 24, no. 2 (February 1944): 14–17. This was a monthly publication of the Coca-Cola Company.

130 Durez advertisement, *Fortune*, July 1943. Spencer, "Practical Product Predictions," 17.

131 Minutes, Directors (Fellows) Meeting of the SID, Inc., March 12, 1945, Industrial Designers Society of America (IDSA) Records, Special Collections Research Center, Syracuse University Libraries, Board of Directors, Minutes of Meetings, 1944–1945, p. 2. Muller-Munk was admitted with four others, including designer Dave Chapman of Chicago, and fellow "academic" Antonin Heythum, director of the Industrial Design Section, California Institute of Technology.

132 SID, meeting minutes, July 11, 1944, IDSA Records.

133 SID, meeting minutes, October 11, 1944, IDSA Records. The original fifteen SID Fellows were Egmont Arens, Norman Bel Geddes, Donald Deskey, Henry Dreyfuss, Lurelle Guild, Raymond Loewy, Raymond Patten, Joseph Platt, John Gordon Rideout, George Sakier, Joseph Sinel, Brooks Stevens, Walter Dorwin Teague, Harold Van Doren, and Russel Wright.

134 "The Clark Building: More Than Half a Century Downtown," *Market Square*, February 29, 1984, 7. The building address is 717 Liberty Avenue.

135 Peter Muller-Munk to Henry Allman, Philadelphia Art Alliance, May 4, 1945, PAA Ms. Coll. 53 F.3369, Annenberg Rare Book & Manuscript Library, University of Pennsylvania. It is unclear when Karlen was first awarded the designation of associate. It may have been earlier than 1945 (the *Bulletin Index* article in July 1943 certainly references him as a partner), but no formal documentation survives. Correspondence between the same parties on March 19, 1945, is on letterhead still featuring the Carnegie Tech address.

136 Costa: *Carnegie Alumnus* 31, no. 1 (September 1945): 13. Nettleton: *Carnegie Alumnus* 30, no. 3 (March 1945): 24. Sink: "Takes Research Post," *Pittsburgh Press*, July 12, 1946, 15; *Carnegie Alumnus* 33, no. 4 (June 1948): 14. Waichler: (later ran her own design firm under her married name Pasinski); PMMA archives. Ward: PMMA archives.

137 They settled on a slot from March 4–April 5, 1946. Peter Muller-Munk to Henry Allman, March 19, 1945; Allman to Muller-Munk, May 2, 1945; and Muller-Munk to Allman, May 4, 1945, PAA Ms. Coll. 53 F.3369.

138 Allman to Muller-Munk, March 20, 1946, PAA Ms. Coll. 53 F.3369. My thanks to Jewel Stern for research on the Art Alliance exhibition.

139 Document titled "Industrial Design by Peter Muller-Munk" included in correspondence is an apparent checklist for the exhibition. PAA Ms. Coll. 53 F.3369.

140 Grafly, "Peter Muller-Munk: Industrial Designer," 8–9.

141 According to his son, Karlen was drafted in March 1945 and shipped out in September of that year; James P. Karlen, conversation with the author, April 14, 2014.

142 Like Karlen, Smith was a standout. In fact, the two won the same student recognition award at Carnegie Tech in back-to-back years (1935 and 1936). Smith was a national scholarship winner of the famed Fisher Body Craftsman's Guild competition. Biography for Lando, Peter Muller-Munk Associates promotional literature, January 1966, PMMA archives.

143 Paul R. Wiedmann, conversation with the author, November 1, 2013; Eric Smith, conversation with the author, May 22, 2014; and James P. Karlen, conversation with the author, April 14, 2014.

144 Peter Muller-Munk to Raymond Smith, Graphics Section, Sch. Facilities Department, AAF School, Orlando, Florida, August 13, 1945; and Raymond Smith to Peter Muller-Munk, September 5, 1945, PMMA archives.

145 Eric Smith, conversation with the author, May 22, 2014.

146 Raymond Augusta Smith, Military Record and Report of Separation, Certificate of Service, February 16, 1946. Courtesy of Eric Smith.

147 The precise date for forming PMMA is not documented. Later PMMA literature often cited it as 1944 or 1945. New letterhead for the Clark Building in spring 1945 reflected Karlen's status as the first associate, but retained the business name "Peter Muller-Munk, Product Design" (see Peter Muller-Munk to Phillip McConnell, June 7, 1945, IDSA Records, Box 43, folder Peter Muller-Munk). The firm was not listed in the Pittsburgh city directory as Peter Muller-Munk Associates until 1947, at which point the letterhead also changed to reflect that title (agreement, Peter Muller-Munk Associates and Raymond Smith, February 1947, PMMA archives).

148 Peter Muller-Munk, "Design for a Percolator or the like," patent filed October 30, 1946, and issued May 4, 1948, D 149,513.

149 "Design Story," *Durez Plastics News*, February 1947, 4.

150 Dorothy Grafly, "Industrial Design," *Design* 48, no. 5 (January 1947): 23.

151 Because examples of the Cafex percolator are exceedingly rare today, a production of 50,000 appears to have been an exaggeration.

152 Peter Muller-Munk to Edgar Kaufmann Jr., October 18, 1946, and Eloise Jane Nettleton to Edgar Kaufmann Jr., November 1, 1946, Museum of Modern Art Archives, *Useful Objects*, 1946 [MoMA Exh. # 336, November 26, 1946–January 26, 1947]. My thanks to Jewel Stern for research on Cafex.

153 See notes 88 and 89.

154 Interview with Elizabeth Rockwell Raphael, conducted by Florence Rosner, December 8, 1984, http://www.contemporarycraft.org/SCC/ERR_Interview.html.

155 Jeannette Jena, "Art Center Has First Show: 'Outlines' Gallery in Boulevard Opens," *Pittsburgh Post-Gazette*, October 13, 1941.

156 *Industrial Design—A New Approach*, exhibition brochure, and "Art: New Arrival," *Bulletin Index*, January 1, 1942, 6. Outlines Gallery scrapbooks, Courtesy of the family of Elizabeth Rockwell Raphael.

157 "Painter to Speak at Gallery of Modern Art," *Jewish Criterion*, January 25, 1942.

158 "Board of Directors, 1943," Outlines Gallery program, 1942–43; "The Modern Movement as Applied to Retailing," flier for a ten-week lecture series, beginning April 8, 1947. Outlines Gallery scrapbooks.

159 Edgar Kaufmann is not designated as either Jr. or Sr., but it is almost certain that Sr. was the board member in question, as his son was in New York City during these years. Outlines Gallery scrapbooks.

160 There is no confirmation of which industrial design object Muller-Munk submitted to the annual. Given the date, however, and the success of the Cafex at MoMA, it is by far the most logical candidate. He is also pictured with it in the article about his withdrawal from AAP. "City's Art Circles Under Fire for 'Ivory Tower' Attitude," *Pittsburgh Press*, March 2, 1947.

161 Ibid.

162 Peter Muller-Munk to Assistant Curator Greta Daniel, Museum of Modern Art, March 27, 1947. Museum of Modern Art Archives, *Useful Objects*, 1946 [MoMA Exh. # 336, November 26, 1946–January 26, 1947]. See also MoMA cataloguing sheet, which describes the object as a gift from Muller-Munk and records the date of acquisition as March 17, 1947. MoMA curatorial files.

The Waring Blendor

1 Howard McLellan, "Sales Strategy That Built a New Business," *American Business* 10 (April 1940): 21.

2 Letter of Agreement, F. J. Osius to Fred Waring, October 27, 1936, Waring Corporation Financial and Legal Files 1930s/1940s, Box 9B03.83, Folio: Fred Waring, The Waring Corporation, Fred Waring Papers, 1922–1984, PSUA 336, Pennsylvania State University. Osius and investor George L. Hollahan had formed the Hollius Company that owned the rights to design patent 88,888. Hollahan later sold his half interest to Waring's corporation and relinquished his twenty shares in Waring's Miracle Mixer Corporation for $11,000. See Letter of Agreement, George L. Hollahan to Ed Lee, June 23, 1937, Waring Corporation Financial and Legal Files 1930s/1940s, Box 9B03.83, Folio: Fred Waring, Fred Waring Papers. Edward J. Lee, vice president, represented Waring in the negotiation with Hollahan; see Ed Lee to Fred Waring, June 24, 1937, Waring Corporation Financial and Legal Files 1930s/1940s, Box 9B03.83, Folio: Fred Waring, Fred Waring Papers. My thanks to Rachel Delphia and Catherine Walworth for their research through the Fred Waring Papers.

3 "A History of the Waring Blendor" attached to letter, Edward J. Lee to Earl Lifshey, July 15, 1970, p. 1, courtesy of Victoria Matranga.

4 Ibid.

5 Quoted in Marilyn Ferguson, "Peter Muller-Munk, 'Industrial Designer,'" *Pittsburgh Sun-Telegraph*, October 27, 1958, sec. 4, 5.

6 F. H. B, "WARING MIXER MOD - B," Blueprint, Air-Way Electric Appliance Corporation, February 15, 1938, Full Scale, Part No. M-100, Waring Corporation Financial and Legal Files 1930s/1940s, Box 9B03.83, Folio: Air-Way, Fred Waring Papers.

7 "7,000 at Restaurant Show," *New York Times*, October 6, 1937, 45; and "A History of the Waring Blendor," Lee to Lifshey, July 15, 1970, p. 2. Initial Waring records show that 981 units were sold in January 1938, Herman Zucker to Waring Mixer Corporation, November 21, 1938, Waring Corporation Financial and Legal Files 1930s/1940s, Box 9B03.83, Folio: Herman Zucker, Certified Public Accountant, Fred Waring Papers.

8 Ed Lee to Air-Way Electric Appliance Corporation, March 1, 1938, Waring Corporation Financial and Legal Files 1930s/1940s, Box 9B03.83, Folio: Air-Way, Fred Waring Papers.

9 A special lid with a fan-shaped finial emblazoned with the words "Ronrico West Indies" was produced for publicity and demonstrations. Ronrico Corporation agreement, February 15, 1938, Waring Corporation Financial and Legal Files 1930s/1940s, Box 9B03.83, Folio: Contracts, Fred Waring Papers; and agreement with Air-Way, March 1, 1938, Box 9B03.83, Folio: Air-Way, Fred Waring Papers.

10 "A History of the Waring Blendor," Lee to Lifshey, July 15, 1970, p. 2.

11 Claire Winslow, "New Type Mixer Reduces Solid to Liquid Form," *Chicago Tribune*, June 26, 1938, sec. 6, 2.

12 "Of course the Hit of the Year Is the Gift of the Season," Waring Mixer Corporation advertisement, *Esquire*, December 1938, 215. The ad lists fifteen stores in fifteen cities selling the mixer. Curiously, in publicity the mixer was almost always illustrated without its lid.

13 Ed Lee to Fred Waring, April 11, 1939, Waring Corporation Financial and Legal Files 1930s/1940s, Box 9B03.83, Folio: Fred Waring, Fred Waring Papers.

14 From surviving examples, it appears that the identifying stamp "Model B" on the underside of the base was continued in the production of the newly named DeLuxe Model.

15 "'I'll Show New York City How,' Says Design Teacher at Tech," *Pittsburgh Sun-Telegraph*, January 6, 1939.

16 "Waring Mixer, Peter Muller-Munk, Designer," *Architectural Forum*, Design Decade special issue 73 (October 1940): 246–47. See also "The Twelfth Brief Case History of a Modern Industrial Designer, Peter Müller-Munk," *Durez Plastic News* 4 (June 1939): 6.

17 The DeLuxe model was still on sale in 1941, when Waring introduced the Model FC1. Because surviving records from 1942 through the sale of the company by Waring in 1944 and the end of World War II in 1945 are incomplete, the year the DeLuxe model was discontinued is uncertain, but it was most likely shortly after the war. See The Waring Corporation Comparative Analysis of Sales in Dollar Values and Quantities for the Years 1939, 1940, and 1941, in Waring Corporation Financial and Legal Files 1930s/1940s, Box 9B03.83, Folio: Herman Zucker, Certified Public Accountant, Fred Waring Papers.

The Postwar "Do-It-Yourself" Movement

1 Steven M. Gelber, "Do-It-Yourself: Constructing, Repairing and Maintaining Domestic Masculinity," *American Quarterly* 49, no. 1 (March 1997): 95.

2 "Do-It-Yourself: The New Billion-Dollar Hobby," *Time*, August 2, 1954, 66.

3 "Do-It and You," *Industrial Design* 1, no. 4 (August 1954): 91.

4 US Bureau of the Census, Historical Statistics of the United States; cited in Gelber, "Do-It-Yourself," 96.

5 William Astor and Charlotte Astor, "Private Associations and Commercial Activities," *Annals of American Academy of Political and Social Science* 313 (September 1957): 96; cited in Gelber, "Do-It-Yourself," 97.

6 "Do-It and You," 87.

7 Exhibition description, *Do-It-Yourself: Home Improvement in 20th-Century America*, National Building Museum, Washington, DC, October 19, 2002–August 17, 2003, http://www.nbm.org/exhibitions-collections/exhibitions/diy.html.

8 "Power Tools: The Newest Home Appliance," *Industrial Design* 1, no. 1 (February 1954): 30–37.

9 For a discussion of the benefits of die casting to PMMA's work for Porter-Cable, see Paul Karlen, "Portable Tools Need Precision in Appearance as Well as in Dimension," *Precision Molding*, February 1954, 47–48. Porter-Cable went from sand casting to die casting (a process with much tighter tolerances). This allowed them to strategically slim cross sections, which resulted in much of the lost weight. The previous version was also aluminum. For a detailed description of the working relationship between PMMA and Porter-Cable's engineers and PMMA's specific design modifications, see "Design of a Portable Saw," *Die Castings*, December 1949, 55.

10 "Design of a Portable Saw," 32–34, 55–56.

11 "Power Tools: The Newest Home Appliance," 36.

12 For Kearney & Trecker, see *Industrial Design* 7, no. 11 (November 1960): 87–89.

13 Staff Report, "Power Positioning and Control for Machine Flexibility and Safety," 101–3. Ergonomics developed during World War II as a study concerned with fitting humans to their surroundings, equipment, and tools, thereby increasing safety and decreasing physical fatigue. This field of study moved into the larger sphere of consumer product design and was famously championed in the 1950s by Henry Dreyfuss, who published his studies in *Designing for People* (1955) and *The Measure of Man* (1960).

14 "Fitting the Machine to the Man: 'Human Engineering' Spurs Productivity," *Dun's Review and Modern Industry* 76, no. 1 (July 1963): 56–57.

PMMA: Product Design

1 Peter Muller-Munk, "Industrial Designers Are Shaping Your Life," *Post-Gazette Tri-State Magazine*, April 24, 1949.

2 Peter Muller-Munk Associates, promotional literature, 1950, PMMA archives.

3 Peter Muller-Munk Associates, promotional literature, November 1955, PMMA archives.

4 Anton G. Parisson, professional résumé, Collection of Joann Parisson Gaus; Peter Muller-Munk Associates, promotional literature, November 1955, PMMA archives. Muller-Munk, Karlen, Smith, and Parisson constituted the senior leadership of the firm well into the 1960s. Parisson was made associate in 1952 and remained a notch above near peers such as Ernst Budke, as evidenced by the fact that only Muller-Munk, Karlen, Smith, and Parisson had bios in company promotional literature during Muller-Munk's lifetime.

5 Peter Muller-Munk, "News for S.I.D. Newsletter," July 16, 1953, Industrial Designers Society of America (IDSA) Records, Special Collections Research Center, Syracuse University Libraries, Box 43, Folder: Muller-Munk. "Peter Muller-Munk Admits New Partner," *Pittsburgh Press*, June 21, 1957.

6 Italian Line News, "M/V Giulio Cesare Arrives Thursday, November 14," press release, November 12, 1957, PMMA archives, Scrapbook 2.

7 It is worth noting that in this period Muller-Munk began to recruit designers from farther afield. Hires in the 1950s were graduates of the Rhode Island School of Design (where Muller-Munk's mentor Raemisch had joined the faculty), the University of Illinois, and Pratt Institute. Although he hired from Carnegie Tech as well, the breadth of his search reflects his commitment to bringing on the best talent rather than showing partiality to the school where he had taught.

8 The 1966 partners were Anderson, Behnk, Budke, Monigle, and Protas; *Pittsburgh Press*, January 6, 1966.

9 Leonard Levitan, e-mail message to Catherine Walworth, May 24, 2015.

10 A letter from Muller-Munk to Russel Wright, May 13, 1952, is on Clark Building letterhead on which that address is crossed out and relabeled "725 Liberty Avenue." IDSA Records, Box 43, Folder: Muller-Munk.

11 Dreck Spurlock Wilson, ed., *African American Architects* (New York: Routledge, 2004), 347–49.

12 For details on staffing and office arrangements, see Peter Muller-Munk Associates, promotional literature, November 1955 and September 1958, PMMA archives.

13 "New Products: Industrial Designers Turn Out Innovations to Pep Up Clients' Sales," *Wall Street Journal*, April 20, 1954.

14 Peter Muller-Munk Associates, promotional literature, 1958, 3, PMMA archives.

15 Peter Muller-Munk Associates, "Product Design," 1, PMMA archives.

16 Peter Muller-Munk Associates, promotional literature, 1948, 1, PMMA archives.

17 "John Peter interviews P. Muller-Munk," sound recording, 1957, Library of Congress, transcription in exhibition files, Carnegie Museum of Art, p. 9.

18 Ibid.

19 Ibid., 3.

20 Peter Muller-Munk Associates, promotional literature, 1952, 1, PMMA archives.

21 Peter Muller-Munk Associates, promotional literature, 1955 draft, 7, PMMA archives.

22 Peter Muller-Munk Associates, promotional literature, 1952 and 1955, PMMA archives.

23 Roy Kohler, "Streamliner by Design," *Pittsburgh Press, Pittsburgh Family Magazine*, March 29, 1953.

24 Kwik-Cup advertisement by Hartford Products, *Good Housekeeping*, December 1947, 253.

25 Appeared in *Pittsburgh Post-Gazette* on April 24, 1949.

26 The publication of the coffee mill in SID's compilation of members' designs for 1949–50 suggests that Silex put Muller-Munk's coffee mill design into production; no extant examples have been located to date. PMMA worked on several iterations of the vacuum coffeemaker. The Constellation carafe also served as the lower half of Silex's vacuum brewing device.

27 For the relationship with Corning, see Society of Industrial Designers, *U.S. Industrial Design: 1949–1950* (New York: Studio Publications, 1950). Monsanto and Durez published competing claims that their black phenolic plastics were utilized in the Silex line, particularly in the carafe handles; see Monsanto Chemicals/Plastics advertisement, reprinted from the *Saturday Evening Post*, August 27, 1949, and "Redesigned Appliances," *Durez Plastics News*, July 1949, 6.

28 Advertisement clipping, *House and Garden*, July 1949, n.p. Clipping, *Durez Molder*, October 1949, n.p. Both in PMMA archives, Scrapbook 2.

29 "Getting Your Grip on Your Products," *Modern Industry* 30, no. 3 (September 15, 1950): n.p.

30 Lodge & Shipley: "Equipment," *Industrial Design* 3, no. 6 (December 1956): 118. Kearney & Trecker: "Case Study II: Milling Machines Share Parts to Cut Costs, Heighten Family Identity," *Industrial Design* 7, no. 12 (December 1960): 87–89. DeWalt: *Industrial Design* 4, no. 11 (November 1957): 113–14; *Industrial Design* 4, no. 12 (December 1957): 107; "Fitting the Machine to the Man: 'Human Engineering' Spurs Productivity," *Dun's Review and Modern Industry* 76, no. 1 (July 1960): 57.

31 "Post-War Design for Industry," *Bulletin Index*, July 9, 1943, 11.

32 Elizabeth J. Beggs, Secretary to Muller-Munk, to Reino Aarnio, Chairman, SID Exhibit Committee, March 28, 1951. IDSA Records, Folder: Nona Triennale di Milan, Friedman, William, 1959. This touring exhibition featured numerous PMMA products, including counters for Veeder-Root and Val Saint Lambert candleholders, among other designs.

33 "Radioear 830 and Design Honored," *Radioear Voice*, no. 130 (November 1954): 8.

34 "The World of Sound in a Matchbox," *Steel Horizons* 18, no. 4 (Fourth Quarter 1956): 14. "Beauty Calls on Deafness: Aspirin-sized Battery Aid Is Pill Madame Ordered," *Pittsburgh Press*, April 1956, PMMA archives, Scrapbook 2.

35 See Sylvania advertisements in *Retailing Daily*, May 3, 1950; *Retailing*, April 1950; and *Plastics World*, September 1950. All in PMMA archives, Scrapbook 2.

36 Schick, advertisement for Lady Schick, *Life*, December 16, 1957.

37 Schick, advertisement for Schick Varsity, *Life*, May 6, 1957. See also Lando Advertising Agency, News Release, "'Peach Fuzz' Crowd Gets Its Own Electric Shaver," n.d., PMMA archives, Lando Binder 1.

38 Schick, advertisement for Schick Powershave, *Life*, October 7, 1957. See also Lando Advertising Agency, News Release, "Introduction of Schick 'Powershave' Climaxes Complete Revision of Line," October 7, 1957, PMMA archives, Lando Binder 1.

39 Schick, advertisement for Lady Schick, *Life*, December 15, 1958. See also Lando Advertising Agency, News Release on Lady Schick (no title), n.d. (but probably late 1958), PMMA archives, Lando Binder 2.

40 Malcolm Townsley and Peter Muller-Munk, "Two Views of Design Progress at Bell & Howell," *Industrial Design* 1, no. 4 (April 1954): 38.

41 Ibid., 38–43. An identical version, but with a more durable aluminum housing, was introduced in 1954 and sold as Model 500. "Why Bell & Howell Uses Butyrate," *Modern Plastics* 30, no. 5 (January 1953): 75–77.

42 Townsley and Muller-Munk, "Two Views of Design Progress at Bell & Howell," 42.

43 Ibid., 41.

44 "The 100 'Best Designed Products,'" *Fortune*, April 1959, 135–41.

45 Alcoa Industrial Design Award, "The Designer Meets the Challenge," *Fortune*, November 1959.

46 "Photographic Equipment: The Famous Super Graphic Emerges Simple, Handsome from a Major Redesign," *Industrial Design* 6, no. 1 (January 1959): 48.

47 Alcoa, advertisement, *Fortune*, November 1959. William E. Inman Sr., "The Graflex 4x5 Super Graphic and Super Speed Graphic," and Ken Metcalf, "Comments on the Super and Super Speed Graphic," *Graflex Historic Quarterly* 14, no. 4 (1999): 1–3.

48 Ken Metcalf, "The Graflex-Made Strobomite, 1957–1962," *Graflex Historic Quarterly* 16, no. 3 (2011): 4. The Strobomite was explicitly marketed (and priced) as an amateur flash, and thus failed with the professionals, who seem to have remained Graflex's primary market.

49 "Photographic Equipment: The Famous Super Graphic Emerges Simple, Handsome from a Major Redesign," 48–49.

50 "Post-War Design for Industry," 10.

51 Peter Muller-Munk, quoted in "Prefabricated Kitchen Units Possible," *Retailing Daily*, January 24, 1956.

52 See trade catalogues: *Série Tricorne* (Seraing: Val Saint Lambert, 1956); *Illustrated Price List Effective July 1, 1956* (Pelham Manor, NY: Vogue Ceramic Industries, 1956); *Val Saint Lambert Fine Belgian Crystal, Illustrated Price List Effective Sept. 15, 1957* (New York: USA Agency and Vogue Ceramics Industries, 1957). See also "'Follow the Fashion' Trend Noted at Glass Exhibit," *Pittsburgh Press*, January 10, 1956, 12; "Belgian Crystal," *Washington Post and Times Herald*, January 29, 1956, F2.

53 "Prefabricated Kitchen Units Possible."

54 Peter Muller-Munk to Raymond Loewy, November 11, 1946, IDSA Records, Box 43, Folder: Muller-Munk.

55 Prior to 1948 the handful of industrial designers in this region were lumped into either the Great Lakes or the Mid-Atlantic chapters. See IDSA Records, SID Present Membership by Regions, October 28, 1947. Early members included Wilbur Henry Adams (Erie, PA), Francis Braun (Cincinnati, OH), Theodore Clement of Eastman Kodak (Rochester, NY), Paul Koons of National Cash Register (Dayton, OH), Onnie Mankii and Viktor Schreckengost (Cleveland, OH), Sam Scherr and Eugene Smith (Akron, OH), E. Russell Swann of the Hoover Company (North Canton, OH), Read Viemeister (Yellow Springs, OH), Robert B. Wemyss (Louisville, KY), and Arthur BecVar et al. of General Electric (also in Louisville). IDSA Records, various documents, 1948–1952, Folder: Chapters.

56 Copies of the newsletter are archived in the IDSA Records.

57 Peter Muller-Munk to Philip J. McConnell, executive secretary of SID, September 7, 1951. IDSA Records, Box 43, Folder: Muller-Munk.

58 Harvard Business School lecture: Peter Muller-Munk to McConnell, March 24, 1952; IDSA Records, Box 43, Folder: Muller-Munk. Contracts: Peter Muller-Munk to J. McLeod Little, William Purcell, Karl Tietjen, and William Winterbottom, February 27, 1952, IDSA Records, Box 43, Folder: Muller-Munk. Ilona's assistance: Robert Hose, acknowledgments over dinner at IDSA National Conference, "10/8/55 2nd Half Fri. PM Hose/Muller-Munk," sound recording, IDSA Records, Box 116.

59 Peter Muller-Munk to Russel Wright, May 13, 1952, IDSA Records, Box 43, Folder: Muller-Munk.

60 Peter Muller-Munk, "Shop Talk No. 6: Why I Belong to the SID" (n.d., pre-1954), 2–3. IDSA Records, Box 43, Folder: Muller-Munk.

61 "News: The Society Changes Its Name," *Industrial Design* 1, no. 5 (October 1955): 12. The name change was approved by a national ballot of members and became effective with the inauguration of the 1955–56 administration in October 1955. Peter Muller-Munk, the President's Report for ASID Annual Meeting, Washington, DC, October 7, 1955, 3, IDSA Records, Box 34, Folder: President's Correspondence 1954–1955.

62 Stenotype Conference Reporting Service, "Society of Industrial Designers, Museum of Modern Art, New York City, Friday Evening, April 22, 1955" (transcript), IDSA Records, Box 94, Folder: Taste Forum, April 1955: "What's Happening to America's Taste?"; Peter Muller-Munk, the President's Report for ASID Annual Meeting, Washington, DC, October 7, 1955, 3, IDSA Records, Box 34, Folder: President's Correspondence 1954–55.

63 After an extended negotiation period, the organizations finally overcame their differences and merged in 1965 to become the Industrial Designers Society of America (IDSA).

64 Peter Muller-Munk to Robert Gruen, November 4, 1954, IDSA Records, Box 34, Folder: SID-IDI-1954 Corres. Peter Muller-Munk, speech at IDSA National Conference, "10/8/55 2nd Half Fri. PM Hose/Muller-Munk," sound recording, IDSA Records, Box 116.

65 Lando Advertising Agency, news release, "Pittsburgh Visited by Prominent Swedish Industrialist," November 13, 1958. PMMA archives, Lando Binder 3.

66 Peter Muller-Munk, the President's Report for ASID Annual Meeting, Washington, DC, October 7, 1955, 5, IDSA Records, Box 34, Folder: President's Correspondence 1954–1955.

67 Audience number from ibid.

68 Ibid., 6.

69 Arthur BecVar to Peter Muller-Munk, June 19, 1956, IDSA Records, Box 34, Folder: Correspondence.

70 Peter Muller-Munk to Arthur BecVar, August 1, 1956, IDSA Records, Box 34, Folder: Correspondence.

71 Peter Muller-Munk, the President's Report for ASID Annual Meeting, Washington, DC, October 7, 1955, 6. Peter Muller-Munk, Report on Meeting of International Coordinating Committee of Industrial Design Societies, Paris, April 11–14, 1956, IDSA Records, Box 34, Folder: Correspondence.

72 For more detail, see Arthur Pulos, *The Industrial Design Adventure: 1940–1975* (Cambridge, MA: MIT Press, 1988), 216.

73 Peter Muller-Munk, Report on Meeting of International Coordinating Committee of Industrial Design Societies, Paris, April 11–14, 1956, IDSA Records, Box 34, Folder: Correspondence.

74 Pulos, *The Industrial Design Adventure*, 216.

75 Ibid., 217.

76 Peter Muller-Munk to Sally Swing, October 25, 1955, IDSA Records, Box 34, Folder: President's Correspondence 1954–1955.

77 Peter Muller-Munk, "Industrial Designers Can Meet the Challenge," *Electrical Manufacturing*, June 1951, 116, 119, 272, 274; "O Wad Some Power the Giftie Gie Us," *Art and Industry* 50, no. 298 (April 1951): 132–37.

78 Peter Muller-Munk, "Workhorse vs. Racehorse," *Steel: The Weekly Magazine of Metalworking*, October 19, 1953, n.p. "European Craftsmen Excel, Pittsburgh Designers Says," *Pittsburgh Press*, October 4, 1953.

79 Peter Muller-Munk, "An Industrial Designer Gives His Views on Successful Co-ordination of … Industrial Design and Engineering Design," *Machine Design*, September 1954, 148–51.

80 Peter Muller-Munk, "Industrial Design as a Tool of Marketing," *Home Appliance Builder*, September 1958, 36–45, an article based on a lecture presented at the 27th Annual Meeting of the Porcelain Enamel Institute, September 25–27, 1958.

81 Marilyn Ferguson, "Peter Muller-Munk, 'Industrial Designer,'" *Pittsburgh Sun-Telegraph*, October 26, 1958, sec. 4, 5. Peter Muller-Munk, "Industrial Design as a Function of Marketing," *Industrial Marketing*, February 1959, 45–47. The newsletter of the American Marketing Association, Pittsburgh Chapter, March 2, 1959, includes a discussion of Muller-Munk's lecture delivered to the group on February 26, 1959. "How Industrial Designers Locate Markets," *Printers' Ink*, November 13, 1959, 68, 69, 73.

82 "Local Merchants to Hear Noted Industrial Designer," *Salem (MA) Evening News*, August 5, 1958; "Salem, Mass., Merchants Gear for More Profits Through Modernization; Witch City Clinic First in Area to Present Complete Updating Story," *New England Electrical News*, September 1958, 32–33; "Noted Planner Warns against Delay in Launching City's 'Operation Uplift,'" *Salem Evening News*, August 14, 1958, 1, 14, 15; Peter Muller-Munk, "Lighting for Industry," from an address at a symposium during the 1st National Lighting Exposition in New York City, Interior Design, April 1958, n.p, PMMA archives, Scrapbook 2; Peter Muller-Munk, "National Lighting Expositions," *Illuminating Engineering*, October 1958, n.p., PMMA archives, Scrapbook 3; Peter Muller-Munk, "How America Influences European Product Development," *Product Engineering*, December 14, 1959, 36–37; Peter Muller-Munk, "Industrial Design: Europe vs. the United States," *Industrial World*, July 1961, 34–36; Peter Muller-Munk [Special Consultant to the European Productivity Agency], "Report to Europe," "Report to Europe II," and "Blueprint for Harmony," reprints from *Industrial Design* bound as brochure, c. 1961, PMMA archives.

83 Peter Muller-Munk, "Think Small," *Charette*, October 1965, 13.

The 1950s "Kitchen Revolution"

1 "There Is More Than Meets the Eye Behind the Design of a Refrigerator," *Westinghouse News*, January 30, 1951.

2 "Men and Business," *Pittsburgh Post-Gazette*, January 5, 1951.

3 "Westinghouse Introduces 9 New Refrigerators, 5 Electric Ranges," *Retailing Daily*, November 13, 1950.

4 Society of Industrial Designers, *Industrial Design in America*, 1954 (New York: Farrar, Straus & Young, 1954), 186.

5 Lawrence M. Hughes, "Westinghouse Comes Back Selling," reprinted in *Sales Management: The Magazine of Marketing*, September 21, 1956, n.p.

6 "1958 Models in Big Appliances," *Business Week*, August 31, 1957, 60.

7 Peter Muller-Munk, "Kitchen Revolution," *New York Times*, May 5, 1957.

8 Peter Muller-Munk, "Designing Built-Ins," *Refrigerating Engineering*, December 1955, 45. Muller-Munk pitched the idea in the fall of 1954 and the concept was given the green light in 1955. The small team of project supervisors included Howard Anderson (ranges), Ernst Budke (laundry), and Roger Protas (refrigerators and freezers), each working under the direction of Raymond Smith, with the help of designers such as Donald Behnk. See "Design at Westinghouse: A Consultant Assists," *Industrial Design* 7, no. 7 (July 1958), and "Westinghouse Makes Its Bid with a Square Deal and a Square Look," *Electrical Merchandising*, October 1957, 150.

9 "Is the Kitchen Disintegrating?," *Industrial Design* 1, no. 4 (August 1954): 64–81.

10 Vera Hahn, "Appliances Seen 'Working Furniture,'" *Home Furnishings Daily*, March 8, 1960.

11 "Refrigerators-Freezers," *Industrial Design* 8, no. 4 (April 1961): 79.

The Color Explosion

1 "Annual Design Review: Trends: Color," *Industrial Design* 2, no. 6 (December 1955), 36.

2 "Report of Executive Committee Meeting with Representatives of Newest Member Bodies," Industrial Designers Society of America (IDSA) Records, Correspondence, 1949–1953, Inter-Society Color Council, Special Collections Research Center, Syracuse University Libraries. The Color Council consisted of various national Industrial Designer's member organizations.

3 The other delegates were Julian Everette, Harper Richards, Hudson Roysher, and Viktor Schreckengost. Philip McConnell to Egmont Arens, September 13, 1949, IDSA Records, Correspondence, 1949–1953, Inter-Society Color Council.

4 See Egmont Arens, "The Dynamic Use of Color," Speech to Inter-Society Color Council, March 8, 1950, IDSA Records, Correspondence, 1949–1953, Inter-Society Color Council.

5 Arthur Gregor, "The Roots of the Product," [source unknown], 59, PMMA archives, Scrapbook 3.

6 Caloric advertisement, *Retailing Daily*, January 4, 1955.

7 "Annual Design Review: Trends: Color," 43.

8 "Introducing the Fabulous New Ranges by Caloric," *Retailing Daily*, January 4, 1955, 132.

9 The shaver's design patent (186,433) is in the name of Raymond A. Smith and Roger Protas. Filed January 14, 1959.

10 Undated press release, Lando Advertising Agency, PMMA archives, Lando Binder 2.

11 Ibid. Author of the landmark book *Functional Color* (1937), Birren had consulted on Walt Disney's Technicolor films in the early 1940s, revolutionized factories with color safety standards during World War II, and transformed postwar commercial products, notably for DuPont and General Electric. See Regina Lee Blaszczyk, *The Color Revolution* (Cambridge, MA: MIT Press, 2012), 222.

12 "Free with every Caloric range … kitchen color plans by Beatrice West," [advertisement] *Sunday Herald*, October 2, 1960; and *Ideas for Westinghouse Confection Color Kitchens* (Westinghouse, 1960), Westinghouse Collection, MSS 424, Detre Library and Archives, Senator John Heinz History Center, Box 94, Folder 2.

13 "Light Panel Ceiling Makes Gay Use of Color and Baffles," *Architectural Forum* 106, no. 4 (April 1957): 178.

14 Peter Muller-Munk [remarks], "The Place of Lighting in Architectural Design," Sylva-Lume News Conference (February 19, 1957), New York City, p. 1, IDSA Records, Box 24, Folder: Lighting.

15 Ibid.

16 Press release, Science Talent Institute, "New Advances in 'Electronic Light' Revealed by Westinghouse Scientist," March 9, 1957. Westinghouse Collection, MSS 424, Detre Library and Archives, Senator John Heinz History Center, Box 83, Folder 6, "Press Releases: 1956–1957," p. 1.

17 "First Full-Scale 'Hot-Cold-Light' Panel Exhibited Here by Westinghouse," Press release, January 19, 1959, PMMA archives, Lando Binder 3.

18 Press release, Science Talent Institute, "Windows of the Future May Provide Light at Night, Westinghouse Scientist Says," September 11, 1957. Westinghouse Collection, MSS 424, Detre Library and Archives, Senator John Heinz History Center, Box 83, Folder 6, "Press Releases: 1956–1957," p. 1.

New Frontiers

1 Peter Muller-Munk, "Transportation and the Balanced City in the Year 2000," transcript of his conference presentation for the First International Conference on Urban Transportation, Pittsburgh, December 1–3, 1966, n.p., Industrial Designers Society of America (IDSA) Records, Special Collections Research Center, Syracuse University Libraries, Box 102, Folder: Peter Muller-Munk.

2 Peter Muller-Munk to Marie Munk, January [illegible], 1964, Marie Munk Papers, Sophia Smith Collection, Smith College, Northampton, MA, Series II, Correspondence, Box 7: folder 5. Our thanks to Jewel Stern for research into family correspondence and for selected translations from the German, particularly the Marie Munk Papers at Smith College, and for her correspondence with Munk's biographer, Oda Cordes, all of which informs various aspects of this chapter.

3 Muller-Munk stated on more than one occasion that he objected to designing "just to sell" where no market existed. Marilyn Ferguson, "Peter Muller-Munk, 'Industrial Designer,'" *Pittsburgh Sun-Telegraph*, October 27, 1958.

4 "The New Wave in Steel Water Tanks Values Esthetics: Water Tanks, Too, Are Changing with the Times," *New York Times*, October 22, 1965. "How Steel Widens Its Targets: Industry That for Years Let Its Products Sell Themselves Now Promotes Offbeat Uses," *Business Week*, March 27, 1965, Marketing sec., 119.

5 For a more thorough analysis of US policy as related to design engagement abroad, see H. Alpay Er, Fatma Korkut, and Özlem Er, "U.S. Involvement in the Development of Design in the Periphery: The Case History of Industrial Design Education in Turkey, 1950s–1970s," *Design Issues* 19, no. 2 (Spring 2003): 17–34.

6 Avrom Fleishman, "Design as a Political Force, Part 2," *Industrial Design* 4, no. 4 (April 1957): 46.

7 Er, Korkut, and Er, "U.S. Involvement in the Development of Design in the Periphery," 20.

8 Dave Chapman (as president of SID) to Secretary of State, December 5, 1950 (marked "Copy," so presumably sent), IDSA Records, Box 100, Folder: US Department of State.

9 Notes of meeting between Chapman, Muller-Munk, and Silberman, IDSA Records, Box 72, Folder: FOA Program on Under Developed Countries, 1955.

10 Brief dated May 4, 1955, FOA to SID, IDSA Records, Box 72, Folder: FOA Program on Under Developed Countries, 1955.

11 Other nations were contracted as follows: Russel Wright Associates (Hong Kong, Taiwan [called Formosa], Thailand, Cambodia, and Vietnam); Walter Dorwin Teague Associates (Greece, Jordan, and Lebanon); Design Research Inc. (Chapman) (Pakistan, Afghanistan, Mexico, Surinam, El Salvador, Jamaica, and Costa Rica); and Smith, Scherr, and McDermott (South Korea). Arthur J. Pulos, *The American Design Adventure: 1940–1975* (Cambridge, MA: MIT Press, 1988), 237. SID played no role in awarding the bids; the proposals were sent directly to Silberman, although SID executive secretary Sally G. Swing compiled a list of interested design firms for the organization's records. Sally G. Swing cover letter to SID membership accompanying Silberman's brief, May 4, 1955, IDSA Records, Box 72, Folder: FOA Program on Under Developed Countries, 1955.

12 For an overview of the International Cooperation Administration, see "The Designer as Economic Diplomat," *Industrial Design* 3, no. 4 (August 1956): 68–73; Fleishman, "Design as a Political Force, Part 2," 37–55; "Expansive Uncle: U.S. Sends Designers to Native Huts to Lend a Hand to Handicrafters/ Foreign Aid Program Aims to Revise Bowls, Bamboo Items for U.S. Consumers," *Wall Street Journal*, July 5, 1957; Conrad Brown, "I.C.A.'s Technical Assistance Program," *Craft Horizons* 18, no. 4 (July–August, 1958): 35–36; and Pulos, *The American Design Adventure*, 236–41.

13 An undated draft agreement between the US federal government and PMMA specifies payments to the contractor not to exceed $100,000 for "Turkey, Pakistan, Israel or other countries that may be designated." Contract PIO/T 99-29-010-3-59010, Small Industry—Product Development, Improvement, and Marketing (draft), between United States of America, Foreign Operations Administration and Peter Muller-Munk Associates, n.d. [1955]. By July 13 the contract had been revised to specify Turkey, Israel, and India.

See J. M. Silberman, Airgram, "Proposed NEA Demonstration Projects for Small Industrial and Handicraft Development: USFOTO CIRC. N A-61; A-71; TOUSFO, Ankara A-305; Tel Aviv 580; New Delhi A-721," International Cooperation Administration, Washington, DC, July 13, 1955. National Archives, Contracts: Peter Muller-Munk; Mission to Israel; Executive Office; Administrative Services Branch; [Unclassified] Central Subject Files, 1952–61; Entry UD 1253; Box 19; RG 469-250/81/22/01.

14 PMMA items for SID newsletter to Sally Swing, April 13, 1956, IDSA Records, Box 43, Folder: Muller-Munk.

15 Ibid.

16 The Indian initiative was later funded by the Ford Foundation and picked up by Charles and Ray Eames. Paul Karlen, "History of Peter Muller-Munk Associates," audio recording, March 15, 1969, Raymond Spilman Papers, Special Collections Research Center, Syracuse University Libraries, Box 92, item 120. "Grand Design for Israel: More Salable Products," *Business Week*, December 15, 1956, 157–58. See also Charles and Ray Eames, "The Eames Report, April 1958," reprinted in *Design Issues* 7, no. 2 (Spring 1991): 63. PMMA was awarded $100,000 for its initial three-nation survey (see note 13). It was reported in 1957 that since the start of the program two years earlier, $600,000 in total contracts had been awarded to the five design firms and the Institute of Contemporary Art, Boston; "Expansive Uncle: U.S. Sends Designers to Native Huts to Lend a Hand to Handicrafters."

17 PMMA's IPDO project operated under US Government Contract PIO/T 71-26-119, cited in International Cooperation Administration, Office of Industrial Resources, *Industrial Activities Bulletin*, August–September 1960, 4.

18 *USOM/Israel: Five Years of Mutual Endeavor* (Tel Aviv: International Cooperation Administration, 1956), available online, http://pdf.usaid.gov/pdf_docs/Pdacr696.pdf. Report as described in "A New State Gets a New Profession," *Industrial Design* 7, no. 4 (April 1960): 66–69.

19 Figures for 1955 showed $87.5 million in exports as compared to $326.5 million in imports; *Business Week*, December 15, 1956, 157–58.

20 Karlen, "History of Peter Muller-Munk Associates."

21 *Business Week*, December 15, 1956, 157.

22 The Israel Product Design Office was the second of two major ICA projects in Israel. The first, as referenced by Muller-Munk in the call to SID members for proposals in May 1955, was an effort by the Institute of Contemporary Art, Boston, focusing on design education in collaboration with the Israeli Institute of Technology (Technion) in Haifa, where they instituted an industrial design curriculum. ICA Boston's director, James Plaut, was also the first US consultant to the Israeli government in industrial design, in 1950. He orchestrated the participation of Israel in trade exhibitions, including the 1954 Milan Triennial. Plaut and ICA Boston/Technion's efforts ran in tandem with PMMA's, but they were separate initiatives. For more on the ICA Boston/Technion program, see "U.S. Gives Design Aid to Israel," *Industrial Design* 3, no. 1 (February 1956), 22; Pulos, *The American Design Adventure*, 241; "A New State Gets a New Profession," 66–69.

23 *Business Week*, December 15, 1956, 157–58; US Information Service, Tel Aviv, Israel, *Daily News Bulletin* 9, no. 207 (September 27, 1957); "A New State Gets a New Profession," 66–69.

24 *Business Week*, December 15, 1956, 157–58; Moshe Dor, "'The Ungly American' in Israel: Robert, Mort and Hatzkel's 'Espresso,'" *Maariv*, September 6, [probably 1959], PMMA archives, Scrapbook 2.

25 "A New State Gets a New Profession," 66–69.

26 Ibid. The fee charged was originally 4,250 I£ per hour, raised to 6,000 and 7,500 I£/hour.

27 Closed November 1, 1956–May 13, 1957; "Expansive Uncle: U.S. Sends Designers to Native Huts to Lend a Hand to Handicrafters." See also "2 Pittsburghers Evacuate Israel," *Pittsburgh Press*, November 2, 1956; "Industrial Designer Cites Israeli Struggle," *Pittsburgh Post-Gazette*, November 20, 1956. The Israeli counterparts, who had been on the job for only four months when the Americans were evacuated in November 1956, kept the office afloat until their return in May 1957.

28 US Information Service, Tel Aviv, Israel, *Daily News Bulletin* 9, no. 207 (September 27, 1957).

29 "List of Clients and Projects of IPDO as of May 5, 1958," National Archives, Contracts: Peter Muller-Munk; Mission to Israel; Executive Office; Administrative Services Branch; [Unclassified] Central Subject Files, 1952–61; Entry UD 1253; Box 19; RG 469-250/81/22/01. See also client 42 ICA, slide cabinet, PMMA archives, and "Trends in Appearance Design ... Israel," *Product Engineering*, August 10, 1959, 46–47.

30 Dor, "'The Ungly American' in Israel," 1. Hatzkel was the first name of the proprietor of Kassit, a famous bohemian café in Tel Aviv.

31 IPDO held a symposium and exhibition on the subject of packaging: see "Trends in Appearance Design," 46–47; Paul Karlen, "1958 Israel Food Packaging Symposium and Exhibit," promotional literature, PMMA archives, Scrapbook 2. "House of Representatives Statement on United States Mutual Aid Program," Congressional Record, Proceedings and Debates of the 85th Congress, First Session, Vol. 103, No. 157, Wednesday, August 28, 1957, n.p. Fact Sheet—ICA Israel, part of March 13, 1958, address to House Committee on Foreign Affairs.

32 "Trends in Appearance Design ... Israel," 46–47. Alternate figures for total clients/projects were reported in ICA, "U.S. Technicians at Work Overseas," *Industrial Activities Bulletin*, August–September 1960, as 59 clients, 126 design assignments, and 271 completed design products.

33 "A New State Gets a New Profession," 66–69; "Trends in Appearance Design ... Israel," 46–47. PMMA's ICA contract ended effective December 31, 1959, per Airgram, June 3, 1959, National Archives, Contracts: Peter Muller-Munk; Mission to Israel; Executive Office; Administrative Services Branch; [Unclassified] Central Subject Files, 1952–61; Entry UD 1253; Box 19, 28; RG 469-250/81/22/01-02.

34 Like all ICA countries, Turkey was a critical part of US Cold War strategy. After Turkish districts along the Soviet frontier were threatened with Soviet takeover, the United States had made it clear that it would protect Turkey. The ICA work was thus an economic arm of a much larger military effort. Er, Korkut, and Er, "U.S. Involvement in the Development of Design in the Periphery," 24–25.

35 Ibid.

36 As in Israel, there was also a design school effort in Turkey called Middle Eastern Technical University (METU); ibid. We are grateful to Dr. Özlem Er, Chairperson, Industrial Designers Society of Turkey Istanbul Branch/ETMK İstanbul, for sharing the following document: David K. Munro, "A Rationale and an Outline for the Establishment of a Department of Industrial Design at the Middle East Technical University, Ankara," unpublished report (Ankara: METU, October 1971).

37 English transcript from *Zafer Demakcasinindir* 9, no. 2931 (October 23, 1957).

38 Brown, "I.C.A.'s Technical Assistance Program," 36. "Küçük sanatlar: Küçük sanatlar geliştirme,"*Akis* (Ankara), November 2, 1957, Kadin [Ladies sec.], 28, and typescript English translation, "Handicrafts: Development of Handicrafts," PMMA archives, Scrapbook 2.

39 English transcript from *Zafer Demakcasinindir* 9, no. 2931 (October 23, 1957).

40 *Carnegie Institute of Technology Faculty Bulletin*, series 1957–1958, no. 2 (September 25, 1957): 1. Peter Muller-Munk, statement, Mutual Security Act of 1958 hearing, see reprint, pp. 168–69.

41 Coverage of a Radio Broadcast, Konya, Anatolian News Service, October 24, 1957. Fact Sheet—Turkey ICA Project, PMMA, November 1957, reprinted in Muller-Munk, Mutual Security Act statement. Also"Küçük el sanatlari sanayii kuruluyor: Bunun için Amerika'dan bir mütehassis geldi," *Hürriyet* (Istanbul), November 2, 1957, and typescript English translation, "Handicraft Industry Is to Be Established: American Expert Arrives to Initiate Project," PMMA archives, Scrapbook 2.

42 Beyond Oksal, the only identified member of the Turkish staff is Leylâ Özön. "Ankara'da Hayirli Bir Adim: Küçük Sanatlar Geliştirme," *Yirminci Asır* (Istanbul), November 14, 1957, 10, and typescript English translation, "The Begining of Useful Work in Ankara: Development of Handicrafts," PMMA archives, Scrapbook 2.

43 "Küçük sanatlar: Küçük sanatlar geliştirme," 28.

44 Brown, "I.C.A.'s Technical Assistance Program," 36.

45 "House of Representatives Statement on United States Mutual Aid Program," n.p. Muller-Munk, statement, Mutual Security Act of 1958 hearing.

46 NBC, *Today Show*, November 15, 1957.

47 *Craft Horizons: Journal of Commerce*, November 15, 1957. Turkish Information Office, "Handcrafts from Turkey for American Markets," *News from Turkey*, October 15, 1958, 3.

48 Pulos, *The American Design Adventure*, 241.

49 "Americans as Advisors," *Industrial Design* 7, no. 2 (February 1960): 18.

50 Peter Muller-Munk to Marie Munk, February 10, 1960. Marie Munk Papers, Sophia Smith Collection, Smith College, Northampton, MA, Series II, Correspondence, Box 7: folder 5.

51 Ilona Muller-Munk had a chronic condition resulting in swelling of her foot. Friends reported that Muller-Munk made her a combination cane/footrest that she could carry with her. Edith H. and James A. Fisher, conversation with Jason Busch and Rachel Delphia, June 2008. Alisoun Kuhn, conversation with Rachel Delphia, March 3, 2014. As early as 1952, a source reported that Ilona visited a Boston clinic to "get her in condition to sail for Europe in August with Peter." Society of Industrial Designers, Allegheny Chapter, "Pittsburgh Patter," *The Allegheny Smog* 2, no. 2 (July 1952): 2. Later, in 1965, Ilona had to use a wheelchair for a period of time. At this point she had a series of surgeries, including at least one on her eyes, and suffered from problems with her vision; Marie Munk to Peter Muller-Munk, January 9, 1965, and September 26, 1965. Marie Munk Papers, Series II, Correspondence, Box 4: folder 27. Peter Muller-Munk to Gertrud Munk, January 26, 1965; and Peter Muller-Munk to Marie Munk, March 9, 1965, and June 3, 1965. Marie Munk Papers, Series II, Correspondence, Box 7: folder 5.

52 Kathleen McLaughlin, "European Industrial Gains Noted: Expert Sights Growth Based on Expected Merger of Rival Trading Blocs," *New York Times*, August 16, 1960. "News: Muller Munk Reports on Tour," *Industrial Design* 7, no. 9 (September 1960): 14. Although press reports had conflicting information about which countries Muller-Munk was to visit (citing the United Kingdom and Greece, for example, but leaving off Belgium), PMMA's Scrapbook 3 contains copies of his lectures, or articles reporting on his tour, in the Austrian, Belgian, Danish, French, and Norwegian press. Only Ireland remains to be confirmed, although all press reports agree on that location as part of the itinerary.

53 Peter Muller-Munk, "Report to Europe," *Industrial Design* 7, no. 11 (November 1960): 52–55; and "Report to Europe II," *Industrial Design* 8, no. 2 (February 1961): 49–51.

54 See Pulos, *The American Design Adventure*, 242; Er, Korkut, and Er, "U.S. Involvement in the Development of Design in the Periphery," 21–22; Jane Fiske Mitarachi, "Design as a Political Force: Pros and Cons of America's Program to Win Friends and Influence Nations through Trade Fair Exhibits Abroad," *Industrial Design* 4, no. 2 (February 1957): 38.

55 See Pulos, *The American Design Adventure*, 243.

56 Sally G. Swing memo to Art BecVar, President ASID, Proceedings of meeting at Henry Dreyfuss Office, March 29, 1956, filed March 30, 1956, Subject International Trade Fairs. IDSA Records, Box 34, Folder: General Correspondence. Memo, ASID Member Offices, from Francis F. Braun, Chairman ASID Interim Committee on the International Trade Fair Program, "Procedure for procuring contracts for the eight forthcoming September trade fairs" (undated), IDSA Records, Box 72, Foreign Design Groups, Folder: International Trade Fairs.

57 Levitan, Wiedmann, and Love in conversation with Rachel Delphia, December 4–5, 2014.

58 "USA International Exhibits Created Here," *Greater Pittsburgh Magazine*, June 1966, 23.

59 Levitan, Wiedmann, and Love in conversation with Rachel Delphia, December 4–5, 2014.

60 PMMA trade fair contracts included Izmir, Turkey, 1957; Poznan, Poland, 1961, 1962, and 1966; Rio de Janeiro, Brazil, 1963; Paris, France, 1964; Zagreb, Yugoslavia, 1964 and 1972; Blackpool and London, England, 1965; Copenhagen, Denmark, 1966; Belgrade, Yugoslavia, 1967 and 1971; Tehran, Iran, 1970; Paris Air Show, 1971. "USA International Exhibits Created Here," *Greater Pittsburgh*

Magazine, June 1966; Peter Muller-Munk Associates, "Exhibition Design Experience: Government and Industry Exhibits" [internal document produced in relation to merger with Wilbur Smith and Associates], c. 1974. Courtesy of James P. Karlen and Elaine K. Crawshaw.

61 "Gateway 4 Leases Announced," *Pittsburgh Press*, March 1, 1964.

62 Incorporation effective July 1, 1965, Staff Memo, July 16, 1965, PMMA archives. PMMA incorporated with nine shareholders: Muller-Munk, Karlen, Smith, Parisson, Anderson, Budke, Behnk, Monigle, and Protas.

63 William S. Dietrich II, "A Very Brief History of Pittsburgh," *Pittsburgh Quarterly*, Summer 2009.

64 For more on the major corporate shift taking place in 1960, see Staff feature in collaboration with R. L. Klapp, chief manufacturing engineer, "Clean Sweep," reprinted from *Production: The Magazine of Manufacturing*, November 1960, n.p. Grand Rapids Public Museum, Bissell Collection, Box 35, Scrapbook 1959–1963.

65 "Industrial Design: New Products: Source of Sales and Growth," *Journal of Commerce*, September 11, 1964, 5–7. PMMA archives, Scrapbook 4. PMMA's expanded corporate service for Bissell and others necessitated a full-fledged graphics department, headed beginning in 1966 by Jerry Rozanski. Diana Riddle in conversation with the authors, December 4, 2014, and May 1, 2015.

66 Muller-Munk, "Report to Europe," 55. Warren DIx, "How Small Manufacturers in Pittsburgh Use Management Consultants," *The Smaller Manufacturers* 15, nos. 11-12 (November–December 1960): 21–22.

67 "Bissell's Floor Cleaner," *Product Engineering*, January 16, 1961, 25.

68 "Shopping This Week in Chicago," *This Week in Chicago*, April 9, 1960. Grand Rapids Public Museum, Bissell Collection, 1991.4, Collection 42, Box 35, Scrapbook 1959–1963.

69 Muller-Munk, "Report to Europe II," 50.

70 American Management Association, "Creativity in Packaging and Design, Peter Muller-Munk Associates," AMA 33rd National Packaging Conference, April 20–22, 1964. PMMA archives, Scrapbook 4.

71 "Haven for Key Men: Muller-Munk Designs Serene Executive Offices for Bissell, Inc., in Grand Rapids," *Contract: The Business Magazine of Commercial/Institutional Design, Planning, Furnishing* 7, no. 7 (July 1966): 68–69.

72 Peter Muller-Munk Associates, "Space Planning and Interior Design," promotional literature, c. 1969, PMMA archives.

73 Ibid.

74 Peter Muller-Munk Associates, "Market Development Design," promotional literature, c. 1969, PMMA archives.

75 Karlen, "History of Peter Muller-Munk Associates." Peter Muller-Munk Associates, "Market Development Design."

76 "New Material, Strong as Steel," *Pittsburgh Sun Telegraph*, June 16, 1957.

77 Bay E. Estes Jr., "Comments on US Steel's Design Project 'A Study in Steel,'" delivered at the Biltmore Hotel, New York City, September 21, 1960, PMMA archives.

78 Sarah C. Nichols et al., *Aluminum by Design* (Pittsburgh: Carnegie Museum of Art, 2000), 246. Aluminum Company of America, *Design Forecast 1 and 2* (Pittsburgh: Alcoa, 1959).

79 Designers recalled covert work on the side for Sam Fahnestock, design director at Alcoa. Kenneth Love and Robert Gaylor, in conversation with Rachel Delphia, December 5, 2014.

80 United States Steel Press Release, "Background Information on 'A Study in Steel,' A New Design Concept Advanced by United States Steel," September 22, 1960. Courtesy of George Scheuring.

81 Bay E. Estes Jr. in "U.S. Steel Exhibits Designs for a Variety of New Steel Products," *Wall Street Journal*, September 22, 1960, 3.

82 A number of their earliest design sketches appeared in "U.S. Steel Launches Design Program," *Steel Magazine*, September 26, 1960, 106–9. For a broad period discussion of steel's pivotal place in the 1950s marketplace, see Charles E. Silberman, "Steel: It's a Brand-New Industry," *Fortune*, December 1960, 123–27, 249–50, 254–56, 261–62, 264.

83 The foam was a product of the Mobay Chemical Company, which would separately contract PMMA for its own market development project a few years later; "Executive Furniture Mates Foam with Steel," *Mobay Polygram* 2, no. 1 (c. 1961–62), PMMA archives, Scrapbook 4.

84 Designed by George Nelson and Robert Propst, this furniture looks similar to PMMA's but featured die-cast aluminum with rubber and plastic laminate work surfaces.

85 Stanley Abercrombie states of Herman Miller's new furniture, "reception in the press was more positive than the reception in the showrooms." Stanley Abercrombie, "Office Supplies: Evolving Furniture for the Evolving Workplace," in *On the Job: Design and the American Office* (New York: Princeton Architectural Press, 2000), 89.

86 Edmour Germain, "Steel Men Urged: Use Steel Desks," *New York World Telegram and Sun*, November 5, 1960.

87 United States Steel, press release for "Study in Steel," 1962. Study in Steel Press Kit, United States Steel Archives.

88 Barbara Barnes, "Steel Comes of Age in Ideas for Living," *Evening Bulletin* (Philadelphia), March 25, 1962, 7. See also "Study in Steel—1962," slide script, PMMA archives, Scrapbook 4.

89 Loretta Ford, "New Kitchen Storage Idea Puts End to Waste Space," *Boston Globe*, March 21, 1962.

90 Ibid.

91 Peter Muller-Munk Associates, "Market Development Design."

92 "The Work of Curtis & Davis," *Interiors* 126, no. 7 (February 1967): 114. The IBM building's civil engineers were Worthington, Skilling, Helle & Jackson of Seattle. This load-bearing design was described as "probably the first real change in multi-office building design since 1903" when the first structural steel-frame building was erected in Chicago. "New IBM Building to Rise in Pittsburgh," *Charette: Pennsylvania Journal of Architecture* 42, no. 1 (January 1962): 21.

93 Albert M. Tannler, *Pittsburgh Architecture in the Twentieth Century* (Pittsburgh: Pittsburgh History & Landmarks Foundation, 2013), 166.

94 "Patterned Block," *Architectural Forum*, November 1962, n.p. PMMA archives, Scrapbook 4.

95 *Industrial Design* featured the Chiaro line in July 1967, December 1967, and again in April 1969.

96 Ghita Cary, "13 Lucky Designs Will Be the Winners," *Chicago Sun-Times: Family Magazine*, December 12, 1967. Chiaro blocks won in the "Window Treatment, Shades and Blinds" category. "Eyes on A.I.D.," *Home Furnishings Daily*, January 8, 1968, 26.

97 "Executive Furniture Mates Foam with Steel."

98 Robert Gaylor, e-mail message to Rachel Delphia, March 5, 2015.

99 "New Manufacturing Systems for Production of Rigid, Flexible Urethane Furniture," *Furniture: Methods & Materials*, August 1970, n.p. "Mobay Pushes New Plastic Process," *Home Furnishings Daily*, August 5, 1970, 5.

100 "Duromer: Joint Designeering Venture between Mobay and PMMA Design Firm Translates Chemical Know-How into Commercial Show-How with World's First Showcase Series of All-Urethane-and-Durome Furniture," *Mobay Polygram*, no. 38 (Summer 1970): 6–7.

101 "Mobay Pushes New Plastic Process," 5.

102 Peter Muller-Munk Associates, "Space Planning and Interior Design Experience," corporate résumé, c. 1973.

103 Highway beautification was the cause célèbre of Lady Bird Johnson, whose activism led to President Lyndon B. Johnson signing the Highway Beautification Act on October 22, 1965.

104 "Design in America," entry form, 1967, IDSA Records, Box 103, Folder: Photos.

105 "Design in America," entry form. Design published in Industrial Designers Society of America, *Design in America*, introduction and text by Ralph Caplan (New York: McGraw-Hill Book Company, 1969), 29.

106 "New Aspects of Service," *Texaco Star* 51, no. 3 (1964): 20.

107 Wes Lerdon recalls driving through multiple states in an F85 Oldsmobile with Glenn Monigle on research trips, scouting out existing service station designs to study. Recounted to Catherine Walworth, January 27, 2015.

108 "New Aspects of Service," 20.

109 William Allan, "Texaco Trying to Get Drivers Out of Seats," *Pittsburgh Press*, October 26, 1964.

110 "New Texaco Station Design," *Houston Post*, January 17, 1967.

111 "Ashland: Look of a Neighbor," *National Petroleum News*, February 1967, n.p. [cut off], PMMA archives, Scrapbook 4; "What Makes the New Look New," *National Petroleum News*, October 1967, 72, PMMA archives, Scrapbook 4.

112 "The Steel Triangle in Pittsburgh's Golden Triangle," *Interiors*, December 1971, 98–99.

113 "Tripleheader," *Industrial Design* 18, no. 10 (December 1971): 63.

114 Bank Building Corporation: Paul Wiedmann, conversation with Rachel Delphia, May 5, 2008. Sheraton bathrooms referenced in *Creative Steel Design: A Quarterly Digest for Designers*, Published by American Iron and Steel Institute 4, no. 1 (1970), PMMA archives, Scrapbook 4.

115 Edith H. and James A. Fisher, conversation with Jason Busch and Rachel Delphia, June 2008.

116 "New Furniture Concept," *Fisher Scientific 1965 Annual Report* (1965): 7.

117 "Fisher Contempra," *The Laboratory* 33, no. 4 (1965): 103, PMMA archives, Scrapbook 4.

118 "Great Scot!," *US Steel News*, October-November 1965, 5. US Steel's transit show was slated to travel to other cities, including St. Louis, Chicago, Houston, Los Angeles, Pittsburgh, Washington, DC, Atlanta, and Detroit.

119 United States Steel, *Dilemma: People in Motion*, company brochure (December 1965); 29, 33, PMMA archives.

120 Richard Carr, "By Rail to the Future," *Design Journal* 223 (July 1967): 28. One criticism of PMMA's design was that the driver's area was left exposed to the passenger area. Patricia Conway George, "Mass Transit: Problem and Promise," *Design Quarterly*, no. 71, theme issue "Mass Transit: Problem and Promise" (1968): 25.

121 United States Steel, *Dilemma: People in Motion*, 22, 24.

122 Muller-Munk, "Transportation and the Balenced City in the Year 2000," n.p.

123 Karin-Margit Muller-Munk, Death Certificate No. 5, 1959, Mairie de Fayence, Arrondissement de Draguignan, France. Margit died on March 24, 1959. Margit and Franz had traveled to Freiburg, Germany, for treatment with Dr. Hans Sarre, a pioneering nephrologist, suggesting that Margit suffered from serious kidney disease. Franz Mombert to Marie Munk, undated; Marie Munk Papers, Series II, Correspondence, Box 7: folder 3. Research by Jewel Stern.

124 Marie Munk to Peter Muller-Munk, February 18, 1961; Marie Munk Papers, Series II, Correspondence, Box 4: folder 27.

125 Peter expressed to his aunt that he never learned how to save money. Marie, in turn, sent $3,000 and offered to advance his inheritance. Multiple letters trace both of their efforts to place Gertrud in the best assisted-living facilities and to cover her expenses. See especially: Peter Muller-Munk to Marie Munk, September 19, 1963; March 9, 1965; and December 30, 1965; Peter Muller-Munk to Idalotte Realty, New York, February 24, 1965; Peter Muller-Munk to Florence Safford, of the Isabella Home, New York, April 6, 1965, and December 17, 1965; and Peter Muller-Munk to Gertrud Muller-Munk, October 20, 1964; January 26, 1965; and March 9, 1965. Marie Munk Papers, Series II, Correspondence, Box 7: folder 5. Marie Munk to Peter Muller-Munk, February 16, 1965; March 15, 1965; and April 30, 1965. Marie Munk Papers, Series II, Correspondence, Box 4: folder 27.

126 Marie Munk to Peter Muller-Munk, December 12, 1964; December 28, 1964; February 23, 1965; March 15, 1965; April 20, 1965; May 23, 1965; and January 21, 1966. Marie Munk Papers, Series II, Correspondence, Box 4: folder 27.

127 Marie Munk to Peter Muller-Munk, February 18, 1961; March 2, 1961; May 10, 1965; July 7, 1965; and November 30, 1965. Marie Munk Papers, Series II, Correspondence, Box 4: folder 27.

128 See note 51.

129 Based on correspondence, Ilona may have suffered from a detached retina, among other ailments. Marie Munk to Peter Muller-Munk, January 9, 1965, and January 16, 1965. Marie Munk Papers, Series II, Correspondence, Box 4: folder 27. Peter Muller-Munk to Gertrud Muller-Munk, January 26, 1965. Peter Muller-Munk to Marie Munk, January 24, 1965. Marie Munk Papers, Series II, Correspondence, Box 7: folder 5.

130 Marie Munk to Peter Muller-Munk, January 9, 1965, and March 15, 1965. Marie Munk Papers, Series II, Correspondence, Box 4; folder 27.

131 Peter Muller-Munk to Marie Munk, December 18? [illegible], 1965. Marie Munk Papers, Series II, Correspondence, Box 7: folder 5.

132 The new partners were: Howard A. Anderson, Donald J. Behnk, Ernst Budke, Glenn W. Monigle, and Roger I. Protas. "Talented Designers Admitted as Partners by Peter Muller-Munk," *Typo Graphic*, February 1966.

133 James R. Mellow, "Activists in the Design Profession ... Peter Muller-Munk Associates," *Industrial Design* 13, no 6 (June 1966): 64–69.

134 Telegram, Peter Muller-Munk to the White House Social Secretary, September 21, 1966, and Guest List/Table Assignments, September 26, 1966, White House Social Office, Social Entertainment, Lyndon B. Johnson Library and Museum, Box 79, folder 9-26-66 Dinner (President and Mrs. Johnson) (Chancellor Erhard of Germany). Peter Muller-Munk to President Lyndon B. Johnson, September 27, 1966, White House Central Files, Lyndon B. Johnson Library and Museum, Box M-629: Folder Muller, P. Our thanks to Jewel Stern for her research in the President Johnson Archives, based on her conversation with Jerry Tallmer, March 22, 2007.

135 "Project Earning Power Receives New Grant," *Braille Monitor*, March 1967.

136 Muller-Munk RSVP'd via telegram for the luncheon: Telegram, Muller-Munk to White House Social Secretary, February 8, 1967. An agenda for February 14, however, is annotated, "wife died last night." The Lyndon B. Johnson Archives contain several documents sadly attesting to the Muller-Munks' deaths. An index card filed under Mr. & Mrs. Muller-Munk records their 1966 dinner engagement with Chancellor Erhard (see note 134). Their death dates are handwritten above their names on the card. Meeting at the White House, February 14, 1967. White House Social File, Social Events Cards; White House Social File, Social Entertainment File, Box 86, "2-14-67 Meeting (Mrs. Johnson)—Project Earning Power"; Mrs. Johnson's Daily Diary, Box 3, "December 1967." Courtesy of the Lyndon Baines Johnson Library, Austin, Texas. Edith H. and James A. Fisher, conversation with Jason Busch and Rachel Delphia, June 2008.

137 Edith H. and James A. Fisher, conversation with Jason Busch and Rachel Delphia, June 2008.

138 Ilona Muller-Munk's remains were cremated. Funeral of Ilona L. Muller-Munk, Records of H. Samson, Inc. (Funeral Home), MSS 260, Detre Library and Archives, Senator John Heinz History Center, Box 32: Folder 3.

139 Edith H. and James A. Fisher, conversation with Jason Busch and Rachel Delphia, June 2008.

140 Writing to Franz Mombert and his second wife, Margot, Marie Munk stated that it was unclear what led Ilona to her final step and surmised possible fear of old age, fear that she was no longer attractive, or even fear that she might end up like her mother, with a German turn of phrase suggesting that Ilona's mother had perhaps suffered dementia: "oder auch Furcht, dass sie wie es ihrer Mutter ging, jahrelang eigentlich nicht mehr auf deser Sinn." Marie Munk to Franz and Margot Mombert, April 5, 1967. Marie Munk Papers, Series II, Correspondence, Box 4: folder 25. Jerry Tallmer, Ilona's son, likewise knew of no reason for his mother's suicide; Jerry Tallmer, conversation with Jewel Stern, March 21, 2007.

141 Dr. Margot Tallmer (wife of Ilona's son, Jonathan Tallmer), conversation with Jewel Stern, May 5, 2007.

142 Jerry Tallmer, conversation with Jewel Stern, March 21, 2007. Tallmer reported to Stern that he had spoken to his mother's physician, Dr. Milton Jena, at the time of her death, and that Jana had told him that there was "no overwhelming reason" for Ilona's suicide.

143 In addition to the Fishers' testimony, Marie Munk also concluded, upon discovering a letter from Peter to Ilona dated December 31, 1966, that Peter had resolved that he could not live without Ilona. Further, Marie suggested that "he had arranged his life too much to please Ilona, and he—I am afraid—had in his genes too much of his father's emotional instability, and too little of my parental strength and courage [Munk genes]." Marie Munk to Ulrich Meisel, March 24, 1967. Marie Munk Papers, Series II, Correspondence, Box 4: folder 21, as cited in Oda Cordes, *Marie Munk und die Stellung der Frau im Recht: Wissenschaftliche Studie über Leben und Werk von Marie Munk in drei Teilen*, 3 vols. (Schwerin, Germany: O. Cordes, 2011), 2:565–66. Translated into English by Oda Cordes for Jewel Stern in e-mail message, October 3, 2013.

144 Edith H. and James A. Fisher, conversation with Jason Busch and Rachel Delphia, June 2008.

145 Marie Munk to Peter Muller-Munk, February 20, 1967. Marie Munk Papers, Series II, Correspondence, Box 4: folder 27.

146 Ann Radion to Marie Munk, February 25, 1967. Marie Munk Papers, Series II, Correspondence, Box 4: folder 27.

147 Oral histories with PMMA employees, December 2014.

148 Cordes, *Marie Munk und die Stellung der Frau im Recht*, 2:565. Cordes cites a personal conversation with Muller-Munk's friend Ulrich Meisel as well as a letter from Marie Munk to Ulrich Meisel, March 24, 1967. Marie Munk Papers, Series II, Correspondence, Box 4: folder 21. Cordes states that the Kuhns were with Muller-Munk on the night of March 12, 1967, but Marie's letter to Meisel (which Cordes cites) appears to be referencing December 31, 1966. Edith Fisher recalls that Muller-Munk told two sets of friends that he was spending the evening of March 12 with the other couple. Fisher in conversation with Rachel Delphia, June 10, 2015.

149 Muller-Munk was discovered in the car in his garage at about 7:30 a.m. on the morning of Monday, March 13, 1967. News obituary, "Fumes Kill Designer Muller-Munk," *Pittsburgh Post-Gazette*, March 14, 1967. Muller-

Munk's remains were cremated. Funeral of Peter Muller-Munk, Records of H. Samson, Inc. (Funeral Home), MSS 260, Detre Library and Archives, Senator John Heinz History Center, Box 32: Folder 3.

150 James R. Mellow, "Peter Muller-Munk, FIDSA, 1904–1967," *Industrial Design* 14, no. 4 (April 1967): 39.

151 Misha Black, "News" column obituary, *Design*, May 1967, 221.

152 Arthur J. Pulos, "Peter Muller-Munk, 1904–1967," obituary in *Industrial Designers Society of American Newsletter*, April–May 1967, 21.

153 Raymond Spilman, "Peter Muller-Munk," manuscript for an obituary for ICSID, Raymond Spilman Papers, Box 20, Folder: Peter Muller-Munk.

The Unisphere

1 The author is indebted to Daniel Short, professor of environmental science, Robert Morris University, who graciously shared substantial primary research on the Unisphere, including findings gleaned from the following archives: New York World's Fair 1964–1965 Corporation Records, Manuscripts and Archives Division, The New York Public Library; Clarke and Rapuano Records, Division of Rare and Manuscript Collections, Cornell University Library; Gilmore David Clarke Papers ca. 1920–1980, Columbia University Avery Library; and Queens Museum, Queens, New York. Short also generously shared his unpublished manuscripts on the subject: Daniel Short, "Unisphere: the Untold Story of the 1964 World's Fair Theme Center," 2015; and Daniel Short and Lori Walters, "Fifty Years of Unisphere" (working paper, School of Engineering Mathematics and Science, Robert Morris University, Moon Township, PA, and Institute for Simulation & Training, University of Central Florida, Orlando, 2014). See also William Robbins, "Doodle Grew into the Unisphere with Help from a Rubber Ball," *New York Times*, August 16, 1964, R1.

2 Editorial, "Fair Is (So Far) Foul," *Industrial Design* 8, no. 3 (March 1961): 27. Robbins, "Doodle Grew into Unisphere," R1.

3 Joint US Steel/Fair Corporation press release, February 14, 1961, United States Steel Archives.

4 Walter Dorwin Teague to Robert Moses, September 23, 1960, New York World's Fair 1964–1965 Corporation Records, 1959–1971, Folder: NYLP Armillary Sphere Q–Z, Theme: Construction, cited in Short and Walters, "Fifty Years of Unisphere."

5 Editorial, "Fair Is (So Far) Foul," 27. Moses's plan, which involved reusing the infrastructure from the 1939 New York World's Fair, was indeed financially motivated. He hoped that with profits from the 1964 fair he could finally achieve the permanent park that had eluded him after the 1939 New York World's Fair ended with a deficit; Robert A. Caro, *The Powerbroker: Robert Moses and the Fall of New York* (New York: Vintage Books, 1975), 1086.

6 Leon Gordon Miller, open letter to Robert Moses, March 27, 1961, Industrial Designers Society of America (IDSA) Records, Special Collections Research Center, Syracuse University Libraries, Box 26, Folder: World's Fair 1964. Miller sent the letter to the *New*

York Times, New York Herald Tribune, Time, Fortune, Wall Street Journal, and *Architectural Forum*, among others. Miller also sent copies directly to New York governor Nelson Rockefeller, to New York's US senators, and to president John F. Kennedy.

7 "News: Designers Resign," *Industrial Design* 8, no. 1 (January 1961): 18.

8 Peter Muller-Munk to Bay E. Estes Jr., February 8, 1961, Gilmore David Clarke Papers ca. 1920–1980, Columbia University Avery Library, Box 2: 1964 World's Fair Correspondence 1960-61. Information provided by Daniel Short.

9 "News: How to Make a Unisphere," *Industrial Design* 9, no. 6 (June 1962): 20, 22.

10 Muller-Munk as mentioned in Austin J. Paddock, "The Unisphere: The New York World's Fair Symbol—Like a Beach Ball Balanced on a Golf Tee," *Typo Graphic*, February 1964, 3.

11 The author is indebted to Daniel Short for sharing a remarkable schematic blueprint of the official Unisphere texture that he discovered at Rigidized Metals Corporation, Buffalo, NY, and that bears PMMA's title block: Ernst Budke, PMMA, Drawing No. B-60-37-28, Full-Scale, "Unisphere Custom Rigidized Metal Pattern," Client: American Bridge Division of US Steel Corporation, October 27, 1961. See also Dick Hirsch, *A Lasting Impression: Rigidized Metals and Its Enduring Idea* (Buffalo, NY: Rigidized Metals Corporation and Stonecraft Publishing, 2014).

12 "News: How to Make a Unisphere," 20, 22.

13 Paul R. Wiedmann to Rachel Delphia, December 11, 2013. Although Muller-Munk was compelled to distance his firm from the project, some designers, like Wiedmann, were proud of the work and lamented the lack of credit they and the firm received.

14 "All's Fair ... A World's Fair Report Comparing '39 and '64," *Industrial Design* 11, no. 3 (March 1964): 51.

15 Peter Muller-Munk, "Improper Credit," *Industrial Design* 11, no.4 (April 1964): 12.

16 PMMA is not mentioned once in the National Historic Landmark Designation report from 1995. US Landmarks Preservation Commission, May 16, 1995, Designation List 263, LP-1925.

Epilogue

1 *Pittsburgh Press*, March 20, 1967, 28.

2 Ibid.

3 Press release, Lando, Inc., by Beverly B. Schenardi for PMMA Inc., Monday, March 20, 1967, PMMA archives.

4 Parisson went to work for Latham, Tyler, and Jensen, in Chicago, in July 1968; "News," *Industrial Design* 17, no. 8 (October 1970): 17.

5 Beverly B. Schenardi, who had managed PMMA's public relations account from her position at Lando Advertising, joined the firm in 1968 and helped produce a suite of promotional brochures for each of PMMA's areas of service.

6 Robert Gaylor, e-mail message to Rachel Delphia, March 19, 2015.

7 Ibid.

8 William Allan, "PMMA Grabs Off Another San Francisco Transit Contract," *Pittsburgh Press*, February 17, 1970.

9 George Rhodes, "Hinged Muni Cars Urged: 78 Units for Subways and Streets," *San Francisco Examiner*, no date. PMMA archives, Scrapbook 4.

10 "Unique Streetcar System Planned for Muni," March 6, 1970. Source unknown. PMMA archives, Scrapbook 3. Paul Karlen and Louis T. Klauder visited about thirty European cities as research study; William Allan, "PMMA to Design San Francisco's New Mass Transit," *Pittsburgh Press*, October 10, 1969.

11 George Scheuring and Paul Karlen, "ACT-1: A Train for People" (final draft article sent to *Industrial Design*, July 25, 1979), 1, PMMA archives. The draft was heavily quoted in "'Testbed' Trains Emphasize Passenger Primary Comforts," *Industrial Design* 26, no. 5 (September–October 1979): 40–43.

12 Kenneth Ellsworth, "ACT-1: Proving Out Rail-Transit Subsystems," *Railway Age*, April 11, 1977, 28–29.

13 For Phase I, prime contractor Garrett/AiResearch provided systems design, rounding out their team by subcontracting PMMA for industrial design, Pullman-Northrop for structure design, and Gibbs & Hill Battelle for technical analysis. Scheuring and Karlen, "ACT-1: A Train for People" (final draft), 2.

14 Ibid.

15 The resulting prototypes were to be tested in Boston, Cleveland, Chicago, New York, and Philadelphia. Peter Muller-Munk Associates, *Advanced Concept Train Phase 1*, brochure, c. 1974.

16 Scheuring and Karlen, "ACT-1: A Train for People" (unedited draft), 6, PMMA archives.

17 Scheuring and Karlen, "ACT-1: A Train for People" (final draft), 8.

18 Scheuring and Karlen, "ACT-1: A Train for People" (unedited draft), 6, 9.

19 Ibid, 9.

20 Paul Karlen, "History of Peter Muller-Munk Associates," audio recording, March 15, 1969, Raymond Spilman Papers, Special Collections Research Center, Syracuse University Libraries, Box 92, item 120.

21 "Design for the Human Environment: Organizing the Visual Aspect of Man-Made Things," *QED Renaissance* 2, no. 3 (March 1971): 28.

22 PMMA advertisement, *Three Rivers Stadium Souvenir Book* (Pittsburgh: Pittsburgh Baseball Club, 1970). Making history yet again, the firm also consulted on the completely redesigned Pirates baseball uniforms. Among other structural modifications, cotton and nylon stretchable fiber replaced the players' traditional wool uniforms, a move that soon became the standard league-wide. Sylvia Sachs, "Pirates Down the Stretch in Drip-Dries," *Pittsburgh Press*, July 24, 1970.

23 Peter Muller-Munk Associates, *Louisiana Stadium & Exposition District*, brochure, after 1975, PMMA archives.

24 Rose DeNeve, "Peter Muller-Munk: Design for the Urban Environment," *Print* 24 (May–June 1970): 62.

25 Peter Muller-Munk Associates, *Design for the Urban Environment*, brochure, n.p. PMMA also designed a cohesive signage system for the Long Island Rail Road, which had an assortment of existing formats throughout their various commuter stations, as well as new train cars.

26 Peter Muller-Munk Associates, Division of Wilbur Smith and Associates, *PAT [Port Authority Transit]*, brochure, n.d., PMMA archives.

27 Ibid.

28 "Pittsburgh Gets 'Color Dynamic' Trolleys," *New York Times*, July 29, 1972.

29 Jack Markowitz, "Peter Muller-Munk Merges," *Pittsburgh Post-Gazette*, December 25, 1973, 20.

30 Ibid. At the time of the merger, WSA had seven hundred employees in twenty US and eight overseas offices.

31 Purchase agreement, PMMA (seller) and WSA (buyer), signed November 30, 1973, PMMA archives.

32 Ibid. Four new associates were named within the PMMA division: H. Kurt Heinz, Curtiss D. Lischer, John (Jack) S. Repko, and George R. Scheuring. All were recent hires (after Muller-Munk's death) save Heinz, who had worked for PMMA in the early 1960s prior to leaving to complete his degree.

33 Markowitz, "Peter Muller-Munk Merges," 20.

34 Significant airport projects included LaGuardia and John F. Kennedy in New York, and Dallas/Forth Worth. Other stadiums included Candlestick Park, San Francisco, and the Houston Arena.

35 Raymond Spilman, "Peter Muller-Munk," manuscript for an obituary for ICSID, Raymond Spilman Papers, Box 20, Folder: Peter Muller-Munk.

36 Peter Muller-Munk, quoted in Betty Morgan, "Peter Muller-Munk," *Home Furnishings Daily*, February 9, 1967. PMMA archives, Scrapbook 4.

Exhibition Checklist:
Silver by Peter Muller-Munk

Coffee service, 1927
Silver, gold, and ebony
Private collection
[P. 25, FIG. 2]

Bowl, c. 1928
Silver
Carnegie Museum of Art,
Pittsburgh, Decorative Arts
Purchase Fund, 87.11.1
[P. 28, FIG. 7]

Bowl, c. 1928
Silver
Collection of the Newark
Museum, 29.472
[P. 34, FIG. 13]

Clock case, c. 1928
Silver
Collection of
Jacqueline Loewe Fowler

Stackable ashtrays, c. 1928–29
Silver
Collection of
Jacqueline Loewe Fowler

Tea set, c. 1928–29
Silver and ivory
Collection of
Jacqueline Loewe Fowler
[P. 38, FIG. 19]

Ashtray set, c. 1928–31
Silver
Museum of Fine Arts, Boston,
The John Axelrod Collection
2014.1417.1–4
[P. 35, FIG. 14]

Telephone pad cover, c. 1928–31
Silver
Museum of Fine Arts, Boston,
The John Axelrod Collection,
2014.1416
[P. 35, FIG. 14]

Bamberger Trophy cup, 1929
Silver and enamel (replaced)
Dallas Museum of Art, Gift of
Sherry Hayslip Smith, Cole Smith,
and Jewel Stern, 2009.51.A-B
[P. 36, FIG. 15]

Candelabra, 1929
Silver
Detroit Institute of Arts, Gift of
Mr. Albert Kahn, 29.454.1–.2
[P. 30, FIG. 10]

Centerpiece and garniture,
c. 1929–30
Silver
Collection of
Jacqueline Loewe Fowler
[P. 22, FIG. 1; P. 39, FIG. 20]

Bowl, c. 1930
Silver
Yale University Art Gallery, Gift of
William Core Duffy, Mus.B. 1952,
Mus.M. 1954, and Mrs. Duffy,
1980.101
[P. 43, FIG. 26]

Bowl, c. 1930–34
Silver
The Museum of Fine Arts,
Houston, Gift of William J. Hill,
2004.1489
[P. 38, FIG. 18]

Tea service with tray, 1931
Nickel-plated silver and ivory
The Metropolitan Museum of
Art, New York, Gift of Mr. & Mrs.
Herbert R. Isenburger, 1978,
1978.439.1–.5
[P. 42, FIG. 24]

Centerpiece, c. 1931
Silver
Collection of
Jacqueline Loewe Fowler
[P. 40, FIG. 22]

Dresser set, c. 1931–34
Silver, mirrored glass, and
animal hair
Private collection, Baltimore,
Maryland
[P. 43, FIG. 25]

Bowl, prototype for Silvermode,
c. 1934
Silver
Collection of James P. Karlen and
Elaine K. Crawshaw
[P. 47, FIG. 32]

**Creamer and sugar bowl from
coffee service**, c. 1934
Silver and wood
Collection of Ken and Debra
Hamlett
[P. 45, FIG. 30]

Silvermode vase, c. 1934
Silver plate
Collection of John C. Waddell
[P. 47, FIG. 34]
Marks: "POOLE SILVER CO /
TAUNTON, MASS. / 0306 /
SILVERMODE / BY MÜLLER-MUNK"

Peter Muller-Munk's silver mark

Exhibition Checklist and Client List, 1930–1973

———

This list is based on various archival sources and is not at all inclusive; no comprehensive client list survived. The specific design categories and dates of activity are listed in italics where known. Objects indented below client listings are included in the exhibition, though not all objects are listed here. If they are illustrated in this volume, page and figure numbers are provided.

Adams Manufacturing Company
unknown project(s), late 1930s or early 1940s

Aldco, Incorporated
beverage coolers, c. 1963

> Cooler, c. 1963
> Carnegie Museum of Art,
> Gift of Jewel Stern, 2014.85.1

> Travel cooler, c. 1963
> Collection of Paul R. Wiedmann

Algonac Marine Hardware Company, Incorporated
unknown project(s), before 1960

Allegheny Ludlum Steel Corporation
market development design (stainless steel) and technical literature, 1940s

> *Over the Horizon* stainless giftware guide, 1941
> Carnegie Museum of Art, Gift of Jewel Stern
> [P. 67, FIG. 15]

> *Magnetic Materials* brochure, 1947
> Museum of Fine Arts, Boston,
> The John Axelrod Collection

> *Welding Stainless Steels* brochure, 1943
> Collection of James P. Karlen and Elaine K. Crawshaw

Allianceware, Incorporated
lavatory sinks, 1960

Aluminum Company of America
unknown project(s), before 1948; *exhibition design*, 1957

American Iron and Steel Institute
water storage tanks, 1965

American Machine and Foundry Company, DeWalt Division, and Mechanics Research Division
radial arm saw, 1957; *Versatran robotic arm*, 1957–60

American Standard
plumbing and heating products, corporate identity graphics, packaging, exhibit design space planning and interior design, 1964–1970s; *Posturemold toilet seat*, 1972

American Steel & Wire
wire fencing, c. 1960

O. Ames Company
tubular steel furniture, children's furniture, 1950s

Armour Alliance Industries
corporate identity graphics, packaging, before 1960

Arthur Young
space planning and interior design, 1970s

Ashland Oil and Refining Company
service station design, 1960s

Attwood Brass Works
marine hardware, 1956–59

> Cleat, 1956
> Carnegie Museum of Art, Gift of Jewel Stern, 2014.85.4
> [P. 105, FIG. 33]

> Seaflite bow light and cleat, 1959
> Carnegie Museum of Art, Gift of Jewel Stern, 2014.85.2–3
> [P. 105, FIGS. 32, 33]

> Seaflite steering wheel, 1959
> Carnegie Museum of Art

Australian Ministry of Transport
mass-transit vehicle design, 1970s

Automatic Canteen Company of America
vending machine(s), 1938–40

Automatic Sprinkler Corporation of America
fire prevention apparatus, c. 1938

Bacharach, Incorporated
air quality measurement instruments, 1967–68

Bank Building Corporation
drive-up teller system, modular bank building designs, 1970s

Bausch & Lomb Optical Company

Balomatic 300 slide projector,
c. 1957
Private collection

Bayer AG (see Mobay)

B-B Pen Company
writing tools, 1950–51

Ballpoint pen, 1950/1951
Private collection

Bell & Howell Company
audiovisual equipment, 1952–57

8 mm movie camera, model 252, 1953
[P. 100, FIG. 26]
8 mm movie projector, model 221, 1953
16 mm movie camera, model 240, 1957
[P. 100, FIG. 27]
Carnegie Museum of Art, Promised Gifts
of Jewel Stern

**Bendix Aviation Corporation, Bendix Radio
Division**
unknown project(s), 1940s

Bissell, Incorporated
*product design, packaging, corporate identity
graphics, interior design, exhibit design,*
c. 1959–68

Sketches, trade fair exhibit design,
1965–66
Collection of Kenneth D. Love

Bissell 400 carpet sweeper and original
packaging, 1962
Carnegie Museum of Art

Bissell Scrub Master and Sweep Master,
1960
Grand Rapids carpet sweeper and
original packaging, 1963

Little Queen housekeeping kit, c. 1966

Little Queen carpet sweeper packaging,
c. 1963
Collection of the Grand Rapids
Public Museum

Little Queen carpet sweeper, c. 1963
Carnegie Museum of Art, Gift of
Jewel Stern, 2015.5.1

Blaw-Knox Corporation, Blaw-Knox Division
unknown project(s), 1940s

Bowser, Incorporated
unknown project(s), 1950s

Budd Company
*mass-transit vehicle design,
Skylounge helicopter passenger
transit, and Skymobile lab*, 1966–67

Calgon, Inc.
shower head, c. 1964

Caloric Appliance Corporation
kitchen ranges, mid-1950s

White Sands 4-burner range, 1955
Carnegie Museum of Art, Gift of Janna
and Richard Taninbaum
[P. 114, FIG. 1]

Catalin Corporation
unknown project(s), late 1930s–1940s

Cincinnati Metalcrafts, Incorporated
unknown project(s), before 1952

Climalene (W. S. Hill Company)
packaging or corporate identity graphics,
before 1955

Coleman Company, Incorporated
portable coolers and thermos,
c. 1964

Crouse Hinds
street lighting, 1960s

James Cunningham, Son, and Company
packaging or corporate identity graphics,
before 1955

Decal Products Company
unknown pottery project(s), 1930

**DeWalt (see American Machine and
Foundry Company)**

R. E. Dietz Company
packaging or corporate identity graphics,
before 1955

Dinsmore Instrument Company
marine and auto compasses, packaging,
1950s–60s

Dow Chemical Company
*market development design (plastics and
magnesium), technical literature*, 1943–45

Dravo Corporation
*corporate identity graphics, space planning
and interior design*, 1960s

DuPont
market development design, 1960s

Dura Co.
unknown project(s) in metal, before 1935

Durez Plastics and Chemicals
market development design, 1943

Ekco Products Company
cookware, c. 1950

Flint-Ware saucepan, 1950,
manufactured c. 1955–60
Carnegie Museum of Art, Gift of
Jewel Stern, 2014.85.5
[P. 91, FIG. 13]

**Elgin American Company (see Illinois
Watch Case Company)**

Elgin National Watch Company
packaging, c. 1938

Eljer Company
sink, lavatory fittings, c. 1948

B. K. Elliot Company
*corporate identity graphics, packaging,
graphic standards manual*, 1960s

Fischer Bed Spring Company
unknown project(s), before 1938

Fisher Scientific
laboratory furniture and equipment, 1960s

Contempra laboratory cabinets, 1964
Carnegie Museum of Natural History

Frick Company
*corporate identity graphics, evaporators,
rotary compressors, exhibit design*, 1960s

Frontier Homes Corporation
mobile homes, 1960s

**Garrett AiResearch Company/United States
Department of Transportation**
Advanced Concept Train, 1972–79

Rendering of the Advanced Concept
Train, c. 1973
Collection of Paul R. Wiedmann
[PP. 152–53, FIG. 4]

**General Bronze Corporation
[Roman Bronze Works]**
desk and smoking set, vases, c. 1931

General Electric Corporation
mass-transit vehicle design, 1970s

Mine Safety Appliances Company
safety equipment products, packaging,
corporate identity graphics, 1950s–60s

> Dustfoe, c. 1967
> Carnegie Museum of Art, Gift of
> Daniel Letson

> V-Gard safety helmet, 1962
> Carnegie Museum of Art
> [P. 92, FIG. 14]

Mobay Chemical Company
market development design (plastics),
1960–1970s

> Cabinet and couch, c. 1969
> Carnegie Museum of Art, Gift of
> Dirk Visser, 1997.54 and 2012.54

> Concept sketches, c. 1969
> Carnegie Museum of Art, Gift of
> Dirk Visser, 97.34

E. A. Myers and Sons
(*see* Radioear)

Nash Motor Company
radiator cap, 1930

Natco Corporation
structural ceramic tile, 1966

National Dairy Products Corporation
market development design
(ice-cream counters), c. 1945

National Forge & Ordnance Company
corporate identity graphics, c. 1960

New Jersey Department of Transportation
(NJDOT)
corporate identity graphics, wayfinding
graphics, mass-transit vehicle design, 1970s

Niagara Frontier Transportation Authority
mass-transit vehicle design, 1970s

NuTone, Incorporated

> Skyline door chime, c. 1947
> Robert Dobrin Collection

Organization for European Economic
Cooperation
international design training/lecture tour,
1960

Otto Milk Company
packaging, 1948–49

Package Machinery Company
candy-wrapping machines, 1950s

Pennwood Company (also
Pennwood Numechron Company)
digital clock(s), 1940s

> Swank clock, model 500, 1940,
> manufactured 1954
> Carnegie Museum of Art, Gift of
> Jewel Stern, 2014.85.12

Peoples Natural Gas Company
space planning and interior design, 1970s

Perfection Stove Company
unknown project(s), 1950s

Philadelphia International Airport
wayfinding graphics, 1970s

Philadelphia Stadium
(John F. Kennedy Stadium)
corporate identity and wayfinding graphics,
late 1960s

Pittsburgh, City of, Planning Department
wayfinding graphics, street lighting, street
furniture, 1970s

Pittsburgh Corning
architectural glass blocks, 1960s

> Chiaro I & II glass blocks, 1967
> Courtesy of Pittsburgh Corning

> Chiaro I & II glass blocks, 1967
> Carnegie Museum of Art, Gift of
> Jewel Stern, 2014.85.17.1–.2

> Intaglio I, II, III, & IV glass blocks, 1962
> Carnegie Museum of Art, Gift of
> Jewel Stern, 2014.85.13–.16

Pittsburgh Plate Glass Company
refractometers, auto glass, exhibit design,
1950s–60s

Pittsburgh Reflector Company
lighting fixture and unknown project(s),
before 1955

Pittsburgh, Stadium Authority of
wayfinding graphics, corporate identity
graphics, space planning and interior design,
and uniforms for Three Rivers Stadium and
Allegheny Club, c. 1967–70

Platinum Products Corporation
cigarette lighters, 1935

> Quarterly lighter, 1935
> Private collection

The Plume and Atwood Manufacturing
Company
unknown project(s), before 1955

Poole Silver Company
Silver-plated tableware, c. 1934

> Silvermode vase, c. 1934
> Collection of John C. Waddell
> [P. 47, FIG. 34]

Port Authority of Allegheny County
Early Action Trolley design, 1970s

Port Authority of New York and New Jersey
wayfinding graphics (La Guardia and John F.
Kennedy Airports), 1970s

Porter-Cable Machine Company
portable power tools, 1948–late 1950s

> Portable electric saw, Guild model A-6,
> 1949
> Carnegie Museum of Art, Gift of
> Jewel Stern, 2014.85.18
> [P. 81, FIG. 5]

> Portable belt sander, model 500, 1950
> Carnegie Museum of Art, Gift of
> Jewel Stern, 2015.5.4
> [P. 81, FIG. 5]

> Finishing sander, Guild model 106, 1951
> Carnegie Museum of Art, Gift of
> Dick Jarmon
> [P. 81, FIG. 5]

> Electric plane, model 126, 1954
> Collection of James P. Karlen and
> Elaine K. Crawshaw

> Portable electric saw, model 108, 1954
> Carnegie Museum of Art
> [P. 81, FIG. 5]

> Router, model 150, 1957
> Carnegie Museum of Art
> [P. 81, FIG. 5]

Poster Products Company
unknown project(s), before 1948

Progress Refrigerator Company

> Portable cooler, 1955
> Carnegie Museum of Art
> [P. 104, FIG. 31]

Prolon Plastics (Division of Pro-phy-lac-tic
Brush Company)
unknown project(s), before 1948

Pro-phy-lac-tic Brush Company
plastic vanity products, late 1930s–40s

> Jewelite mirror, c. 1939
> Carnegie Museum of Art, Gift of
> Jewel Stern, 2014.85.19

Pro Plane
stereo cabinets, 1950s

Radioear Corporation (E. A. Myers and Sons)
hearing aids, corporate identity graphics, c. 1940–late 1950s

Radioear 45 hearing aid, 1942

Permo-Magnetic Multipower hearing aid, 1946

Starlet hearing aid, model 62, 1949

Zephyr hearing aid, model 82, 1952

Radioear 830 hearing aid, 1954

Lady America 840 hearing aid, 1956

Radioear 850 hearing aid in original case, 1957
The Kenneth Berger Hearing Aid Museum and Archives, Kent State University

Lady America hearing aid eyeglasses, model 840, 1956
The Hearing Aid Museum, Stewartstown, PA

Revere Copper and Brass, Incorporated

Normandie pitcher, 1935
Carnegie Museum of Art, Decorative Arts Purchase Fund, 87.29.1
[P. 49, FIG. 35]

Robertshaw Thermostat Company
unknown project(s), before 1948

Rockwell Manufacturing (see Porter-Cable Machine Company)

Rockwell-Standard Corporation
gas meters, plumbing tools, corporate identity graphics, 1950s–60s

Rospatch Corporation
corporate identity graphics, 1960s

C. F. Rumpp & Sons
leather goods, before 1935

Sargent & Company
padlocks, 1940s

Scaife Company
unknown project(s), 1950s

Schick, Incorporated
electric shavers, 1957–58

Varsity electric shaver, 1957
Carnegie Museum of Art, Gift of Jewel Stern, 2014.85.21
[PP. 98–99, FIG. 24]

Lady Schick Futura electric shavers (frost white and blush rose), 1958
Carnegie Museum of Art
[P. 115, FIG. 2]

Lady Schick Futura electric shaver with box (turquoise), 1958
Carnegie Museum of Art, Gift of Jewel Stern, 2014.85.22
[PP. 98–99, FIG. 24; P. 115, FIG. 2]

Powershave electric shaver, 1957
Carnegie Museum of Art, Gift of Jewel Stern, 2014.85.23
[PP. 98–99, FIG. 24]

Shenango Pottery Company
unknown project(s), before 1948

Shepler Manufacturing Company
unknown project(s), before 1955

Sheraton Corporation
prefabricated hotel bathrooms, c. 1970

Shumann Equipment Company
unknown project(s), before 1948

Silex Company
small appliances and housewares, late 1940s–early 1950s

Air-Lift steam iron, 1949
Carnegie Museum of Art, Gift of Jewel Stern, 2015.5.5
[P. 91, FIG. 12]

Candlelight coffee warmer, 1948–49
Carnegie Museum of Art, Gift of Jewel Stern, 2014.85.25
[P. 89, FIG. 8]

Constellation carafe, 1949
Carnegie Museum of Art, Gift of Jewel Stern, 2014.85.24
[P. 89, FIG. 8]

Double-burner electric range, 1950
The Lilane and David M. Stewart Program for Modern Design, Gift of Dr. Sze
[P. 90, FIG. 9]

Sinclair-Koppers Company
carton closures, stackable tumblers, drink carriers, late 1960s

Smith Metal Arts Company
unknown project(s), before 1948

Standard Oil of Ohio (Sohio)
service station design, 1961–62

Stanley Tools
portable electric tools, 1960s

Sterling Faucet Company
faucets, 1960s

Sylvania Electric Products
radios, lighting products, Sylva-Lume luminous ceiling, 1950s

Radio, model 510B, 1950
Carnegie Museum of Art, Gift of Jewel Stern, 2014.85.26
[P. 96, FIG. 22]

Sun Gun movie lamp, 1960
Carnegie Museum of Art, Gift of Jewel Stern, 2015.5.6.
[P. 100, FIG. 26]

Symington-Wayne Corporation (see Wayne Pump Company)

Tasa Coal Company
portable shelters, 1960s

Taylorcrafts, Incorporated
unknown project(s), before 1955

Tek Hughes, Incorporated
brushes, 1930s–40s

Texaco
corporate logo, station design, exhibition design, touring center interior design, 1960s

Drawing of Texaco station prototype, Matawan, NJ, c. 1963
Collection of Paul R. Wiedmann
[P. 137, FIG. 26]

Display sign, c. 1964
Carnegie Museum of Art, Purchase: Gift of Kenneth D. Love

Three Rivers Improvement & Development Corporation
Allegheny River Recreation Study, 1970s

Three Rivers Stadium (see Pittsburgh, Stadium Authority of)

Towel King Cabinet Company
continuous-roll linen towel dispenser, 1957

Tracy Manufacturing Company
unknown project(s), 1940s?

Turkey, Government of (*see* United States, Department of State)

U-Need-A-Pak Products Corporation
vending machine, 1938

United States Bureau of Mines
unknown project(s), c. 1940s

United States Department of Commerce, Office of International Trade Fairs
international trade fair design, 1957–1970s

United States Department of State, International Cooperation Administration
foreign technical assistance contracts, India, Israel, and Turkey, 1955–60

United States Department of Transportation, Urban Mass Transit Administration (*see* Garrett AiResearch Company)

United States Department of War
technical literature, 1940s

United States Glass Company
unknown project(s), 1930s

United States Steel Corporation
market development design (steel), the Unisphere, mass-transit vehicle design, corporate identity graphics, space planning and interior design, 1950s–70s

Urban Redevelopment Authority of Pittsburgh
wayfinding graphics, 1960s

Val Saint Lambert
contemporary crystal, 1956

> Tricorne ashtray, large bowl, smoking set, 1956
> Dallas Museum of Art, Gift of Jewel Stern, 2010.45.8, 2010.45.7, 2010.45.10.1–.2

> Tricorne candleholders, creamer and sugar, 1956
> Carnegie Museum of Art, Gift of Jewel Stern, 2015.5.7.1–.3, 2015.5.9.1–.2
> [P. 107, FIG. 34]

> Tricorne dish, 1956
> Collection of James P. Karlen and Elaine K. Crawshaw

Veeder-Root, Incorporated
computational devices

> Vary-Tally multiple-unit reset counter, series 1490, 1953, manufactured 2011
> Carnegie Museum of Art, Gift of Jewel Stern, 2014.85.27
> [P. 92, FIG. 15]

Volupté, Incorporated
dressing table accessories, 1934

> Hand mirror, 1934
> Carnegie Museum of Art, Gift of Jewel Stern, 2015.5.8
> [P. 44, FIG. 27]

Walters Manufacturing Company
packaging or corporate identity graphics, before 1955

Walworth Company
unknown project(s), before 1941

Waring Corporation

> Blendor, model B, 1937
> Private collection
> [P. 76, FIG. 3]

Wayne Pump Company (Symington-Wayne)
gasoline pumps, 1950s–60s

> Wayne 500 series gasoline pump, 1950 (restored)
> Carnegie Museum of Art
> [P. 93, FIG. 17]

Westinghouse Electric Corporation
major appliances, small appliances, exhibition design, Rayescent lighting panels, 1949–c. 1964

> DFC-10 Frost Free refrigerator, 1951
> Carnegie Museum of Art
> [P. 94, FIG. 18; P. 110, FIG. 1]

> Portable radio, model H-349P5, 1951
> Carnegie Museum of Art
> [P. 97, FIG. 23]

> Freez-File freezer, 1953
> Carnegie Museum of Art

Wilbur Smith Associates
bridge railings, 1964

Wolcospray, Incorporated
packaging or corporate identity graphics, before 1955

Timeline

1904   June 25, Klaus-Peter Wilhelm Müller is born in Charlottenburg, a town on the western outskirts of Berlin

1923–26   Apprentices with silversmith Waldemar Raemisch, professor at the Vereinigte Staatsschulen für freie und angewandte Kunst (Unified State Schools for Fine and Applied Art), Berlin

Studies liberal arts at Friedrich-Wilhelms-Universität, Berlin

1926   August 14, arrives in New York City

August 25, begins work as silversmith at Tiffany & Co., Newark, New Jersey

1927   July 30, leaves Tiffany & Co.

Opens independent silver studio, 148 West Fourth Street, New York

December 4, first exhibition of silver in New York opens at Dudensing Galleries, 5 East Fifty-Seventh Street, New York

1928   Solo silver display, R. H. Macy's *International Exposition of Art in Industry*

1929   Silver included in *The Architect and the Industrial Arts: An Exhibition of Contemporary American Design*, Metropolitan Museum of Art, New York

Silver included in *Modern American Design in Metal*, Newark Museum; a silver bowl is acquired by the museum

1932   Participates in symposium on design education, "Choosing a Life Career in the Design Arts," organized by New York Regional Art Council and National Alliance of Art in Industry

1933   Summer, teaches metalcraft, Oswego State Normal School, Oswego, New York

1934   October 26, Marries Ilona Loewenthal Tallmer in New York City

Silvermode line and Laura Lee Linder desk accessories included in *Contemporary American Industrial Art*, Metropolitan Museum of Art, New York

Carnegie Institute of Technology (Carnegie Tech) establishes a new Industrial Design Bachelor's Degree within its Department of Painting and Design

1935   Designs the Normandie pitcher for Revere Copper and Brass

August, moves to Pittsburgh to accept post as assistant professor of Industrial Design at Carnegie Tech

1936   Becomes a citizen of the United States

1937   Exhibits silver, Exposition Internationale des Arts et des Techniques dans la Vie Moderne, Paris

Exhibits silver candelabra (commissioned by the Detroit Institute of Arts, 1928) in crafts section, Annual Exhibition of the Associated Artists of Pittsburgh; receives Grogan Company Prize

1938   Hires Robert (Paul) Karlen, first employee; begins formal consultancy, Peter Muller-Munk, Product Design, from his Carnegie Tech office

1939   Exhibits silver, Golden Gate International Exposition, San Francisco

1940   Promoted by Carnegie Tech to associate professor of Industrial Design

1941   Exhibits silver, *With Hammer and Tongs: Malleable Metals in Diverse Designs*, Cooper Union Museum for the Arts of Decoration, New York

1943   By July, has moved office to Murray Avenue in Pittsburgh's Squirrel Hill neighborhood

1944   Society of Industrial Designers (SID) incorporated in New York

1944–45   Takes a faculty leave of absence from Carnegie Tech

1945   Elected to membership in SID

Resigns teaching post; establishes full-time design practice

Moves office to Clark Building, 717 Liberty Avenue, in downtown Pittsburgh

1946   Solo exhibition of industrial designs, Philadelphia Art Alliance

Cafex percolator exhibited in *Useful Objects, 1946*, Museum of Modern Art, New York

Hires Raymond A. Smith

1946–47 The firm adopts the name Peter Muller-Munk Associates (PMMA)

The Museum of Modern Art is the first museum to acquire a Muller-Munk industrial design, the Cafex percolator

1948 PMMA leadership is formalized under three associates: Muller-Munk, Paul Karlen, and Raymond Smith

Hires Anton Parisson

1949 PMMA adds major accounts with Porter-Cable and Westinghouse

1951 Muller-Munk elected to Board of Directors, SID

Exhibits photographs of industrial designs with SID, Milan Triennial

Silex Company double hotplate included in *Industrie und Handwerk schaffen neues Hausgerät in USA*, Landesgewerbemuseum, Stuttgart, organized by Museum of Modern Art, New York

1952 PMMA relocates to Gamble Building, 725 Liberty Avenue

1953 PMMA becomes a formal business partnership comprising Peter and Ilona Muller-Munk, Paul Karlen, and Raymond Smith

1953–55 Muller-Munk serves as vice president and then president of SID

1956 Elected Fellow in American Society of Industrial Designers

PMMA establishes Israel Product Design Office (IPDO) in Haifa (later in Tel Aviv)

1957 Muller-Munk cofounds International Council of Societies of Industrial Design (ICSID); serves as president, 1957–59

PMMA establishes Turkish Handicraft Development Office (THDO) in Ankara

November, Muller-Munk appears on NBC's *Today Show* as a guest of Dave Garroway

1958 Brussels World's Fair, Muller-Munk serves as Industrial Design adviser to the US Commissioner General

1959 Named Man of the Year by the Pittsburgh chapter of the US Junior Chamber (Jaycees) for contributing to Pittsburgh's industrial and civic progress in the field of art

1959–60 Six industrial designs included in *20th Century Design: U.S.A.*, traveling exhibition, cosponsored by eight museums

1960 Six-month lecture tour, Organization for European Economic Cooperation (OEEC)

1964 PMMA moves office to Four Gateway Center

1964–65 The New York World's Fair opens with the Unisphere as its symbol

1965 Effective July 1, PMMA incorporates as Peter Muller-Munk Associates, Inc., with nine shareholders

1966 Ilona and Peter Muller-Munk attend the White House state dinner honoring Ludwig Erhard, Chancellor of the Federal Republic of Germany

1967 February 12, Ilona Muller-Munk commits suicide

March 13, Peter Muller-Munk commits suicide

PMMA restructures under Paul Karlen, Chairman of the Board

1974 Effective January 1, 1974, Peter Muller-Munk Associates merges and becomes a Division of Wilbur Smith Associates, an engineering and urban planning consultancy based in Columbia, South Carolina

197

List of Patents

Muller-Munk, P. 1937. *Design for a mirror or similar article*. US Patent Des. 107,543, filed Oct. 22, 1937, and issued Dec. 21, 1937.

Muller-Munk, P. 1937. *Design for a brush or similar article*. US Patent Des. 107,544, filed Oct. 22, 1937, and issued Dec. 21, 1937.

Muller-Munk, P. 1939. *Design for a hair brush (2)*. US Patent Des. 114,195, Des. 114,196, filed Feb. 2, 1939, and issued Apr. 11, 1939.

Muller-Munk, P. 1939. *Design for a bath brush or the like (2)*. US Patent Des. 114,197, Dec. 114,198, filed Feb. 2, 1939, and issued Apr. 11, 1939.

Muller-Munk, P. 1939. *Design for a hair brush or the like*. US Patent Des. 114,344, filed Feb. 2, 1939, and issued Apr. 18, 1939.

Muller-Munk, P. 1939. *Design for a hair brush*. US Patent Des. 115,967, filed Feb. 2, 1939, and issued Aug. 1, 1939.

Muller-Munk, P. 1939. *Design for a hair brush or the like*. US Patent Des. 117,108, filed July 15, 1939, and issued Oct. 10, 1939.

Muller-Munk, P. 1940. *Design for a clock*. US Patent Des. 120,740, filed Jan. 4, 1940, and issued May 28, 1940.

Muller-Munk, P. 1943. *Design for a padlock (5)*. US Patent Des. 137,274, Des. 137,275, Des. 137,276, Des. 137,277, Des. 137,278, filed Nov. 29, 1943, and issued Feb. 15, 1944.

Muller-Munk, P. 1945. Design for a vanity case. US Patent Des. 145,100, filed Sept. 12, 1945, and issued June 25, 1946.

Muller-Munk, P. 1946. *Design for a percolator or the like*. US Patent Des. 149,513, filed Oct. 30, 1946, and issued May 4, 1948.

Muller-Munk, P. 1947. *Design for a beverage brewing device*. US Patent Des. 152,284, filed Feb. 4, 1947, and issued Jan. 4, 1949.

Muller-Munk, P. 1947. *Design for a hairbrush*. US Patent Des. 149,965, filed Aug. 9, 1947, and issued June 15, 1948.

Muller-Munk, P. 1947. *Design for a hairbrush*. US Patent Des. 155,310, filed Aug. 9, 1947, and issued Sept. 20, 1949.

Muller-Munk, P. 1947. *Hairbrush*. US Patent Des. 156,757, filed Aug. 9, 1947, and issued Jan. 3, 1950.

Muller-Munk, P. 1947. *Design for an electric stove*. US Patent Des. 154,418, filed Aug. 15, 1947, and issued July 5, 1949.

Muller-Munk, P. 1947. *Design for a coffee maker*. US Patent Des. 156,147, filed Sept. 5, 1947, and issued Nov. 22, 1949.

Muller-Munk, P. 1948. *Shelf Lavatory*. US Patent Des. 157,278, filed Jan. 30, 1948, and issued Feb. 14, 1950.

Muller-Munk, P. 1948. *Design for a coffee warmer or similar article*. US Patent Des. 155,354, filed Feb. 17, 1948, and issued Sept. 27, 1949.

Muller-Munk, P. 1948. *Cooking utensil*. US Patent Des. 155,442, filed Apr. 1948, and issued Oct. 4, 1949.

Muller-Munk, P. 1948. *Container for dairy products and soft drinks*. US Patent Des. 163,132, filed Mar. 24, 1948, and issued May 1, 1951.

Muller-Munk, P. 1948. *Design for a beverage serving utensil (2)*. US Patent Des. 155,438, Des. 155,439, filed Apr. 20, 1948, and issued Oct. 4, 1949.

Muller-Munk, P. 1948. *Design for a percolator knob (2)*. US Patent Des. 155,440, Des. 155,441, filed Apr. 20, 1948, and issued Oct. 4, 1949.

Muller-Munk, P. 1948. *Covered cooking utensil*. US Patent Des. 159,918, filed Apr. 20, 1948, and issued Aug. 29, 1950.

Muller-Munk, P. 1948. *Cooking utensil cover* (3). US Patent Des. 160,647, Des. 160,648, filed Apr. 20, Des. 160,649, filed Apr. 20, 1948, and issued Oct. 24, 1950.

Muller-Munk, P. 1948. *Lavatory fitting*. US Patent Des. 162,678, filed June 29, 1948, and issued Mar. 27, 1951.

Emmons, A. N., and P. Muller-Munk. 1949. *Portable electric hand saw*. US Patent Des. 165,062, filed Apr. 23, 1949, and issued Nov. 6, 1951.

Stoner, A. M., and P. Muller-Munk. 1949. *Lathe chuck*. US Patent Des. 161,552, filed June 24, 1949, and issued Jan. 2, 1951.

Muller-Munk, P., and C. Delafontaine. 1950. *Razor*. US Patent Des. 161,779, filed Sept. 6, 1950, and issued Jan. 30, 1951.

Muller-Munk, P. 1950. *Housing for fluid dispensing apparatus*. US Patent Des. 163,764, filed Nov. 30, 1950, and issued June 26, 1951.

Emmons, A. N., and P. Muller-Munk. 1951. *Portable power operated sanding machine*. US Patent Des. 166,148, filed Jan. 27, 1951, and issued Mar. 11, 1952.

Muller-Munk, P. 1951. *Refrigerator*. US Patent Des. 165,096, filed Feb. 1, 1951, and issued Nov. 6, 1951.

Muller-Munk, P. 1951. *Spindle nose collet chuck*. US Patent Des. 167,473, filed Feb. 9, 1951, and issued Aug. 12, 1952.

Muller-Munk, P. 1951. *Standard for motion-picture projectors or the like*. US Patent Des. 166,988, filed May 19, 1951, and issued June 10, 1952.

Muller-Munk, P. 1952. *Refrigerator cabinet*. US Patent Des. 168,583, filed Feb. 5, 1952, and issued Jan. 6, 1953.

Muller-Munk, P. 1953. *Case for motion picture projectors or the like*. US Patent Des. 175,035, filed Apr. 16, 1953, and issued June 28, 1955.

Behnk, D. J. 1953. *Index File Unit*. US Patent Des. 171,481, filed May 27, 1953, and issued Feb. 16, 1954.

Muller-Munk, P. 1953. *Case for motion picture projectors or the like*. US Patent Des. 175,036, filed Sept. 14, 1953, and issued June 28, 1955.

Muller-Munk, P. 1953. *Combined automatic coffee maker and dispenser*. US Patent Des. 173,909, filed Oct. 16, 1953, and issued Jan. 25, 1955.

Muller-Munk, P. 1953. *Case for motion picture cameras or the like*. US Patent Des. 178,533, filed Nov. 6, 1953, and issued Aug. 14, 1956.

Muller-Munk, P. 1953. *Refrigerator cabinet*. US Patent Des. 173,536, filed Dec. 7, 1953, and issued Nov. 23, 1954.

Parisson, A. G., and D. J. Behnk. 1957. *Slide projector*. US Patent Des. 181,312, filed Feb. 20, 1957, and issued Oct. 29, 1957.

Parisson, A., and R. Protas. 1957. *Radial arm tool for sawing, planing or the like*. US Patent Des. 186,423, filed June 19, 1957, and issued Oct. 20, 1959.

Smith, R. A., and R. I. Protas. 1957. *Electric shaver*. US Patent Des. 182,935, filed Oct. 17, 1957, and issued May 27, 1958.

Behnk, D. J. 1958. *Marine flagstaff*. US Patent Des. 185,656, filed May 14, 1958, and issued July 14, 1959.

Behnk, D. J. 1958. *Cleat for a boat or the like*. US Patent Des. 186,799, filed May 14, 1958, and issued Dec. 1, 1959.

Behnk, D. J., and G. W. Monigle. 1958. *Combined marine light and flagstaff*. US Patent Des. 186,906, filed May 14, 1958, and issued Dec. 22, 1959.

Behnk, D. J., and G. W. Monigle. 1958. *Marine light*. US Patent Des. 185,621, filed May 15, 1958, and issued July 7, 1959.

Monigle, G. W. 1958. *Steering wheel*. US Patent Des. 186,001, filed May 15, 1958, and issued Aug. 25, 1959.

Smith, R. A., and R. I. Protas. 1959. *Electric shaver*. US Patent Des. 186,433, filed Jan. 14, 1959, and issued Oct. 27, 1959.

Behnk, D. J., and R. O'Neil. 1959. *Wire tying machine*. US Patent Des. 189,935, filed Mar. 17, 1959, and issued Mar. 21, 1961.

Anderson, H. A. 1959. *Convertible retractible sponge mop*. US Patent 3,076,216, filed Aug. 26, 1959, and issued Feb. 5, 1963.

Smith, R. A., and E. Budke III. 1960. *Lathe chuck*. US Patent Des. 189,992, filed Jan. 5, 1960, and issued Mar. 28, 1961.

Yonkers, R. A., R. W. Herring, and H. A. Anderson. 1960. *Combination electric vacuum cleaner and floor scrubber*. US Patent 3,079,626, filed Mar. 21, 1960, and issued Mar. 5, 1963.

Anderson, H. A. 1960. *Combined cleaner and drier for floors or the like*. US Patent Des. 191,300, filed Mar. 31, 1960, and issued Sept. 12, 1961.

Smith, R. A., and R. I. Protas. 1962. *Safety hat*. US Patent Des. 194,305, filed Feb. 9, 1962, and issued Jan. 1, 1963.

Anderson, H. A. 1962. *Combination fluid dispenser and brush for cleaning upholstery or the like*. US Patent Des. 195,081, filed May 14, 1962, and issued Apr. 23, 1963.

Anderson, H. A. 1962. *Housing for a carpet sweeper*. US Patent Des. 196,035, filed Sept. 21, 1962, and issued Aug. 20, 1963.

Lindberg, C. A., and H. A. Anderson. 1963. *Vacuum cleaner with removable filter bag*. US Patent 3,184,778, filed Jan. 4, 1963, and issued May 25, 1965.

Anderson, H. A. 1963. *Bottle*. US Patent Des. 197,191, filed Feb. 6, 1963, and issued Dec. 24, 1963.

Anderson, H. A. 1963. *Dispensing applicator for cleaning upholstery*. US Patent Des. 196,707, filed Feb. 15, 1963, and issued Oct. 29, 1963.

Smith, R. A., and H. A. Anderson. 1963. *Cooking oven*. US Patent 3,169,520, filed Apr. 10, 1963, and issued Feb. 16, 1965.

Love, K. D., W. E. Lerdon, and D. J. Behnk. 1964. *Portable shelter with panel storage floor members*. US Patent 3,330,081, filed Sept. 14, 1964, and issued July 11, 1967.

Stoner, A. M., R. C. Schneider, and R. L. Paquin. 1964. *Beverage can cooler*. US Patent 3,302,427, filed Dec. 28, 1964, and issued Feb. 7, 1967.

Anderson, H. A., and R. A. Yonkers. 1966. *Implement handle*. US Patent Des. 208, 997, filed Aug. 15, 1966, and issued Oct. 24, 1967.

Anderson, H. A. 1966. *Portable manually operated rug shampooer*. US Patent Des. 207,632, filed Aug. 24, 1966, and issued May 16, 1967.

Smith, R. A., G. W. Monigle, and R. B. Gaylor Jr. 1967. *Gasoline dispenser*. US Patent Des. 209,918, filed Jan. 31, 1967, and issued Jan. 16, 1968.

Anderson, H. A. 1967. *Housing for a carpet sweeper*. US Patent Des. 210,241, filed Feb. 23, 1967, and issued Feb. 20, 1968.

Behnk, D. J., and W. E. Lerdon. 1967. *Translucent building block or the like*. US Patent Des. 210,373, filed Apr. 19, 1967, and issued Mar. 5, 1968.

Protas, R. I. 1967. *Safety hat*. US Patent Des. 214,861, filed Nov. 9, 1967, and issued Aug. 12, 1969.

Bell, T. A., and G. W. Monigle. 1967. *Respirator*. US Patent Des. 213,810, filed Dec. 11, 1967, and issued Apr. 8, 1969.

Anderson, H. A. 1968. *Head for a dust mop*. US Patent Des. 214,287, filed Feb. 9, 1968, and issued May 27, 1969.

Anderson, H. A. 1968. *Mop with pad securing means*. US Patent 3,528,076, filed Feb. 9, 1968, and issued Sept. 8, 1970.

Peter Muller-Munk Associates Employee List

This list is not comprehensive but represents an effort to capture employees referenced in the firm's archival documents between 1938 (the year of Muller-Munk's first formal office) and 1975. For some, only a single date is listed, indicating that the employee was cited during that year but that starting and ending dates are unavailable. Descriptors after the name suggest general roles within the firm; they do not reflect formal job titles nor do they indicate that the individual held that role for the duration of his/her tenure. Employees are grouped by decade of first mention and listed alphabetically within.

1930S

Peter Muller-Munk
designer, founder, 1938–67

Robert (Paul) Karlen
designer, 1938–78

Ilona Muller-Munk
office manager, 1938–c. 1950

Arnold L'Heureux Proellochs
designer, 1938

1940S

Ernst Budke III
designer, 1949–73

Marion L. Costa
designer, 1945–46

Eloise J. Nettleton
executive secretary,
1945–at least 1948

Anton G. Parisson
designer, 1948–68

Mark E. Sink
designer, 1946

Raymond A. Smith
designer, 1946–71

Irene Waichler [later Pasinski]
designer, 1945

Robert C. Ward
renderer, 1945–55

James Robert Winkworth
designer, 1940

1950S

Kenneth F. Altfather
model maker, 1959–70

Howard A. Anderson
designer, 1953–69

Elizabeth Beggs
executive secretary, 1951

Donald J. Behnk
designer, 1952–69

Robert C. Boone
client services, c. 1952

Bill Borland
head of model shop,
late 1950s–late 1960s

Vincent Cooper
designer, 1959–60

D. Lee Dusell
designer, 1957–58

Samuel L. Fahnestock
designer, 1951–55

Robert Gabriel
designer, 1957–58

Irma R. Gusky
executive secretary, 1951–52

H. Kurt Heinz
designer, 1958–63 (temp/part time/seasonal); 1964–74

Frederick M. Hill
designer, 1956–60

Kendall F. Jones
1956

Bruno Kersten
1956–58

Leonard Levitan
designer, 1956–65

Richard R. Lewellen
designer, 1959–64

Richard L. Martin
designer, 1959–62

Glenn W. Monigle
designer, 1957–69

Harold E. North
designer, 1959–60

George Oka
designer, late 1950s–early 1960s

Norma S. Protas
designer, ?–1956; 1976

Roger I. Protas
designer, 1954–69

Ann Radion
executive secretary, c. 1953–68

Robert J. Renaud
designer, 1950–64

William Richards
executive assistant, research director, 1955–at least 1966

Mort Rothenberg
designer, 1956–60

Richard C. Schneider
designer, 1958–60; 1962–67

Herbert G. Seel
designer, 1959–at least 1977

Walton E. Sparks
designer, 1959–64

William E. Stumpf
designer, 1959–62

Dana Charles Thayer
designer, 1958–59

Kenneth A. Van Dyck
executive manager, 1953–54

Arnold S. Wasserman
designer, 1956–59

Mrs. R. D. Wettach
1950

Ray B. Wheeler Jr.
designer, 1954–56

Paul R. Wiedmann
designer, 1959–97

Robert G. Wilson Jr.
designer, 1957–58

1960s

Michael Adams
designer, late 1960s

Richard D. Albright
controller, 1963–?

Louis Asti
designer, c. 1963–at least 1966

William Babcock
designer, 1961

Alex Bally
designer, 1967–68

Ted A. Bell
designer, 1959–at least 1968

Roma W. Darden
executive secretary, 1968–69

Ned DeForrest
designer, 1960–2003

David T. Dubbink
designer, 1961–?

Robert B. Gaylor Jr.
designer, 1963–71

Denis Johnson
designer, 1966–72

Robert Kapp
designer, c. 1965–70

Wesley E. Lerdon
designer, 1962–65

Curtiss D. Lischer
designer, 1968–76; 1997–2004

Raymond A. Loturco
designer, 1962–68

Kenneth D. Love
designer, 1963–73

Walter V. Mansfeld
model maker, 1960–70

Lawrence A. Marek
designer, 1961–63

John (Jack) Ernest Martin Jr.
photographer, 1968–70

J. David Meyer Jr.
designer, 1967–69

David G. Moore
designer, 1961–62

Emett Morava
designer, early 1960s

William James O'Neil Jr.
designer, 1964–68

David Y. Pond
designer, 1963–64

Bernard Porto
designer, 1963–at least 1966

Ben Presutti
model maker, 1960s

Christopher B. Pugh
designer, 1969–71

Peter Tighe Quinn
designer, 1961–?

John (Jack) S. Repko
designer, 1969–74

Diana Riddle
designer, 1963–65; 1967–76

clockwise

Roger Protas presenting Westinghouse refrigerator design concepts, c. 1960

PMMA party in the design area of Gateway 4 offices, c. 1968. Left to right: Ann Radion leaning, Raymond Smith serves himself and Denis Johnson a drink, with Ted Bell, Peter Zorn, and William O'Neil at far right; Left to right in back: Kenneth Love, unidentified woman (Paul Karlen's secretary), and Howard Anderson.

Kenneth Love, Raymond Smith, Paul Karlen, Paul Wiedmann, and Ernst Budke in Muller-Munk's former office (then Paul Karlen's), c. 1969

Jerome W. Rozanski
designer, 1961–64

Beverly B. Schenardi
director of marketing communications, 1968–c. 1970

George R. Scheuring
designer, 1967–2006

John B. Schmid Jr.
designer, 1961–62

Alex F. Sekely
designer, 1963–at least 1967; 1974–?

Donald Sentner
model maker, c. 1968–74

Dominic Strafalace
model maker, c. 1961–early 1970s

James A. Strafalace Sr.
model maker, c. 1957–early 1970s

Donald M. Streiff
designer, 1961–?

Jeffrey L. Thompson
designer, 1968–71

John E. Thomson
designer, before 1960; 1961–63

Stefan A. Unger
designer, 1963–?

Dennis Walczak
model maker, 1965–66

Ruth B. Whittaker
stenographer, 1962–63

Frank D. Wilson
designer, 1963

Wayne Wurzer
model maker, 1961–75

Peter Zorn
designer, 1965–68

1970S

Ida M. Dunofsky
designer, 1972–73

Leslie Ann Whitlinger
secretary, 1971–74

―――――――――

above, left to right

Left to right: George Scheuring, Paul Karlen, Paul Wiedmann, Herbert Seel, unidentified man, Curtiss Lischer, unidentified women, Kenneth Love, Kurt Heinz, unidentified woman, Jack Repko, unidentified woman, Michael Adams, Ned DeForrest, unidentified woman, Diana Riddle, unidentified woman, and the office's cardboard cutout, c. 1971

Anton Parisson admires a PMMA designer's concept for Bausch & Lomb Balometric slide projector, c. 1956

201

Index

Studio, The, 37
sugar bowls. *See* silver wares
Sundberg-Ferar, 151
Supersol, 122, *123*
    packaging, *123*
Surinam, 184n11
Sweden, 26, 108, 109, 176n26, 177n63
Swing, Sally G., 184n11
Sylvania Electric Products, Inc., 95, 168
    radio, model 510B, 95, *96*
    Sun Gun movie lamp, *100*
    Sylva-Lume luminescent ceiling, 116–17, *116*
Syracuse University, 10, 59
systems and infrastructure, 108, 120, 141

T

Taiwan, 125, 184n11
Tallmer, Albert F., 45, 46, 178n127
Tallmer, Ilona Marion Loewenthal. *See* Muller-Munk, Ilona
Tallmer, Jerry, 45, 46, 142, 178nn127–28
Tallmer, Jonathan, 45, 46, 178n128
Taylor, Crombie, 73
Teague, Walter Dorwin, 55, 67, 106, 121, 145, 151, 181n133, 184n11
tea sets/services. *See* silver wares
technical literature, 63, 66
Technicolor, 184n11
Tehran, 185n60
Texaco, 127
    logo, 136, *136*
    service station prototypes, 136–38, *137*
Thailand, 168, 184n11
Thomas, Ann, *96*
Thompson, Jane, 180n57
Tiffany & Co., 9, 24, 175n5, 175n7, 196
Time, 79, *79*, 187n6
Tito, Marshal, 120
Today Show, 125, 197
Town and Country, 25–26, 42–43
trade fairs, 92, 120, *120*, *124*, 125–26, *125*, 185n60
transportation design, 141, 142, 156
    See also mass transit
Treasure House: Museums of the Empire State, 10
Truman, Harry S., 120
Turkey
    ICA initiative in, 122–25, *123*, 168, 169, 184n13, 185n34, 185n36, 197
    trade fairs in, *124*, 125, 185n60
Twain, Mark, 18
12th Exhibition of American Industrial Art, 42, 177n79, 177nn85–86
20th Century Design: U.S.A., 197

U

U-Need-a-Pak Products Corporation, vending machine, 64, *65*
United Kingdom, 108, 185n52
United States, 10, 27, 44, 45, 48, 52, 56, 65, 108, 120, 122, 124, 125, 159, 168, 180n50, 185n34, 196
United States Steel (US Steel), 79, 126, 127, 128–33, 138, 150, 168
    Concepts in Steel brochure, *132*, 133
    IBM tower wall concept, 133, *133*
    Power Styling program, 120
    Steel Car of Tomorrow (SCOT), 139–41, *141*, *148*, 150, 151, 186n118
    Study in Steel campaigns, 130–32, *131*, 134
    Unisphere, 11, 133, *144*, 145–46, *145*, *146*, *147*, 187n6, 187n13, 187n16, 197
    US Steel Tower, 138–39, *138*, *139*
    vinyl-clad steel campaign, 128, *130*

University of Illinois, 182n7
University of Pittsburgh, 52, 62
Unterrichtsanstalt des Königlichen Kunstgewerbe-museums (School of the Royal Museum of Applied Arts), 20
Urban, Joseph, 32
urban planning, 52, 141, 151, 197
US Department of Agriculture, 125
US Department of Commerce, 108, 120
    Office of International Trade Fairs (OITF), 120, *124*, 125–26, *125*
US Department of State. *See* International Cooperation Administration
US Department of Transportation (USDOT)
    Advanced Concept Train (ACT-1), 151, *151*, *152–53*, 188n11, 188n13, 188n15
US Department of War, 65–66, 69
Useful Objects, 1946, 70–73, 196
US Glass Company, 181n98

V

Vago, Pierre, 108, *109*
Valentiner, W. R. (Wilhelm Rheinhold), 29
Val Saint Lambert, 105
    Tricorne candleholders, 105, *107*, 183n32
Vance, Vivian, *111*
Van Doren, Harold, 66, 69, 181n133
vanity sets, 43, *43*, 46, 64, 70, 72, 177n96, 178n137
vases. *See* silver wares
Veeder-Root, Incorporated, 92, 183n32
Vary-Tally multiple unit reset counter, series 1490, *92*
vehicle design. *See* mass transit
vending machines, 64, *65*
Vereinigte Staatsschulen für freie und angewandte Kunst (Unified State Schools for Fine and Applied Art), 20, 21, 27, 175n48, 196
Vienna, 26, 35
Viénot, Jacques, 108
Vietnam, 184n11
Virginia Museum of Fine Arts, 63
Vogue, 27, 32
Volupté, Incorporated, 59
    vanity set, *44*, 46, 60
Vytlacil, Vaclav, 179n16

W

Waichler, Irene, 68, 181n136, 199
Wakeman, R. L., 180n61
Wall Street Journal, 86, 187n6
Wandervögel, 19
Warburg, Siegmund, 27
Ward, Robert C., 68, 199
Waring, Fred, 75–76, *77*, 182n2, 182n17
Waring Corporation, 182n2, 182n17
    Waring Blendor, 9, 10, 11, 63, 69, *74*, 75–76, *76*, *77*, 164n2, 182n7, 182n9, 182n12, 182n14, 182n17
wayfinding graphics, 120, 126, 151–55, *154*, 156, 188n25
Wayne Pump Company (Symington-Wayne), 91
    Wayne 500 gas pump, *92*, *93*
Weber, Kem, 33, 175n52
Weimar Republic, 24
Werkbund, 20
Werkschulen, Cologne, 32
Wertheim, 18
West, Beatrice, 116
West Germany, 108

Westinghouse Electric Corporation, 53, 54, 64, *82*, 86, 91, 92–95, 111–13, *112*, 116, 126, 127, 168, 179n15, 184n8, 197, 200
    Center Drawer Refrigerator, 95, *113*
    DFC-10 Frost Free refrigerator, 92, *94*, 110
    Freez-File, *111*, 122
    portable radio, model H-349P5, *97*
    radio, *96*
    Rayescent panels, 117, *117*
    room-divider refrigerator, *113*
Wheeler, David, 106
Wiedmann, Carole, 120
Wiedmann, Paul R., 11, 85, *120*, 125, 156, 168, 187n13, 200, *200*
Wiener Werkstätte, 48
Wilbur Smith Associates (WSA), 156, 197
Wilhelm II, 18, 19, 24
Wilk, Christopher, 48
Winkworth, James, 180n61, 199
Winterbottom, William, *109*, 180n61
With Hammer and Tongs: Malleable Metals in Diverse Designs, silver exhibited in, 63, 196
WMF (Württembergische Metallwarenfabrik), 37
Wolfe, Thomas, 169
Wooley, James T., 180n85
world's fairs, 11, 54, 63, 65, 113, 133, *144*, 145–46, 178n14, 187nn5–6, 197
World War I, 20, 24
World War II, 9, 11, 76, 79, 111, 182n12, 182n17, 184n11
Worthington, Skilling, Helle & Jackson, 186n92
Wright, Frank Lloyd, 62
Wright, Russel, 10, 106, 121, 181n133, 184n11

Y

Yale University Art Gallery, bowl, 43, *43*
Yolen, Will, 181n110
Yugoslavia, 120, 125, 185n60

Z

Zagreb, Yugoslavia, trade fair in, *120*, 125, 185n60
Zavada, Frank, 180n61
Zeidman, Robert S., 180n55
Zeitner, Herbert, 21
Zimmerman, Marie, 29
Zorn, Peter, 200, 201
Zuntz, Nathan, 19
Zybasheff, Boris, *Time* cover, 79, *79*

Illustration Credits

P. 6: Peter Muller-Munk presents camera designs to client Graflex, as published in *Fortune*, November 1959, PMMA archives; p. 8: Water towers envisioned as grand observation decks in a parklike setting for the American Iron and Steel Institute, 1964–65, PMMA archives; p. 12: A woman reading in front of a wall of Chiaro glass blocks, designed for Pittsburgh Corning, 1967, PMMA archives.

Berlin

Fig. 1: Courtesy of Carnegie Mellon University Archives; fig. 2: Prints and Photographs Division, Photochrom Prints Collection, Library of Congress; fig. 3: © Humboldt University of Berlin, Porträtsammlung: Franz Müller; fig. 4: Courtesy of Cleveland Public Library, Special Collections Department.

New York: Silver to Industrial Design

Figs. 1, 7, 19–20, 22, 27, 32, 35: Photo: Tom Little; fig. 2: Photo: Tony De Camillo; fig. 3: Sigurd Fischer Archive, Prints and Photographs Division collection, Library of Congress, 267N17; fig. 4: *Charm* 9 (April 1928), 16, PMMA archives; fig. 5: *The Antiquarian* 10 (May 1928), 87, Courtesy of Carnegie Library of Pittsburgh; fig. 6: Sigurd Fischer Archive, Prints and Photographs Division collection, Library of Congress, 267N4; figs. 8–9: *Newport Bulletin, Official Weekly Publication of the Newport Casino*, August 6, 1928; fig. 10: Detroit Institute of Arts, USA / Gift of Mr. Albert Kahn / Bridgeman Images; fig. 11: *Deutsche Kunst und Dekoration* (December 1927), 229, Courtesy of Cleveland Public Library, Special Collections Department; fig. 12: Image © The Metropolitan Museum of Art, Image source: Art Resource, NY; fig. 13: Collection of the Newark

Museum, 29.472, Photo: Richard Goodbody; fig. 14: Photograph © 2015 Museum of Fine Arts, Boston; fig. 15: Image courtesy of Dallas Museum of Art, Photo: Brad Flowers; figs. 16–17: PMMA archives; fig. 18: William Hill Land & Cattle Company collection / MFA Houston, Image provided by Bridgeman; fig. 21: Reproduction by permission of the Buffalo & Erie County Public Library, Buffalo, New York; fig. 23: *The Jeweler's Circular* (October 1931), Courtesy of The Meriden Historical Society; fig. 24: Image © The Metropolitan Museum of Art, Image source: Art Resource, NY; fig. 25: Image courtesy of Jewel Stern; fig. 26: Yale University Art Gallery; fig. 28: Digital Image © 2015 Museum Associates / LACMA, Licenses by Art Resource, NY, Photo © Estate of Margaret Bourke-White/Licensed by VAGA, New York, NY; fig. 29: University of Notre Dame Archives; fig. 30: Picture courtesy of Heritage Auctions, www.HA.com; fig. 31: *House & Garden* 67 (January 1935), PMMA archives; fig. 33: *Gift and Art Buyer* 31 (January 1935), 57; fig. 34: Image courtesy of Yale University Art Gallery.

Professor Muller-Munk, Industrial Designer

Fig. 1: Allegheny Conference on Community Development Photographs, Detre Library & Archives, Senator John Heinz History Center; figs. 2–3: Courtesy of Carnegie Mellon University Archives; fig. 4: Courtesy of Carnegie Mellon University, College of Fine Arts, School of Design; fig. 5: *Design* 40 (December 1938), Courtesy of Carnegie Mellon University Libraries; fig. 6: *Pittsburgh Post-Gazette*, June 6, 1936, PMMA archives; fig. 7: *Modern Plastics* (April 1936), Courtesy of Carnegie Library of Pittsburgh; fig. 8: *Architectural Forum* (July 1936), Courtesy of Carnegie Mellon University Libraries; fig. 9: *The Pittsburgh Press*, October 12, 1936, Courtesy of Carnegie Library of Pittsburgh; fig. 10: Special Collections Research Center, Syracuse University Libraries, Photo © Estate of Margaret Bourke-White/Licensed by VAGA, New York, NY; fig. 11: United States Patent and Trademark Office; figs. 12, 18: Special Collections Research Center, Syracuse University Libraries; fig. 13: *Modern Plastics* (February 1940), Courtesy of Carnegie Library of Pittsburgh; fig. 14: Courtesy of Kent State University; fig. 15: Carnegie Museum of Art, Promised Gift of Jewel Stern; fig. 16: *Popular Mechanics*, July 1942, Courtesy of Robert Lanza, Pittsburgh; fig. 19: *Design* (May 1946), Courtesy of Carnegie Mellon University Libraries; fig. 20: *Fortune* (July 1943), Carnegie Museum of Art, Promised Gift of Jewel Stern; fig. 21: Courtesy of the Family of Raymond A. Smith; fig. 22: Photo: Tom Little; fig. 23: *Life*, October 14, 1946, Carnegie Museum of Art; fig. 24: PMMA archives.

The Waring Blendor

Figs. 1, 4–5: Fred Waring's America, Penn State University Archives, Pennsylvania State University Libraries; fig. 2: United States Patent and Trademark Office; fig. 3: Image courtesy of Dallas Museum of Art, Photo: Brad Flowers.

The Postwar "Do-It-Yourself" Movement

Fig. 1: *Life*, December 1954, Courtesy of Carnegie Library of Pittsburgh; fig. 2: *Time*, August 2, 1954 © 1954 Time Inc. Used under license; fig. 3: *Life*, September 5, 1955, PMMA archives; fig. 4: PMMA archives; fig. 5: Photo: Tom Little.

PMMA: Product Design

Figs. 1, 4, 36: PMMA archives; fig. 2: "Industrial Design and Engineering Design," *Machine Design* (September 1954), PMMA archives; fig. 3: Courtesy of the Family of J. Craig and Sally Kuhn; fig. 5: *Domus* 312 (November 1955), PMMA archives; fig. 6: *Modern Industry* (August 15, 1949), Courtesy of Carnegie Mellon University Libraries; figs. 7–9, 13–15, 17–18, 22–26, 29, 31–33: Photo: Tom Little; fig. 10: Courtesy of Carnegie Library of Pittsburgh; figs. 11, 16, 35: Special Collections Research Center, Syracuse University Libraries; figs. 12, 34: Image courtesy of Dallas Museum of Art, Photo: Brad Flowers; fig. 16: Society of Industrial Designers, *U.S. Industrial Design* (New York: Studio Publications, 1951), 123, Courtesy of Carnegie Library of Pittsburgh; fig. 19: Courtesy of Family of Anton Parisson, PMMA archives; fig. 20: Life, 1956, Carnegie Museum of Art, Promised Gift of Jewel Stern; fig. 21: *Pittsburgh Sun-Telegraph*, March 2, 1952, PMMA archives; figs. 27, 34: Image courtesy of Dallas Museum of Art, Photo: Brad Flowers; fig. 28: *Modern Plastics* (January 1953), PMMA archives; fig. 30: Carnegie Museum of Art, Promised Gift of Jewel Stern.

The 1950s "Kitchen Revolution"

Fig. 1: Photo: Tom Little; fig. 2: Courtesy of CBS Broadcasting Inc.; figs. 3, 5: PMMA archives, Courtesy of Westinghouse Electric Corporation; fig. 4: Image courtesy of Carnegie Library of Pittsburgh, Courtesy of Westinghouse Electric Corporation; fig. 6: Carnegie Museum of Art, Promised Gift of Jewel Stern.

The Color Explosion

Figs. 1–2: Photo: Tom Little; fig. 3: Special Collections Research Center, Syracuse University Libraries; fig. 4: PMMA archives.

New Frontiers

Figs. 1, 17–20, 29–30, 32–33: PMMA archives © United States Steel Corporation. Used with Permission; fig. 2: Courtesy of Paul R. and Carole Wiedmann; figs. 3, 5–14, 27, 31: PMMA archives; fig. 4: Original photograph by Israel Haramati; digital image from the Harvard Judaica Collection of the Harvard Library, Harvard University; fig. 15: Image courtesy of Dallas Museum of Art, Photo: Brad Flowers; fig. 16: *Pittsburgh Sun-Telegraph*, June 16, 1957, PMMA archives © United States Steel Corporation. Used with Permission; fig. 21: © 2006 Carnegie Museum of Art, Charles "Teenie" Harris Archive; fig. 22: Courtesy of Pittsburgh Corning; figs. 25, 27: PMMA archives; fig. 26: Courtesy of Paul R. Wiedmann; fig. 28: Allegheny Conference on Community Development Photographs, Detre Library & Archives, Senator John Heinz History Center.

The Unisphere

Fig. 1: *Industrial Design* 2 (March 1964), Courtesy of Carnegie Mellon University Libraries; figs. 2–3: © United States Steel Corporation. Used with Permission; figs. 4–5: Photo: Rachel Delphia.

Epilogue

Figs. 1–10: PMMA archives; fig. 11: Courtesy of the Family of J. Craig and Sally Kuhn.

Reprints

Pp. 160–63: PMMA archives; pp. 164–65: Manuscripts and Archives Division, The New York Public Library, Astor, Lenox and Tilden Foundations.

Staff

Pp. 200–1: PMMA archives.

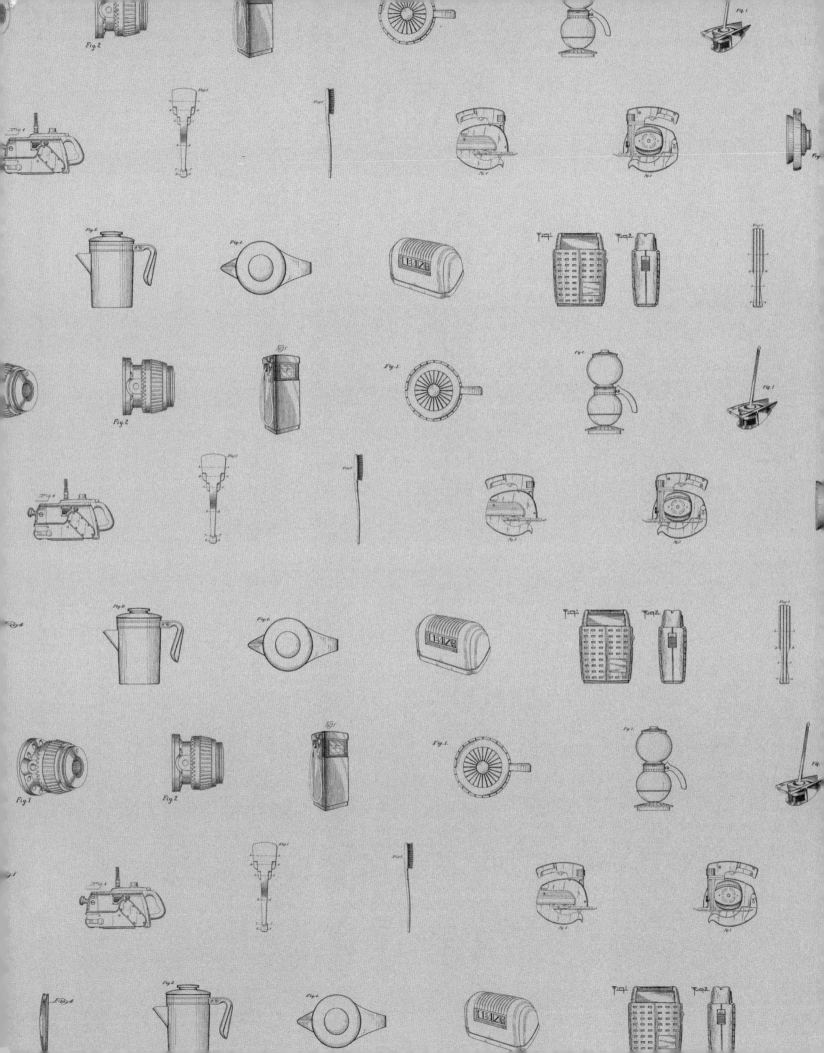